D1035514

Russian Imperialism from Ivan the Great to the Revolution

Russian Imperialism from Ivan the Great to the Revolution

Edited by Taras Hunczak

with an introduction by Hans Kohn

RUTGERS UNIVERSITY PRESS
New Brunswick, New Jersey

Second Printing

Manufactured in the United States of America by Quinn & Boden Company, Rahway, New Jersey

Library of Congress Cataloging in Publication Data

Hunczak, Taras, 1932– comp.
Russian imperialism from Ivan the Great to the revolution.

To the memory of Hans Kohn, 1891–1971.
CONTENTS: Hunczak, T. Foreword.—Kohn, H. Introduction.—Huttenbach, H. R. The origins of Russian imperialism. [etc.]
1. Russian—Territorial expansion. 2. Kohn, Hans, 1891–1971. I. Kohn, Hans, 1891–1971. II. Title.
DK43.H86 327'.11'0947 74-809
ISBN 0-8135-0737-5

To the memory of Hans Kohn,
a great scholar and an inspiring teacher
(1891–1971)

Contents

MAPS

Foreword

> The policy of Russia is changeless. . . . Its methods, its tactics, its maneuvers, may change, but the polar star of its policy—world domination—is a fixed star.
>
> —Karl Marx, 1867

Karl Marx's observation is only one of many expressions of awareness of Russian expansionism and imperialism through history. Indeed, it has been estimated that the original Russian state, which, according to Professor V. O. Kliuchevskii, controlled an area of some 15,000 square miles in 1462, expanded at the rate of fifty square miles a day for four hundred years, creating in the process the largest unbroken political unit. In 1914 it occupied an area of 8,660,000 square miles, or more than one seventh of the land surface of the globe. From the Carpathian Mountains to Kamchatka and from the Arctic Ocean in the North to Persia in the South, the ethnic Russians established dominion over a large number of nations and other racial and religious groups. Had one taken a trip from Warsaw to Vladivostok in 1914, one would have traversed some 7,000 miles and seen a variety of peoples who actually outnumbered the dominant Russians.

The statistics on Russian imperialism are overwhelming. Yet, aside from a few general statements, there exists no comprehensive study of the spectacular growth of the Russian imperial colossus. It seems that because the Russian empire was a continental state, its expansion has been viewed largely as a process of unification and consolidation. This basic misconception has led many students of history to deal with the Russian empire as a national rather than a multinational state. A notable exception to this approach is Professor Hugh Seton-Watson's *The Russian Empire, 1801–1917,* in which he deals with the totality of its population rather than primarily with its dominant segment.

Like other empires, Russia had its empire builders in autocratic rulers, military adventurers, and the nobility. They, like their Western counterparts, aimed at increasing their power, wealth, glory, and national prestige. The drive that led Cecil Rhodes to say, "I would annex the planets if I could" impelled the Russian empire builders into the Baltic region, the steppes of the Ukraine, the taiga and the inhospitable tundra of North Siberia. Ironically, even the Russian peasants who fled the social, economic, and religious oppression of the tsarist state eventually became a tool of Russian imperialism as the state caught up with them.

Russian Imperialism from Ivan the Great to the Revolution is intended to provide a carefully researched and authoritative volume on the expansion of the Russian empire, and thereby offer the first comprehensive history of Russian imperialism. It covers the period from the decline of the Mongol empire to the Bolshevik Revolution.

The editor has understood imperialism to be the extension of power and influence by one nation or state over other nations, territories, or groups of people, but at no time did he suggest this or any other definition of imperialism to the distinguished international group of authors who appear in this volume. Whatever their differences of approach, the authors proceeded from this basic understanding of the meaning of Russian imperialism, and they have defined that concept by exploring its content in the actual historical process.

The book is divided into two sections: the first attempts to explain the sources of Russian imperialistic behavior within the Russian historical context; the second discusses the implementation of plans and objectives as the Russian empire builders advanced northwestward to the waters of the Baltic, southward to the Black Sea and the Caspian Sea, and eastward through Siberia to the Pacific Ocean.

The transliteration of proper nouns used in this book follows the Library of Congress (modified) system. An exception was made with people and places that are well known in Western literature. My principal source for the transliteration of places was the *Columbia Lippincott Gazetteer of the World*. Unless otherwise indicated, dates are given according to the Gregorian Calendar.

I express my thanks to the many friends and colleagues whose support and interest helped in bringing the preparation of this book to a successful conclusion. I am particularly grateful to the staffs of the Dana Library of Rutgers University and the Slavonic Division of the

New York Public Library, especially Svitlana Lutska and Roman Ilnytzkyj, for their assistance.

I also thank Velhagen and Klasing, publishers of *F. W. Putzger Historischer Weltatlas,* who gave permission to adapt their maps for this book, and Professor Edward Fox of Cornell University, who was generous with advice and help in this matter. The maps were planned and executed by Mrs. Luba Prokop of the American Geographical Society.

Taras Hunczak

Chatham, New Jersey
July, 1973

Russian Imperialism from Ivan the Great to the Revolution

the pyramids my people built stand to this day; whilst the dustheaps on which ye slave, and which ye call empires, scatter in the wind even as ye pile your dead sons' bodies on them to make yet more dust.

—Bernard Shaw

Caesar and Cleopatra

HANS KOHN

Introduction

I

The question of continuity and change and of their interrelationship is a fundamental problem for the comparative historian. The methods, objectives, and ideological implications of contemporary Russian imperialism are debatable. In contrast, the historian can discuss with greater authority the nature and manifestations of pre-1917 Russian imperialism since the basic political currents of the earlier period can be readily documented and analyzed in their historical setting. It is very clear that there has been an imperialism of tsarist Russia at least since the days of Peter the Great. He was Tsar and Emperor, and these titles are both proudly connected with imperial ideas. He wished to make Russia a competitor with Western imperialist states, and for that purpose he instituted the reforms that made his reign famous. He understood one thing: that imperialism was a manifestation of great vitality. And he intended to transform a semi-Oriental country of inert masses into a dynamic one of explorers and activists.

Imperialism and empire are words used today mostly in a pejorative sense. That was not the case in the past. For many centuries, empire meant the Roman empire, which in the hands of the princeps and commander in chief of all armed forces became the self-appointed but widely recognized guardian of universal peace. In spite of the passing of the respublica Romana into an autocracy, a process completed by Constantine in the fourth century, Dante in his *De monarchia* saw in the Roman empire and in the Roman Church the pillars of a universal order of peace and happiness, a common end for the *civilitas generis humanis*. Charles V was the last ruler to wish to reestablish the empire in fulfillment of Dante's image based upon the unity of Christendom and Empire. In the sixteenth century the vision of universal empire was threatened simultaneously by the Turks, by Luther, and by the fresh vistas opened up by Ferdinand Magellan's circumnavigation of the globe.

Under Constantine the center of the empire had shifted from Rome to the old Greek colony of Byzantium—Constantinople—from pagan foundations to consecration by Christian bishops. Though the empire remained in theory one and indivisible, there were soon two emperors and two seats of imperial power and Christian *sacerdotium*. Thus the foundations of a Holy Roman Empire rose first at the gateway to the East, and soon another seat was established in the West. The factual division of the one empire became openly manifest in 800 with the coronation of the Frankish King Charlemagne in Rome as Emperor of the West. From then on there were two empires and soon two Catholic churches, hostile to each other, competing for the role of the one empire, the one church. From 962 German kings represented the Holy Roman Empire in the West; under the influence of rising nation-states the empire shrank more and more, the designation of Emperor becoming a hollow though hallowed title, until Napoleon I tried to restore the Carolingian empire and indirectly put an end to the Holy Roman Empire of the West. Until 1453, however, the Roman empire survived in an unbroken legitimate line, and in Christian Orthodoxy in Constantinople. When this second Rome fell to the Islamic Turks, a third Rome rose up in Orthodox Moscow, Holy Russia, continuing in some ways the heritage of Byzantium. In 1807 Napoleon as Emperor of the West met with Alexander I of Russia as Emperor of the East.

The words "empire" and "imperialism" lost their universal connotation in the course of the nineteenth century, and imperial institutions continued to divest themselves of direct religious ties. There came a time of competing empires and imperialisms. Russia and the United States, Britain and France, Holland and Belgium, expanded, as Spain and Portugal had done in the preceding centuries, as Germany and Italy were to do around the turn of the century. At the beginning of the twentieth century a climax occurred in the atmosphere of imperialism. The German economist Moritz Julius Bonn wrote in the early 1930's: "in the last third of the nineteenth century imperialism as a [general] movement arose and resulted in the creation of the great colonial empires of Great Britain, Russia and the United States. Contemporary imperialism is simply the most recent form of that primitive drive for power which has led kings and nations onward ever since the pharaohs upon the path of acquisition of ever increasing masses of territory and of political power. The countermovement [pacifism and the League of Nations] is today neither morally nor politically in the ascendancy." [1]

A French scholar also noted the intensification of imperialism in recent times, but he stressed the efforts to support it ideologically as a "mission civilisatrice," as a continuation of former universal attempts in the age of industrial expansion. "It is in the outbreak of nationalist fever following the events of 1870 and 1871," wrote Henri Brunschvig, "that one has to look for the true reasons of expansion. France, which since 1815 had considered colonization to be an important element of its national prestige in the face of England, showed itself even more jealous of this prestige in the aftermath of its defeat. . . . Colonial imperialism belongs to the vast movement of Westernization of the globe which, from the fifteenth century, pushed the European peoples, masters of ever more perfected techniques, to model the world in their image. It is probable that this evolution would have been accomplished without the colonial conquest and its abuses. But it is certain that in that case the process would have been slower." [2]

Empire building is an age-old historical phenomenon. In dealing with the age of developed capitalism the English liberal-socialist John A. Hobson in his book *Imperialism,* which appeared in London in 1902, stressed the economic aspects of imperialism, but he also recognized that the three P's—Pride, Pugnacity, and Prestige—were motivating forces of the movement. A more intensified economic interpretation, fitted into the categories of Marxism, was given by Lenin in his *Imperializm kak noveishii etap kapitalizma* (1917), which appeared a few years later in an English translation, *Imperialism, the Latest Stage in the Development of Capitalism.* Lenin analyzed this stage as the "monopoly" or the "moribund" stage of capitalism, with its essential need to export capital, to invest in underdeveloped lands rich in raw materials and cheap labor, and to open up new markets for the products of highly industrialized and financially strong countries.

An entirely different, philosophical, explanation of imperialism was given in the works of Ernest Sellières, who in numerous books—especially in *La Philosophie de l'impérialisme,* which appeared in four volumes from 1903 to 1908—stressed the romantic side of imperialism. Its modern sources he saw in social Darwinism, in the biological *élan vital,* in Nietzsche's will-to-power.

These aspects were also stressed in Britain and the United States around the turn of the century. A well-written popular book, *The Expansion of England* (1883) by Sir John Robert Seeley, expressed and stimulated a widespread feeling of the period. In December, 1898, at the end of the Spanish-American War, Rudyard Kipling wrote his poem "The White Man's Burden." Published the following month in a New York paper, it gave support to the wave of imperialism that had engulfed the heartland of America. A progressive senator from Indiana, Albert Jeremiah Beveridge, a lifelong passionate defender of labor and of the poorer classes, proclaimed the duty of extending "our empire—the empire of liberty and law, of commerce and communication, of social order and the gospel of our Lord—the star of empire, of the civilization of the world." In his Emporia (Kansas) *Gazette,* William Allen White wrote on March 20, 1899, that Yankee domination was the civilizing salvation for the Cubans as well as for the Chinese.[3]

II

Each imperialism was *sui generis,* depending on geographical features, on historical traditions, on social structures. Nevertheless, all imperialisms had many features in common. Russian imperialism was no exception. For all its distinctive characteristics, it is similar to European and American imperialism of modern times. In the nineteenth century Russia and the United States were very different; yet to the Europeans both were often strange, little known, even incomprehensible. Equally, Russians and Americans often felt like strangers in Europe. Distrust was widespread on both sides.

Franz Freiherr von Kuhn, Austrian minister of war from 1868 to 1874, told Emperor Franz Josef on July 20, 1870: "Sooner or later we shall have to wage war [against Russia], the sooner the better. . . . If we postpone it, we shall find Russia growing stronger every year because she is proceeding feverishly with her armament and her building of roads. . . . We must weaken this giant and confine him to Asia, otherwise the earth will sooner or later be divided up among two powers, the North Americans and the Russians." [4]

On the other hand, a German and a Pennsylvanian of German origin, Theodore Poesche and Charles Goepp, published in 1853 a book called *The New Rome or the United States of the World,* in which they voiced the disappointment caused by the defeat of the revolutions of 1848 and 1849 in the Germanies. All people, the authors wrote, as they throw off the yoke of their tyrants, should demand admission into the American states, a league of states that lives under a free constitution which was the starting point of a World Republic. As a first step, the new "co-republic" should annex the Caribbean and Central America all the way to Panama, and Hawaii and the whole of the British empire, and it should universalize the English language.[5]

In the nineteenth century distrust and competition were as great between empires as between nations. The United States and Britain, Britain and France, Britain and Russia, later Germany and the older empires, faced each other as potential enemies. To the Russian people Napoleon represented the West and the Antichrist, the Rome which wished to repeat in 1812 the humiliation inflicted upon the Orthodox East by the Fourth Crusade in 1204.[6]

After Russia's victory over Napoleon, one of the more intelligent diplomatic observers at the Congress of Vienna, Friedrich von Gentz, its secretary and Metternich's adviser, noted in 1815: "Napoleon's downfall was a pure and unqualified advantage for Russia; for the rest of Europe, and especially for the states bordering on Russia, it was largely balanced by the increased strength that Russia secured for herself at the expense of the general equilibrium. . . . For this great power there is virtually no further real danger; if she attacks her neighbors, her greatest risk is merely that she may fail in her purposes and have to postpone her venture to a more favorable time. The difficulty of penetrating to Russia's interior is now so generally recognized that only lunacy and despair could any longer prompt an attempt to destroy this great Empire. While the other states of Europe exhausted themselves in the struggle against Napoleon, Russia, which allied herself with him, understood well how to extract the most solid benefits from the ephemeral union. It would be easy for her to fall upon her neighbors, for she has so many greedy and ambitious reasons for trying it, and, if the expression be allowed, such substantially centrifugal habits, that war, which others regard as a necessary evil, will always be to the Russians a matter of choice, of emotions and of speculation." [7]

When Russian soldiers entered Paris in 1814, Russia stood at the pinnacle of power, yet did not undertake what Peter, ineptly enough, had begun: to stimulate the dynamic participation of the masses, to lift them out of their lethargy. The energy of the people was not aroused until one hundred and thirty years later, when the Germans, unmindful of Gentz's warning, penetrated the heartland of Russia with the design of destroying the Slavs as a people and as an organized power. Despite Germany's aggression and arrogance, the Russian forces entered Berlin and Vienna in 1945.

This was an entirely unexpected outcome of Germany's over-confident militarism. It is true that the fear of Russian expansion to the west expressed by Gentz in 1815 was shared by many Europeans in the nineteenth century, often in the most exaggerated terms. Thus Karl Marx warned in the New York *Daily Tribune* of April 12, 1853, against England's allowing the conquest of Constantinople by the Russians: "Having come thus far on the way to universal empire, is it probable that this gigantic and swollen power will pause in its career? Circumstances, if not her own will, forbid it. . . . As surely as conquest follows conquest and annexation follows annexation, so would the conquest of Turkey by Russia certainly be only the prelude to the annexation of Hungary, Prussia, Galicia, and to the ultimate realization of the Slavonic empire which certain fanatical Pan-Slavonic philosophers dream of." Adding to this anticipation of the domino theory, Marx, one week later in the same paper, painted a lurid picture of subversive Russian Pan-Orthodox and Pan-Slavonic agents in the Balkans. Again, in an article in the New York *Daily Tribune* on May 5, 1855, Marx declared that he was convinced, on the strength of secret reports, that "Pan-Slavism is now, from a creed, turned into a political programme, or rather a vast political menace, with 800,000 bayonets to support it." [8]

The French liberal historian Jules Michelet similarly stressed the danger of subversive Russian propaganda that allegedly aimed at paralyzing the intellectual and moral understanding of the potential victims. "This dissolvant force, this cold poison that she circulates little by little and that slackens the nerve of life, demoralizes her future victims, renders them defenseless," is of an infinite variety, wrote

Michelet in 1851, under the influence of his Polish friends. "Yesterday it [Russian propaganda] told us: I am [true] Christianity; tomorrow it will tell us: I am [true] Socialism." In 1863 Michelet protested against the subordination of the Poles by the Russians: "la tribu finno-tatare, le Kremlin byzantino-mongol." [9]

Michelet and Mazzini were liberals who regarded the Habsburg empire with great disfavor. On the other hand, as the Czech historian František Palacky, one of the great awakeners of the "dormant" Czech people in the Habsburg realm, rejected the invitation for Czech participation in the German National Assembly in Frankfurt am Main, he stressed his belief in the necessary existence of the Habsburg empire and his fear of Russia. The Czechs, he wrote on April 11, 1848, wished to maintain the Habsburg empire. Its "preservation, integrity, and consolidation is, and must be, a great and important matter not only for my own nation but for the whole of Europe, indeed for mankind and civilization itself. Allow me to express myself briefly on this point. You know what power it is that holds the whole great eastern part of our continent; you know that this power, which already has grown to vast dimensions, increases and expands by its own strength every decade to a far greater area than is possible for the Western countries; that as its own center is inaccessible to almost any attack, it has become, and for a long time has been, a threat to its neighbors, and that although it has open access to the north, it is nevertheless led by natural instinct to go on expanding southwards, and will so continue; that every one of its steps forward on this path threatens with ever hastened speed to produce a *universal monarchy,* that is to say, an infinite and inexpressible evil. . . ." [10]

T. G. Masaryk was long a faithful follower of Palacky's belief in the necessity of preserving a reformed Austrian empire in the interest of the non-Russian Slavs and of European peace. Yet in the feverish atmosphere of World War I he abandoned his realism for wishful thinking—as did many others. In a confidential memorandum on the future independence of Bohemia, he insisted that Bohemia and the peace of Europe no longer needed a federative Austria. In April, 1915, he wrote: "Since the military spirit and oppressive propensities of nations have grown relatively weaker, and as there is some good hope that the war [of 1914] will bring about a longer time of peace [1870 was followed by a forty-five-year peace], Bohemia can, during that time, relatively easily be consolidated. The necessary protection against hostile neighbors free Bohemia can get from alliances with equally threatened neighbors or with friendly neighbors. Bohemia will be contiguous with Poland and Russia, and perhaps with Serbia."

Masaryk was better acquainted with the backwardness of Russia than Palacky, but in predicting an alliance with Poland he showed a strange naïveté. As soon as Czechs and Poles became independent, the two Slav nations showed a profound dislike for each other. In this same memorandum of 1915, prepared for British (not Russian) statesmen, Masaryk, himself a critic of Russia and no adherent of dynastic loyalties, recognized that "the Bohemian people . . . are thoroughly Russophile." And so strong was the monarchical spirit in Europe before the great turning point of 1917 that Masaryk went on: "A Russian dynasty, in whatever form, would be most popular [in Bohemia]. At any rate the Bohemian politicians wish the establishment of the kingdom of Bohemia in full accordance with Russia. Russia's wishes and plans will be of determining influence." [11]

III

Throughout the nineteenth century, some publicists in the West grossly overestimated the power and the aggressiveness of the Russian empire; similarly, some Russian nationalists far overrated Russia's strength and mission. Today, Russia's success in training its people and developing an advanced technology and immense industrial complex, together with the inventiveness of its military and political leadership in the life and death struggle with Germany, rank it as one of the greatest powers on earth. But the claims made in 1837 by the Russian historian Michael Pogodin (and published in 1867) sound as preposterous as the fears of some Western observers of the time:

"Russia, what country can compare with her in magnitude?" he asked. "Which one merely by half? . . . Where is there a people as numerous as that? . . .

"Russia is . . . a country that even in her present state of development abounds in all products . . . a world in itself, self-contained, independent, with no need of supplementation. Many of her products are of a kind that each by itself could in the course of time have been the source of wealth for the whole empires. . . .

". . . What a short time ago it was that we started thinking of factories—and yet how well they have developed! . . . All these physical and spiritual forces form a gigantic machine . . . directed by the hand of one single man, the Russian Tsar, who with one motion can start it at any moment, who can give it any direction, any speed he wishes. . . .

"I ask: who can compare with us? Whom will we not force into submission? Is not the political fate of the world in our hands whenever we want to decide it one way or the other?

"The truth of my words will be even more evident if one considers the conditions in other European countries. . . . In contrast to Russian strength, unity, and harmony, there is nothing but quarrel, division, and weakness, against which our greatness stands out still more—as light against shadow. . . .

". . . Who dares pretend that the goal of humanity has been achieved or kept in sight by any of the states of Europe? . . . Corruption of morals in France, laziness in Italy, cruelty in Spain, egoism in England, are characteristic of these countries. Are these by any chance compatible with . . . the ideal society, the City of God? It is the Golden Calf, the mammon, to which without exception the whole world pays homage. Should there not be a higher level of a new European civilization, of Christian civilization? . . . America cares solely for profit; to be sure, she has grown rich, but she will hardly ever bring forth anything great . . . of universal significance. . . .

"[Russia is] chosen to consummate . . . the development of humanity, to embody all the various human achievements . . . in one great synthesis. . . . [Russia] alone can prove not only that science, liberty, art, knowledge, industry, and wealth are the goal of mankind, but that there is something higher than scholarship, trade, and education, freedom and riches—the true enlightenment in the spirit of Christianity, the Divine Word, which alone can impart to man earthly and heavenly happiness." [12]

Another vision of the greatness of the Russian empire was given in Nicholas Danilevskii's *Rossiia i Evropa* (1869), a book enthusiastically acclaimed by Dostoevsky. Danilevskii was convinced that Europe was united in opposing Russia. Europe had led civilization for centuries but now was declining, and for that reason feared Russia, its potential successor, though the latter was neither aggressive nor hostile to liberty. The West, heir to the Roman tradition of domination and violence, manifested this spirit in all its great historical enterprises.

On the other hand, Danilevskii argued, neither force nor intolerance had been dominant traits of Slav civilization. It proceeded not by conflict but by harmony and peace, and in the acceptance of Christianity as well as in the emancipation of serfs, in the colonization and cultivation of vast tracts of land, and in the introduction of great liberal reforms. Russia must accept all the science of the West, but use it in a different spirit, in a spirit of social justice, "to provide the popular masses with a just socioeconomic structure." Danilevskii believed that for historical reasons the expansion of Western nations had little in common with the expansion of Russia. Whereas Western imperialism enslaved peoples and numbed their cultural growth, Russian expansion was a mission of peace.[13]

IV

The fears of some Western Europeans and the grandiose expectations of some Russians about Russia's empire and its mission proved equally unfounded. From 1815 to 1917 the western frontiers of the Russian empire in Europe remained on the whole unchanged. The Russian expansion in Asia during this time was matched in a similar expansion of Western empires in Asia and Africa. That Russian imperial expansion had a characteristic mystique, as well as a concrete political history, will be apparent in the course of this book.

Inasmuch as the latter part of the nineteenth century was an age of imperialism, of conflicting empires and conflicting ideologies, of mutual distrust, it bore similarities to some other historical epochs. Unprecedented, however, were the technological complexity and destructive potential of the new armaments, the participation of great masses of people in military and industrial enterprises, the shrinking of distances in time and space, and the dynamism of scientific progress. By the end of the nineteenth century, the armaments race was clearly recognized as a danger for the future of mankind. Alfred Bernhard Nobel, the inventor of dynamite, established the Nobel Peace Prize, its first recipients (1901) being Jean Henri Dunant, the Swiss founder of the International Red Cross, and the French economist Frédéric Passy, who founded the International League of Peace.

In 1899 the Russian government took the initiative in calling a peace conference to meet that year in The Hague. The representatives of twenty-six states participated, "sincerely seeking to make the great idea of universal peace triumph over the elements of trouble and discord." In his invitation to the conference, the Russian foreign minister, Count Nicholas Muraviev, pointed out that the ever increasing burden of armaments strikes at the root of prosperity. "Hundreds of millions are spent in acquiring terrible engines of destruction, which though today regarded as the last word of science, are destined tomorrow to lose all value in consequence of some fresh discovery in the same field. . . . The continual danger which lies in this accumulation of war material is transforming the armed peace of our days into a crushing burden which the peoples have more and more difficulty in bearing. It appears evident, then, that if this state of affairs be prolonged, it will inevitably lead to the very cataclysm which it is desired to avert, and the impending horrors of which are fearful to every human thought.

"In checking these increasing armaments and in seeking the means of averting the calamities which threaten the entire world lies the supreme duty today resting upon all States."[14] This was written almost half a century before the United States dropped the first atomic bombs on two Japanese cities.

The Hague disarmament conference proved futile. Reconvened in 1907 after the Russo-Japanese War, again by the initiative of the Russian government, the conference ended with pious wishes against the foreseeable further dehumanization of war, proposals for the prohibition of shocking inhumanities, which then appeared as possibilities—bombardments from the air, use of asphyxiating gases and of antipersonnel bullets. Even these rather modest wishes in the pre-atomic and pre-napalm age were disregarded. A third conference, expected to meet in 1915, never met. The Russian empire perished, as Count Muraviev had foreseen, in the horrors of a war that was started lightheartedly in the capitals of Germany, Austria, and Russia. The Russian Revolution of 1917 profoundly transformed Russian imperialism, and indirectly imperialism and empires elsewhere.

V

The growth of the Russian empire in the last three centuries before the Revolution is comparable in some respects to the vast territorial expansion of the thirteen British colonies which became the United States of America. Russia expanded primarily on its eastern and southern frontiers, where "potentially rich territories were either under the domination of internally unstable" governments, or "sparsely populated by nomadic or seminomadic groups without any permanent political institutions." Similar conditions, to the west and south, existed for the United States. "Russia expanded between 1761 and 1856 at a rate of thirty square miles a day. During approximately the same number of years (1790 to 1890), the United States expanded at double that rate, or sixty square miles a day." [15] The Louisiana Purchase, the annexation of Texas, the Mexican War and the treaty of Guadalupe Hidalgo, the Oregon treaty, the acquisition of Alaska, marked the great events in this continuous expansion before 1890. Then followed the American expansion in the Caribbean and in the Pacific Ocean. Finally the United States became a far-flung empire with worldwide influence and responsibilities.

The expansion of both the United States and Russia had an ideological character. The American ideology was based mainly on the ideas of the Enlightenment; the Russian was based on Orthodox Christianity and the rejection of the Enlightenment.

The latter was best expressed in the writings of Constantine Pobedonostsev, who was for a quarter of a century (1881 to 1905), "the most influential man in Russia . . . earning an international reputation as the prime mover of the policies of Russification, clerical control of education, compulsory conversion to Orthodoxy, and the persecution of all dissenters." [16] He rejected all "modern thought—liberalism, democracy, socialism, popular sovereignty, freedom of press and of religion, separation of state and church"—as firmly as did Pope Pius IX in his *Syllabus of the Principal Errors of Our Age* (encyclical *Quanta Cura,* December 8, 1864).

Pobedonostsev, an enthusiastic supporter of autocracy, thought representative or parliamentary governments destructive of national unity, strength, and morality. In a parliamentary democracy, he argued, "the people lose all importance for its representatives, until the time arrives when it is to be played upon again. Then false and flattering and lying phrases are lavished as before; some are suborned by bribery, others terrified by threats—the long chain of manoeuvres spun which forms an invariable factor of parliamentarism." [17]

The Americans saw themselves from the beginning as opponents of monarchy, of political or religious absolutism, as republicans and democrats. In 1794 the president of Yale College, Timothy Dwight, published a poem "Greenfield Hill," named after his Connecticut parish. In it he compared the West (American) with the East (Europe).

O blissful visions of the happy West!
O how unlike the miseries of the East!
There, in sad realms of desolating war,
Fell Despotism ascends his iron car;
Printed in blood, o'er all the moving throne,
The motto glows, of "Millions Made For One."[18]

The ideological differences between the two empires were expressed in another way. The Russian empire contained many different people, but it was mainly a closed society which did not readily or very often open its gates to fill its open spaces. This made it difficult to enter, difficult to leave. The United States on the whole was a nation of open gateways, and millions from abroad participated in the vast forward movement with its beckoning opportunities. Individual liberty, social mobility, personal initiative, distinguished the Americans in the minds of the Europeans from their own more tradition-bound societies. The Russian radicals, from Nicholas Chernyshevskii to Lenin, wished in that sense to "Americanize" Russia.

In Chernyshevskii's famous didactic novel of the 1860's, *What Is To Be Done?* to which he gave the subtitle *Tales about the New People,*[19] Vera Pavlovna anticipates the position of the American Women's Liberation movement of the 1970's. It so happened that her aspiration had an American origin. Rakhmetov, Chernyshevskii's mysterious hero, the representative of the coming generation, travels abroad to study the countries and peoples of Central and Western Europe. Chernyshevskii does not say much about this new hero, but one thing is "absolutely necessary" to him, to visit the United States, "a country which he must study more than any other. There he would remain a long time, perhaps more than a year, and perhaps forever . . . but it was more likely that in three years he would return to Russia, as it seemed to him that at that time it would be necessary to be back."[20] It took more than three years.

To the Russian radicals, children of the Enlightenment but also fettered by the absolutist authoritarian traditions of the Russian state and church, America was the distant fulfillment of that West which had given them the visions of active participation, the gospel of the dignity of labor, the revolutionary expectation of a new society and a new man. Russia's vast empire of tsarist times did not realize its potentials, but rather continued to preserve a semi-Oriental society in which the people counted for little and literacy was low. In our period of the Westernization of the globe, Russia, at least since Peter the Great, offered the first example of the Westernization of an underdeveloped country. Many of its problems had been familiar to Western lands in their long period of transition from a medieval, tradition- and custom-bound society to modernity and mobility.

The pathways between the Atlantic shore of North America and Western Europe have been kept open for the interchange of peoples and ideas. The United States fought the two world wars of the twentieth century largely to this end. Russia was geographically in a much less fortunate position. The way to the East lay open beginning with Ivan III and Ivan IV, and so did the way to the Arctic North; but when Peter the Great ascended the throne, he found the paths to the West and to the South closed by three powerful empires of his day, the Swedish in the northwest, the Polo-Lithuanian in the center, the Turkish in the south. In the two hundred years between 1710 and 1910 the Russian empire gained control of its approaches westward, as well as control of the Baltic Sea and of the landway across the Belorussian, Lithuanian, and Polish lands, and even access to the southwest as it gained influence in the former Turkish provinces of the Balkans and on the shores of the Black Sea.

In World War I, in tsarist Russia's secret treaties with its Western allies, Russia hoped to win the citadel of Orthodox Christianity, Constantinople, and to unite the Second and Third Romes, as Napoleon I had tried to build his Western empire on the two great columns of Paris and the First Rome. This hope was not realized; the Germans defeated Russia and the Allies fabricated a *cordon sanitaire* as a defense against the new Third Rome of the proletariat. This *cordon sanitaire* consisted of weak states, at loggerheads with each other. Most of them very quickly abandoned the Wilsonian democracy of 1919 for a more or less fascist or authoritarian regime, so that the lot of the peasant masses was scarcely changed. The Russian empire survived in a radically changed form, but its new development was interrupted by German aggression and by Stalin's semi-Oriental despotism, a throwback in some ways to the times of Ivan IV.

As of 1972, the Union of Soviet Socialist Republics—the former Russian empire—has survived for fifty-five years, a very long time for a revolutionary government, but since Russia's victory of World War II the *cordon sanitaire* countries, many of which fought on the German side, have not been incorporated into a planned utopia of a World

Union of Soviet Socialist Republics. They develop in their own way, guided by the differently interpreted ideology of Marxism-Leninism and adhering partly to their own traditions. They still form a *cordon sanitaire,* but it is no longer directed against Russia but rather protects her from, and connects her with, the West. It is possible that in the future, as in centuries long past, the Russian empire may feel threatened from the East, from which it has felt safe since Ivan IV. This is mere speculation as to one of the many trials that may be in store for the former tsarist empire and for mankind. Whatever these trials turn out to be, historical factors and trends cannot but continue to bear strongly on the future.

HENRY R. HUTTENBACH

The Origins of Russian Imperialism

The dramatic presence of Russia straddling the Eurasian continent has tempted many an observer to investigate the historical background to the formation of the world's largest political unit. In recent years especially, the emergence of the Soviet Union and the extension of its influence beyond its borders have stimulated a large number of studies of the forces that generated Russia's desire for territorial expansion and global power. Ever since the appearance of Peter the Great's Russian empire on the world scene at the beginning of the eighteenth century, Europe and Asia have been uncomfortably aware of the Russian presence.

Shortly after World War II, when Soviet imperialism erected an East European satellite system, Philip E. Mosely suggested that the phenomenon of Russian expansionism had historical roots that so far antedated present ambitions dictated by communism as to originate with Peter the Great's imperial vision.[1] In 1952, when Russian power had become indisputably entrenched in Eastern Europe, Oscar Halecki, the distinguished Polish historian, went further and tried to show that underlying the Soviet drive into that region was an older *Drang nach Westen* derived from pre-Petrine Russia.[2] In reply to those "who see exclusively communism with its program of world revolution" [3] as the motivating force behind Russian aggrandizement, Halecki argued for the reality of a postwar Russia operating in accordance with an old pattern of Russian national imperialism in Eastern Europe that had begun with the rise of Muscovy in the fifteenth century. That same year, Nicholas Riasanovsky countered Halecki's pro-Polish interpretation by pointing out that Russia's penchant for territorial acquisition was preceded by a far older Polish *Drang nach Osten* into Russian-inhabited regions, beginning with Boleslav I's seizure of Russian lands in the eleventh century and culminating with the Polish intervention during the Time of Troubles in the early seventeenth century.[4] Indeed, Riasanovsky maintained, much of Russia's territorial conquest was *in response* to foreign attacks.

This dialogue may have established a balance of imperialisms, but it by no means discounted the fact of a long history of Russian expansionism with its own ideological rationales. Imperialism in its modern usage, as defined by John A. Hobson to describe the imposition of the will of one state upon another as practiced in the nineteenth century by the industrialized European nations,[5] may not be exactly applicable to the growth of Russia in its early centuries, certainly not prior to Peter the Great.[6] However, Russia did expand over the course of several centuries with extraordinary rapidity. The origins and stimuli of this phenomenon still remain unclear to laymen and perplexing to historians.

It is the purpose of this chapter to inquire whether early Russian rulers and people acted in accordance with a consistent policy and an evolving tradition of expansion that can be interpreted as the nucleus of a doctrine of national growth prior to the emergence of Peter the Great's Eurasian empire and its policy of conquest. Whether the ingredients of such a doctrine carried over into the modern period at the end of the seventeenth century is not in question here; however, a survey of this preimperialist period should help in assessing whether modern Russian imperialism, tsarist or Soviet, bears any similarity to Russian doctrines and policies of former times. Only then can the question of the evolutionary or revolutionary character of recent Russian expansionism be satisfactorily answered.

Russia's Geographical Setting and Expansionism

In considering the historical evolution of Russian concepts of aggrandizement, it is well to bear in mind the environmental factors that affected the shaping of these ideas. Topography and other natural features can either hinder or further a people's desire to enlarge its borders. Whereas mountain ranges, deserts, and jungles can act as barriers to restrict ambitions of conquest, great plains set no natural limits, and rivers and mountain passes provide ready avenues to adjoining territories.

Russia began in the great Eurasian plain and in due course embraced virtually all of the flat stretch of land extending from the Baltic to the Pacific. The Russian survival in and ultimate conquest of the steppe is one of the great dramas of history. The absence of natural barriers is the basic condition of the Russian setting. Indeed, few commentators of Russian history have ignored the constant influence that the boundless "ocean" of steppe land has had upon its inhabitants, not only in sparking an adventurous spirit to reach out beyond far horizons but also in forming the fundamental character of Russian society.

Best known, perhaps, is the theory of Robert J. Kerner, who, stressing the disadvantages of Russia's landlocked condition, strove to explain Russian expansionism in terms of a constant struggle to gain access to the world's major oceans. This urge to the sea, he noted, was facilitated by a gift of nature, a network of rivers whose portages allowed easy transfer from one to the other and accelerated the move southward to the Black Sea and eastward across Siberia. "Each [group], whatever its ideology, utilized them [the portages]." [7] According to Kerner, no matter what social and governmental system prevailed, eventually each one responded to the character of the environment and moved along the waterways provided by nature. The geographical factor, he reasoned, "vitally helped shape the course of Russian history." [8]

Even the philosophically inclined Nicholas Berdiaev, in search of a metaphysical answer to the meaning of Russian history, found it difficult to ignore the overwhelming significance of Russian geography. Though he was no friend of the Russian state that grew out of the Eurasian plain, he recognized that it was a product of the struggle for control of a vast territory. Self-preservation, he observed, forced the Russians to push off invaders and to entrench themselves firmly in their habitat, but since it afforded them precious little natural protection,[9] they were constantly pressed to expand their borders to keep their enemies at bay.

The influence of geography on Russia's historical evolution was more clearly spelled out by Boris Brutkus. The great expanse of the Russian plain with its long, unprotected borders made it extremely vulnerable to enemy attacks. This basic geographical factor also caused a cultural isolation that forced the Russians to seek contacts with centers to the west. Even more pertinent to this theme was Brutkus' third point: the thinly populated Eurasian plain offered the Eastern Slavs an unparalleled opportunity for continuous colonization eastward.[10]

This last observation he credited to V. O. Kliuchevskii, who had astutely recognized that the primary characteristic of Russian expansionism attributable to the natural setting was the centuries-long process of Slavic colonization of the Eurasian plain. This process, he noted, had begun with the earliest Slavs to arrive in the Dnieper valley and continued until well into the nineteenth century. In Kliuchevskii's estimation, Russia grew largely on account of the steady process of Slavic migration. "The primary truth of Russian history has been colonization, and all other factors have been either directly or indirectly related to it." [11] A. Kizevetter has given particular attention to this phenomenon as the fundamental historical truth underlying all others that molded the largest state in the world.[12]

Slavic Colonization

Chronologically, Slavic colonization, voluntary and involuntary, of the Eurasian plain preceded all other manifestations of Russian expansionism. In general, the Slavic peasantry was driven ever deeper into the interior and towards the Arctic Circle by three overriding considerations: the search for lands secure from nomadic attacks; the desire for free land; and the hope of escaping the state's tax collectors and recruiters. From the moment the Eastern Slavic tribes reached the Dnieper valley in the sixth century, they took advantage of the river basin to enlarge their territorial domain. They moved easily as far south as the Black Sea coast and northward to the upper Volga until they were stopped by Finnish tribes and the Bulgar state on the middle Volga. By the eighth century, though, they had been pushed back from the Black Sea littoral by a new nomadic invader, the Magyars. This setback motivated one of the major aggressive policies of early Kievan Rus, the reconquest of the entire lower Dnieper, whose right bank, formerly settled by the Slavic Ulichi tribe, was then controlled by the nomadic Pechenegs, who had replaced the Magyars.

The next stage of extensive Slavic colonization began in the late eleventh century as a result of the increasing instability of life in the southern steppe around Kiev. The pressures of the Polovtsi nomads drove waves of Slavs northeastward, and many moved well past the old line of Slavic settlement extending from Beloozero through Iaroslavl and Murom into predominantly Finno-Ugrian populated regions of the Chud and Merians. Thereby they laid the foundations for the large and powerful principality of Vladimir-Suzdal, the heartland of Mongol Russia, in which Muscovy was spawned.[13]

During the Mongol era, though Slavic expansionism was restricted to the North, it by no means diminished. Thousands of refugee peasants fled to Karelia to escape the Mongol terror, thereby providing the Novgorodian republic with an opportunity to consolidate its claim to this region. Muscovy, in contrast, in order to entrench itself in the Beloozero region against the claims of its rival Novgorod, colonized the northern territory with former slaves and bondsmen whom it freed on the condition that they settle in and around Beloozero.

The fourth wave of Slavic migration, which anteceded any official political consolidation and laid the groundwork for subsequent frontier extensions, started in the middle of the sixteenth century shortly after the final disintegration of the Mongol empire and Ivan IV's conquest of the entire Volga valley. In reaction to the extreme demands of taxation and recruitment put upon the peasantry by the endless Livonian War (1558 to 1581), and also in response to an old dream of returning to the fertile lands to the south, thousands of Muscovite peasants migrated southward, largely into the no-man's-land of the Don and Donets valleys. In terms of chronological sequence, this movement was well ahead of Ivan IV's system of fortifications, which began with the famous Line of 1571, a series of southern *ostrogi* (forts) to fend off Tatar attacks behind which he established peasant settlements (*slobody*).[14] As the original settlers moved further south, they set up new Cossack communities, well beyond the grasp of the agents of the Muscovite government. Thus, the initial fact of Russian expansion towards the Black Sea was prepared by an advance contingent of semi-fugitive peasants, without whom the process of conquest and of annexation would have been considerably retarded.

A final wave of peasant migration that greatly facilitated political consolidation came about in the late sixteenth and early seventeenth centuries in response to the opening of Siberia with its lure of free land and, once again, in reaction to the burdens of taxation and recruitment that weighed more and more heavily upon the entire peasant population of Muscovy. Strictly speaking, this migration followed on the heels of the fur merchants;[15] however, until the government pursued its own policy of colonization, peasant migration numerically far exceeded the official Muscovite presence represented by the trader and the clergy, and at all times far outnumbered the settlers imported by the state.[16] Spontaneous settlement slackened relatively early in the seventeenth century with the consolidation of the Romanov serf system. Henceforth the state strictly determined the rate of flow of its peasants into Siberia. Nevertheless, the original Russian penetration of Siberia, especially West Siberia, took place in conjunction with *voluntary* peasant migration.

In almost all instances, the Russian peasant preceded the state official and thus was a true pioneer in the huge Eurasian steppe. In his quest for fertile land or for security from the nomad or state levies, the adventurous Russian peasant extended the physical horizons of his people. Unwittingly, he also prepared the way for the very state he sought to evade. The more he moved ahead of the authorities, the more he encouraged the acceleration of official Russian expansionism.

Trade and the Expansion of Russia

The next stimulus to Russian expansion was the drive for possession of regions rich in trade commodities and for control of trade routes between major international markets. This of all factors remained the most constant in the dynamics of Russian expansionism. It motivated the Viking merchant-adventurers, whose overlordship greatly influenced the consolidation of the East Slavic tribes into a semifeudal, urban-based society with Kiev as its political and cultural center.

The Varangians (as the Vikings became known in Russian history) provided the main expansionist drive after the initial Slavic migration had come to a halt towards the end of the eighth century. In pursuit of commercial fortunes, the Varangians discovered the Slavs' potential strategic significance to international trade. Their territory could be used as a trade route linking the markets of Baghdad and Constantinople with those of the Carolingian empire. It was this dream of forming a huge commercial empire that inspired the direction of Kievan Rus expansionism in its first centuries. As soon as the Varangians had welded the Eastern Slavs from Novgorod to Kiev into a malleable power base, they embarked on a long campaign to conquer the surrounding trade routes.[17]

The dramatic effort by Sviatoslav I of Kiev (962 to 972) to expand his Dnieper empire westward to the Danube and eastward to the Volga climaxed this period. Much like Charlemagne, who battled to extend his power beyond the original Frankish base, Sviatoslav planned to establish a realm that included numerous other peoples besides the Slavs. Like his Carolingian counterpart, Sviatoslav devised a detailed and systematic plan of conquest,[18] beginning with a military neutralization of the Khazars by the capture of the Sarkel fortress on the Don in 963, and culminating in his campaign in 968 against the Bulgarians on the Danube.[19]

It was in the midst of this campaign in 969 that Sviatoslav divulged the primary reason for his battles, namely, the capture of international trade. For this, he was willing to transfer his capital from Kiev to Pereiaslavets: "I do not care to remain in Kiev, but should prefer to live in Pereiaslavets on the Danube, since that is the center of my realm, where all riches are concentrated: gold, silks, wine, and various fruits from Greece, silver and horses from Hungary and Bohemia, and from Russia furs, wax, honey, and slaves." [20]

In the end he failed. None of his successors managed to aggrandize the Eastern Slavic domain much beyond the original Novgorod-Kiev axis, with the exception of Vladimir, who in 981 conquered eastern Galicia to gain access to the Vistula basin and its trade route potential.[21] A last glimmer of the Varangian-inspired dream to erect a riverine trade empire across West Eurasia during Kievan days is seen in the early thirteenth century, shortly before the Mongol conquest. Grand Prince Iurii II of Vladimir and his brother Prince Iaroslav of Novgorod cooperated in an effort to create a Baltic-Caspian trade route: Iurii fought the Bulgars on the middle Volga and founded a strategic outpost, Nizhni-Novgorod; and Iaroslav fought a successful campaign against the Karelian Finns.

It is to Novgorod that one must look for any really dramatic Russian expansion in the name of trade following the mighty effort exerted by Sviatoslav I in the tenth century. During the eleventh and twelfth centuries, prior to the Mongol invasion, Novgorodian fur trappers and tribute collectors moved along the White Sea littoral northward as far as the Kola peninsula approximately to the present Russo-Norwegian frontier.[22] Eastward, they moved to the Pechora valley and to the Urals through the territory of the Ugrians. Indicative of the origin of territorial expansion of the princes of Novgorod is the 1137 code of Prince Sviatoslav Olgovich, which lists the rivers flowing into the White Sea claimed by him.[23] The adventurous advance of these princes of a merchant republic revealed an intimate knowledge of the complex river network.[24] In the Mongol period, in the thirteenth and fourteenth centuries, Novgorodian merchant trade along the Arctic Circle expanded greatly, ultimately including a coastal route to the mouth of the Ob.[25] At this point, the Novgorodian expansion collided with Muscovite fur trading interests, above all in the Pechora region, and ultimately, in the fifteenth century, after a bitter duel, had to give way to the more dynamic Muscovite expansionism, which had the advantage of denser population. So began the next stage of this category of Eastern Slavic aggrandizement.

Trade interests now fell under Muscovite auspices and came to a head as an international issue in the pivotal reign of Ivan IV (1533 to 1584). Whereas the swift conquest of Kazan in 1552 was cloaked in the guise of a Christian crusade against the Muslims,[26] that of Astrakhan in 1554 and 1556 was overtly pursued to open the entire Volga valley to Muscovite trade.[27] Ivan next turned towards the Baltic, where the Swedes were threatening to dash his hope of establishing a Baltic-Caspian axis, a dream first contemplated by his grandfather, Ivan III.[28] As a result of the revolutionary change of trade routes threatened by recent Portuguese and Spanish explorations, Muscovy was in danger of being pushed to the periphery of European trade activities.[29] Ivan IV had to make Muscovy both accessible to Europe and within reach of Asia in order to prevent economic isolation. Such a prospect derived from the mid-sixteenth century politics of several nations, especially Sweden and Poland, which sought to exclude Muscovy from the strategic Baltic coast.

Consequently, Ivan launched his costly Livonian War [30] in a bid for a Muscovite port on the Baltic coast. As long as he held Narva, the war proved a potentially profitable enterprise,[31] but because of the triple opposition to Ivan's presence on the Baltic, from Poland, Lithuania, and Sweden, Ivan's beachhead in Livonia had to be constantly enlarged to make it militarily defensible. This factor forced him to keep the war going despite peace offers in 1565. The 1566 Zemskii Sobor's decision to continue the war was taken largely as a result of the advice given by the seventy-five Muscovite merchant-delegates (who made up one fifth of the assembled delegates, and who participated for the first time in a council of state alongside the traditional advisers, the boiars and the upper clergy).

The final stages of Muscovy's pre-Petrine territorial expansion, largely stimulated by trade interests, culminated in the conquest of nearly all of Siberia. Following the pattern of the Novgorodian fur merchants, traders licensed by Moscow penetrated deep into the interior, then to be followed by Muscovite government officials and, of course, by the Church. For at least the first fifty years after the destruction of the Volga khanates of Kazan and Astrakhan and the opening of the East, Muscovite penetration of Siberia was achieved by a combination of merchant endeavors and Cossack adventurism. Though granted a government monopoly, the Stroganovs pushed well beyond the original land staked out for their exploitation in pursuit of the seemingly endless wealth of Siberia. In their quests, they were assisted by Ermak Timofeevich and his Don Cossack mercenaries,[32] and the tacit approval of Moscow.

The state was never far behind. As early as 1555, Muscovy had begun to impose its will on the peoples to the east through a system of tribute vassalage (*iasaq*).[33] In extending privilege rights to merchants such as the Stroganovs, it retained a controlling hand from the beginning and by 1590 had troops stationed permanently in West Siberia to quell local uprisings. By 1613, under the Romanovs, travel distances were so great that Russians found they could not survive without state support. They knew bitter want during the Time of Troubles when grain supplies so dwindled as to threaten them with starvation. Henceforth, the march east, though primarily in pursuit of trade, proceeded in conjunction with state supervision, best symbolized by the promotion of the Siberian section (*stol*) (founded in 1599) to a full-fledged department (*prikaz*) in 1614, which received complete autonomy in 1637. The state worked in close cooperation with its merchants, not only in consolidating its hold on Siberia but in sponsoring expeditions ever eastward in search of furs. The process culminated in 1648 with Semen Dezhnev's rounding of the northeastern tip of the Eurasian continent through the Bering Straits. Thereafter Muscovy could reach across the sea to the American continent, though this adventure did not begin until after Peter the Great.

Religion and Russian Expansionism

In their own minds, the Russians were less Slavs (a characteristic of which they were little conscious until the nineteenth century) than they were Orthodox Christians. Until the great schism of the seventeenth century, Russians shared a single faith which influenced both their spiritual and their political lives. From the time of their conversion in 988, Christianity became inextricably woven into the pattern of their lives, inspiring and shaping their private and public actions. Above all, Christianity gave them a world view that enabled them to orient themselves to the peoples around them: the Muslims to the east and the Roman Catholics to the west. Both posed a threat to their political and, therefore, to their religious survival.

Ever since Vladimir I, the first Christian prince, Rus princes conceived their role in religious terms. Indeed, the most renowned were often rewarded not only with the legendary honors due warrior heroes but also with admission to the calendar of saints.[34] It is not surprising that most of the Kievan and Muscovite military action against nations of other religions was undertaken in the form of crusades: new territories were seized to extend the frontiers of Orthodox Christianity. Thus, apart from the expansionism brought on by the aggressiveness stimulated by geographical restrictions and the greed aroused by economic desires, one must take into consideration yet another dimension of Russian expansionism, namely, the zeal born of religious messianism. Given a long encirclement by powers of other religions, Orthodox Christianity became a constant in the conquering rationale of pre-Petrine Russia.

In describing the Kievan Rus preparations to attack the Polovtsian nomads who controlled the steppe south of Kiev, the *Russian Primary Chronicle* explicitly states that the Rus mind looked upon the endeavor as a crusading venture. As long as they fought the Polovtsi pagan in the name of the true faith, the Rus had nothing to fear: "For great is the power of the Cross. By the Cross are vanquished the powers of the Devil. The Cross helps our princes in combat, and the faithful who are protected by the Cross conquer in battle the foes who oppose them." [35] Throughout their numerous campaigns against the Polovtsi, the Rus princes rallied their troops as Christian armies. In 1102 they set out on their campaign as if on a divine assignment: "God inspired the princes of Rus' with a noble project, for they resolved to attack the Polovtsians and invade their territory." [36] In 1111 they envisioned themselves as the children of Israel about to conquer the Promised Land in calling on the Angel of the Lord to go before them.[37] In 1185, during the famous battle commemorated in the *Song of the Host of*

Igor, the Rus saw themselves fighting as God's soldiers: "Fighting for the Christians against the pagans." [38]

On the other frontier, to the southwest in Galicia and Volynia, Orthodox Christianity instilled similar attitudes in the Rus *vis-à-vis* the Catholic world. Early in the thirteenth century, hard-pressed Prince Roman proudly rejected allegiance to the Pope: "Is the Pope's Christian sword different from mine? As long as I possess mine I have need of no other." [39] And in 1214, when Prince Mstislav of Novgorod extended his power to Galicia, he did so as the liberator of Orthodox Christians from the Catholic Hungarians; the population complemented his claim by rising up in his behalf.

Much of the political revival during the long Mongol overlordship was due to the religious zeal that sprang up within the Rus peoples, and this their rulers were able to tap in their own rise to political independence. Thanks to the memory of Alexander Nevskii, grand prince of Novgorod, as the saintly victor over the Catholic Germans and Swedes, the Russian princes who turned to fight the Mongols in the name of the only true faith stood to inherit an important mantle.[40] The first to earn the title of successor to Alexander Nevskii was Prince Dmitrii Donskoi, famed for his victory over the Mongols at Kulikovo in 1380. Both according to the literary narration, the *Zadonshchina* of the priest Sophronia of Riazan, and the later official Muscovite rendition,[41] the battle was undertaken as a religious obligation to save the Orthodox Christians from the Muslims. Indeed, the venture had been given the solemn blessing of Saint Sergei Radonezh, then the most revered religious figure in Mongol Russia. "Go against the godless," he told Dmitrii, "and with God's assistance you will conquer and return safe to your homeland with great glory. . . . Go without hesitation, my lord, daringly against their ferocity, do not fear, God will help you in all." [42]

Muscovy's unification of the northeastern principalities was also undertaken in the name of Orthodoxy. Ivan III's annexation of the Republic of Novgorod in the 1470's and of the Grand Principality of Tver in 1485 were both executed on the excuse that Catholic Lithuania might otherwise extend its influence into these Orthodox Christian regions. Even the official *casus belli* when he attacked Lithuania in 1500 was phrased in terms of the increasing pressure Catholic authorities put on Orthodox citizens to submit to the Uniate formula spelled out by Rome in the Council of Florence in 1439.[43] Similarly, Ivan IV's conquests of Kazan and Astrakhan were done as much in the name of religion as they were for mercantile interests, as is indicated by the famous icon *The Church Triumphant* in the Tretiakov Gallery in Moscow. This icon shows Tsar Ivan side by side with the Archangel Michael and Dmitrii Donskoi, suggesting Ivan's spiritual descent in a holy tradition of saintly Orthodox conquerors. No less zealously did Ivan fight the Livonians and the Polish-Lithuanians as his ungodly enemies. Over and over again he portrayed himself as the guardian of the true faith, accordingly entrusted with the task of reuniting the Christian world in emulation of his great predecessor, the Emperor Constantine.[44]

Although the religious principle never prevailed at the expense of political interests, it always served as a useful rationale, if only to disguise more earthly motives underlying Muscovite acquisitions. Nevertheless, the cautious and practical rulers of Muscovy should not be looked at too cynically. Their religious proclamations were not sheer camouflage. As devout Christians, they never completely separated religion from politics: the former dictated a constant commitment, and the latter called for prudence and patience. Thus the ideal and the real were harmonized in the minds of the Muscovite princes and tsars.

The Russian Church, on its side, never ceased goading the civil authorities to expand the borders of Muscovy. From the moment the Russian metropolitans took up residence in Moscow in 1328, they increasingly lent their moral support to the aggrandizing ambitions of the princes of Muscovy. The head of the Russian Church bore the title Metropolitan of Kiev and of all Rus, and his technical jurisdiction extended well beyond the frontiers of Muscovy, so that it could only be to his advantage to bring his large diocese within the confines of a single political order. The Russian hierarchy's vision of an enlarged Muscovy became even more urgent with the establishment of a separate metropolitanate in Kiev in 1458 under Catholic Lithuanian auspices to offset the Moscow election of a metropolitan ten years earlier as a result of the crisis brought on by the Council of Ferrara-Florence. With the threat of losing the Ukraine to the Uniate movement, Muscovy's metropolitans and the entire clergy called insistently for the conquest of the Ukraine and the liberation and unification of all Orthodox Rus. And when the fall of Constantinople left Muscovy as the only autonomous Orthodox Christian political order, the voices of the Church grew ever louder in their effort to shape imperial Muscovite ideology. Though not successful in influencing directly Muscovite territorial ambitions, they were able to inject a dynamic sense of messianism and religious mission into Muscovite foreign policy. In 1492, Metropolitan Zosima wrote Ivan III that "Moscow and all the Rus lands were the new city of Constantinople," the new Orthodox empire.[45] In 1510, Abbot Filofei wrote Vasilii III declaring Moscow to be the new Rome, heir to the spiritual and physical heritage of Rome and Byzantium,[46] an event coinciding with the monk Savva's announcement that the princes of Muscovy were the direct descendants of the Roman emperors.[47]

In disseminating the grandiose concept of Moscow as the new Eternal City, heir of Rome and Constantinople, the Church hierarchy conveniently conveyed to the Muscovite princes the fact of their divinely sanctioned obligation to fashion out of Muscovy a new Christian empire, without, however, specifically delineating its frontiers.[48] This very vagueness proved, in the end, a useful device for justifying many expeditions of conquest aimed at other than Orthodox-populated regions. In the case of Ivan IV, the warring tsar never once doubted that "the Russian piety" [49] placed Muscovy above all other states in its inherent virtue, and hence in its organic growth, which he saw as the fulfillment of Divine Will. Ever since the fall of Byzantium in 1453 the new millennium, which began in 1492, belonged to Orthodox Muscovy. Providential history clearly pointed towards Moscow. As Abbot Filofei explained in reference to Muscovy's annexation of Pskov, Muscovy was carrying out the positive will of God.[50] In aggrandizing itself, Filofei extrapolated, Muscovy was laying the foundations of a new Christian empire, of which it was the preordained head in light of the religious discreditation and political demise of Byzantium and the concomitant rise and triumph of Muscovy.[51]

Whereas a slavish acceptance of the Third Rome theory as the basis of Muscovite foreign policy was never the case, the influence of the fundamental *Weltanschauung* that it exerted upon the official thinking was considerable. As early as the reign of Vasilii III (1505 to 1533), Muscovy's leading diplomatic figure, Dmitrii Gerasimov, fell prey to the temptations of Filofei's formula.[52] As Moscow's ambassador to Rome, his public pronouncement that Moscow was the new *urbis orbis* could not but have stirred profound anxieties. By the reign of Ivan IV, the entire court was imbued with an air of Christian superiority and self-righteousness, which on the one hand increased the desire to expel the Protestants from the Baltic (which Muscovy contended historically belonged to it), and on the other hand reinforced a policy of extensive Christian colonization in the Muslim lands to the east.

In the seventeenth century, the Church had even greater opportunity to steer Muscovite foreign policy when Patriarch Filaret reigned cojointly with his son Tsar Michael Romanov. To the day of his death in 1633, Filaret laid plans for the day when Romanov Muscovy should carry its wars against Poland, not only to revenge Poland's interventions during the Time of Troubles but also to bring a militant Orthodoxy to battle militant Polish Catholicism. In so doing, he was strongly backed by the populace, which saw Poland as the personification of the anti-Christ.[53] Filaret was so determined in his ambition that he followed this course at the expense of the Orthodox Christians in Kiev, whose appeals he shunned in 1625.[54] With the accession of Patriarch Nikon in 1652, Muscovy turned more towards the Orthodox East, and the plan to liberate coreligionists in that region took shape. Once Poland had been neutralized and the eastern Ukraine annexed, this ambition began to fit into the realistic schemes of Muscovy, namely, a war with Turkey. Such a prospect had been avoided for over one hundred and fifty years.[55] By 1700 the principle of an aggressive Christian monarch and the world ambitions of the Russian Orthodox Church, which had been merging since the fourteenth century,[56] finally became fully compatible—in part, no doubt, because the tsars felt Russia to be strong enough to challenge the Ottomans. The key to the Balkan peninsula was its Orthodox peoples; a call for their liberation might give Russian trade an exit through the strategic Bosporus.

Russian Expansion and Dynastic Ambitions

Rus princes never forgot that they belonged to the great House of Rurik, a dynasty founded by the legendary Danish Viking prince who came to eastern Baltic shores in the middle of the ninth century. Throughout Kievan times, descendants of Rurik held sway in the expanding realm. After the death of Grand Prince Iaroslav in 1054, the right to rule the various principalities of Kiev and the line of succession to the city of Kiev were restricted to the successors of Iaroslav. The Rurikids conceived of themselves as the legitimate heirs to Kievan Rus. With the decline of Rurikid power in Kiev and the concomitant rise of Vladimir-Suzdal, the political center shifted, but not the monopoly of the Rurikids.

During the Mongol invasion and overlordship, the House of Vladimir-Suzdal (descendants of Iaroslav's son Vsevolod) sought to gain permanent possession of the title of Grand Prince and, thereby, inherit the legacy of Rurik. For a century, however, their efforts were thwarted by the successful challenge of the House of Tver, itself a subbranch of the Rurik line originating from Vladimir-Suzdal. Tver's efforts were finally defeated by the Muscovite princes, who, beginning with Grand Prince Ivan Kalita (1328 to 1341), wrested the Mongol charter, the *iarlyk,* from Tver and thereafter, with but one brief exception in 1375, held the title continuously.

Ivan I, not content with the title alone, augmented it to "Gosudar Vseia Rusi." [57] Thereby he elevated himself to the rank of *primus inter pares* and claimed obeisance from a domain as extensive as that of the metropolitan from whom he had borrowed the title and who had just taken up his residence in Moscow. In so doing, Ivan announced that the Rurikid inheritance previously seated in Kiev and then moved to Vladimir and Suzdal had now been established in Moscow. Over the course of three centuries, his successors were able to secure this claim.

It is significant that the territorial ambitions to reconstruct the former Kievan empire and to bring the Rurikid realms under one monarch again were reflected in the periodic modifications of the titles adopted by the princes of Muscovy. From reign to reign, a subtle but important change would occur, indicative of the imperial ideology developed by the Muscovite branch of the Rurikid as they pursued their goal of reclaiming their *otchina* (patrimony), a vision of a territory that expanded from generation to generation.

At first, the grand princes of Muscovy used their new title cautiously, restricting it to inter-princely affairs to accomplish the first step in their long-range plan, namely, to establish their primacy among the Orthodox princes under Mongol jurisdiction. Thus, Grand Prince Simeon, Ivan's successor, employed it in 1350 in his dealings with Novgorod.[58] Dmitrii Donskoi, the hero of Kulikovo, received the accolade "Gatherer of the Russian Lands." [59] Vasilii I (1389 to 1425) returned to Ivan Kalita's formula.[60] Following the tumultuous years of Vasilii II (1425 to 1462), in which the existence of Muscovy was seriously threatened, Ivan III the Great (1462 to 1505) again promoted Muscovy's steady advance as the primary Russian principality in the Northeast. As he annexed Novgorod and Tver, Ivan proudly flourished his title: Grand Prince of all the Russias.[61]

Then, turning to his neighbors in the West, Ivan the Great started to employ his title in his dealings with them. Beginning in 1483, Ivan heralded himself to the Livonians as the legitimate ruler of all the Russias.[62] Two years later, in his struggle with Lithuania to impose his will on Tver, Ivan formally identified himself as monarch of all the Russians [63] in defiance of a similar claim made by the grand duke of Lithuania, who styled himself as "Dux terras Russiae." The use of the title was tantamount to a declaration of war, and war did break out in 1500, a war in which strategic territory was at stake.

In 1493, in his dealings with the German Emperor, Ivan the Great for the first time used his provocative title with a major European power.[64] By that time, Muscovite imperial ideology had taken yet another symbolic step to communicate its historical claims. Since 1473, Ivan had on various occasions resorted to the title Tsar, a Russian corruption of Caesar, in reference to the fact that the Rurikid genealogy linked the House of Muscovy to the ancient Roman emperors.[65] To impress the Emperor (who also saw himself as the successor of the Roman Imperium), Ivan made use of the two-headed eagle insignia. As a reinforcement to the Romanization of Muscovite imperial ideology, a learned priest from Tver, Spiridon (later the monk Savva), proposed a new historical genealogy for the House of Muscovy. According to him, Rurik had been a brother of Pruss, the founder of Prussia, thereby making the Rurikid direct descendants of the Roman Emperor Augustus.[66]

As Muscovite territorial acquisitions demonstrated, the adoption and strategic use of titles and their complementary ideology constituted not only a desire to express equality with other rulers but an overt announcement of expansionist designs from which Muscovy would not be deterred. Nor was this lost on Muscovy's enemies. In 1519, for example, the grand master of the Teutonic Order (knowing that Livonia was considered a part of "all the Russias") hoped to deflect Vasilii III's territorial ambitions southeastward by encouraging him "to fight for his Constantinopolitan inheritance." [67] no doubt assuming that the much-publicized Third Rome theory had altered Muscovy's territorial ambitions. But neither Vasilii III nor his successor Ivan IV the Terrible was to be influenced by that ploy.[68]

As a final dimension to the Muscovite imperial policy, Muscovy's rulers were increasingly aware of themselves as successors to the heritage of the Golden Horde. As the power of the Kipchak capital of Sarai dwindled, four potential political centers emerged: the Crimea in 1427, Kazan in 1437, Astrakhan in 1466, and, finally, Muscovy in 1480. Thereafter began the battle for the Volga valley, the backbone of the Golden Horde's empire.

Muscovy, no less than the three khanates, strove to gain possession of this vital trade artery. Although its Volga campaigns were partially fought as a Christian crusade to spur on the Orthodox Russians, the rulers of Muscovy engaged in this Eastern campaign as the logical heirs to the ruins of the former Golden Horde. Indeed, as has been amply demonstrated by Michael Cherniavsky, the title Tsar was first of all synonymous with Khan long before the Russian mind associated it with the idea of the Roman Caesar.[69] Thus, when a chronicle referred to Dmitrii Donskoi as "tsar," it implied that he had attained the stature of a khan, an independent monarch.[70] It was after his successful campaign against Kazan that Ivan III adopted the title for the first time.[71] And when Ivan IV conquered Kazan and Astrakhan as tsar, he did so as the true successor to the khan of the Golden Horde.[72] As Cherniavsky showed, the title Tsar in the Russian political language of the day carried with it the idea of a sovereignty which had been the khan's until 1480, and which was then transferred to the grand prince himself; the latter, in adopting the title, did so after imposing his own sovereignty upon the Kazanis. Similarly, Ivan IV imposed his will on the Astrakhanis in the middle of the sixteenth century. In 1556, when turning to Livonia, Ivan did so not only as "Gosudar Vseia Rusi" but also as the legitimate ruler of his newly acquired provinces in the Volga valley. He justified his right to the title Tsar (that is to say, Khan), since it had described the previous rulers of the region which he had just conquered and annexed.

Thus, if the rulers of Muscovy marched westward as the descendants of the Roman emperors and the spiritual heirs of the Byzantine emperors, they marched eastward as the successors of the khans of that great Eurasian empire of the Mongols of which they had once been a part. As mid-sixteenth century Muscovite political theory indicates, there was no reluctance in Orthodox Russia to recognize the prestige of great Muslim rulers. Even as Ivan embarked on his great expeditions against Kazan as the newly crowned tsar of Russia, Ivan Peresvetov urged him, if Ivan desired rapid success, to emulate the most successful conqueror of the day, namely, Sultan Mohammed the Great, before whom all Europe trembled.[73] Consequently, the rulers of

Muscovy, an *imperium mundi in statu nascendi,* tapped the gamut of possibilities offered them by their own rich past—by Kievan Rus as well as by imperial Rome and by the empire of Jenghiz Khan—in order to formulate an imperial ideology that could better their territorial ambitions.

The Emergence of Muscovite Foreign Policy

From the standpoint of *Realpolitik,* wherein power reigns supreme and is the ultimate criterion determining the expansion and contraction of states, the elements discussed so far serve only as ideological rationales, supplying but secondary stimuli to the expansionist ambitions of a state. In the case of Muscovy, the urge to enlarge its borders sprang from a simple desire—the instinct to survive, a response to the hazards posed by topography.

Given the absence of natural protective frontiers behind which the state could find reasonable security, and given the irreconcilable tensions between Muscovy and its neighbors, Muscovy chose among the few options in its struggle for political survival to put as much distance as possible between itself and its enemies. The multinational and multicultural composition of the peoples in its dominions made Muscovy extremely sensitive to disorders beyond its frontiers that might spill over into Muscovy. Combined, these fears of foreign invasion and imported uprisings encouraged Muscovy's foreign policy planners to move ever outward. The process had no comparable historical precedent. Out of the quest for national security Muscovite foreign policy was born, and upon its dramatic successes the Russian empire of Peter the Great was founded.

From the time Muscovy emerged as an independent political unit free from Mongol overlordship, its rulers resorted to the technique of territorial expansion as a means of defense. Even the early annexations of adjacent principalities can be interpreted in these terms: Novgorod and Tver—to prevent Lithuanian expansion; Riazan—to diminish the chances of a Tatar invasion. In pursuit of his goal to secure Muscovy's new independence, Ivan III laid down the basic outlines of a foreign policy that proved valid for over two centuries.

Recognizing the technological superiority of Europe, Ivan knew that Muscovy's future depended on full participation in its scientific achievements, and such a decision demanded unrestricted access to the

European centers of learning.[74] Setting his sights accordingly, Ivan III clarified the principles of all future Muscovite foreign policy. First and foremost, Muscovy had to be assured of the neutrality of the peoples to the east if it was to avoid military encirclement in its efforts to march west. Second, Muscovy had to isolate its Western enemies by means of shrewd diplomacy in order to avert an international war with which Muscovy could not cope. Third, Muscovy had to be prepared to fight its enemies alone and not count on victory with the assistance of an ally. In preparing for and conducting his war with Lithuania, Ivan was to give classical expression to these principles: in a series of military expeditions against Kazan, Ivan demonstrated Muscovy's military superiority sufficiently to discourage its interference; thanks to his patient negotiations with the khanate of Crimea, Ivan won assurance of its temporary neutrality; and, finally, after careful diplomatic settlements with Moldavia, Hungary, and Denmark, among others, Ivan deprived Lithuania of military allies, thereby allowing him to fight the war alone to win important territorial concessions for Muscovy.[75]

Vasilii III soon understood the accuracy and brilliance of his father's foreign policy both in his acceptance of it and in his failure to observe all its principles faithfully. In the first part of his reign, in pursuit of the Western expansion advised by Ivan III, Vasilii III honored the conditions maintained by his father, with the result that Muscovy captured Smolensk in 1514. In the second half of his reign, however, Vasilii failed to keep the Crimea neutral. Therefore, even as he attempted to conduct an aggressive war against Lithuania, he also had to contend with attacks from the Crimea. Many of the advantages gained by Ivan were rapidly eroded as Muscovy's stance *vis-à-vis* the West was hampered by growing disorder in the steppe to the south. In order to quiet the vulnerable steppe frontier, Vasilii resorted to building fortifications deeper and deeper into the plain and inaugurated a policy of counterattacks, without, however, postponing his push against Lithuania. Thereby he left a legacy of impending war on two fronts to the regents of the young Ivan IV in 1533.[76]

By the time Ivan IV assumed some control over Muscovy's foreign policy in 1547, Muscovy was threatened both by Lithuania and by the Crimea. The young tsar's troubles were compounded by the resurgence of Kazan at the instigation of the Crimea.[77] During the first decade of his reign, Ivan and his advisers slowly returned to an acceptance of the rules Ivan III had recognized as essential for a viable Muscovite foreign policy. In the context of a pact with Lithuania assuring it that Muscovy harbored no further territorial intentions, Muscovy focused upon Kazan in a series of campaigns that culminated in the historic conquest of 1552. Then, in order to assure safety for its trade with Persia and Central Asia, Muscovy imposed its will on the entire Volga valley, none of whose inhabitants was strong enough to maintain order along the exposed river banks. Thus in order to keep peace along a river vital to its economic growth, Muscovy absorbed the entire region and won reasonable guarantee of a secure eastern flank before turning back to its primary purpose of forging a direct link with Central Europe.[78]

It was at this juncture in Ivan the Terrible's reign that he and his advisers split over the next step in foreign policy. Whereas Ivan favored an immediate move upon the Baltic as the logical continuation of the Volga conquests, several of his advisers counseled a war with the Crimea to eliminate the danger from the South once and for all. Wisely, Ivan avoided this course, correctly reasoning that it would involve the Ottoman Empire, an opponent Muscovy could not challenge at the time.[79] Instead, Ivan sought to tame the steppe and dissuade the Crimea from attacking by mounting annual deterrent attacks against the khanate.[80] At the same time, Ivan turned boldly westward and prepared for conquest on the Baltic, through which passed a considerable portion of Muscovy's trade with Europe. With the weakening of the power of the Teutonic Knights and the disintegration of Livonia, Poland and Sweden vied for control of this strategic coastline. Muscovy's old rivalries with both Sweden and Poland made them equally unacceptable as the successor power in Livonia. Both states had actively pursued a policy of denying Muscovy a place on the Baltic ever since Ivan III had built Ivangorod opposite Narva in 1492. In the long run, Ivan had no choice but to take the initiative in seizing Livonia before his enemies could blockade his trade routes to the markets of Europe.

If Ivan's decision to engage in a conquest of Livonia was correct and true to form in the tradition of his grandfather, his diplomatic preparations were unsatisfactory and reflected his lack of patience as compared to Ivan III. Instead of waiting until Muscovite diplomacy had assured him of a limited war, Ivan plunged into war; and in his rush to conquer all of Livonia (not just a satisfactory beachhead to protect Muscovy's trade) he involved Muscovy in a protracted international war that ended in his humiliating defeat almost a quarter of a century later.[81] As the war dragged on, Lithuania, Poland, and Sweden were actively drawn into the contest for Livonia against a steadily weakening Muscovy deprived of military allies of its own. In the middle of the war, Ivan's defenses in the South broke down and the Crimea dealt Muscovy a dreadful blow in 1571 by putting the city of Moscow to the torch. By the time he died in 1584, the price for having ignored the tactics of Ivan III's foreign policy was a Muscovy compelled to share borders with a merged Poland-Lithuania (by the treaty of Lublin in 1569) and a powerful Sweden which had rid itself of Danish domination. Together, they posed an ominous threat to the very existence of Muscovy: Poland, as the Eastern outpost of Counter-Reformation Catholicism, was poised to eliminate Muscovy as an Orthodox Christian state. Sweden, as an emerging European monarchical nation, was on the verge of making *mare nostrum* out of the Baltic, and, to achieve that goal, decided to deny Muscovy contact with the sea, including its White Sea outlets.

No experience more deeply impressed the fallacies and fatalities of foreign policy on the Muscovite consciousness than the tragic decade of the Time of Troubles (1605 to 1613). Almost simultaneously, all of Muscovy's enemies descended upon it, determined to erase it from the political map, or at least to reduce it to a peripheral state of no consequence in Eastern Europe. Sweden made good its claims along the Baltic and temporarily occupied Novgorod and its territories. Poland directly and indirectly (in the guise of supporting pretenders) entered the capital itself and threatened to make Muscovy a new outpost for Polish ambitions. From the South, Cossack armies poured out of the Dnieper and Don valleys in search of adventure and booty, and thereby worsened the trauma of the Time of Troubles. Only heroic resistance and fortuitous circumstances saved Muscovy from annihilation. The new dynasty, the Romanovs, and the architects of their foreign policy could not but approach the revival of Muscovy with extreme caution, pondering the lessons of the terrible times.

Until 1633 Patriarch Filaret was the leading figure in Muscovite foreign policy planning.[82] On the whole, patience and caution characterized his philosophy, and its spirit endured to the end of the reign of Michael Romanov in 1645. After working out peace terms with Sweden in 1617 and Poland in 1619, Muscovy could at long last anticipate a relative balance of power: Sweden and Poland together could overcome Muscovy, but alone, neither was strong enough to defeat it; Muscovy, however, was not even capable of defeating either one individually. Given this precarious stalemate, it was essential that Muscovite policy concentrate on preventing a Polish-Swedish alliance. By exploiting the rivalries between the two countries, Muscovy could keep them at bay and gain valuable time in which to recuperate before resuming its westward expansion.

Once this was recognized as a means of keeping the peace, the path to winning future wars also became clear. Since under no circumstances must Muscovy face more than one of its enemies at a time, they must be confronted in the order best suited to Muscovy's strengths and long-range interests. As in the past, two concerns dictated Muscovite territorial aspirations in the interests of national security: tranquil and secure borders, and outlets to the sea. The former looked to stability in the South, where different groups of Cossacks kept the land in constant disorder in their struggle for territory in competition with Poland, Muscovy, and the Crimea. Since total Muscovite intervention in the Crimea would involve the Ottoman Empire, the southern conquest must be delayed, even though it was the key to control over the sprawling steppe. The latter goal ultimately spelled a war with Sweden, and such could be contemplated only if Poland were kept out, a matter contingent on Poland's being forcibly subordinated to Muscovite military superiority. In other words, the way to the Baltic (and unavoidable war with Sweden) lay via confrontation with Poland first; subjection of the steppe and a challenge of the Ottoman Empire constituted a complementary and even longer-range consideration. This, in a nutshell, was the orientation of the Romanov foreign policy during the seventeenth century; and with but minor exceptions, it was scrupulously observed by all its statesmen from Filaret through Michael D. Voloshininov, Almaz Ivanov, and Afanasii Ordyn-Nashchokin, the advisers of Tsar Alexis. As for the East, where their interests lay only secondarily, they gave it their attention only when opportunities in the West permitted. With that began a pendular process of aggressive expansion westward and eastward which continued with but minor variations into the twentieth century.

Not until 1633 did Muscovy attempt to launch a new era of expansion westward. In that year it declared war on Poland, hoping to exploit the death of its king to regain Smolensk. By 1634 Muscovy had learned that its armies were still no match for the Polish armies. After the peace was signed, it returned to its former attitude of avoiding war, no matter how tempting the invitations to intervene (and there were several from Kiev and the various Cossack communities during the 1620's). Just as Muscovy deceptively assured and reassured Sweden that its interests in Poland involved not the Baltic coast but the Ukraine, it continually informed the Ottomans that it had no major ambitions in the steppe with respect to the Black Sea. As a gesture of its reliability, it refused in 1645 to accept the Don Cossacks' offer to annex the Azov region they had seized from the Crimea in the name of the tsar in 1637.

Only after years of careful military expansion and modernization did Muscovy decide to make a move against Poland, and this was in the context of the Dnieper Cossack independence movement in the middle of the century. Unable to secure their independence through their own efforts, the Dnieper Cossacks were forced to appeal to Muscovy. Its agreement to guarantee their independence brought on a war with Poland that lasted on and off until 1667. With the peace of Andrusovo, Muscovy reasserted its military primacy over Poland and at long last gained control of the Ukraine as far west as the left bank of the river Dnieper, including Kiev. This represented a major step in imposing control over the entire restless southern plains.

To the east chronic troubles with the Kalmucks and Bashkirs plagued Muscovy in the 1630's and 1640's. In the early 1640's the Kalmucks attacked the Bashkirs and in 1643 entered the lower Volga valley, besieged Astrakhan, and continued on into the Northern Caucasus. Faced with the need to pacify the frontier beyond the Volga, but not wishing to jeopardize their campaign against Poland, Muscovite authorities devised a plan to neutralize the Kalmuck-Bashkir region. In 1655 the Kalmuck armies were pressed into the war in the Ukraine, primarily to participate in deterrent expeditions against the Crimeans and, thereby, to free the Muscovite armies for battle with Poland. In 1664, during a lull in the war with Poland, a major Bashkir uprising was quelled, and at the conclusion of the war with Poland in 1667 Muscovy took steps to integrate the region east of the Volga into its state system. Under the supervision of the *voevoda* of Tobolsk, P. I. Godunov, administrative controls were established as far east as the Ob watershed to protect trade routes to Central Asia and distant China. And because of the lasting peace with Poland, Muscovy maintained its Eastern momentum, extending its official presence to the borders of China, with which it finally signed the treaty of Nerchinsk in 1689. This treaty designated the territory north of the Amur as a Muscovite sphere of influence and laid the groundwork for the absorption of the whole of Siberia.

In the interim, Muscovy's Western foreign policy was gravely modified. After the death of Tsar Alexis in 1676, there appeared a new architect of Muscovite foreign policy in the person of Prince Vasilii Golitsyn.[83] In his estimation, in contradiction to past opinions, Muscovy ought first to attend to the chronic disorder in the steppe. Internecine Cossack rivalries inflamed by Crimean intervention and occasional Turkish condonation (and even participation) seriously retarded the economic development of the fertile Ukrainian plains. He decided, therefore, that a solution to this problem took precedence over preparations to put Muscovy on the Baltic (which called for a costly war with Sweden).

To this end, Golitsyn departed from two previously tried and tested principles of Muscovite foreign policy, namely *not* to aim for the Black Sea until after the Baltic Sea outlet had been secured and *never* to rely on an alliance to achieve these ends. Instead, Golitsyn felt that in the context of a European alliance Muscovy could share in the gradual upset of the military balance of power between Europe and the Ottoman Empire in order to reach the Black Sea coast. The dramatic victory of Poland and Austria over the Turks in 1683 persuaded Golitsyn that the turning tide also favored Muscovy. Along with Venice, Poland, Austria, and Rome, Golitsyn involved Muscovy in a latter-day crusade in the belief that it would serve Muscovite interests in the Ukraine. On two occasions, Golitsyn led large Muscovite armies against the Ottomans, only to learn that while victory was assured technologically superior Europe, it was not yet within the grasp of Muscovy and its only partially modernized armies. Thus, in 1687, Golitsyn suffered a humiliating defeat, having been totally outmaneuvered; and again, in 1689, he led a military expedition which at best was nothing but bluster and had an embarrassing outcome.

Specifically, the two episodes contributed indirectly to the downfall of the regency of Sophia Alekseevna and directly to the political demise of Golitsyn, allowing Peter I to occupy the throne as the sole ruler of Russia.

The advent of Peter, however, did not immediately reverse the errors in Muscovy's foreign policy as practiced by Golitsyn.[84] Instead, the youthful Peter resolved to continue the unfinished war with Turkey, a goal he pursued with great energy. Nevertheless, despite his contention that better management was all that Muscovy needed in its conduct of the war, Peter fared no better than his predecessor. In his first campaign in 1695, Peter failed to reach the elusive Black Sea. In his second campaign, he did manage to capture the Azov region in 1696, but Muscovy still remained blocked from the sea by the Turkish-controlled Strait of Kerch. Determined to win, Peter looked for a grand alliance to expel the Turks from the northern shores of the Black Sea. Whereupon Peter set out for Europe on his famous voyage in quest of allies.

Much to his chagrin, Peter learned that no one of any consequence in Europe had any interest in his project. He was therefore forced to begin a modification of Muscovy's foreign policy strategy as he had inherited it. Less by design than from circumstance, largely because his trip to Europe had put him in touch with a plan to form an alliance against Sweden and overthrow its monopoly control of that sea, Peter chose to make the Baltic Sea his first objective. Typically, Peter hurled himself headlong into this new venture. Assured of Polish cooperation, Peter hurried to war in 1700 counting heavily upon his allies, Poland and Denmark. The end result was a war that dragged on for the rest of his reign and forced Peter to adjust all his domestic reforms to his military needs. Like Ivan IV, instead of contenting himself with a limited stretch of the Baltic coast, Peter lost perspective on the strategic necessities and pushed the war to its extreme conclusion. Russia was to become master of the Baltic, and Sweden was to be reduced to a tertiary power. But by prolonging the war far beyond Russia's national interests Peter magnified the war's importance in European eyes. It irrevocably upset the balance of power, so much so that it permanently distorted Russia's significance in Europe. By pushing Russia deep into Europe and excluding Sweden as a meaningful partner in the pattern of alliance, Peter permanently entangled Russia in the web of European alliances and counteralliances which was to generate war after war of no conceivable benefit to Russian national interests, but from which Russia dared not withdraw for fear of an unfavorable power alignment.

By his unplanned conduct of the war with Sweden, Peter made Russia a potential friend or foe of every European power. His forceful manner of pushing Russia's frontiers outward in other directions merely aggravated the situation. Any Russian advance set Russia on a collision course with one European power or another, however distant the project. The war with Turkey was no longer simply a struggle for the Black Sea coast but a contest for the Balkans, and the Balkan issue aroused the fears of the Habsburg empire. Peter's victories over Persia and several Central Asian khanates were no longer remote battles in the heart of the Eurasian continent but, from England's point of view, Russian advances towards the Indian subcontinent and the Indian Ocean, which England regarded as its domain. Russia's penetration of Alaska and advance along the Pacific coast brought it into conflict with the Spanish empire, as well as with English interests. Thus, thanks to the brilliant but immodest acquisitions of Peter, Russian aggrandizement became a matter of world concern and called for entirely new techniques in the conduct of Russian foreign policy.

Not only could Russia no longer afford to stay outside the alliance system but Russia's security depended (if only in the minds of its foreign policy planners) more and more upon strong allies. Furthermore, Peter's conquests, instead of easing, compounded the centuries-long sense of insecurity induced by the absence of formidable geographical barriers. As with Ivan IV, the victories had brought Russia closer to the center of Europe, but all the powers—Austria, England, France, and Prussia—not only regarded Russia as a major danger but harbored profound Russophobic sentiments. The foreign affairs of the empire had indeed to be skillfully managed if European anti-Russian forces were to be stifled. Though the Russian empire was greater than ever when Peter the Great died, so was its sense of insecurity *vis-à-vis* Europe. The process of aggrandizement begun in the days of Ivan III against the Lithuanians and the Tatars had by no means diminished its fears; on the contrary, they became more acute during the days of the empire.

The Traditional, Thematic Character of Russian Expansionism

In retrospect, it cannot be said that the character of Russian expansionism prior to Peter the Great had any distinctive historical qualities that set it apart from the expansionist forces operating elsewhere in Europe. Diplomatic observers in Poland-Lithuania, in the Habsburg empire, and in the Ottoman Empire did not find the Muscovite ambitions mysterious or out of the ordinary. Compared to the territorial aspirations in these realms, Russian expansionism was no more than another political challenge that had to be accommodated in the complex balance of power structures developing in Eastern Europe. The Habsburgs also struggled to gain direct access to a coastal port. In turn, the Sultans also fought for control of transcontinental trade routes. Like the Russians, the Poles used the cover of a religious crusade to push Muscovy eastward. And each of these four powers sought to conquer regions claimed by their respective ruling dynasties on the basis of historical precedent. It would, therefore, be inconsistent with the facts and detrimental to historical analysis to look upon Russian expansionism as anything other than a variant of one of the major political movements with like goals in Eastern Europe.

Nor should the Muscovite aspirations for the former empire of the Golden Horde tempt one to see a particular non-European element in Russian imperialism that would remove it from the general dynamics of interpower struggles in Europe. The power vacuum created by the disintegration of the Mongol empire naturally impelled Muscovy to adapt the political role of the Mongols to its own end. As Muscovy began to receive the benefits of European technology it enjoyed a growing superiority over the more feudal and nomadic societies it encountered in the East, an advantage which facilitated its eastward march. From the perspective of these peoples and nations, the encroachments of Muscovy were onerous but hardly unexpected. Over and over in the past, they had experienced the retreat of one overlord only to witness the rise of another. This time the new master arrived from the West. They did not have to endure the instant, heavy-handed imposition of Muscovite institutions, as did the Ukraine, White Russia, and the Baltic regions; the cultural and social autonomy allowed them, made the Muscovite yoke bearable. This, however, did not discourage them from frequent rebellions; as in the mutinous Ukraine, Muscovy was ultimately forced to increase its presence. In the end, the degree of Muscovite entrenchment was about the same in the West and in the East because the same basic forces were operating throughout the empire. And, to keep Russia's territorial growth in at least quantitative perspective, one should bear in mind tiny England's no less significant and dramatic territorial acquisitions on every continent over several centuries.

EMANUEL SARKISYANZ

Russian Imperialism Reconsidered

The Image

According to George Orwell, the belligerent blocks of "1984" shall take it for granted that history is to be rewritten at each change of alliances—in such a way that the opponent of the moment shall be made to appear as the enemy of always. This mood is at least as old as the Age of the Masses and is not confined to particular ideologies. Even Dean Acheson, at the height of the Cold War, spoke of half a millennium of Russia's history in terms of a long sequence of conquests and imperialistic expansion. It is true that he was immediately contradicted in "letters to the Editor" (we are still far from 1984). One letter to the New York *Times* pointed out that other imperialisms had been no less expansive.

Still the notion that tsarist imperialism has a unique character remains deeply rooted. From the time of the Napoleonic Wars, and earlier, a political mythology has grown up around it. So much so that even Russian-American scholars, for example the late Michael Karpovich, felt defensive about it, to the point of discouraging reference to Russian messianism, even as a religious phenomenon, out of apprehension that calling attention to it might strengthen foreign convictions about the traditional aggressiveness of the Russian mentality. There was—and perhaps still is—considerable reason for such caution. Secularized man has as great a problem in replacing mentally the part so long played in the panorama of history by Almighty Providence as he has in finding a modern substitute for the personification of evil.

Soon after the proclamation of the Cult of Reason in Western Europe, qualities of diabolical cunning or inscrutable motives for an international plot with unseen forces came to be attributed to the gigantic and therefore fear-inspiring empire of the tsar. Peter the Great's alleged blueprints for subversive Russian intrigue, conquest, and aggrandizement were first communicated to the Directoire of revolutionary France by the Polish refugee General M. Sokolnicki. Between 1812 and 1836, rumor converted them into forgery. Yet the so-called Testament of Peter the Great continued to circulate, seeming to present Russia's conquests of the eighteenth century as proof that its tsars aspired to world domination. Karl Marx apparently believed it to be the genuine document. Napoleon III popularized it as a propagandistic tool of power politics. The Testament was a favorite source for Victorian journalists during conflicts or tensions with Russia, for instance in 1877; and it was quite seriously quoted in the United States as recently as 1948.

Napoleon I, even in exile at Saint Helena, kept warning Europe that it would fall under the knout of the tsar, that Europe would "turn Cossack"—and Britain would lose India to Russia. In fact, the imperial interests of the powers that defeated Napoleon were to collide with tsarist imperialism: Britain saw itself threatened by Russia's approaches to the Mediterranean; Austria (and to a lesser extent Prussia) feared the Southern and Western Slavs' political connections with Russia.

These Western empires, as well as the land of Napoleon, produced most of the publicity about the sinister designs of tsarist imperialism. During the first quarter of the nineteenth century, when criticism of the antiliberal neoabsolutist regimes was dangerous, the conservative forces in Western and Central Europe were customarily accused of serving Russia. In 1819 the German writer August von Kotzebue was murdered by a nationalist student on suspicion of being a tsarist agent. Post-Napoleonic frustration of German national unification aspirations generated notions about an omnipotent conspiracy of Russian diplomacy (which allegedly had strongly contributed to defeating liberalism in Spain, Italy, and Central Europe). It was hard to resign oneself to history's not being directed by some unseen power.

Even in mid-century the Russian empire remained the antisymbol of such representative liberal German political writers as Jakob Fallmerayer and Heinrich von Gagern. They believed that the struggle against the Russian East was inevitable. It was to be an apocalyptic struggle between Despotism and Freedom "as the Greeks knew it." Marx and Engels demanded war against the Russian empire, which even in their thought tended to assume features of a political myth. It was psychologically quite understandable that for honest middle-class European liberals the very boundlessness of Russia, with its autocrats, nomads, and sectarian self-burners, had something sinister and uncanny. Thus, in 1851 Aurelio Buddeus warned his Germans that stopping the Revolutions in Europe would be the only means to save the West from the Asiatic Russian empire, and that it should be the sacred duty of European statesmen to defend Culture (as they knew it) against the Slavs, the European and the Asiatic being the main antagonistic factors of history. Similarly for Karl Diezel, Slavdom seemed an irreconcilable opposite to Germandom—in terms of anti-individualism against individualism. And Diezel prophesied in 1852 that the "half-putrefied" Russian people would end up in Communism and that a revolutionary Russian empire would be still more dangerous for Europe than the one of the tsars.

A French writer Astolphe, Marquis de Custine, warned against the dangers that threatened Europe from the empire of the schismatic tsars at a time when internal subversion imperiled the Faith within the West. In contrast, Thomas Carlyle expected (as late as 1855) that salvation from the internal anarchy that afflicted Europe would come from Russia and its discipline. Such associations of the Asiatic Russian empire with ideologies of Europe's potential civil war (generally with the conservative and occasionally with the revolutionary side) continued until the fall of tsardom.

Of less romantic nature was a British image of tsarist imperialism that had been perpetuated in Anglo-Saxon public opinion since the nineteenth century. It was about as old as the puritanization of British public opinion, with its sense of cant, and is correspondingly based on an unconscious (or at least unadmitted) dichotomy of premises that is taken for granted even today: the rival empire's expansion is judged *morally;* one's own empire's expansion is judged *pragmatically.* The motto, "The right to interfere in the affairs of independent states is founded on this single principle, that as self-preservation is the first duty, so it supersedes all other obligations . . . ," was formulated in 1836 by Sir John McNeill, an associate of Henry John Temple, Viscount Palmerston, and British envoy to Persia, who proclaimed the principle "My Country right or wrong."

Proposals for a preventive war against the Russian empire appeared in British political writing after 1828, particularly under the influence of David Urquhart's *Danger to India.* Revealing also are the titles of the books *Designs of Russia* and *The Practicability of an Invasion of British India,* published in 1828 and 1829 by a Colonel de Lacy Evans. So much did they impress Edward Law, Earl of Ellenborough, subsequently governor-general of British India, that he determined to open Central Asia for Britain before Russia could reach it. Lord Ellenborough was representative of an important stream of British thought, as for example when he declared that he saw in the sufferings of Russian soldiers (in 1829) "the judgement of Providence on unprincipled ambition" and that "every success of theirs . . . makes my heart bleed. I consider it a victory gained over me, as Asia is mine." According to McNeill (and Palmerston, Ellenborough, and their successors) the Muslim peoples of Central Asia dreaded the power of the Russian empire and looked to Britain "for countenance."

In this spirit much of British historiography on India (but not only on India) calls identical actions and policies "defense of legitimate interests" if performed by Britain, but terms them "intrigues" if performed by a rival power, such as the tsarist empire. Suspicion of Russia became so deeply ingrained in British India that it continued unabated even during the periods of British-Russian cooperation in Europe. A traditional British view took it for granted that Russian expansion could not be compared with British expansion, the latter being merely protective and the former always an aggressive challenge to Great Britain.

Pamphleteers so accustomed the British public to a sinister image of tsarist imperialism that every disturbance in Asia was likely to be attributed to Russian designs. A gigantic army (of unknown size) was thought to stand prepared to execute the boundless ambitions of the tsars. Against such a background, a British journalist had no hesitation in reporting that "along the vast frontier of China the grass is every morning examined for traces of footsteps!" English explorers of the Russian peril to India (for example, Captain Alexander Burnes, who braved even the terrors of the khanate of Bukhara in 1832) usually found those dangers they had been sent to discover.

In turn, tsarist diplomacy continued to use the argument that Russia was advancing into Asia to spread the blessings of civilization, Europe's civilization. Such was the claim that had admitted St. Petersburg to membership in the concert of European powers in the Age of Enlightenment. St. Petersburg's self-assumed mission of enlightening backward Asia was encouraged by Germans from Leibniz to Bismarck. Bismarck's purpose was to manipulate Russia's expansion away from Europe. In Central Asia, tsarist imperialism of the nineteenth century used the argument that the vicinity of nomads was bound to force civilized states to expand until they reached the frontier of another civilized state. In the case of Russia's drive into Central Asia, it was the frontier of Persia. Alexander Gorchakov, Alexander II's foreign minister, compared in 1864 this expansion of Russia to that of the United States (in the West), France (in North Africa), the Netherlands and Britain (in India), and considered it motivated "less by ambition than . . . by necessity." The underlying notion that the existence of a power vacuum justifies penetration or annexation survived the Age of Imperialism into the present. Also still current is another part of McNeill's formula of 1836 describing the mode of Russian penetration: that it proceeds from the disorganization of coveted areas by secret agents to the fomenting of public disorders and then to military occupation. This was not a correct description of the methods used by Russia at that time (it anticipated the methods of another age), but it corresponded to the image of Russian imperialism held by champions of the rival British imperialism.

Russia's central position in Eurasia has allowed and even invited alternating recession and expansion in opposite directions, towards Europe or towards Eastern Asia. Muscovy's own independence had to be secured against an alliance of a European and an Asian power, the Lithuanian-Tatar coalition (1480). During the sixteenth century, although Ivan IV's Muscovy failed to break through to the Baltic maritime accesses to Renaissance Europe, it was successful in the military conquest and Cossack colonization of Siberia. Advancing mainly along the great rivers of northeastern Eurasia, the Russians reached the Pacific coast by 1639.

The radical modernization of Russia's political and military structure enabled Peter the Great to conquer the Baltic coast from Sweden. Thereby the Russian empire, which in Muscovite days was considered relevant to Western Christendom merely because of its potential solidarity against the Ottoman Turkish menace, forced its way into the concert of European powers. As one of them, it vainly sought to establish a foothold in the rear of Turkey, in the dissolving Persia of 1722.

Further eastward in Asia, it consolidated its South Siberian frontier with China (in 1727) and accepted the voluntary subjection of a portion of the Kazakh steppe nomads in 1730. The main obstacles to Russian expansion in the eighteenth century were the allies of France, Poland, and Turkey. From Poland, in 1772 and in 1793, Russia annexed the balance of the Ukrainian and White Russian-speaking territories. And the defeats of the Ottoman Empire enabled Russia by 1774 to regain the northern coast of the Black Sea, an area through which the medieval Kievan state had received much of its stimulation from Byzantium, and from which its population had been pushed away by Turkic nomads since the eleventh century. The last of the originally nomadic Turkic powers to raid European Russia (as late as the eighteenth century) was Tatar Crimea. By annexing it in 1783, the Russian state practically reached its natural borders and removed the last existing threats to its central areas.

If the previous expansion of Russia could claim defensive features, the subsequent territorial aggrandizement of the St. Petersburg empire passed from the defensive into the offensive and assumed definite characteristics of aggressive imperialism. The antirevolutionary coalition situation gave the Empress Catherine II an occasion to annex the core region of eastern Poland (1795); and by the settlement with Napoleon, Tsar Alexander I gained Finland from Sweden. The Greek Orthodox Georgian monarchies and the Monophysite Armenians of Transcaucasia desired a Russian protectorate against Muslim Persia but found instead their main areas annexed by the Russian empire between 1800 and 1828. Likewise from Persia, Russian military victories gained Daghestan, and northern Azerbaijan and control of the Caspian (1813).

At the Congress of Vienna (1814 to 1815) the tsar was still mainly represented by ethnic non-Russian Europeans. But under the ideologized autocracy of Nicolas I the bureaucratic centralization of the empire brought Russification policies which produced early stirrings of modern nationalism among the empire's non-Russian population. Entire armies of the tsar perished in the struggle against the Muslim crusading movement of Shamil of Daghestan. Breaking the resistance of the Muslim peoples of the Northern Caucasus (1859 to 1864) and annexing the Amur and Ussuri extensions of southeastern Siberia from China (1850 to 1860) served to compensate in part for the failure of Russian expansionist aspirations toward Constantinople that resulted from the Western allies' victory in the Crimean War (1854 to 1856). In the same period Russia finally consolidated its hold over the Kazakh steppes, from the Chinese border to the Caspian.

Between 1864 and 1873 Russian armies subdued the Uzbek oasis states of Kokand, Bukhara, and Khiva. The latter two survived the Russian monarchy as Russian protectorates, and the former, with its Kirghiz vassals, was annexed by Tsar Alexander II in 1876. Kokand's core region of Ferghana became the center of Russian Turkestan and the empire's main cotton-producing area. The subjection of the last independent Turkoman tribes between 1880 and 1884 brought Russian imperialism to its present limits in Central Asia—after a collision with British-backed Afghanistan in 1885 which almost ignited a Russo-British war.

Checked by British imperialism in the South and German-Austrian in the West, Russian imperialism found outlets in Chinese Manchuria and Korea in the 1890's. Its collision with and defeat by the rival Japanese imperialism in 1904 and 1905 prepared the ground for the revolutionary disintegration and collapse of tsarism between 1905 and 1917.

Russian Messianism, Popular Sentiment, and Economic Factors

Aside from two limited periods of crisis, tsarist imperialism was not strongly motivated by ideology, at least in the St. Petersburg period. The last occasion on which Russian religious enthusiasm had a decisive influence on offensive warfare may have been the conquest of Tatar Kazan by Ivan the Terrible in 1552. It marked Russia's victory over a religious as well as a political antagonist (the Tatars) and initiated Russian annexation of the Tatar states. The folk image of Russia's numerous wars with the Ottoman Turks (the infidel "Basurmane") was less colored by crusade-like conceptions. The upsurge of militant faith that largely inspired the struggle to free Orthodox Moscow from Roman Catholic Polish occupation in 1612 took place in a situation of basically defensive warfare and cannot be associated with Russian imperialism.

The sixteenth-century concept of Holy Russia, of the Muscovite Third Rome, hardly affected Muscovite foreign policy or the Romanov tsar's war and peace with Catholic Poland or Austria. There is no evidence that Muscovite foreign policy was determined by messianic concepts. With respect to Muscovite imperial expansion, both achieved and attempted, the sixteenth- and seventeenth-century wars of territorial acquisition were pragmatically rather than ideologically motivated. Imperial Muscovy's universalist state ideal of the messianic Third Rome, on the other hand, evolved out of essentially eschatological concepts that had even less bearing on Russian imperialism than did the medieval concept of Holy Roman Empire ("Reich") of the Germanic peoples on German imperialism in terms of aggressive territorial expansion. It is because the chiliastic outlook embodied in the theory of the Third Rome has had enormous influence on the development of Russian social thought that it has become simplistic convention to identify the tradition of the Third Rome with Russian imperialism.

It is not correct to assume that it was in its capacity of Third Rome that Moscow desired to recover Constantinople, the Second Rome. Even less correct is such a generalization for the St. Petersburg empire (with the exception of the episode of the Russo-Turkish War of 1877 to 1878 for thinkers such as Dostoevsky). The strong interest that the empire builders Peter I and Catherine II took in Constantinople and the Orthodox Slavs obeyed secular reasons of state. St. Petersburg's imperial Russia was ruled by a modernized secular élite culturally far removed from the Muscovite masses and their universalistic outlook. Foreign policy, imperialist and otherwise, concerned not the people but the state. Thus the state was far removed from the people, and foreign policy much more so.

This was true deep into the nineteenth century. Russian public opinion (which barely existed before the 1830's) affected the empire's foreign relations and wars of territorial expansion even less than its domestic policies. The people were in no position to restrain the Petersburg variety of imperialism in the age of secret and cabinet diplomacy —of enlightened absolutism. The tsar's government exercised even greater power in foreign policy decisions than other European absolute monarchs or constitutional policy makers in the Age of Imperialism.

Unlike insular Britain and overpopulated Holland, whose prosperity had grown after overseas imperialist expansion, the Russian empire with its great Eurasian plains never vitally depended on imperialist accomplishments. Russian foreign trade—of little importance for Russia's economy—was not an important factor in tsarist imperialism.

Aside from the conquest initiative and the largely spontaneous Rus-

sian peasant colonization of Siberia, St. Petersburg's imperialistic ventures sprang mainly from personal decisions of the tsar, from dynastic moves or competitive actions in the game of international diplomacy. Not until the late nineteenth century was Russia's imperialism derived from internal economic or political needs or the pressures of Russian public opinion. The Empress Elizabeth's involvement of Russia in the Seven Years War in 1756 because of a personal offense to her by Prussia's Frederick II and Tsar Paul I's championing of the Order of the Knighthood of Malta are examples of Russia's involvement in Central and Mediterranean Europe for personal or dynastic reasons. From the Napoleonic period the tsars personally conducted imperial foreign policy. This particularly applies to Alexander I and Nicholas I in the half century between 1801 and 1855, but it largely holds even for the last tsar. Even the postimperial Provisional Government's disastrous decision to leave Russia involved in World War I on the side of the French and British empires is reputed to have been taken by a small number of persons associated with Alexander Kerensky's personal circle, the so-called Star Chamber.

The three decades of systematically antiliberal, antirevolutionary, and monarchist Russian foreign policy of 1825 to 1855 represent the one and probably the only period of Russian imperialism that was consistently motivated by an ideology. In this period of Nicholas I, aggressive expansionist or foreign interventionist policies were conceived not so much in promotion of Russia's national interest as in support of abstract and supranational principles to be enforced internationally: the doctrine of the divine right of monarchs as reiterated by the Holy Alliance of 1815. If this Russia of Nicholas I acted as an imperialistic power, its imperialism was motivated more by the personal and ideological than by economic factors.

As for that tsar, the struggle of "legitimate" rulers against the forces of revolution was a struggle of right against wrong, and he made even less distinction between his empire's international concerns and the properly internal affairs of other countries than does the Soviet Union within its sphere of influence or the United States within the Western Hemisphere. He adhered to an imperialism that refrained from intervention, or intervened without using opportunities for annexation, provided that the governments concerned were in his terms "legitimate under God." The imperial interventionist policies of Nicholas I were so consistent with his belief in the divine right of monarchy

that he was capable of acting contrary to his own empire's interests on occasion. Thus the tsar opposed the Greek coup d'état of 1843, although its main following favored the Russian empire and expected help from it. In fact, the tsar opposed the coup because it was directed against a prince, Otto of Wittelsbach (Otto I of Greece), even though Nicholas I disliked that prince. An example of Nicholas' aggressive military intervention abroad for the sake of monarchist principles of legitimacy and not for the sake of Russian imperialism was the crushing of the Polish rising in the Free City of Cracow by Russian forces in 1846. The tsar did not annex Cracow to Russian Poland but invited Austria to annex it.

On the other hand, the Russian empire of Nicholas I anticipated twentieth-century imperialist opposition to the self-determination of peoples, and proceeded to implement systematically a policy of cultural and linguistic conformity. Thus, if the legitimist ideology of Nicholas I had a restraining effect on Russian imperialism in terms of expansion and territorial annexations, it did accelerate the imperialist domestic policy of forcing non-Russian subjects of the tsar on the road to compulsory Russification.

The principle of foreign rulers' legitimacy was applied by Nicholas I, at least until the last two years of his reign, even to the Muslim Sultan-Caliph: the Russian autocrat refused to profit from revolts in the Ottoman Empire. He even supported the Sultan Mahmud II when Muhammad 'Ali of Egypt, his vassal, was on the point of invading Anatolia in 1832. And in 1844 the tsar discouraged even Christian opposition to the Muslim monarch's rule—to the point of disappointing Russian nationalists such as Michael Pogodin. When the fellow Orthodox Rumanians of Wallachia and Moldavia revolted against the Turkish rule in 1848, Russian forces crushed the revolt and occupied the two Danubian principalities in the name of the Ottoman Empire; Nicholas I did not use this opportunity to annex the Rumanian states to the Russian empire.

When eventually, in 1854, he did resume imperial Russia's expansion towards Constantinople and the Straits of the Bosporus and the Dardanelles—an expansion that Empress Catherine II associated with the restoration of the Byzantine empire—the tsar wanted it to be known that he was fighting "not for conquest" but "for Christianity." He was, apparently sincerely, surprised to see other Christian monarchs fighting in the Crimea on the side of the Ottoman Crescent. He wrote

in resignation that only "perishing as a martyr of the Faith" was being left to him.

The imperialism of the tsars did not benefit abroad from the conservative principles it professed. Tsarist imperialism had almost no ideological following in foreign countries, no organized support comparable to Communist Russia's international party network. Its conservative admirers in Western and Central Europe failed to assist its expansion (as their heirs were to assist the expansion of the fascist empires when the latent conflict between European revolution and reaction had advanced to a more acute stage). After 1855 the international solidarity of monarchs, implicit in the conservative doctrine, ceased determining imperial Russia's foreign policies. Before the century ended, Russia was to replace its long cooperation with the conservative Hohenzollern and Habsburg monarchy by an alliance with liberal France. This anti-ideological turn in the international alignments of tsarist Russia was necessary to preserve Europe's balance of power in the heyday of imperialism. Post-1855 tsarist imperialism was restrained by the imperative to avoid military and political risks of the kind incurred in fighting the Crimean War, that is, against an alliance of Western powers.

The restraints to military ambitions customarily came from the ministry of finance, and perhaps the main restraint to late tsarist imperialism was economic. Yet, economics played an extremely subordinate role in the *driving motivation* of that Russian imperialism. The Russian empire was not dominated by the interests of the middle classes, the strata most swayed by economic motivations. Its ruling classes held economic privilege by virtue of political power, and not power by virtue of wealth, as was the case in the industrial empires of the West. Among the inherent contradictions of monarchist Russia was the aspiration to catch up with the industrial liberal empires, economically and imperially. Diplomatically, within the concert of European powers, Russia's imperialist interests did operate on a plane of equality with those of the middle-class industrial powers.

Under the last three tsars, foreign policies, including those that entailed imperialist ventures, began to be affected to some extent by Russian public opinion. In the 1860's and 1870's, as the intelligentsia turned against the tsars' government, imperial policies came to require the backing of at least the nationalist part of public opinion. For example, influential journalistic support of tsarist imperialism was given by Michael Katkov, a Russian conservative of the Tory type in the reign of Alexander III.

In contrast, Russian revolutionary thought largely ignored imperial foreign policies—unless they had a bearing on anti-imperialist movements of popular liberation. For this reason, the Russian Populists backed the emancipation struggle of the Southern Slavs, while imperial Russia waged war on Turkey on their behalf in 1877 and 1878. When British pressure, through Germany's intermediacy at the Congress of Berlin, forced Russia to abandon a considerable part of what its soldiers had gained, Russian public opinion followed Russian imperialism in turning against Austrian and German imperialism. In the unfavorable international situation following 1878 and the upsurge of the Narodnik revolutionary struggle against the monarchy, the tsarist government was not loath to see domestic frustration directed against rival imperialist powers.

Isolated by Germany's refusal to renew the mutual Reinsurance treaty in 1890, Petersburg autocracy, which had just triumphed over revolutionary Populism, was approached by the similarly isolated French republic. French loans secured the assistance of the Russian empire's military manpower against potential German imperialism. Underdeveloped Russia was greatly dependent on Western capital for investments in return for forced exports. Exporting even at the price of starvation (since the scarcity at home produced inflated grain prices) was not unheard of in the Russia of the 1890's. As in more recent times, the export of grain, though it jeopardized rural welfare, was to provide the resources required for the modernization that was needed to uphold the Russian empire's standing as one of the great powers of the European concert. At the turn of the century, Count Sergei Witte, finance minister and then prime minister under Nicholas II, attempted to coordinate the direction of Russian imperialist drives with the domestic requirements of industrialization. His aim was to achieve a kind of capitalist reconstruction together with territorial expansion, preferably in uncontested directions, away from Europe. Such an enterprise had no precedents in the history of Russian imperialism and did not endure. The "peaceful" Russian penetration of the Far East brought Russian imperialism into collision with Japanese imperialism.

In the estimation of Nicholas II's minister of the interior, Viacheslav von Plehve, Russia's war with Japan in 1904 and 1905 would serve as a safety valve against accumulated internal revolutionary tensions. In reality it ushered in the Russian Revolution. Russian public opinion did not rally behind the monarchy for the sake of ensuring the victory of Russian imperialism over its Japanese rival. Even at this zenith of the Age of Imperialism, tsarist imperialism was not propelled to the same peaks of national feeling or nationalist ideology of the middle classes as its Western counterparts, for instance British and German imperialism. Unlike the educated élite behind the other imperialist powers, the Russian intelligentsia on the whole failed to profess national self-interest above universal humanitarian values. It was precisely the relatively cosmopolitan outlook of the Russian intelligentsia, dominated by Western culture, that limited the appeals of chauvinism and imperialism in Russia.

To a certain extent this also resulted from the non-Russian (largely Baltic German) ethnic composition of the tsarist ministry of foreign affairs and diplomatic service, the Baltic German tradition being "good tsarist but not good Russian." At the height of Europe's Age of Imperialism, the directions taken by Russian imperialism were determined not so much by Slavophile nationalism or echoes of Byzantine or Muscovite traditions of universalistic imperial mission as by pragmatic considerations of the balance of power. By the early years of the twentieth century, international treaty links came to restrict even the tsar's scope of negotiations. When in 1905 the German Emperor had induced Nicholas II to sign a treaty that would have contradicted Russia's alliance with France of 1891 to 1894, the tsar found no minister willing to countersign this treaty of Björkö. The same applied to the tsars' desire to reorient St. Petersburg's foreign alliances in accordance with antirevolutionary ideology.

In 1906 Count Vladimir Lamsdorff, at that time Russia's foreign minister, suggested in a secret memorandum that Russia should, jointly with the German empire and the Vatican, act against liberal France, allegedly "an instrument of world Jewry represented by the Alliance Israélite Universelle" (which was alleged to consider Russia "an obstacle to its world domination"). Nicholas II commented that he agreed and instructed that negotiations along these lines be started immediately. But the next foreign minister, Alexander Izvolskii, paid no attention to the absurd scheme—whose very presuppositions depended on a forgery. During the previous year the last tsar had been shown the notorious "Protocols of the Wise Men of Zion," and he called them "prophetic" and praised "their depth of insight," seriously believing the Revolution of 1905 to be directed by agents of "Zion." Upon Prime Minister Peter Stolypin's investigation of the "Protocols" and their exposure as crude forgery, the tsar forbade the use of this material for anti-Jewish propaganda, because, as he put it, he rejected the use of evil means. Only to an extremely limited extent did late tsarist regimes attempt to make use of international anti-Semitism.

By the summer of 1914 the imperial Russian regime could not afford another diplomatic failure: tsardom no longer reflected the outlook of the majority of the Russian people. The imperialist decision that decisively accelerated the end of the Petersburg period was the decision to risk war with the Central Powers. It was partly dictated by Russia's internal political situation, real or fancied. Yet in spite of the popular enthusiasm for national defense when Germany declared war on Russia, Russian imperialist aspirations remained much more remote from the Russian people than did the semiconstitutionalized and semi-folk government (its elected Duma and its peasant court favorite, the monk Rasputin). In the crisis situation of World War I the late Muscovite ("Third Rome") eschatological messianism began to reverberate in political directions of imperialism. Once sparked by imported Marxism, it exploded into the visionary message of World Revolution. Tsarist imperialism was the first to suffer the fate of the unideological Western imperialisms. The unrealistic foreign policy decisions made in the last years of the imperial regime culminated in the spring of 1917 in the determination to continue the world war on the side of the Entente powers. Thus democratic Russia's (just as in a different way American) war efforts to make the world safe for Democracy were utilized to make the world safer for the British and French empires.

A generation of doctrinaire Russian revolutionaries had to pass from the scene before the Petersburg imperialism could be transposed into a neo-Muscovite and totalitarian imperialism based on the manipulation of mass society in terms of the proletarian myth. Stalin's Russian empire, like old Muscovy in "pre-capitalist encirclement" (as Ivo Lederer calls it), saw itself besieged in a hostile world of the European power system—to which Russia had ceased to belong soon after November, 1917, when its capital was returned from St. Petersburg (Petrograd) to Moscow. Since most of the Westernized élite was eliminated by the Bolsheviks, the Soviet system was largely evolved by the relatively non-Westernized strata of Russia. The victory of the

Marxist minority faction of the Russian Revolution, that is, of the most Occidentalized of Russian revolutionary ideologies, resulted in nothing less than the de-Westernization of Russia. In the new Moscow, the old Muscovite antagonism to the Latin West indirectly revived in the form of capitalistic attitudes. The failure of the Communists in Central Europe temporarily isolated Russia from the Occident.

Tsarist Power Experiments in Africa

Russian military interest in the Egyptian army today has antecedents in the anti-Ottoman Mediterranean expansion policies of Catherine II, who in 1784 hoped to station Russian troops in Alexandria, and by 1786 succeeded in placing Russian soldiers within the Mamluk army. Under Nicholas I, in 1847, Egypt received a Russian technical aid mission (with mining experts to set up gold-washing operations). However, opportunities for supporting independence movements of Muslim Ottoman provinces were scorned under the Nicholas I's legitimist imperial policies (which discouraged Muhammad 'Ali's emancipation aspirations for Egypt). Against this background, the offers of the next tsar to support Egypt against the Ottoman Empire were not accepted by the Khedive Ismail I. Although the Russian general Rostislav Fadeev had served in 1875 and 1876 as military adviser to the viceroy of Egypt and almost became his army's commander, Russian forces in Bulgaria in the Russo-Turkish War of 1877 to 1878 were confronted by Egyptian units which fought on the Ottoman side.

Nor was Russian interest in Ethiopia much more successful. This last enclave of East African Christendom was threatened by the tide of Islam at the culmination of Ottoman power in the early sixteenth century. In the course of Russia's military designs against the Ottoman barrier to southern maritime outlets in the late seventeenth century, Ethiopia was envisaged as a potential Russian ally. There were ambitions to unite the Ethiopian Monophysite Church with Russian Orthodoxy. Such late Muscovite schemes were revived in the context of Petersburg's imperialism on the eve of the division of Africa among the colonial powers. A member of the Russian ecclesiastical mission to Jerusalem recommended that Ethiopia be used as Russia's main African base against the power of Islam.

In this enterprise it was intended that Ethiopia should become the core of Russia's prospective sphere of influence in Africa. But the

Ethiopian ruler Theodore, mindful of the Coptic kingdom's experience with the sixteenth-century Catholic mission as a spearhead of Portuguese imperialism, suspected that Russian missionaries too would be followed by their soldiers. His successor, John IV, hoped, however, to cooperate with Russia against the Ottoman Empire, which was still a Red Sea power at the end of the nineteenth century. Bismarck's encouragement of Russian involvement in Africa (whereby Russia might be distracted from its European expansionist interests) made the scheme suspect in Petersburg. The main promotion for Russian imperialist involvement in East Africa came from post-Slavophile circles. The well-known attempt of the Cossack Ataman Ashinov to establish a Russian colony on the Red Sea coast in 1888 and 1889 failed inasmuch as the Russian government did not wish to back an enterprise that entailed interfering with the French sphere of influence. When Germany's Italian allies invaded Ethiopia in 1896, the Russian Red Cross sent a first aid unit to Ethiopia. The fact that the Russian hospital establishment in the Ethiopian capital lasted long beyond that war aroused British suspicions of Russia's designs: at the turn of the century even bandages and pills sent to "natives" by a rival empire were objects of suspicion in the British press.

The wariness of the British at this time may be understood against the background of the Boer War of 1899 to 1902, in which Russian imperialism appeared to encourage resistance to British imperialism in Africa. The Boer general Joubert Pienaar even recommended that Russia, instead of Britain, should become the dominant power in South Africa, a project that was approved by Tsar Nicholas II but—not surprisingly—had no results. Such schemes never really brought Russia into open competition with the British empire, as was the case in Asia.

Anglo-Russian Rivalries in Muslim Central Asia

The rivalry between Russia and Great Britain in their imperialistic enterprise is one of the great themes of nineteenth-century history and a crucial factor in early American-Russian relations. The main object of this rivalry was India, which the British suspected Russia of coveting. Although no tsarist government (after Paul I and his eccentric "marching" order of January, 1801, when he ordered 20,000

Cossacks to invade India) ever seriously planned to invade India, it is true that some Russian agents occasionally did toy with such projects. It is also true that a number of Indian princely states, notably Kashmir in 1867 and Indore in 1871, did send embassies to Russia to request the tsar's support for their resistance against British hegemony. The more realistic and responsible British empire builders were in fact less alarmed by the improbable possibility of a Russian advance into India than they were by a more probable strengthening of Indian opposition against Britain that might result from Russia's domination of Central Asia—with which India had historical links. Such a view was expressed, for example in 1854, by Sir Charles Wood, British secretary of state for India from 1859 to 1866.

Persia, on the other hand, had since the early nineteenth century been pressured and even invaded both by the Russians and by the British. Russia sought outlets to the Persian Gulf, and Great Britain was mainly concerned with protecting the western flank of British India. The standard works in English on this topic tend to establish a rather one-sided picture of a Persia suffering less through British than through tsarist machinations, the latter being represented as the main obstacle to Iran's progress. The currency of this notion is attributable to the selective nature of the standard sources. Those in the English language stress the English viewpoint, and those based on Russian archives by the early Soviet regime expose the darkest side of tsarist designs.

For example, Persia's anti-British agitation against the concession that Shah Nasr-ed-Din granted the naturalized Englishman Paul Julius von Reuter in 1872 is conventionally depicted as a fruit of Russian intrigue. It is hardly necessary to assume that the Persians required a Russian stimulus to force cancellation of the concession since the shah was in effect handing over to a British subject not only railway building and banking rights but also rights to all of Persia's minerals (except for precious metals).

As Britain's rival, Russia did of course benefit from Persian resistance to this and later concessions to British imperialist interests. But had Persia felt itself victimized more by tsarist imperialism than by British pressure, it would not have stubbornly insisted on entering the Crimean War and the Russo-Turkish War of 1877 to 1878 on the side of Russia against Britain's protégé, Turkey. The fact that during both wars Russia had difficulty dissuading the shah from entering the struggle on its side is attested by Russian diplomatic correspondence of the time but is rarely—if at all—mentioned in the standard literature in English. If Russia was the main obstacle to nineteenth-century Persia's progress towards modernization, how does one explain the large number of Russian loan words in the Persian language denoting objects of modern technology? If tsarist Russia's ultimate design in Persia was conquest, as it had been in the Uzbek khanates, contemporary Persian opinion did not see it this way. Otherwise there would not have been jubilation in Persia over the Russian conquest of Khiva in 1873, which resulted in the freeing and repatriation of many thousands of Persian slaves held in that Uzbek capital; nor would the Persians have relished Russia's subjection of the remaining Turkoman tribesmen in the early 1880's.

Russia's connivance with Britain to divide Persia into spheres of influence (in 1907 and 1915) sacrificed a weaker country to the solidarity of Anglo-Russian imperialism against German imperialism. This was committed in the spirit of an age that believed in the survival of the fittest and in the limitation of such morality as was then accepted in international law to transactions among members of the European state system. The practices of that day cannot of course be judged without recognizing that even in today's anti-imperialistic age the great powers that champion the self-determination of peoples are not always visibly outraged by violations of this allegedly universal human right (in places where the preservation of certain spheres of influence might otherwise be adversely affected).

As a formality that would be observed in similar circumstances today, the Russian foreign ministry proclaimed in 1868 that its government *regretted* the military occupation of Samarkand and would terminate it "as soon as possible." Pious professions of intentions such as these were repeated by Great Britain upon its occupation of Egypt in 1882 and later. As the tribute that Might pays to Right, they are to be taken with as large a grain of salt as possible.

Just as it is still the practice of great powers to encourage weak countries within an imperial rival's sphere of influence to resist that rival power (on the strength of promises of support), so in 1878 Russian imperial interests encouraged Shir Ali of Afghanistan to resist British demands. (Involving Britain in Central Asia was to distract British power from Turkey and the Straits.) He followed this encouragement, trusting in Russia's promise of support; but since he received none, Afghanistan lost its second war with Britain—and hence its sovereignty. Unlike the situation in the mid-1860's, when the Russian military's will to advance into Central Asia prevailed over the caution of the ministry of foreign affairs (and in the case of General Michael Cherniaev's storming of Tashkent, even over the antiexpansionist instructions of Tsar Alexander II), the tsarist military did not take the responsibility for war with Britain in 1878. An Anglo-Russian war was beyond the economic capabilities of Russian imperialism, although Russian Turkestan's Governor-General C. P. Kaufman had assembled 20,000 men, the largest tsarist force ever mobilized in Central Asia for an eventuality of conflict with British India. Russian colonial officers found more scope for military prowess in police actions against natives. The massacres of the Yomud Turkomans ordered by Kaufman in 1873 and the massacre of the Tekke Turkomans under General Michael Skobelev in 1881 accorded with contemporary "pacification" practices in other colonial territories of Western powers.

The Pan-Slavist Image of Russian Imperialism and the Balkans

Nor were the Balkan goals of tsarist policies dictated by Russian economic interests. Although Russia needed access to the Straits for the export of southern grain from the middle of the nineteenth century, Russian capital investments in that area were not encouraged by the St. Petersburg government. Yet Balkan politics became the central theme of Russian imperialism. With the stabilization of Russia's Western borders by the Congress of Vienna in 1814 and 1815, the tsardom's westward expansion was confined to southeastern Europe for about a century. For this reason profession of the Greek Orthodox faith and Slavic ethnic links took on increased political significance.

Very soon, the notion of Pan-Slavism connoted for Westerners apprehensive of Russia's design any doctrine of Russia's mission to renovate Europe, be it by its Orthodox Christianity, its Slavic vitality, its peasant revolution, or its docile discipline—or it could mean any sort of claim of Russian superiority. Even educated Western and Central Europeans imagined Pan-Slavism to be a creation or device of the Russian government. This notion is still current, in spite of the fact that not Russian agents but Slovak and Czech thinkers (Jan Kollár, František Palacky) were the originators of Pan-Slavism (though they did have a seventeenth-century Croatian Catholic predecessor in George Križanič). As an expectation of protective or liberating action for all Slavs to come from the Russian empire, Pan-Slavism was much more popular among the Southern Slavs under Ottoman Turkish rule and the Czechs under Austrian rule than it ever became in Russia. Russia's potential helpers in enemy territory, Czech, Serbian, Montenegrin, and Bulgarian Pan-Slavists, represented about as much of a Fifth Column as tsarist imperialism ever had.

Accordingly, fears of Pan-Slavism were so exaggerated in the German and Austrian press from the 1830's, and particularly after Russia's alliance with France in 1893, that commentaries on the apathy that Russian society displayed toward this creed were hardly believed. In truth, even though Pan-Slavism was the most popular cause ever taken up by Russian imperialism, the championing of the Serbs and other Slavs was never a mass movement in Russia. (Recall for a moment how passive and noncommittal was the response of "a man of the people," a gardener, in Tolstoy's *Anna Karenina,* when asked what he thought about going to war for the sake of Slavic solidarity. And this was at the height of Pan-Slavic sentiment, in 1877.) Pan-Slavism in Russia was not much more than an intellectual trend in public opinion; it was not a government program. Only in 1877 and 1878 did Pan-Slavist public opinion briefly attain the strength of a lobby capable of influencing government decision.

Not until the crisis situation at the time of Germany's declaration of war on Russia in the next century did Pan-Slavism reach the scope of a popular mood. But Western, particularly German and Austrian, public opinion did and still does vastly overestimate the influence of Pan-Slav ambitions or sentiments on tsarist imperialism. The influence of Pan-Slavism on pre-1914 Russian imperialism was as much overestimated by Central European journalism as the influence of the Pan-German League (Alldeutscher Verband) on William II's German imperialism by British and French opinion.

In practice, pragmatic considerations for the balance of power outweighed any Pan-Slavist sentiments—where they were cherished at all among St. Petersburg decision makers. Cautious not to upset the balance of power by destroying Turkey, and not to risk a war against its supporters, the Russian empire scorned the opportunities it had for seizing the Straits in 1878, 1897, and 1912, that is, during its last victorious war against the Ottomans, during the Greek-Turkish struggle over Crete, and during the First Balkan War, which put an end to Ottoman dominion in Europe.

Other obstacles to Pan-Slavist empire building were the nationalisms of non-Slavic peoples of the Balkans, such as the Rumanians, not to mention the rival nationalisms of the Orthodox Southern Slavs themselves. The Orthodox Rumanian experience with Russian occupations as they had recurred in Russo-Turkish wars brought disappointment, especially to educated modern Rumanians with their pan-Latin or at least pro-French predilections. Aside from this, the Southern Slavic ties of Russia were countered by hostility of long standing between the Serbians and the Bulgarians. Serbian and Bulgarian, no less than Rumanian, nationalist politicians hoped to be able to utilize tsarist imperialism for their own purposes (as "noncommitted" statesmen of the Third World hope to use the Soviet Union). Their opportunities were so much the greater because the Russian occupation of the Rumanian principalities, Moldavia and Wallachia (1829 to 1834), and of Bulgaria (1878 and 1879) not only failed to implant the tsarist autocratic political model but had the side effect of encouraging the liberal movement. Both Serbia and Bulgaria departed from St. Petersburg's internal pattern and ultimately gave up alliance with Russia altogether.

It is clear that the diplomacy of these Southern Slavic monarchies —with the exception of tiny Montenegro—failed to reciprocate Russian Pan-Slavist affection. After the Congress of Berlin of 1878 both Serbia and the much-favored Bulgaria turned from Russia's to Austria's sphere of influence. Although the overthrow of the pro-Austrian Obrenovich dynasty in 1903 returned Serbia to the Russian connection, it was not so much Pan-Slav attraction to tsarist imperialism as the pressure of Habsburg imperialism that caused the shift.

An internal Russian barrier to the political effectiveness of Pan-Slavist sentiment was the autocracy itself. Domestically, the tsarist government could not make any more use of Pan-Slavist agitation than of any other agitation, since this would have presupposed that popular demands and popular claims were entitled to consideration in policy decisions (thereby to reduce the privilege of autocracy). This was particularly the case in the reign of Nicholas I (1825 to 1855), but in the period of his successors, Alexander II and Alexander III, the government managed at times to manipulate Pan-Slavist opinion. Under Nicholas II, a few days before the outbreak of World War I, Kaiser William II used the argument about the dangers of conspiratorial Pan-Slavism to the established thrones in an attempt to dissuade the tsar from helping Serbia. When the tsar nevertheless did, Pan-Slavist nationalism seemed briefly to popularize the imperial policies, at least defensively.

Tsarist Imperialism and the Far East

The Russian public showed no more interest in St. Petersburg's imperial mission in the Far East than in Pan-Slavism. The St. Petersburg empire never developed an ideology for its drive into Asia that would compare with the British imperialist slogan about the White Man's Burden. Formulas insisting on the mission to spread Western civilization were occasionally used for publicity purposes. But they never became an integral part of the outlook of the Russian people. Throughout the St. Petersburg period the Russian élite had a European frame of reference. In spite of Russia's geographical links with Asia, the Orient was viewed through European eyes.

Even ideologies that sought to reject Western values, notably Slavophilism, still conceived of Russia as a part of European Christendom, even though opposed to the Latin Occident. The outburst of Asianism in Russian symbolist literature and monarchist journalism, around and after the turn of the century, was an important phenomenon of Russian intellectual history, leading towards post-tsarist Eurasianism on the White side and revolutionary Scythism on the Red side, but it had only ephemeral relevance to contemporary tsarist imperialism. The main protagonist was Prince Esper Ukhtomskii, who before Nicholas II's accession accompanied him on his tour of the Far East. After the construction of the Trans-Siberian Railroad, Ukhtomskii encouraged the tsardom's expansion into East Asia. He wrote, for example, that in Asia the Russian empire could not be bound by any border but the sea, by virtue of the affinity of antimaterialistic and anti-Occidental Russian outlooks with Asian spirituality. This affinity, he declared, was manifested in the un-Western and more Asian institution of Russia's autocratic tsardom. According to him, "the only lawful Lord of the East" was to be the one "adorned in legendary splendor with the crowns of . . . Kazan, Astrakhan, and Sibir, merged into a single crown." Writing in 1900, at the time of the Boxer Rebellion in China, Ukhtomskii envisaged a time when "Russia would decide the eternal contest between Europe and Asia in favor of Asia," because of what he alleged to be Russia's fraternal links with the East.

Such idealizations of Asian values found appeal in some monarchist circles attracted by the fact of the survival of absolute monarchies in Asia at a time when autocracy was threatened in Russia. Russian liberals and radicals regarded the tsardom as a relic of the Mongol yoke. In fact, the Muscovite heritage implying service obligations to the crown for all subjects (the gentry originally being compensated with land) that underlay much of the pre-Soviet social order had its counterparts not in European feudalism or capitalism but in what Karl A. Wittfogel refers to as Asian "hydraulic despotism."

Unavoidable, of course, was the trauma of mutual strangeness when Russian conquerors and colonists encountered Asiatics. Yet, unlike the overseas expansion of Western European colonial powers in the sixteenth and seventeenth centuries, Russia's expansion through northern Asia, towards the Far East, did not consist of sudden incursions but was only the climax of a long prior evolution of East Slavic absorption of the Eurasian forest tribes or steppe nomads through conquest, intermarriage, and agricultural colonization. Thus the Russian conquests of Siberia continued the process of Muscovite absorption of the Tatar states. Though Muscovy's first encounter with China was followed by a struggle (1655 to 1658) in which the Manchu rulers of the Chinese were victorious, this produced nothing like the trauma of Britain's Opium War on China. In contrast to the almost contemporary Jesuit mission in the Far East, the Russian ecclesiastical mission in Peking was not suspected of imperialist designs.

As to China's territory, the Russian empire had given up designs on it in 1689. They were not resumed until 1847, when Count Nicholas Muraviev-Amurskii, governor-general of Eastern Siberia (1847 to 1861), aspired to build up a Russian maritime empire on the Pacific. With the support of Tsar Alexander II, this Russian liberal and admirer of the United States prevailed over the cautious ministry of foreign affairs in favor of landing Russian forces at the estuary of the Amur River (1849). In the Crimean War, Russia's Pacific coastal positions proved less vulnerable to British attack than those on the Black Sea. Checked in the West by the treaty of Paris in 1856, the Russian empire resumed its Far Eastern expansion through the foundation of Vladivostok, a city whose name means "Sway over the East," and through the treaty of Peking, which confirmed its annexation of the Amur and Ussuri regions (1860). These concessions to Russia were not wrested from China by armed force, as were those forced by Britain in 1842 and 1858, but Russian imperialism did benefit from the weakening of the Chinese empire by British imperialism.

Less well known is St. Petersburg's encouragement of Lamaist Buddhism and its effect of promoting the tsar's popularity in the Mongolian and Tibetan areas under Manchu imperial suzerainty. Russia's western Mongolian Kalmucks (of the Volga estuary) and the northern Mongolian Buriats (of the Baikal region) profess Lamaism. The latter were converted to it after they had come under Russian rule, in the eighteenth century. From about that time Lamaist subjects looked upon the Russian monarchs as Bodhisattvas, potential Buddhas. In the nineteenth century this Buddhist image of tsardom spread to Lamaist peoples beyond Russia's frontiers. With this in mind, Russia's ministry of foreign affairs opposed the anti-Lamaist proselytizing and Russifying policies of the ministry of the interior, which were designed to isolate Russia's Lamaists from those of China's sphere. Thus the advantages of centralizing control of subject peoples clashed with those to be derived from attracting foreign coreligionists to the Russian empire as early as the 1830's and the 1850's (as they were to clash again in the 1920's). Between 1900 and 1904, the Dalai Lama of Tibet preferred collaboration with the tsardom to Chinese suzerainty.

Did Tsarist Imperialism Constitute a "Prison of Peoples"?

The non-Russian nationalities that fell under tsarist rule may be divided into those which were pressed into the Russian empire by brute force and those which initially had asked to be accepted as subjects of the tsar so as to receive protection against other powers whose threat to them was more immediate and more feared or more resented than the Russian alternative. Even among the Tatars of the Kazan khanate a considerable part had sided with Muscovy against rival Ottoman-oriented Tatar factions after the middle of the fifteenth and in the early sixteenth centuries. In 1546 the Chuvash on the western bank of the Volga voluntarily submitted to Muscovy in order to escape Kazan Tatar domination. In 1557 both the Kabardians of the Northern Caucasus, long threatened by the Crimean Tatars, and the Bashkirs of the

Ural, who felt threatened by the rival nomadic Nogai, asked to be accepted as subjects of the tsar. In 1645, 1655, 1661, and 1673 the Kalmucks, established on the Volga, voluntarily submitted to Muscovy to collaborate against rival nomadic hordes such as those of the Kazakhs. That the Ukrainian Cossacks in 1654 submitted to Orthodox Russia because Catholic Polish domination seemed to them a heavier burden is well documented.

During the Muscovite conquests in Siberia the Russians were spontaneously assisted by Tungus (for example, in 1640) and lesser peoples of the forest zone because they felt more immediately threatened by Buriat and Yakut horse nomads who had exacted a heavy tribute from them. In the steppe zone it was again and again the struggle between rival nomadic hordes that induced the weaker side to tip the balance in its favor by offering allegiance to the tsar. In 1730 a part of the Kazakhs, whose pastures were being devastated through the westward expansion of the Dzungar (Oirat) Mongols, preferred to accept Russia's protectorate.

As an alternative to domination by Muslim Persia and Turkey, the main Georgian kingdom arranged a protectorate treaty with Russia in 1783. In 1806 and 1815 the northern Ossetians (in the Northern Caucasus) wanted to become Russian subjects to escape the previous Kabardian domination. Eastern Armenia welcomed in 1828 the occupation armies of the tsar as a long-desired alternative to those of the shah. Even among the Turkoman tribes, some of whom were the last people to be conquered by Petersburg (1880 to 1884), a large number had much earlier voluntarily requested Russian domination (in preference to that of Persia or Uzbek Khiva): notably various Caspian Turkoman tribal groups as early as 1677, 1745, and 1802, 5,600 Chowdur Turkomans in 1811, and by 1850 about 115,000 Chowdur and Yomud Turkomans. Between 1863 and 1867 almost all northern Kirghiz tribes voluntarily submitted to Russia for protection against the expansion of Uzbek Kokand.

This is not to say that the many peoples who voluntarily submitted to the Russian tsardom remained content under Russian imperialism and never tried to free themselves from its domination. Almost all of them had cause to rebel at one time or another, frequently because they were subjected to Russian annexation or colonization instead of protective tsarist overlordship. Following is an enumeration of these attempts in order of their original submissions to Russia:

The Kazan Tatars revolted against the Russian conquerors in the years 1572 to 1584, the Chuvash rose against Muscovy between 1606 and 1610. Bashkir uprisings took place from 1662 to 1664, 1681 to 1683, and 1704 to 1711. Tungus attempts at resistance were made in 1649 and 1650, 1666, and 1678 to 1684. The Kabardians had to be subdued by Russian armies in 1768, 1777 to 1779, and 1805. In 1771 the majority of the Volga Kalmucks broke off from the Russian empire, braving pursuit and starvation on the way (to return into what had been Dzungaria, depopulated by Chinese genocide of the other Oirats). Around 1672 many, if not most, of the Ukrainian Cossacks preferred even the Sultan's overlordship to the tsar's. Kazakh independence struggles against Russian interference or occupation started as early as 1785 and continued until 1869 and 1916. There were Ossetian risings against tsarist Russian policies in 1802, 1804, 1809, and 1850. A conspiracy to separate Georgia from Russia was suppressed in 1832. Yomud Turkomans rose even against superior Russian might, notably in 1873 and 1915, and the southern Kirghiz in 1875 and 1916. Even among the Christian Armenian victims of Turkey, tsarist imperialism was resisted by guerrilla-like methods from 1903 to 1905.

Pressures for Russification were the main grievances of the Georgians and Armenians. In the North the policies of Russification, particularly under Alexander III and Nicholas II during the quarter of a century of 1881 to 1905, received most unfavorable publicity because they interfered with German preponderance in the Baltic regions. There the mainly rural Latvians and Estonians had remained at the mercy of Baltic German nobility and burghers, even after the areas passed to Russia in the early eighteenth century. As a matter of fact, the Baltic Germans continued to hold a disproportionately large number of the highest positions in the St. Petersburg empire. It was through the weakening of this group under tsarist Russification policies (which in turn must be seen against the background of Germany's rival imperialism from the 1870's) that the emergence of an Estonian and Latvian nationhood became possible, notably in the educational, cultural, and economic spheres.

On the other hand, the ethnic and denominational imperialism that prompted the Russification pressures under the last two tsars also produced what is known as the most notorious phenomenon of the late tsarist empire: it stimulated not only sharpened anti-Jewish legislation but also encouragement of bloody pogroms against minority groups, particularly the Jews in southern Russia. Middle-class Germany was so shocked by them that a representative part of the German press echoed the slogans that such brutality against the Jews could happen *only* in a land as barbaric and un-European as Russia.

Less unequivocal was the Russian public's rejection of tsarist imperialism where it applied to the Poles. Here Russian opinion depended on political affiliation. Even the Russian liberals (Kadets) were not willing to concede more than restricted autonomy to the Poles, whereas the socialistic groups affirmed Poland's right to self-government. And it cannot be forgotten that Alexander Herzen, father of Russian revolutionary Populism, sacrificed his popularity with the Russian public by declaring his solidarity with the fighters for Poland's independence in 1863, although this Polish independence war was also fought for Poland's claims to West Ukrainian and West Belorussian territories. Polish imperialism was historically a rival of Russian imperialism and between 1609 and 1611 almost succeeded in supplanting the latter in Eastern Europe. Nor can a judgment on tsarist imperialist injustice to the Polish people ignore the oppressive discrimination practiced against the largely Orthodox Ukrainians and Belorussians in pre-tsarist and post-tsarist Poland.

No such history of hostilities separated the Finns from Russia. As a duchy of the St. Petersburg monarchy (after 1809), Finland in fact had more self-government than during the preceding seven centuries of Swedish rule. Nonetheless, the Finnish élite remained culturally Swedish, and it inherited attitudes of a Sweden which had lost its imperial position to Russian imperialism at the beginning of the eighteenth century. To this was added resentment over the abolition of Finland's autonomy and constitutionalism at the last high point of autocracy under Nicholas II (in 1899).

Yet, when all is said, it is an indisputable (but little-known) fact that until the dissolution of Russia in 1918 the Poles and Finns were the only two subject nations to demand separation from the Russian state. All the other non-Russian peoples (if one disregards a small number of Georgian and Crimean Tatar exiles abroad who were on the side of the Central Powers), even those anti-Russian Muslims of Daghestan and Uzbek Kokand who had been most recently conquered by tsarist imperialism, demanded only autonomy within a federalized Russian democracy. The Ukrainians, for example, abandoned this line of thinking only after the Bolshevik invasion of the Ukraine. This fact, more than any other, was responsible for the Rada's proclamation of complete independence and sovereignty on January 25, 1918.

Russian Imperial Colonialism in Siberia

Muscovite imperialism in eastern Eurasia used methods of indirect rule as early as any other colonial power. The aborigines of Siberia were made tributary to but did not become subjects of the tsars. The conquerors hardly interfered in their internal affairs. Where an incipient political power élite already existed (as among the Yakuts and Buriats), it was strengthened. Muscovite imperialism attempted not to destroy but to use the institutions of the conquered peoples. Muscovy took the clan elders of the Siberian peoples it subdued into its service —mainly as collectors of fur tribute (*iasaq*).

Although the *iasaq* probably offered the most important single motive for the tsardom's expansion into Siberia, it was, according to government instructions, not to be collected from the poor, the sick, and the crippled. Like the Indians of Spanish America, the Siberian peoples were to be treated as wards of the state who required protection. If their complaints reached the tsar, they were eventually answered, and the crimes of Muscovite colonialism were punished by the government itself. Many of the governors of Muscovite Siberia ended their careers as defendants before the tsar's courts, for example, Peter Zinoviev and Prince Ivan Gagarin of Iakutsk at the end of the seventeenth century. And yet, in practice, the ineffectiveness of central government control over local Russian abuses in Siberia reduced the humanitarian elements of Muscovite colonial policies to mere pious intentions. Disregarding the instructions of their government, the Muscovite government officials and pioneers in Siberia oppressed and exploited the "pagans," extorting many more furs than the regulations required. The Russians who entered Siberia, including officials, soldiers, and even priests, were from the very beginning swayed by greed and mercantile motives. Some of the Siberian "pagans," who by the nature of their land and their way of life had but a precarious subsistence, were reduced to selling their last miserable possessions or even their wives and children—if these last were not abducted for ransom.

The Siberian peoples resisted not only by making complaints to the tsar but also by migrating and by resorting to arms. In northeastern Siberia their resistance was not broken until the eighteenth century.

Russian punitive expeditions used methods of intimidation and terrorism. In order to ensure submission, the Muscovite fortresses used to take hostages from each individual clan. They were frequently kept in irons, until this institution was abolished in 1769. In contrast, it was precisely at the time of the Enlightenment that slavery in Russian Siberia reached its peak. In vain had the semimedieval Muscovite tsars attempted to prevent the enslavement of the Siberian aborigines. In 1599 Tsar Boris Godunov ordered the release of enslaved Siberians. Even though traffic in slaves was prohibited under penalty of death, the slave trade continued in Siberia. Eventually, by 1702, that is from the beginning of the St. Petersburg empire, the possession of slaves was officially recognized in Russian legislation. Until the early nineteenth century the slave trade was the most important business activity along the Southwest Siberian Fortification Line. It was not until 1826—earlier than in British India (1833) and much earlier than in the United States—that slavery was finally prohibited in the whole of Russian Siberia.

The excuse used for the keeping of slaves prior to 1826 was that they could be converted to Christianity. Such forced conversions were prohibited in Muscovite Siberia after 1625. On the other hand, Siberian converts were exempted from the fur tribute and entitled to enlist in Russian garrisons on the same basis as Russians. Nevertheless, forced conversions occurred under the enlightened absolutism of Peter I and his immediate successors, whose secular state policies looked to standardizing the empire's subjects denominationally.

Like the Portuguese and unlike the British colonials, the Russians freely intermarried with the native peoples. They took Tungus wives and Buriat ones on the Angara River and in Transbaikalia. The last barrier separating the aborigines from the Russians fell as the former were absorbed into the common religion. The Russian empire had—and still has—an ideological and not a biological criterion of identity. The criterion for belonging to the imperium was profession of the Orthodox faith, not race of birth. And the tsardom's imperial ideal remained the absorption of its colonial subjects into the Russian people.

In practice the mutual adaptation of the aborigines and the Russians of Siberia was already far advanced by the time Siberia was actually integrated into the Russian empire. Its Russians had been isolated from the European part of the empire for a long time. It was through the immigration of Russian farmers, fleeing from serfdom in the seventeenth century, that Siberia was freed from chronic famines. By the end of that century the Russian colonists constituted the majority of Siberia's population. And into the nineteenth century it preserved many Muscovite traits.

Typically, Russian administrators in Siberia exercised enormous arbitrary powers, and these were not reduced until St. Petersburg's beginning liberalization during the Napoleonic period. After 1708 the powers of governors-general encompassed the whole of Siberia. Ivan Pestel filled this office without leaving Petersburg; here he would intercept complaints against such subordinates as Treskin, governor of Irkutsk, who forced the Buriats of Lake Baikal to sell their herds to provide hired labor to build a road. Worse still, he connived with grain merchants, whose bread speculations produced a major famine. Only after this, in 1808, did the Irkutsk intelligentsia, supported by some Irkutsk merchants, succeed in smuggling a messenger to St. Petersburg to transmit these grievances. Ultimately, Governor-General Pestel, who was prepared to ignore even the instructions of the central government, was dismissed, but not until 1819. Meanwhile the town commander of Nizheudinsk went about in a coach pulled by subordinates who had dared to complain against him.

Aside from the evils of such arbitrariness, the eighteenth century brought further empoverishment to the aborigines of Siberia. Both epidemics and the destruction of game for the sake of furs diminished the population and even caused the extinction of entire tribes. Even the large cattle breeding and agricultural peoples of southern Siberia suffered thereby. The decline of their numbers worsened the situation of the survivors, for they remained collectively responsible for the same fur tribute. To a considerable extent they fell into debt bondage to Russian merchants.

Eventually the independence movements of Britain's and Spain's American colonies prompted Tsar Alexander I to reform the administration of Siberia. In 1819 he made the relatively liberal Michael Speranskii its governor-general. The latter investigated and reported: "If in Tobolsk every official should have been indicted, here in Tomsk there is nothing to do except have every single one of them hanged!" Finally 681 Siberian officials were indicted. Speranskii in 1822 gave Siberia an administrative status that remained in force until 1917. It sought to protect the Siberian peoples against arbitrary abuses. The nomadic ones were to preserve their autonomy. The sedentary ones were given the status of Russian peasants, but were still exempted from military service. Russian colonists were not to be admitted on their land.

In practice, these guarantees were not fulfilled. Thus the northern and northwestern Buriats were forced out of their pasturelands by Russian agricultural colonization. The settlement of Russian agriculturalists undermined the extensive nomad economy and thereby the Buriats' livelihood. The Tungus with their hunting economy suffered even more. The guarantees of usufruct of the nomads' pastures were not observed (after they had been declared property of the Russian state). When the emancipation of the Russian serfs in 1861 accelerated the Russian peasant colonization of Siberia, the livelihood of the nomadic peoples of the steppe zone was threatened even more. This produced ethnic antagonisms between them and the Russian colonists.

Russian Colonialism in Tsarist Central Asia

Much the same thing happened in the Kazakh areas adjoining southwestern Siberia. Russian peasant settlement started in Kazakhstan after 1866. This colonization increased during the famine of 1891 and 1892 in European Russia. Three years later Russians constituted 10 percent of the inhabitants of Semirechie (Dzhety-Su), but they owned all of its agricultural land. After the Revolution of 1905, the policy of Peter Stolypin sought to relieve peasant pressure on landlords in European Russia by dispatching peasant colonists to both Siberia and the steppe areas. This caused the Kazakh nomads drastic losses in pasturelands, and they were gradually pushed back towards desert areas. Between 1902 and 1913 the Kazakh people declined by almost one tenth.

Similar was the fate of the Kirghiz under Russian colonization. The Kirghiz nomads were sometimes left with no more land than was given to the Russian agricultural settlers who began to arrive in 1868. Such Russian colonists were often organized as Cossacks, and in that case they were privileged by receiving grants of the most fertile lands. Their life was very different from that of the impoverished Russian peasants who emigrated after the famines of 1891 and 1898. To accommodate the colonization that Stolypin promoted in an attempt to avoid European Russia's agrarian revolution, entire Kirghiz groups were pushed into the steppes and mountains. In the present Frunze

(Pishpek) area the Kirghiz lost more than 700,000 hectares of their most fertile pastures to Russian colonization. More and more Kirghiz peoples were thereby reduced to the status of hired farmhands. In the decade 1903 to 1913 the Kirghiz peoples lost by famine and emigration about 10 percent of their numbers. By 1914, on the other hand, 131 Russian and Ukrainian settlements had grown up in the Kirghiz areas.

Such mass Russian settlement of the steppe zone does not mean that tsarist imperialism in Central Asia could not fully rely upon the solidarity of the European colonial minority against the subdued native majority. The Russian colonists were relatively devoid of race consciousness and had already started to intermarry with Kazakhs and Kirghiz. If some tsarist administrators occasionally declared that the Russians were the ruling people of the empire ("by virtue of the sacrifices they had undergone in its conquest") and that the native subjects were expected to conform, this did not give the colonials a consciousness of being an imperial race, or produce a solidarity of the "imperial people" against the "lesser breeds." This applied more to the Russian-acculturated parts of Kazakhstan and Kirghizia than to the strongly Muslim Uzbek lands. Thus when, in 1916, the Kirghiz (and other Central Asian peoples) rose against a Petersburg labor-drafting decree (opposed by the on-the-spot colonial authorities), a number of Russian peasants fought and died on the Kirghiz side: of four Russians known to have died for the self-determination of the native subjects, one had been three times decorated by the tsar and another was a village headman.

Even in the colonial capital of Russian Turkestan, in Tashkent where the Russian population had few contacts with the Uzbek and Tajik Sarts, Russian party affiliations made the Europeans less than fully united and empire-conscious. It is true that the native self-administration, subordinated as it was to the governor-general of Russian Turkestan, was not really representative. The peoples of Turkestan were grossly underrepresented in Tashkent's municipal council and in the imperial Duma of 1906 (from which they were excluded altogether in 1907). Yet from 1871 the official educational policy of the colonial government aimed at lessening the distance between Muslims and Russians. In contrast to contemporary British Indian patterns, the schools were meant to reconcile natives and Russians. However, their effect was slight.

On the whole, the Russians clustered in a few of Turkestan's urban centers, and lived apart from the natives. The latter's modernists were stimulated less by the Russians than by Russian Tatars and the Young Turks. However, not all such Muslim modernists opposed Russian colonial rule: like British India, Russian Turkestan had its share of pro-empire natives. Among its nineteenth-century modernists were such pro-Russian writers as Zakir Furqat and Karimbek Sharifbek-oghli Kamil; the one praised electric lights and Russian secondary schools and the other the enlightenment expected from the Russians in general.

Although under Russian rule Muhammad's descendants, the dignitaries of the annexed khanate of Kokand, had lost their privileges and the lands of Muslim endowments were no longer exempt from taxation, the mass of the farmers were charged less taxes than under Kokandian rule. Initially this reconciled the rural population to Russian colonial rule, but soon the introduction of cotton as a cash crop made Russian Turkestan (like Egypt under British occupation) dependent on food imports from Russia for its sustenance and the world markets for its prosperity. The transition to a money economy brought speculation among investors and indebtedness for producers, so that by 1912 a third of the peasants of Ferghana had lost their land by mortgaging and foreclosures (comparable to the situation in British Burma). In this most developed part of Russian Turkestan, potters, smiths, weavers, and other artisans were ruined by imports of industrial products. Forced into agriculture, they increased the population pressure on the land. In spite of the growing population, the Russian colonial administration made little effort to irrigate more land.

Against this background, the infidel rule of the Russians was opposed by dervish sheikhs of medieval cast. One of them led 1,500 disciples in a holy war against the colonial power in 1898—which got him hanged and the property of his followers confiscated: Trial by jury and other restrictions on arbitrary rule, which had been introduced into Russia proper at the time of its conquest of Turkestan, had not been extended to this colony, with the result that many of the corrupt practices that had been abolished in European Russia by the 1860's continued unabated in Turkestan. Such a time lag in reforms between the metropolitan centers and the colonies of imperial powers is a familiar phenomenon.

Likewise, premodern social structures in underdeveloped states controlled by imperialist powers were frozen and carefully preserved through methods of indirect rule. Two extreme cases were the states of Bukhara and Khiva under the overlordship of tsardom. Initially they were to be Russian Turkestan's buffer states, counterparts of the Afghan buffer state of British India. Like Afghanistan, Bukhara was relieved of the conduct of its foreign relations, and Khiva's semiencirclement by Russian territory deprived it of occasions for such. Though Russian administrative interference was greater in Khiva than in Bukhara, its impact was smaller. Both Uzbek vassal states were obliged to abolish slavery and to admit Russian garrisons. In the case of Khiva, the Russian military protected the Uzbek against the warlike Turkoman minority of its subjects. In the case of Bukhara, they protected the despotic Uzbek emir against dynastic rivals and rebellious vassals. Both protectorates were much less reformed by Russian imperialism than were the native states of India (other than Bhutan and Nepal) by British imperialism. Thus in Khiva nomadic militancy remained a threat, and in Bukhara the medieval Muslim scholastic tradition endured. Uncanonical innovations, such as a Russian-built railroad or a purified water supply, were not permitted to touch the city of Bukhara. When Bukhara was discovered to be a focus of epidemics threatening Russia and a delegation of Russian government physicians gave the Bukharan theologians a microscopic view of their water, they were told that lenses could delude and that only God could send or stop diseases. In spite of the liberal critics of Bukhara's refusals to progress and imperialist urgings to incorporate Bukhara, St. Petersburg preferred not to interfere beyond a bare minimum—mainly for reasons of economy. Even so, opposition to both the original tsarist conquest of Bukhara of 1866 to 1868 and the final Soviet conquest of 1920 came mainly from social forces of medieval Islam.

Tsarist Imperialism in the Multinational Caucasus

Resistance to both the first tsarist and the last Soviet Russian conquests of the Northern Caucasus also derived from Islam. The Muslim mountain tribes were subdued with fire and sword by the tsarist General A. P. Ermolov in the years 1816 to 1827; he destroyed crops and burnt entire villages. Yet—notably among the semifeudal Kabardians—Russian pacification policies tended to favor the dependent peasants over their lords if the latter happened to be the main force of resistance against the Russian conquest. The late eighteenth-century penetration of tsarist imperialism beyond the Caucasus attached Daghestan's petty states through a kind of protectorate system, with Russian officers acting as political agents of the British type at the native courts. The Muslim crusading movement of the murids that rose against the historical Daghestani dynasties and their collaboration with the infidels could be considered a nativist reaction against the penetration of Russian imperialism were it not for the fact that the (Bukharan-inspired) murid movement did not reach Daghestan until after the Russian invasion and was almost as alien to its traditions as were the Russians. Shamil, the great imam of Daghestan's murids, probably killed more Daghestanis than he did Russian soldiers (from 1834). He destroyed the monarchies of Daghestan and forced its peoples into unity against Russia in the name of a pietistic, militant Muslim esoteric order. Entire armies of the Russian empire perished in the struggle against Shamil's murid empire of Daghestan.

His surrender to Russia in 1859 was followed by the expulsion or voluntary emigration of Northern Caucasian Muslims to Turkey. The genocide that occurred during this exit of the Islamized Circassians in 1864 made this conquest probably the darkest chapter in nineteenth-century Russian imperialism. In Daghestan itself the Russian empire, adopting measures much like those of the British in Bengal in the late eighteenth century, turned the old élite into dependents by restoring the dynasties and vassalages which the murids had overthrown. Though they ceased to rule once Daghestan was annexed and directly administered by the Russian empire, they remained powerful landowners. What had been service "fiefs" of revenue collection assignments were converted into private land holdings, the owners being entitled to the labor of the peasant farmers on the land.

Through similar economic policies the Russian empire attached to itself the landed Muslim elites of northern Azerbaijan. There were hardly any mass risings against Russian rule in this area because denominational hostilities for a long time counterbalanced the links of Turkish-speaking Azerbaijan with the anti-Russian Ottoman empire. Tsarist policies of encouraging Western investment made possible the rise of the Islamic world's first industrial urban center in Azerbaijani territory: the oil-producing metropolis of Baku, which after 1875 developed into the world's second largest source of oil, became a cosmopolitan, capitalistic, and proletarianized enclave in patriarchal, rural Azerbaijan.

Earlier, at the time of Russia's conquest of Transcaucasia from Persia (1813 to 1828), Armenian aspirations had served the expansionist goals of tsarist imperialism. Eastern Armenia, annexed by Russia in 1828, increased its population through Armenian immigration from Persian and Ottoman territories. Out of its core Nicholas I organized an Armenian territorial entity—which he dissolved in 1840. Among individual Russified Armenians in the service of the tsardom, Michael Loris-Melikov became prominent as a general and minister under Alexander II. It was this tsar's failure to hold portions of old Armenia that had been wrested from Ottoman control and occupied by Russian armies in 1877 and 1878 that caused the modernizing Armenian intelligentsia (who initially were associated with Russian revolutionary Populism) to evolve more nationalistic goals. When, under Alexander III in the 1890's, tsarist expansionism shifted to the Far East and thereby avoided antagonizing the Ottoman Sultan, Abdul Hamid II (who had started systematic massacres of Armenians), Armenian revolutionary activities turned against agents of Russification, though not against eastern Armenia's remaining in the Russian empire. The center of Armenian nationalism was the Georgian capital of Tiflis, where the chief currents of Russian Armenian modernization developed.

Georgia, which shared the Orthodox faith of the Russian State Church, came closer to full integration in the St. Petersburg empire than did Armenia. In 1811, St. Petersburg's Holy Synod started taking over the Georgian Church. Georgia's autonomy was taken away and its regional feudal institution was forced into line with the bureaucratic centralization of the St. Petersburg empire. All this antagonized even pro-Russian Georgians. Peasants and aristocrats revolted together against Russian imperialism again and again between 1804 and 1820, particularly in 1812. Yet, the tsar was by no means exploiting Georgia: on the contrary, the Russian occupation there was a deficit enterprise. When Nicholas I personally inspected the situation in Georgia in 1837 he soon discovered that the people were prevented from approaching him with complaints. The tsar accepted 1,400 complaints and took immediate sanctions against the most corrupt and arbitrary of his administrators. M. S. Vorontsov, his viceroy from 1845 to 1854, gave Georgians scope for self-realization, at least in the cultural sphere.

The Georgian aristocracy, having failed in its anti-Russian conspiracy of 1832, reconciled itself to the rule of the tsar, who had confirmed most of its feudal privileges. (Even Alexander II, who freed the Georgian serfs, did not give them land as he had to the Russian peasants.) An important part of Georgia's aristocratic élite had merged with the ruling class of the Russian empire. The Georgian generals P. I. Bagration (one of the victors over Napoleon) and P. D. Tsitsianov (one of the tsarist conquerors of Transcaucasia), for example, were absorbed into the St. Petersburg élite as members of the upper class of one of the empire's non-Russian nations. Even an originally Lamaist Kalmuck family, the Dondukovs, were so absorbed.

But in Georgia, as in other parts of the empire, tsarist imperialism tended to rely on a social stratum that was economically undermined by its very incorporation into the empire. The Georgian aristocracy became impoverished still more rapidly than did its Russian counterpart. As its wealth passed to the Armenian bourgeoisie, the scions of Georgian feudalism came to champion Marxist democratization. And it was left to an antidemocratic Georgian Marxist to restore a post-tsarist Russian-dominated empire: Joseph Vissarionovich Dzhugashvili, better known as Stalin.

TARAS HUNCZAK

Pan-Slavism or Pan-Russianism

And the domes of ancient Sophia
In the transformed Byzantium
Once more Christ's altar will enshrine!
Kneel down before it, O Tsar of Russia
Then rise as Tsar of all the Slavs.
—Fedor Tiutchev [1]

Pan-Slavism originated among the Western Slavs, who were under a profound influence of Western, particularly German, writers and philosophers of the Romantic era. From Johann Gottfried von Herder, the submerged Czechs and Slovaks and later the Poles, Ukrainians, and Southern Slavs had learned that they were bound by linguistic affinity and a Slavic *Volksgeist*. Central to Herder's teaching was the role of language in the development of national consciousness. Indeed, he taught that for the not yet fully developed nations, language, as the medium of creativity and the record of their past, was the very source of their identity.[2] When these ideas penetrated the Slavic world, a basis for cultural Pan-Slavism and national renascence was established. In time these currents were to prove mutually exclusive.

Pan-Slavism, as a consciously directed quest for common sources of ethnic kinship, was also a product of psychological and political need. The Slavic nations, which found themselves in an inferior cultural and political position *vis-à-vis* their Western neighbors, experienced a compelling need to identify themselves with a large and powerful family. This was to compensate for their inferiority and provide them with a new source of strength. The prospect of a bright future in the Slavic family was perhaps most eloquently described by the Slovak poet Svetozar Hurban-Vajansky:

> I am proud, proud of being a Slav.
> My beloved fatherland
> Counts one hundred million inhabitants.
> It commands half of the globe.
> With the Slav language
> You can travel in the four quarters of the Universe.
> One of our brothers cultivates the palm tree,
> Another contemplates the eternal ice,
> The third ploughs the seas.
> I am proud, proud of being a Slav.[3]

The main objectives of the early Pan-Slavs, particularly the Czechs, the Slovaks, and the Ukrainians, were cultural and political freedom, which they hoped to pursue within a federation of other free and equal Slavic nations. These nations, as well as the Southern Slavs, having lost their statehood long ago, had no claims to primacy or leadership; indeed, they would be satisfied with a status of equality.

Pan-Slavism of these politically weaker Slavic nations differed markedly from the Polish and especially the Russian understanding of the nature of Slavic solidarity. The Poles, who had just lost their independence as a result of the partition of 1795, felt that they had a special mission to fulfill in Eastern Europe. They therefore demanded for themselves a position of leadership among the Slavs. Adam Mickiewicz in his work *Księgi Narodu polskiego i pielgrzymstwa polskiego* (*The Books of the Polish Nation*) (1832) exalted his country above all the others, for it alone was the embodiment of freedom. His cosmic idea of Polish mission was an extension of the Christian concept of redemption through suffering and death. Within the framework of the poet's vision, the resurrection of Poland would herald the liberation and salvation of mankind and inaugurate an era of universal peace. Similar messianic views were voiced by Zygmunt Krasinski and Julius Slowacki.

Polish claims to hegemony among the Slavs, a position the Poles hoped to use against Russia, provided a serious rival to Russian messianism. This clash of messianic aspirations, complemented by the growing feeling of nationalism among the Slavic nations, created an atmosphere in which genuine supranational considerations proved untenable. Although one should not discount the earnestness of some of the nineteenth-century thinkers who preached a universal gospel, the messianic political movements seem to have served as a façade for other more limited objectives. Russian Pan-Slavism is a case in point.

As an extension of Slavophile ideology into the political sphere, Russian Pan-Slavism was but another phase in the unfolding of Russian national consciousness.[4] It was a product of the cross-fertilization of the currents of Romanticism and the era of Napoleon with its summons of the masses, conditioned by the peculiarities of Russia's historical development. The Russians, hitherto submissive and passive, were stirred to a new life, a life of searching for a usable past in the hope of establishing their identity.

Slavophilism and Pan-Slavism reflected Russia's quest for national identity and national mission from two different perspectives. Alexander Herzen, perhaps the most profound of the nineteenth-century Russian thinkers, thought of "Slavophilism or Russianism, not as theory or teaching, but as the offended national feeling . . . , as a reaction to the foreign influence that existed from the moment Peter I caused the first beard to be shaved." [5]

It was this wounded pride and the feeling of inferiority that made the Russians examine their heritage, hoping to find something that would restore their self-respect and dignity in the eyes of others. This necessitated a journey into the Russian past, and this they undertook with vigor and determination. The results of the Russian national introspection imperceptibly divided the Russian intelligentsia into two fairly clearly defined groups of Westerners and Slavophiles.

The former, more profoundly influenced by the achievements of the West, saw Russia's salvation in the acceptance of Western values, culture, and liberal ideals. Peter Chaadaev, who acted as a catalyst in the great debate over the nature of Russian history in the second quarter of the nineteenth century, found nothing worthwhile or inspiring in Russia's recorded past. "We have not known an age of exuberant activity and of the exalted play of moral forces among the people as others have. The period in our social life which corresponds to this moment was characterized by a dull and dreary existence, without vigor or energy, which was enlivened only by abuse and softened only by servitude. There are no charming recollections and no gracious images in our memory, no lasting lessons in our national tradition. . . .

Alone of all the peoples in the world," he concluded, "we have not given anything to the world, and we have not learned anything from the world. . . . We have contributed nothing to the progress of the human spirit, we have disfigured it." [6]

Chaadaev's eloquent though overstated indictment of Russia's past, "a shot that rang out in the dark night," [7] inflamed the wounded national pride, producing at the same time a violent reaction in government circles. Polemics, which engaged the most active Russian minds, took a new turn. Inspired by the position of *Moskvitianin,* a nationalist monthly which voiced the blind hatred of everything foreign of its founder, Michael Pogodin, the defenders of the Russian heritage turned their attacks against the West and its allegedly corrupting influence on Russian culture. Thus one important element of the Slavophile and subsequently Pan-Slavist ideology came into existence. According to Friedrich Hertz, this element, the struggle against foreign influence, played a significant role in the emergence of nationalism among the Slavs in general.[8] As their ideology crystallized, other elements were added to this anti-Western Slavophile orientation. The Slavophile philosophers insisted that the basic differences of the two worlds, East and West, created an unbridgeable precipice between them. Their heirs, the Pan-Slavs, felt that this dialectical situation could only be resolved in an armed conflict in which the decadent West should perish and victorious Russia should remain to lead the field.

Besides this negative aspect of their ideology, the Slavophiles evolved a whole system of values that were in harmony with their conception of the nature of the Russian nation, its institutions, and its providential mission. Under the influence of the Western Romantics, they delved into their history and discovered a myriad of institutions and character traits that enhanced their self-esteem.[9]

As had other nationalist movements, the Slavophiles sought a wider base for their ideology. The answer to this need was the discovery of the simple Russian people, the *narod,* who in their state of simplicity and backwardness preserved all those personal and social virtues that were believed to be specifically Russian.[10] They allegedly preserved the humility and communality of the Russian spirit, and these traits, the Slavophiles held to be incongruous with the egoism and individualism that afflicted the Western world.[11] It was this emphasis on the primacy of the collective and the communal over the individual as a principle of harmony and brotherhood that contained for the Slavophiles a promise of spiritual regeneration for Russia and the world.

The focal point of the Slavophile ideology was the Russian Orthodox Church with its universal message of truth, love, and internal freedom.[12] For the Slavophiles, the Church was the very principle of the inner national life, intrinsically related to personal and family relations, social institutions, and ethical concepts.[13]

An extension of Orthodoxy into the socioethical sphere found its logical expression in the peasant commune.[14] It corresponded to the Slavophile conception of the organic progression from man to family, to commune and nation, toward social and moral wholeness.[15]

Constantine Aksakov gave what was perhaps the best description of the commune: "A commune is a union of the people, who have renounced their egoism, their individuality, and who express their common accord; this is an act of love, a noble Christian act, which expresses itself more or less clearly in its various other manifestations. A commune thus represents a moral choir, and just as in a choir a voice is not lost, but follows the general pattern and is heard in the harmony of all voices; so in the commune the individual is not lost, but renounces his exclusiveness in favor of the general accord—and there arises the noble phenomenon of harmonious, joint existence of rational beings (consciousnesses); there arises a brotherhood, a commune—a triumph of human spirit." [16]

These Romantic considerations of Russian *sobornost* or wholeness as a product of the organic principle that permeated Russian life at every level [17] helped to usher in the Russian messianic idea.[18] It was reinforced by Hegelian notions of the unity of the historical development of civilization, wherein, in different periods, one nation is given the mission of revealing the absolute spirit. The Slavophiles felt that it was Russia's destiny to save the world. This universalism, true of all messianic aspirations, was tempered by their desire to identify Russia with the Orthodox Church, its institutions, and the ideals that were to regenerate mankind.[19]

Various aspects of the Slavophile ideology went into the making of Russian nationalism whose apotheosis was messianism. However, the enhanced feeling of self-esteem they zealously sought and cultivated by projecting their own values and ideals [20] into the annals of Russia's past proved to be the very antithesis of the Russian claim to universalism. Indeed, the development of nationalism led Russia in the direction of exclusiveness and chauvinism.

Vladimir Solovev described this mutually exclusive relationship as follows: "The worship of one's own people as the preeminent bearer of universal truth; then the worship of these people as an elemental force, irrespective of universal truth; finally the worship of those national limitations and anomalies that separate the people with a direct negation of the very ideal of universal truth—these are the three consecutive phases of our nationalism represented by the Slavophiles, Michael Katkov, and the new obscurantists, respectively. The first were purely fantastic in their doctrine, the second was a realist with fantasy, and the last are realists without any fantasy, but also without any shame." [21]

The Slavophiles, although distinguished from other Russian nationalists by their attitude toward state, emancipation of the serfs, and education, shared with them a profound attachment to all those elements of Russia's past that gave it national identity, power, and a claim to universality. Caught in the tide of nascent nationalism, they displayed only the scantiest interest in the other Slavs. And even on those rare occasions their references to the other Slavs were invariably related to Russia's size and strength, and therefore its natural right to hegemony among other members of the Slavic family.[22]

The first Russian awareness of the other Slavs (who, Russians thought, could be added to the Russian empire with the help of the Russian army) was displayed early in 1821 by Michael Pogodin, a zealous nationalist.[23] Ten years later a nationalist of Western orientation and a foremost bard of Russia, Alexander Pushkin, wrote a poem "To the Slanderers of Russia," answering those who supported the Polish rebels in their fight against Russia. He ended his poem, which can be considered as a Russian counterpart to Kipling's "White Man's Burden," declaring that the Slavic rivers should join the Russian sea. In these words Pushkin expressed what was to become the credo of the Russian Pan-Slavists. Any attempt at separateness of the Poles in 1831 or of the Ukrainian Pan-Slavs at a later period was met by a Russian phalanx of opposition.[24]

This Russian centralism, particularly of the Slavophiles, was duly noticed by other Slavs. Perhaps the most eloquent critic of this tendency was Karel Havliček, a gifted Czech journalist and a devoted Pan-

Slav. In search of a better understanding of his Slavic brothers, Havliček traveled to Warsaw and then to Moscow. The results of his journey were disheartening; he left for the Slavic lands an ardent Pan-Slav only to learn of the narrow, selfish interests of the two countries. Havliček's illusions of fraternal concern were quickly dashed, and he "returned to Prague, as a Czech, a simple determined Czech, even with some secret sour feeling against the name Slav, which a better knowledge of Russia and Poland had made suspect to me." In his article, which he wrote in 1846, Havliček honestly admitted: "The freezing temperature in Russia and other aspects of Russian life extinguished the last spark of Pan-Slav love in me." [25]

Havliček was particularly disturbed by what he correctly considered to be the most dangerous aspect of Russian Pan-Slavism: the consuming desire to dominate others. "The Russian Pan-Slavs believe," said Havliček, "that we and the Illyrians would like to be under their domination!! They are firmly convinced that they will one day control all Slav lands!!! They now look forward with joy to their future vineyards in Dalmatia. These gentlemen have started everywhere to say and write Slav instead of Russian, so that later they will again be able to say Russian instead of Slav. . . . I can . . . testify that the Russians think of the other Slavs in no brotherly fashion, but dishonestly and egoistically. . . ." [26] In view of the increasing Russian claims to primacy to the exclusion of other Slavs, Havliček's criticisms were well founded.

The process of national introversion, which resulted in the crystallization of the Russian national idea and expressed itself in cultural nationalism, was given a new turn by the outbreak of the Crimean War.[27] The threat to the prestige and the integrity of the Russian empire mobilized the Slavophiles, causing them to abandon their utopian approach to political problems. Their previous speculation about the alien and inimical West was suddenly affirmed by the pro-Turkish anti-Russian Western coalition. In the effort to help their besieged fatherland, the Slavophiles sought for other sources of strength. They discovered them in their radical social, cultural, religious, and linguistic affinity with the other Slavs. Alienated from the West, Pogodin found Russia's strength and its mission in the Slavic community.[28]

Under these circumstances the feeble Pan-Slavic trends of the earlier period became an expression of the rising Russian nationalism.

The Slavophiles and kindred groups who in the past had examined their heritage to the exclusion of others now plunged into a new activity. Under the pressure of international events they began to project in the other Slavs those qualities they found to be specifically Slavic, that is, Russian. This shift did not signal the emergence of an entirely new movement; rather, it represented a change of emphasis and direction in the Slavophile ideology, to which some new elements were added. Although the newly oriented movement was very often composed of the same men, it soon became known as Pan-Slavism or Pan-Russianism.[29] To the Slavophile conception of history (of mutually exclusive Romano-Germanic and Slavic worlds, of Russia's messianism and of Orthodoxy as the true religion of Slavdom) Pan-Slavism added the element of intense preoccupation with the Slavic question as seen from a political vantage point.

This political preoccupation of the Slavophiles, for whom state and politics were a necessary evil, brought them closer to the supporters of official nationality, champions of the Russian state idea.[30] Beginning with the Crimean War the ideas of these groups were modified until they coalesced into a Pan-Slav credo. At its very basis was the idea of Slavic political unification. Only now it was lifted from the realm of folk culture and ethnography, factors that had played an important role in the earlier period. The idea that cultural rapprochement should precede a political unification of the Slavs gave way to belief in a political solution to the Slavic question. Its proponents insisted that only upon political unification would the original cultural unity of the Slavs be restored. Since they stressed a purely political solution of the Pan-Slav problem, they also favored the use of force, direct action, and, where feasible, a policy of intervention.

The foremost exponent of this militant Russian Pan-Slavism and the first to emphasize its nature was Michael Pogodin. Although of plebeian origin, Pogodin rose to become a well-known historian and journalist, achieving a position of public prominence. The ideas he articulated so clearly and forcefully antedated the Great Divide in Russian history—the Crimean War. In 1837 Pogodin addressed a "Letter on Russian History" to the future Tsar Alexander I giving vent to his nationalist Pan-Slav sentiments. Dazzled by the size and power of the Russian empire, which was controlled and directed by a single man,[31] Pogodin prophesied the fulfillment of Russian mission—the creation of a universal monarchy.[32] "Russia—what a marvelous phenomenon on the world stage . . . which country can compare with [it in] magnitude? . . . A population of 60 million people, aside from those who have not been counted. . . . Let us add to this multitude 30 million more of our brothers and cousins, the Slavs, . . . in whose veins the same blood flows as in ours, who speak the same language as we do, . . . Slavs who in spite of geographic and political separation form by origin and language a spiritual entity with us. . . . I cannot think any longer, I am overwhelmed by this vision. . . ." In the course of his elaboration of other sources of strength, Pogodin posed a rhetorical question of extraordinary political and historical significance. *"Who can compare with us? Whom will we not force into submission? Is not the political destiny of the world in our hands whenever we want to decide it one way or the other?"* (italics mine).

Having discussed the superior qualities of Russia and the Russians, Pogodin returned to the question of Slavic solidarity in order to claim Russian primacy in the fulfillment of the Slavic mission. "But which of the Slav tribes occupies the first rank today? Which tribe can by its number, its language and the totality of its qualities be considered the representative of the entire Slav world? Which offers the best pledge for the future good? . . . .

"My heart trembles with joy, oh Russia, oh my Fatherland! Is it not you? Oh, if it were only you! You, you are chosen to consummate, to crown the development of humanity, to embody all the various human achievements . . . in one great synthesis, to bring harmony to the ancient and modern civilizations, to reconcile heart with reason, to establish real justice and peace. . . ." [33]

Pogodin's conception of Pan-Slavism demanded an unqualified subordination to Russia. Those Slavs who would join under the flag of the tsar of Russia, accept the Russian language, law, and Orthodoxy, would be accepted as brothers. However, "he who is not ours," continued Pogodin, "we shall force to become ours, or leave him to be consumed by the German, Hungarian, or even the Turk." [34]

Pogodin's faith in the providential character of Russia's mission because of Russia's grandeur and uniqueness was shared by the other members of the Pan-Slav circle. Among them we find Iurii Samarin, Stephen Shevyrev, Vladimir Lamanskii, Ivan Aksakov, Alexander Hilferding, Nicholas Danilevskii, and Fedor Dostoevsky.

A statesman and administrator, Samarin voiced the consuming centralism of his group in a letter to a friend in May, 1842. He thought that it was erroneous to seek "Slavic spirit" in a union of Slavic tribes. The objective of the Slavic movement according to Samarin was "to elevate Russia and in her manifest concentration and the completeness of the Slavic spirit without any onesidedness. . . . Only in Russia the Slavic spirit attained self-awareness emanating from self-denial. . . . I do not think that Russia can get anything new that she does not already possess from the Slavic tribes. On the contrary, their liberation from their tribal one-sidedness and the actualization within themselves of the all-Slavic essence is possible only under one condition—realization of their self-awareness through Russia." [35]

Stephen Shevyrev, a close friend of Pogodin's, stated the Russian objective in relation to the Slavs more openly and more succinctly. He simply said what the Russians need is that "all the other Slavs should become Russian, rather than that we Russians should seek some other basis." [36]

These views coincided with the position of the imperial government, which favored the incipient Russian nationalism even though it feared any popular movement. In this matter, the early exponents of Russian Pan-Salvism differed from the government only in that the first favored an expansive set of ideas that they hoped to translate into action, whereas the government, desiring to remain faithful to the concert of Europe, urged the Russians to concern themselves with their own affairs.

The most articulate expression of the government's position on this question can be found in Count S. Uvarov's circular of 1847: "Everything that we have in Russia belongs to us alone, without the participation of other Slavic peoples who now stretch their hands toward us and beg for protection, not so much from an inspiration of brotherly love as from the calculations of a petty and not always disinterested egoism. . . .

"Is not the name of the Russian more glorious for us, that famous name of ours which, since the foundation of our state, has been repeated and is being repeated by millions of people in their social life? Let the name of the Russian be heard in the universities as it is heard among the Russian people which, without any cunning philosophizing, without the imagined Slavdom, has retained the faith of our fathers, the language, the ways, the customs, the entire nationality. . . ." [37]

This self-centered nationalism was also characteristic of such zealous Pan-Slavs as Ivan Aksakov, who in 1849 openly expressed his lack of confidence in Pan-Slavism. "We do not believe in Pan-Slavism," he admitted candidly. As Aksakov saw it, there were too many differences and conflicts of interest among the various Slavs. As one of the possible solutions, he saw the fusion of all the other Slavs with Russia. "I admit," he concluded, "that of all the Slavs, the Russians are the ones that most concern me." [38]

The Crimean War, a *Götterdämmerung* long expected by the Russian nationalists, strengthened the Slavophile contention that relations between the West and Russia were fundamentally antithetical.[39] Alexis S. Khomiakov, a foremost Slavophile polemicist and lay theologian, viewed the conflict as a "holy war" which, as the agent of Divine Providence, would usher in a new era. It would mark the triumph of "the Russian or rather the Slav" and of the Orthodox principles that henceforth should enlighten humanity.[40]

More politically oriented, Pogodin sought the attainment of Russia's objectives, not in the acts of Divine Providence, but in the strength of numbers. Although deeply aware of Russia's isolation, he felt that there was hope of support from its natural allies—the 80 million Slavs living outside the Russian empire.[41] His war aims were also more mundane than those of Khomiakov. He expected the Russians to capture Constantinople and make it the capital of a Slavic federation under the Russian aegis.[42]

The visionary anticipation and a long-time objective of the Russian Balkan policy were frustrated on the battlefields of the Crimea. Russia lost the war in its own backyard, at least temporarily frustrating its ambitions for hegemony in the Black Sea area and denying it control over the coveted Straits. This debacle forced the Russians in the government and outside it to reassess their domestic situation as well as their attitude towards the neighboring states and the outworn international formulas of legitimacy and divine right of kings that Nicholas I adhered to so tenuously. These developments favored the Pan-Slavic cause in Russia.

In the years following the Crimean War, the Russian Pan-Slavists sought to discover and "to define the sources of Slavic unity, to endow the Slavic movement with an ideological direction, to propagate the Slavic cause, and to win friends for their ideology." [43] Their objectives were more political than ever, and yet because of their recent traumatic experience and the humiliating political setback that Russia had suffered, the Pan-Slavists, like the Slavophiles, espoused the priority of a cultural unification. Since the cultural aspect of their activities constituted merely the intermediate step, however, their ultimate objective was transparent in all their undertakings. The complete subordination of their efforts to political ends became so suspect to the other Slavs that the work of the Russian Pan-Slavs could not meet with success.

Perhaps the most dedicated and the most prolific popularizer of Russian Pan-Slavism was Ivan Aksakov. He was the embodiment of the evolving Russian idea that passed from the pietistic stage of the Slavophiles to the militancy and activism of Pan-Slavism. With the death of many of the leading lights of the former Moscow Slavophile circle, Aksakov became the natural heir and the chief spokesman of the Slavophile ideas in their new setting.[44] Aksakov's more active involvement in the Slavic issue began in 1858 when he became editor of the *Russkaia Beseda*. Although, as a measure of expedience, the articles published by him were mostly historical in nature, Aksakov hoped that they would gain a political significance by creating and promoting a feeling of Slavic solidarity.[45]

Aksakov reached a position of influence and social prestige largely through his activities in the Moscow Slavic Benevolent Committee, first as its secretary treasurer and then as its president after Pogodin's death in 1875. The organization had grown in size and importance since its establishment in 1858, and the work of the Moscow committee and its branches in other cities was facilitated by liberal grants of funds from the Asiatic department of the foreign ministry, the ministry of public education, the Holy Synod of the Russian Orthodox Church, and the imperial family.[46] One of its major functions was to provide aid to Orthodox Churches and schools outside the empire in the form of funds, books, supplies, and student scholarships.

In general, the various committees remained faithful to their avowed objectives; they engaged in philanthropy and the dissemination of the Russian language and literature among the other Slavs.[47] Like the foreign aid programs of our day, however, committee operations were not based entirely on altruism. Indeed, the very active participation of the government, particularly of the Asiatic department of the foreign ministry, which also dealt with Balkan affairs, in the various facets of the committees' activities is indicative of the political objectives the government hoped to attain. That this Russian philanthropy, aside from its purely humanitarian aspect, was a long-term political investment was subtly hinted by Egor Kovalevskii, a department chief of the Asiatic department of the foreign ministry, in a letter to the first president of the Moscow Slavic Benevolent Committee, A. N. Bakhmetev, when he said that the activities conducted by the committee "will undoubtedly yield a harvest in the future." [48] The "harvest," as N. M. Druzhinin sees it, was to strengthen the Russian influence in the Balkans and then among the Slavs in general.[49]

Language occupied a prominent place in the arsenal of the Russian Pan-Slavists in their search for cultural rapprochement with the other Slavs. Influenced by the earlier Romantic views on the role of language in the process of unification through understanding, the Russian and several non-Russian Pan-Slavs urged the adoption of a single literary language. Their insistence that only the Russian language qualified as the vessel of Slavic solidarity revealed more clearly than any other aspect of their activities the political centralism of the Russian Pan-Slavic programs. In their desire to establish the primacy of the Russian language the Russian Pan-Slavs invoked various arguments, some of which were of questionable validity. They cited history and tradition, size and strength, utility and necessity, and even the "nobility" of the Russian language in order to convince the other Slavs that salvation and progress lay with the acceptance of the Russian language.

Pogodin openly linked linguistic uniformity to the Pan-Slavic political program when he urged the Slavs to adopt the Russian language, for "God has foreordained a wondrous destiny for it by having put it in the mouths of that people which has been consecrated to primacy over all the people of the Slavic, and perhaps of the European, world!" [50] Similarly Vladimir Lamanskii, a professor of Slavic philosophy at the University of St. Petersburg, urged the Slavs to give up their linguistic autonomy and recognize the hegemony of one Slavic language, that is, Russian, his hope being that this would contribute to the spread of Russian culture and influence.[51]

Anton Budilovich, professor of Russian and Church Slavonic at Warsaw University, speaking for a linguistic unification of the Slavs in 1877, argued that the all-Slavic language did not die; it merely changed under the influence of various conditions. Among the Slavic literary languages, "only the Russian developed from the basis of the Old or Church Slavonic language, succeeded to all its legends and to all its rights. . . . Only the Russian nation," he continued, "remained a faithful preserver of the Slavic heritage, both in Church matters and in literature, gaining thereby for its literary language a historical right to be called 'all-Slavic.' "[52]

Budilovich maintained that the struggle for existence of the several lesser Slavic languages, competing with the German or Italian or Russian languages, was hopeless. "As concerns the Russian language," he said, "its future is sufficiently assured even now because of the numerous Russian-speaking population, the size of their territory, and the strength of the Russian state, and finally because of the thousand-year history of our literary language, the heir to the blessing of the Slavic Apostles." For a Pan-Slavist who was supposedly seeking for sources of unity, Budilovich came to the amazing conclusion that "the Russian language, because of its history, its character, and its position, has very little in common with any of the other literary languages of the Slavs."[53]

Budilovich was obviously not concerned with Slavic linguistic ties when he wrote these words. His goal was a Russian political hegemony in which the Russian language should serve as a midwife to realize the ultimate objective. "Thus the idea of the Russian language as the all-Slavic language," observes Professor Druzhinin, "became an expression of the thesis of the Russian hegemony in the Slavic movement."[54]

It is in the context of this political objective of the Russian Pan-Slavs that one must view their negative attitude toward the languages of such major Slavic groups in the Russian empire as the Ukrainians and White Russians. The Russians could not logically approve of or tolerate other Slavic languages within their own state since these could correspond to the political aspirations of non-Russian groups. The English writer Malachy Postlethwayt touched the very essence of the problem when he wrote in 1757 that "it is a law founded on the very nature of colonies that they ought to have no other culture or arts wherein to rival the arts and culture of the parent country."[55]

Support of the official policy of Russification of the Western provinces of the empire, that is, territories occupied by the Baltic people, Belorussians, Ukrainians, and a large Jewish minority, was wholly in keeping with the objectives of the Russian Pan-Slavists. Since they favored the strengthening of the Russian influence in the various parts of the multinational Russian empire, they opposed all forms of nascent nationalism or even of national consciousness of the subject nations. Thus, for example, Ivan Aksakov condemned Ukrainophilism, the nineteenth-century cultural nationalism of the Ukrainians, considering them "willing and conscious traitors to the Russian cause. . . ." [56] He felt that the Russian language, culture, and powerful state gave the Ukrainians the highest of aspirations. The development of the Ukrainian nationalism was therefore an absurdity which, like the nationalism of other minorities, "threatened the integrity of the Russian empire and his [Aksakov's] dreams of a Slavic millennium." [57]

Perhaps most revealing in terms of the long-range objectives of the Russian Pan-Slavists was their attitude toward the Polish question. Should Poland be independent or should it be ruled by Russia? It was this "Fateful Question," as Nicholas Strakhov called it, that conveyed to the other Slavs the profound difference between the high-sounding declarations of brotherly love and Slavic solidarity and the banal reality. Alexander Hilferding, an ardent Pan-Slavist and apologist of the Russian policy in Poland, commented on the crux of this problem in July, 1863: "Poland places Russia into a constant state of contradiction with herself and thereby deprives her of freedom of action. . . . We strive to believe that the direct holy calling (mission) of Russia is protection of the Slavic nations, representing them before Europe, cooperating in their liberation. And again we must look back at Poland, for if we wanted to forget about her, our enemies would point her out to us reminding us accusingly: 'Physician, heal thyself.' . . . Everywhere, on all paths, Poland forces Russia to contradict herself, her mission, her political hopes and aspirations." [58]

Having lamented what must have been a traumatic experience for the Russian Pan-Slavists, Hilferding came to the surprising conclusion that despite the numerous difficulties Russia should not give up Poland. He contended that Russia should keep Poland not only out of national or state egoism but also for the sake of Russia's Western provinces.[59]

Torn between the *Wahrheit und Dichtung* of Russian Pan-Slavism, Ivan Aksakov acknowledged the right of the Poles "to strive to unite all the Poles into one Poland." [60] At the same time, however, he advocated a solution of the Polish question through Russification, expropriation of the Polish landowners outside the limits of ethnic Poland, replacing the Polish officials with Russians, subverting Catholicism with Orthodoxy, and making education serve Russian political objectives.[61]

Iurii Samarin gave the Polish question the aura of an ideological struggle between the two worlds represented by Polish Catholicism and Russian Orthodoxy. As one of the early members of the Moscow Slavophile circle, Samarin remained faithful to its teachings, and these he applied in dealing with the Poles. Thus, for example, he acknowledged Poland's right to an unhampered cultural development, but without recognizing its right to an independent political existence. For Samarin, the fact that a people possessed all the attributes of national individuality did not necessarily entitle them to political independence.[62]

General Rostislav Fadeev, a man widely known for his Pan-Slavic views, was disturbed by the effect the Russo-Polish relations would have on the future development of Pan-Slavism. He argued therefore: "the perpetuation of the present state of things in Poland, elevated into a principle, will frighten the Slav world and destroy all confidence in Russia at its very root. The Slavs, who to this day fear the phantom of an insatiable Russian ambition, would consider our brotherly call as a stratagem. An insurrection of the Poles, although possible against Russia, would become impossible against a Federation that shall have surrounded their country on all sides." [63]

Besides this purely strategic consideration, Fadeev thought that moral restraint would prevent the Poles from revolting against the tsar since he would stand at the head of the future Slavic federation. Revolt against the head of the Slavic family would be construed as an act of treason. The logical conclusion of Fadeev's argument was that once the Poles found "themselves not on the borders, but in the center of a country which sympathetically [accepted] the priority of Russia in a general Confederation," they would have no choice but to submit.[64]

For Fadeev, as for other Russian Pan-Slavists, the solution of the Polish question was connected with the future of Russia's Western provinces, by which he meant primarily the Ukrainian and Belorussian principalities west of the Dnieper River. General Fadeev maintained that a thorough Russification of these "six purely Russian provinces" was a *sine qua non* for a successful solution of the Polish problem.[65]

It is safe to assume that Fadeev and other Russians who proposed to Russify the "purely Russian provinces" were neither naïve nor ignorant in making such self-contradictory statements. They merely stretched the truth in order to justify their policies, which were directly opposed to what they promised the other Slavs outside the Russian empire.

That the Russian Pan-Slavism had little if any chance to win converts to its ideas among the other Slavs became obvious during the Moscow Slav Congress of 1867. Despite the great efforts of the Russians and the government's blessing of the undertaking, the Moscow

Congress of 1867 was not as representative as that of Prague of 1848, nor did it yield the results anticipated.[66] Apart from numerous toasts, high-sounding platitudes, and declarations of Slavic solidarity, the 1867 Congress did not have any positive accomplishments. The spirit of the conspicuously absent Poles hovered over the assembled delegates not only because of the recent Polish uprising but also because news arrived from Paris that a Polish émigré had attempted to assassinate Tsar Alexander II, then in France on a state visit. In this atmosphere any useful discussion of Slavic solidarity was out of the question.

The hosts fared no better in questions of linguistic and cultural unity which they tried to promote. Despite the eloquent pleas of Professor Lamanskii of St. Petersburg, Professor P. A. Lavrovskii of Kharkov University, Count D. A. Tolstoi, minister of public education, S. I. Barsken, rector of Moscow University, and others, for a common language, culture, and religion, the other Slavs rejected the Russian centralism in favor of their own tradition, their own heritage.[67] František Rieger, a leading member of the Czech delegation, was the most outspoken champion of the idea that Slavic solidarity should consist, not in the negation of the individuality the various Slavs had developed in the course of their thousand-year history, but in a mutual brotherly assistance. His alternative to complete unification was "diversity in harmony." [68]

Rieger thus touched upon what was the source of discord in the Pan-Slav movement. His statement could be contrasted with Fedor Tiutchev's ideas on the true meaning of Pan-Slavism. Tiutchev, the great bard of Russian Pan-Slavism, wrote to Samarin on May 15, 1867: "Everything depends on how the Slavs understand and feel their relations with Russia. . . . If they see in Russia only a friendly, allied, helpful, however . . . a foreign power, then nothing has been accomplished and we are far from [our] goal. And that goal will be reached only when they sincerely understand that they are one with Russia, when they feel that they are tied to her by that dependence, with that organic community, which unites all the component parts of an entity into something truly living." [69]

The organic centralism of Tiutchev was not only a product of his poetic fancy; it corresponded to the goals and aspirations of the Russian Pan-Slavists. Although the Russians did not prepare a formal political platform to be discussed at the Moscow Slav Congress, they aired their political objectives indirectly by translating and publishing Ludovit Stur's book *Slavianstvo i mir budushchego* (Slavdom and the World of the Future) in time for the Congress.[70] Stur's work was ideally suited for the Russian purposes, for in calling upon the Slavs to unite with the Russians, to accept Orthodoxy and the Russian language, he did so as a non-Russian.

The Moscow Slav Congress was obviously preceded by a considerable preparation. When it met, "the Russian Pan-Slavists made an attempt to win hegemony in the Slavic movement." Their efforts were fruitless, however. "To turn the Slavic Committee [the Moscow Slavic Benevolent Committee] into a central committee of an all-Slavic organization proved impossible." As a result of this failure the Moscow Slavic Benevolent Committee, together with its branches in other cities, returned to its previous role.[71]

The Russian Pan-Slavists of the post-Crimean War period found their support and inspirations in such indefatigable journalists as Ivan Aksakov and Michael Katkov, in the creative genius of Fedor Dostoevsky, and in the writings of Nicholas Danilevskii, all of whom found many ideological heirs among the political practitioners. Aksakov, who represented a natural living link between two phases of the Russian nationalism, and Dostoevsky continued to proselytize in the Slavophile tradition. Dostoevsky, particularly, renewed the Slavophile claim of Russian messianism. Like the early Slavophiles, he gloried in Russia, its Orthodox religion, and its people. For the thoroughgoing nationalist that Dostoevsky was, these diverse elements coalesced into a picture of Russia as the land of the "God-bearing people." [72] Dostoevsky defined his integral nationalism in an unpublished dialogue between the characters Shatov and Stavrogin (*The Devils*) in the course of which Shatov stated that "man for him is a Russian only, God for him is only the Russian God, custom only Russian custom." [73]

Dostoevsky's nationalist creed may have been the basis of the mystic religious messianism he ascribed to the Russian people and not vice versa, for this is stated clearly by his *alter ego* Shatov: "If a great people does not believe that truth resides in it alone (in itself alone and in it exclusively), if it does not believe that it alone is able and has been chosen to raise up and save everybody by its own truth, it is at once transformed into ethnographical material, and not into a great people. A truly great people can never reconcile itself to playing second fiddle in the affairs of humanity, not even to playing an important part, but always and exclusively the chief part. If it loses that faith, it is no longer a nation." [74]

It is within this purely nationalist objective that Dostoevsky's conception of Russian messianism with all its contradictions and claims to world leadership becomes more comprehensible. These claims were a natural extension into the pan-human and Pan-Slavic spheres.[75] Having reduced "God to a simple attribute of nationality," Dostoevsky in effect negated the universality of Christianity.[76] Instead, he preached a belligerent exclusivism as the natural and healthy order of things. Dostoevsky felt that whereas the national identities of other people rested on false gods, Russia was the repository of truth, for it alone worshiped the true God.[77] Russia's mission was to unite, "to regenerate and save the world in the name of a new [Russian] God. . . ." [78]

Pan-Slavism was accorded a prominent place in Dostoevsky's vision of Russia's future: Its cornerstone, he maintained, had been laid in 1472 by Ivan III of Moscow when he married Sophia Paleologus, the heiress of Constantinople. By this act, wrote Dostoevsky, he "laid the first stone for the future hegemony of the East, . . . not only of a great state but [of] a whole new world, destined to renew Christianity by Pan-Slavism and Pan-Orthodoxy. . . ." [79] That did not mean, however, that Dostoevsky conceived of Pan-Slavism as a Slavic solidarity based on reciprocity and equality. On the contrary, when Danilevskii suggested that Constantinople should be shared equally with the other Slavs, Dostoevsky rejected the proposal. One should not compare Russians with other Slavs. The Russians were superior to other Slavs, not only separately but all combined.[80] Pan-Slavism, therefore, was not an end in itself, but rather an intermediary step that Dostoevsky hoped would hasten the advent of the Russian millennium.

Dostoevsky's ideas coincided with those of his contemporary Nicholas Danilevskii. Upon reading Danilevskii's *Rossiia i Evropa* (1869), Dostoevsky was struck by the likeness of Danilevskii's views to his own. "Danilevskii's article," he wrote to his friend and editor of the journal *Zaria,* Nicholas Strakhov, "is so in harmony with my own views and convictions that here and there I stand amazed at the identity of our conclusions. . . ." [81]

This identity of views was not accidental. It was founded on their basic Slavophile conception of the nature of Russian Orthodoxy, on the peculiar characteristics of the Russian people and their institutions, and on the notion of the irreconcilability of Europe and Russia. Their Manichean conception of history led Dostoevsky and Danilevskii to a nationalist messianism in which Russia appeared as a new Israel, and the Russians the Chosen People. "From an objective, factual viewpoint," wrote Danilevskii, "the Russians and the majority of the Slavs became, with the Greeks, chief guardians of the living traditions of religious truth—Orthodoxy—and in this way the continuators of the high calling, which was the destiny of Israel and of Byzantium, to be the chosen people." [82]

To invest his understanding of Russian messianism with scientific respectability, Danilevskii borrowed or developed a historical philosophical theory that sought to explain the past and project the future. In it Danilevskii discounted unity and continuity of historical development, postulating instead of a cyclical theory, according to which history passes through independent cycles, a succession of historical cultural types, each characterizing a given era. One of those was Europe or German-Roman civilization, which was to be replaced by the Slavic historical cultural type. During this phase, Slavdom, which Danilevskii identified with Russia, would bring about "a synthesis of all aspects of cultural activity—aspects which were elaborated, either in isolation or in incomplete union, by its precursors on the historical scene." [83] To mount this drama, which would usher in a pan-human civilization, Russia needed the support of the other Slavs. This led Danilevskii to espouse Pan-Slavism and promote the Slavic union that he thought was a necessary precondition for the fulfillment of the Slav civilization.

Since he connected the achievement of Pan-Slav union with a favorable solution of the Eastern question,[84] Danilevskii divested himself of metaphysical Slavophilism and adopted the then prevalent Bismarckian *Realpolitik*. He no longer abhorred war as a means of solving problems, as had the Slavophiles of the previous generation. On the contrary, Danilevskii, like General Rostislav Fadeev, Constantine Leontiev, and Count Nicholas Ignatiev, thought that the question of Slavic union as well as the Eastern question would be resolved by the military confrontation of Russia and Europe.[85] The conflict not only would bring victory to Russia and the Slavs but also would produce a salutary psychological effect. In the course of the struggle the Slavs would unite in a common effort against the West, and this would hasten the cause of Pan-Slavism. In fighting the West, the Slavs would cleanse themselves of their subservience to Western ideas, Western culture, and Western institutions.

The Pan-Slav union that Danilevskii envisioned would unite geopolitically and morally all the people occupying the territory from the Pacific Ocean to the Adriatic Sea and from the Arctic Ocean to the Aegean Sea.[86] Out of geopolitical considerations even such non-Slavs as the Rumanians, Magyars, and Greeks would have to join and remain in the projected Pan-Slavic federation. Having been wedged by historical destiny into the Slavic mass, these non-Slav nations, according to Danilevskii, were for better or for worse inseparably bound to the Slavs.[87]

Russia was given the most prominent position in Danilevskii's grand design. Indeed, because of Russia's size, military power, wealth, and political prestige, it was to become the natural leader of the Slavs. In order to help the Slavs against the hostile West, Danilevskii, expressing the prevalent attitude of the Russian public, demanded a very close federal union under Russia's political hegemony.[88] In the proposed federation Russia would not intervene in the internal affairs of the member states, but would merely help them to resolve all their conflicts amicably and justly.[89] Danilevskii considered the successful establishment of the proposed Slavic federation under Russian leadership, with its capital in Constantinople, the only intelligent solution of the Eastern question.[90]

On the practical side Russia would gain several important advantages. Strategically, Russian control of Constantinople and of the Straits would make Russia's southern border secure and inaccessible to states with powerful navies.[91] Danilevskii also thought that Russian control of Constantinople would be of great moral advantage to Russia. Russia could exercise a profound influence from this center of Orthodoxy with its great historical heritage. Indeed, it was from this seat that Russia would succeed in its great historical mission. It would initiate a new, all-Slavic era of world history.[92]

Danilevskii's political objectives, stripped of the high-sounding verbiage, found a worthy champion in Count Ignatiev. As director of the foreign ministry's Asiatic department, which included the Balkans, from 1861 to 1864, and Russia's envoy to Constantinople from 1864 to 1877, Ignatiev was in a position to represent Pan-Slavism at the highest governmental level.[93] Perhaps even more significant, Ignatiev as a career diplomat could and did work toward the realization of the plans and aspirations of two generations of Russian Pan-Slavists.

The principal tasks confronting Russian foreign policy, as Ignatiev saw it, were the revision of the unfavorable treaty of Paris of 1856, gaining control over Constantinople and the Straits, and the attainment of Slavic solidarity under the leadership of Russia.[94] With an unusual frankness, Ignatiev made it abundantly clear that Russian support of other Slavs was justified only if it would further Russian political objectives. "Austrian and Turkish Slavs," said Ignatiev, "should be our allies and tools of our policy against the Germans. Only to attain this goal can Russia make sacrifices for them. . . ." There was nothing altruistic about Ignatiev's Pan-Slavism. Indeed, he considered it not only unwise but criminal to concentrate on liberating the Slavs. For Ignatiev such a policy entailed confusing the means with the end.[95]

Ignatiev remained faithful to his ideas and ideals despite the opposition of his chief, Prince Alexander Gorchakov. "All my activities from 1861 to 1877 in Turkey and among the Slavs," wrote Ignatiev, "were inspired by the above thoughts . . . that Russia alone should rule the Balkan peninsula and the Black Sea, . . . that the Eastern nations should turn their sight exclusively toward Russia, placing their future in dependence of her. . . ." [96]

Developments in the Balkans between 1876 and 1878 gave Ignatiev's expectations an aura of reality. The Bulgarians, who were subjected to heavy repressive measures after their unsuccessful revolt against the Turks, and the Serbs, who suffered repeated defeats, looked toward Russia for help. They were not disappointed, for despite the lukewarm attitude of official Russia, particularly the tsar and his chancellor, Gorchakov, who sought a peaceful solution of the Balkan crisis, highly placed members of the court, the hierarchy of the Orthodox Church, and members of the Pan-Slav committees zealously furthered the Slav cause. They collected money for relief purposes in the streets, in churches, and at public gatherings.[97] Perhaps the most active was the Moscow Slavic Benevolent Committee, which, besides gathering funds, actively recruited volunteers, particularly officers, for the Serbian army. In an atmosphere of public exaltation about 5,000 men joined up to fight the Turks.[98]

The pro-Slav movement in Russia was on the crescendo throughout the summer of 1876, and although it never became a mass movement, it did succeed in engaging a dedicated educated minority in the principal cities. Here lay its importance and its influence. It included teachers, professors, journalists, writers, officials, and men of other professions—in short, men who were articulate enough to propagate their ideas, exercising thereby a profound influence on Russian public opinion.

Amid the effusions of sympathy for their southern brethren and the numerous memoranda addressed to the government urging it to act, expressions of concern for Russia's self-interest in a favorable solution of the Eastern question occupied a prominent position. Most revealing in this respect was General Fadeev's memorandum of June, 1876, which demanded a unilateral Russian solution of the Eastern question by seizing the Straits and establishing control over the Balkans.[99] Three months later, Fadeev reiterated his view, urging a shift of emphasis from Serbia to Bulgaria to enable Russia to solve the Eastern question in its own interests.[100]

Similarly, Ivan Aksakov, the moving spirit behind the activities of the Moscow Slavic Benevolent Committee, thought in terms of the primacy of Russian interests. In writing to General Michael Cherniaev, therefore, Aksakov admonished the ambitious general not to become involved in Serbo-Bulgarian affairs so as to favor the Serbs against the Bulgarians. "You are a Russian, and we Russians must stand above Bulgarians and Serbs and take a broader view. For Russia, the Bulgarians and their independence are no less dear than the Serbs and their independence. . . . The interests of Russia stand above all else, since what is beneficial for Russia also benefits the Serb, the Bulgarian, and all of Slavdom." [101]

Aksakov's concern that Cherniaev might become a convert to the Serb cause at the expense of Russia was groundless. Cherniaev's mission to Serbia was motivated by his desire to direct the Slav crusade against Turkey in such a way as to benefit Russia. His statement to Aksakov of January, 1877, dispels any notion of Cherniaev's altruism in going to Serbia: "If I had had [1,000,000 rubles] at the beginning of the War, I could have made out of Serbia an extremely useful tool in the hands of the Russian government." [102] That this was not a passing whim is attested by another observation he made to Aksakov describing the political possibilities as they would develop after the anticipated coup d'état. Cherniaev wrote: "The influence of Russia upon Serbia would be real and rest on firm foundations: the chief of state and the entire people sympathize with Russia. The ministers gradually could be named from Russians. Hostile parties would disappear, and one of the Slav states would become de facto a Russian province." [103]

The aspirations of the leading Russian Pan-Slavists did not escape the attention of careful observers. The political leaders of the Southern Slavs simply did not comment publicly, lest they antagonize the very people on whose help they depended. In other words, both sides used each other for grossly selfish ends under the camouflage of Pan-Slavic solidarity.[104] In private comments, however, some of the Southern Slavs, among them Jovan Ristic, the foreign minister of Serbia, gave vent to their sentiments. Of particular interest was Ristic's comment to the effect that the Russian Slavophiles were in reality "true Russophiles who regarded small Slav peoples as nice mouthfuls to satiate Russian insatiability." [105]

The limited national objectives pursued by the Russian Pan-Slavs as well as by the Southern Slavs at a time of crisis revealed the true nature of the supranational solidarity that Pan-Slavism was supposed to represent. Now more than at any other time it became obvious that one could not speak "of a Pan-Slav movement, but, . . . of local pan-movements, a Pan-Russian, a Pan-Serbian or a Pan-Polish movement, each one at times using Pan-Slav slogans to win the sympathy of other Slavs or to establish its control over them." [106]

The Pan-Russian and the various local pan-movements represented in reality varying degrees of emerging nationalism. Between Pan-Russianism and the other pan-movements, however, there was a basic difference. The Russians, unlike the other Slavs, had a powerful state and a sense of mission that emanated from it. Their nationalism was therefore assertive and aggressive, demanding a dominant role for Russia among the other Slavs. In this, Pan-Russianism complemented the expansive foreign policy of the state under the camouflage of Pan-Slavism.[107] Thus the Russian state's objectives, strengthened by a four-hundred-year tradition of expansion,[108] proved more powerful than the ideal of Pan-Slavic solidarity. Like other great and noble utopias, Pan-Slavism was divorced from the realities of life, having lost sight of man's preoccupation with self-interest.

RAGNHILD MARIE HATTON

Russia and the Baltic

Moscow's goal of reaching the shores of the Baltic, the waters of which—in the words of Tsar Ivan IV—were worth their weight in gold,[1] was set during the fifteenth-century expansion of the principality. The very position of the principality (known to us only after 1147, when it is first mentioned in a chronicle), astride the river and portage networks of the vast lands of the Rus,[2] encouraged economic ties that facilitated territorial growth as soon as the hold of the Mongols began to weaken. By outright purchase, by gradual colonization, by skillful and often ruthless diplomacy, and by direct conquest when opportunity arose, Moscow's rulers extended the area under their control.

In retrospect there seems something inevitable about the expansion. From its situation on the Moskva River in the heartland—the *Mezhdurechie*—bounded by the upper Volga and the Oka, Moscow had access to the Volga, the Msta, the Dnieper, the Western Dvina, and the Lovat. To the west and north of the Valdai Hills, three routes led to the Baltic: along the Dvina into the Gulf of Riga; over Lake Ilmen, the Volkhov River, Lake Ladoga, and the mighty Neva into the Gulf of Finland; along the Velikaia River to Lake Pskov and the Narva River into the southern part of the Gulf of Finland. To the northeast of Moscow, tributaries of the Volga brought contact with the Northern (Severnaia) Dvina basin with its egress in the White Sea. Further east, the Pechora and Kama rivers led to the Ob basin and the Pacific. To the south, tributaries of the Oka reached out to the Don, and ultimately to the Sea of Azov. No wonder therefore that the urge to the seas, to the Baltic, the Black Sea, and the Pacific, dictated by political considerations as well as by the geocommercial position of the water routes and man-made canals, has been one of the dominant themes in Russian history. "Moscow must either dominate or suffocate." [3]

Conscious long-term aims along these waterborne lines of expansion to the open seas took time to formulate, and they were fashioned as much by the accident of history as by the geocommercial factors. The very lineage of the first known ruler of the Moscow principality, Daniel Nevskii, later served to give moral support in the struggle for access to the Baltic. Was he not the son of that Prince Alexander of Novgorod honored with the name of Nevskii (of the Neva), who in 1240 had defeated the Swedes on the bank of that river and thus put a stop—for a considerable time—to their hopes of building a town on the Narva? But Daniel himself, though he doubled the size of the Moscow principality before his death in 1303, was, as were many of the rulers after him, too preoccupied with expanding the nucleus of his state nearer home to give a thought to conquests so far afield. Expansion in a northeasterly and a southeasterly direction, where neighboring principalities were small and relatively weak, was in any case easier to accomplish than expansion to the west. Here lay powerful states with control of the Baltic littoral. Lithuania, which had profited from Mongol weakness even more spectacularly and speedily than Moscow, stretched from the Black Sea to the Baltic. It governed many Rus peoples within its boundaries and dominated, with Poland, the shores of the central Baltic. Though the ports it controlled were the outlets for non-Russian rivers, the Niemen and the Vistula and their tributaries, Lithuania was in effect in command of the southwestern half of the Valdai Hills portage system from the Western Dvina to the Dnieper and from the Dnieper to the Volga system.

The eastern shores of the Baltic as well as the southern shores of the Gulf of Finland were dominated by the Knights of the Order of the Sword, which, under the aegis of the Holy Roman Emperor of the German Nation, had penetrated beyond the territory of its brother order, the Teutonic Knights of East Prussia, into Courland, Livonia, and part of Estonia on a Christian crusade and stayed to govern in the interests of religion and profit.[4] The Knights of the Order of the Sword were usually referred to as the Livonian Knights to distinguish them from the Teutonic Knights; and "Livonia" often implied also Estonia and Courland, where the Knights were influential. Their control was not absolute, inasmuch as they shared it with the burghers of the towns, who were nearly all German by descent and culture, and with the powerful archbishop of Riga.

The northern littoral of the Finnish Gulf was part of the Swedish state, Finland being a grand duchy integrated into that state since the early Middle Ages, again as a result of missionary activities from Sweden coupled with the search for trade.

Closer to Moscow, indeed as buffer states between that principality and the West but also as obstacles to expansion to the Baltic, were the independent Rus republics to Novgorod and Pskov. Novgorod had a large fur trading empire to the northeast which it had not been able to colonize because its own population was relatively small. Its main military effort had been expended principally against the Swedes and Finns, where bitter border raids for the Karelian isthmus had been the order of the day from the 1260's onwards.[5] The Swedish-founded Vyborg (Finnish Vipurii) was besieged time and again, though it never fell; the Novgorod-built fortress of Kexholm (now called Priozersk) changed hands several times. Novgorod was favored in hard winters when cavalry could speed across ice-bound lakes and marshes, whereas the Swedish-Finnish cause was advanced in summers when the government found the money to reinforce garrisons by sea. The struggle had somewhat abated by the time Novgorod was conquered by Moscow in 1485. On the whole it had ended with benefit to Sweden-Finland: Novgorod kept Nöteborg (Oreshek in Russian, now called Petrokrepost), on its nearly impregnable position on an island in the Neva, but each side had agreed to respect the other's access to the Ladoga-Neva route; Vyborg had maintained its existence, and Finnish expansion in Karelia had been accepted. The struggle was reopened, however, when the new masters of Novgorod refused to recognize the compromise arrived at.

Long before this time the princes of Moscow had become powerful enough to style themselves Grand Dukes of Muscovy and ambitious enough to begin to think of all the lands inhabited by the Rus as their *otchina,* their patrimony. This ambition was deepened by the responsibility they felt for the defense of the Orthodox Church wherever Rus peoples were in danger, real or assumed, of being converted to the Church of Rome, as was the case in Lithuania and in those Rus states

East-Central and Eastern Europe about 1550

Drawn by L. Prokop

that were in touch with Lithuania. It was a Novgorod treaty (provoked by fear of Muscovy) with Casimir, king of Poland and grand duke of Lithuania, which gave Ivan III (1402 to 1505) an excuse to make the first attack on the republic in 1471. Victorious, he appropriated considerable areas of land but left the town of Novgorod nominally independent on condition that it renounce all dealings with its Western neighbors. When this promise was not kept, a final campaign was launched which ended the town's independence. In 1494 Ivan closed the Hanseatic office, a symbolic gesture which pointed to future plans to exploit that trade which had once been Novgorod's glory and the foundation of its riches.[6]

Several features of the conquest and incorporation of Novgorod became typical, in greater or lesser degree, of Russian imperialism in its expansion to and on the Baltic. First, the opportunity for conquest came through divisions inside Novgorod itself, and these were skillfully exploited by Moscow. The republic, its trade in decline, was split into hostile factions, and Ivan III was able to appear as the supporter of the poor pro-Muscovite masses against the rich oligarchy; the latter sought Lithuanian-Polish help to stave off Ivan's design and even appealed in the same errand to the Knights of Livonia. Second, the process of absorption was a gradual one, advance, retreat, and renewed offensive being geared to changing circumstances. Third, the final campaign and its aftermath were carried through with great ruthlessness: mass executions and deportations took place, and at least 8,000 of the wealthiest citizens were forcibly removed to Muscovy and replaced by Ivan's nominees, including merchants from Moscow.[7]

That Muscovy regarded the conquest of Novgorod as a step towards access to the Baltic (as well as to exploitation of the trading empire of Novgorod to the northeast) is demonstrated by Ivan III's early but unsuccessful attempt to drive the Finns from the newly settled areas of Karelia (1479), by the long siege of Vyborg (1495), and by his invasion of Livonia (1481). On meeting stiff opposition, however, he turned away, leaving Ivangorod on the Narva (the town he had built in 1491 and they had taken in 1496) in Swedish hands; Vyborg and the recently constructed Nyslott (1475) remained intact and Livonia undiminished. Instead he took up the struggle with Lithuania for the Smolensk and Ukraine areas, demonstrating yet another characteristic of Muscovite expansion: since there were so many directions in which the territorial aggrandizement (with consequent opportunities for trade and greater income from tolls) could operate, it was politic to shift the field of conflict if returns were slow. Reabsorption of the Rus peoples who were Lithuanian subjects into Muscovy seemed particularly tempting at this time, since by his second marriage in 1472 to a niece of the last Byzantine Emperor, Ivan III felt that the mantle of Byzantium had descended on him with its holy duty to defend the faith. His lack of success against Lithuania had a bearing on the Baltic issue inasmuch as the trade routes of Lithuania gave access to that sea; his failure there compounded that suffered in Livonia and Sweden-Finland.

Yet his clear delineation of goals to be reached, as well as of methods to be used, is significant, and Ivan III's English biographer has rightly stressed that in spite of his lack of success in the post-1485 years he was one of the few Russian rulers to be honored with the epithet "the Great."[8] He shares this honor with Peter the Great and Catherine the Great, who also were bent on Russian empire building. He had gained Novgorod with its outlet to the Gulf of Finland and had put Pskov and the remaining independent Russian principalities in such isolated positions that they soon chose to submit to Muscovy rather than fight him and his successors.[9] From that time on the mission of Moscow as the Third Rome was much talked of, and the Roman title of Caesar began to replace that of Grand Duke in its Russian form, Tsar.[10]

The title caused some trouble in diplomatic interchanges once Ivan IV, a grandson of Ivan III, had been crowned in 1547 with full Byzantine rites and with the formal designation of Tsar. Other rulers were reluctant to use it, since Ivan (like his father and grandfather) was likely to squeeze the most out of any concession in respect of forms of address. Neighboring princes were also disturbed by Ivan's habit of refusing to receive their envoys, referring them instead to his officials in Novgorod or Pskov. Did his behavior, they wondered, imply a trap? If they acquiesced, would he later argue that they had accepted his territorial overlordship by putting themselves on the same level as his subjects, even if these had the title of viceroys?

That the suspicions of Sweden-Finland and of the Livonian Knights were not without foundation was borne out by Ivan's attack on Karelia in 1554 and on Livonia in 1558. The aims were those of his grandfather: to prevent Swedish-Finnish settlements from expanding into territories which, unpopulated or not, he regarded as part of the old Novgorod republic; to strengthen his hold on the Finnish Gulf by taking Vyborg from the Swedes; and, if possible, to remove Narva and Dorpat (Tartu) from the sphere of influence of the Livonian Knights. He was beaten back from Vyborg in 1555 (and had to make a forty-year truce with Gustavus Vasa); but in Livonia he succeeded for a period of twenty-five years. The spread of the Reformation to the East Baltic had undermined the power of the Livonian Knights,[11] and differing opinions on how to govern and defend the territories for which they had for so long been the military shield weakened the whole area. As it split into Estonia, Livonia, and Courland, policy on these matters diverged even more. The moment was ripe, and Ivan IV took Dorpat and Narva in 1558, though Reval (Tallinn) held out against him.

In the face of Ivan IV's advance, appeals for help were sent in all directions: to Frederick II of Denmark, as representative of a Baltic power which had once had a footing in Estonia; to Sweden-Finland, where Eric XIV, the eldest son of Gustavus Vasa, was king but where his brother John governed Finland as its duke; and to Sigismund Augustus, king of Poland and grand duke of Lithuania. All these rulers responded and took under their protection the areas most accessible to them: Denmark, the island of Ösel and (temporarily) part of Estonia; Sweden, western Estonia; Poland-Lithuania, East Prussia (later lost to Brandenburg), Courland, and Livonia. In every case their protection was later altered to various forms of incorporation.

In their turn these rulers appealed to the maritime powers of Europe, and particularly to the English and the Dutch, to blockade Narva as long as the Russians were in control of the port.[12] They had little or no success, for Narva (never part of the Hanseatic League) had built up a flourishing trade by undercutting the other Baltic ports in matters of tolls and dues, and this trade the Western powers were not anxious to forego. The tone of the appeals is worth noting, however, since here, for the first time, a sharp fear of Russian imperialism makes itself felt in the Polish and Swedish proposals for countermeasures to deny a potentially formidable rival access to Western expertise and technology. The Livonian Knights had attempted to exercise some control over the importation of arms and the passage of craftsmen into Muscovy, and Ivan and his advisers had desired control of a port in order to free themselves of such restraints as well as to encourage trade. It is unlikely that Muscovy's Western neighbors had specific information about the expansion and colonization that stretched the borders of the Russian state nearly to the Pacific during Ivan IV's reign, but the broad outlines of ambitious schemes that would link the trade of India and China and Persia with one or more Russian Baltic ports were well known and stiffened Polish and Swedish resistance to Ivan's plans in the East Baltic.[13]

The Muscovite hold on Narva was doomed once Poland and Sweden were free to take joint action. Eric XIV of Sweden-Finland had stopped the Russian advance by taking control of western Estonia and had declared Narva to be in a state of blockade in 1562; but he was then side-tracked by Frederick II of Denmark, who declared war on him and received help from a Poland resentful of the Swedish presence in Estonia.[14] Eric's deposition in 1568 by his brother John brought peace with Denmark-Norway and an alliance with Stephen Báthory (king of Poland from 1575 to 1586). John III was anxious for cooperation with Poland-Lithuania for dynastic as well as strategic and commercial reasons. He had married Catherine Jagiełło, a sister of the late King Sigismund Augustus of Poland-Lithuania; and she hoped that their son, christened Sigismund and brought up as a Catholic, would one day be elected king of the two parts of the Commonwealth which had been united in 1569 (thus formalizing the custom that Poland and Lithuania had observed since the 1380's of electing the same ruler).

In the ensuing war against Ivan IV, defeats in the field forced Muscovy to armistices in 1582 and 1583 acknowledging Livonia as Polish and Estonia (where the Danish occupation on the mainland, but not of Ösel, had been ended) as Swedish as far as the Narva River and including Narva. John III's hold over Kexholm and most of Ingria was also admitted,[15] though Ivan kept a small foothold in Ingria on either side of the Neva since Nöteborg had withstood Swedish attempts at conquest. When formal peace was made in 1595 at Teusina (Täyssinä), Catherine's ambitions for her son had come to fruition: Sigismund Vasa had been elected Báthory's successor in 1586 and had also succeeded his father as king of Sweden in 1592. Circumstances were, however, more propitious for Ivan IV than this might seem to imply; for Sigismund's position in Sweden was weak, his attempts to reintroduce Catholicism having met with stiff opposition. Whereas the peace therefore confirmed the armistices in respect of Polish Livonia and Swedish Estonia, it widened Russian access to the Gulf of Finland by restoring Swedish-held Ingria and Kexholm and settling the border in Karelia along the lines of Finnish and Muscovite inhabitants.

Sigismund's loss of the Swedish throne and the accession of his uncle, Charles IX, in 1604,[16] inaugurated a long period of Polish-Swedish struggles, since Sigismund and his sons kept their claim to Sweden alive. To the Catholic powers of Europe they were the true rulers, who ought to be restored as the elder branch of the House of Vasa; and Charles IX, and his son Gustavus Adolphus, they regarded as Lutheran usurpers of the cadet branch. The threat from the Polish Vasas, supported by the Counter-Reformation, undoubtedly intensified Swedish expansion and empire building in the Baltic. The fear of Russo-Polish cooperation to dislodge Sweden from the Gulf of Finland altogether (Russia to take southern Finland and eastern Estonia with Narva, Poland the rest) had some justification: as early as 1590 the Commonwealth had laid claim to Estonia, and Boris Godunov had attempted (unsuccessfully) to launch an attack on Narva with Polish-Lithuanian help.

Encirclement from the east was a frightening prospect to a Sweden already encircled to the south and west by Denmark-Norway, with only the smallest and most insecure outlet to Kattegat at Älvsborg at the mouth of the Göta River. Denmark not only controlled both sides of the Sound but possessed several islands in the Baltic—Bornholm and Gotland of old, Ösel as its share of the spoils from the break-up of the East Baltic states—and was therefore a formidable enemy, against whom the Swedes found it difficult to make headway.

Swedish efforts were concentrated in the east, for financial as well as for strategic reasons: the income from the tolls of Narva was already making a sizable contribution to the Swedish budget,[17] though a good deal of the trade from the Russian hinterland found ways to avoid Narva, either by using other Baltic ports or by taking the route to Arkhangelsk. The hope of forcing more Russian trade over Swedish-controlled ports is evident in Charles IX's suggestion that the White Sea area might be conquered so that Arkhangelsk, the center of Russian trade with the West, might become Swedish, but the distances involved in such a project were vast and it was deemed more feasible to concentrate on enlarging the Baltic bridgehead. The prospect of *dominium maris baltici,* with lucrative tolls and dues from many ports rather than one, was a lodestar for some, though certainly not for all, men of influence in Stockholm.

Fears and hopes alike are mingled in the Swedish intervention in the Russian Time of Troubles after the death of Boris Godunov in 1605, when, to prevent a Polish candidate from becoming tsar, a Swedish army answered Muscovy's call for help. The army did indeed reach Moscow in 1610, and suggestions for the incorporation of the whole province of Novgorod in the Swedish empire and for a permanent link between Sweden and Russia in the form of a Vasa tsar (as secundogeniture in the reigning Swedish dynasty) were made. Such talk, vague though it was, was brought to an abrupt halt by the election of Michael Romanov as tsar—a consequence both of national reaction against all foreigners and of Swedish inability to help Vasilii Shuiskii to a military decision. But the Swedish armies maintained themselves in the Ingria and Kexholm regions, though Charles IX found himself with a war with Denmark on his hands and had to starve the Russian front.

His son Gustavus Adolphus, king of Sweden from 1611, decided to reach a speedy armistice with Denmark. It is a measure of his scale or priorities that he was content to leave Älvsborg, the one outlet to the Western seas, to the Danes (to be redeemed within four years at a cost of a million riksdaler) in order to free himself for the Eastern front. His military successes there were not outstanding, his two sieges of Pskov being failures, but he brought fresh armies into play, and this, in conjunction with the conquests in Ingria and Karelia of Jacob de la Gardie and Gustaf Horn in his father's reign, ensured that these provinces (Muscovy's remaining foothold on the Gulf) were in their entirety ceded by Tsar Michael at the Peace of Stolbovo in 1617. Gustavus Adolphus contemplated with pleasure the map of the redrawn frontier, which now went through Lake Ladoga: "the Russian bear won't find it so easy to jump that ditch." [18]

It is from 1617 that Swedish imperialism is traditionally dated,[19] though to the king and his chancellor, Axel Oxenstierna, the need to gain security at a time when Muscovy was weak was more operative than thoughts of expansion for reasons of trade and income. Oxenstierna had stiffened the attitude of the chief Swedish negotiator, de la Gardie, during the long negotiations by urging him to remember: "We have in the Russians a false and at the same time a mighty neighbor; in whom by reason of the guile and treachery which he has (as it were) drunk with his mother's milk, no faith is to be reposed; but who by reason of his power is terrible not to us only, but to many of his neighbors. . . . That we should now not only let go, but ourselves help him to his legs again, before his feathers be somewhat plucked and his condition a little embarrassed (but we on the other hand somewhat strengthened and improved) is what seems not only to be unsafe and prejudicial, but despicable and censurable, and on its heels will follow a tardy and ineffectual repentance." [20]

The search for security for Finland and against an outflanking attack by Poland-Lithuania was uppermost in the minds of those who controlled Swedish policy; but historians are justified in using the label "imperialism," not only because strategic considerations form a significant factor in all imperialistic countries but also because it is from 1617 onwards, with Sweden's rapid expansion at the expense of Poland-Lithuania,[21] that an economic theory of empire was fully developed, if never fully implemented.

The Swedes prided themselves on possessing more civilized standards than the "barbaric and insolent" Muscovites, and their imperialism was not of the kind that terrorized the conquered peoples. Rather, they assumed responsibility for them: a fortnight's grace was given the well-to-do inhabitants of the ceded areas to decide whether they wished to leave, with their wealth, for Muscovy.

Sweden's military successes against Denmark-Norway, during the Thirty Years War and in the 1650's, confirmed its standing as the foremost Baltic power: in 1645 Gotland and Ösel were handed over; in 1658 Danish and Norwegian peninsular provinces were ceded, giving Sweden wide access to the Western seas as well as control of one side of the Sound and, with it, exemption from Sound dues.[22]

Denmark had tried to keep Russian anti-Swedish feeling alive in the years after 1617; but several reasons combined to deny its diplomatic efforts any immediate effect: Gustavus Adolphus cultivated Russian friendship throughout his reign, and the regents for his daughter continued this policy. Moscow and Stockholm were joined by anti-Polish sentiment,[23] and Russian efforts were in any case concentrated on repairing the ravages of the Time of Troubles at home. In time, however, resentment at the 1617 peace and at Swedish successes since then was voiced in Moscow. Charles X Gustavus justified his attack on Poland-Lithuania in 1655 by that state's having refused to join him in a preventive war on Muscovy which he deemed necessary because of Russian plans of revenge for Stolbovo.[24]

His aggressiveness gave impetus to men like the Russian foreign minister, Afanasii Ordyn-Nashchokin, who had long argued that Moscow must reassert its status in the Baltic against Sweden and against Poland. During Charles X's campaigns in Poland and against Denmark, part of Livonia and Ingria was easily captured by the Muscovites. Fleets were built on Lake Ladoga and on the Dvina. Nyen (the town founded by Gustavus Adolphus in 1632 on the northern bank of the Neva as an administrative and trade center for Ingria to secure the Swedish hold) was destroyed in 1656. Ordyn-Nashchokin was made viceroy of the conquered territory and made no secret of his plan to put the coast from Narva to Vyborg under Muscovy, nor of his desire to secure the Duchy of Courland as a Russian naval base in the Baltic. The number of pro-Swedish subjects deported from Finland, Karelia, and Ingria during the war was very large; from Finland and Karelia alone 8,000 families were forcibly removed.[25]

The Russian position, like the Polish, was, however, weakened by the fact that the Swedish stronghold of Riga held out; and once Sweden (after the death of Charles X Gustavus) had made peace at Oliva with Poland-Lithuania, essentially restoring the status quo (but with the added advantage for Sweden that the Polish Vasas relinquished their claim to the Swedish throne), Russia found it expedient to make peace with the regents of Charles XI's minority at Kardis (June, 1661). Here the Swedish negotiators, though willing to permit Muscovy's traders in Sweden and its empire, proved adamant on the overlordship of land on the East Baltic: the Stolbovo peace must be restored in its entirety. Muscovy thus remained without a foothold on the Baltic, and once more it concentrated its efforts in Poland-Lithuania on the Smolensk and the Ukraine. Russian reluctance to acquiesce in the northern settlement is evident in the constant quarrels over the interpretation of the thirty articles of the Kardis treaty, and in perpetual complaints of Sweden's infringements of some of these articles. Moscow still feared Swedish power, however, and agreed in 1666 to make the treaty "permanent" and to accept Swedish diplomats in the capital on a permanent basis, though Ordyn-Nashchokin did his best secretly to counteract Sweden's position.

The fall of Ordyn-Nashchokin in 1670 has frequently been seen as the defeat of a Moscow faction which favored Baltic expansion and the success of another which urged advance into Tatar and Turkish territory. Such a view is oversimplified. Ordyn-Nashchokin had won his greatest laurels in the armistice of Andrusovo (1668), which permitted Muscovy to keep the Smolensk area for thirteen and a half years and acquiesced in the Russian protection of the Ukrainian Cossacks; but he, as well as his successors in office, especially Artamon Matveev, were at one in bringing pressure to bear wherever success seemed likely, whether in the North, the West, or the South. What is certain is that Muscovy, active on its southern frontiers, could not make full use of the opportunity on the Baltic offered by Swedish involvement (1675 to 1679) in the Dutch war on the side of Louis XIV of France.

Even so, Danish embassies which preached joint action against Sweden during this war had their effect in Moscow. The Russians noted with pleasure that whereas one hundred years earlier Russia's neighbors had scorned Muscovy's claims to Baltic land, now they supported these claims and urged it to press them.[26] Not only Denmark, but Courland (which suffered from Swedish attempts to strangle the trade of its ports)[27] and the Dutch republic (out of a dislike of Swedish monopoly of export from the East Baltic) looked forward to the prospect of the tsar's retaking at least part of what Sweden had conquered in Karelia, Ingria, Estonia, and Livonia.[28]

Such moral support strengthened the hands of Moscow in the 1679 to 1681 negotiations with Sweden over interpretation of the Kardis articles. It was argued that the king of Sweden, in matters of titles to be accorded to the tsar, had broken that treaty and that the only satisfactory compensation for such slights would be sacrifice of land in Ingria. Tell us, the Russian negotiators were instructed to ask, with what right have you taken the land of Ingria? Threats were liberally employed. The Swedish protocol records, "We know the road to Vyborg very well, and we might even find that to Uppsala."[29] Preoccupations in the South (the first Russo-Turkish War had broken out in 1677) prevented the tsar from translating such threats into reality when the Swedish negotiators refused to yield: in October, 1683, the treaty of Kardis was confirmed, with great pomp and circumstance, by a Russian embassy in Stockholm; and a Swedish embassy traveled to Moscow to confirm the treaty on Charles XI's behalf in June, 1684. Russian expansionism turned to the southern frontier again, but this time as a partner in the Holy League against Turkey.

Two factors brought Russian policy in the Baltic to offensive action before the southern thrust had exhausted itself. One was Tsar

Peter's becoming convinced during his Western tour of 1697 and 1698 that the War of the Holy League could not be revived since the Emperor Leopold I, replete with victories and concerned with his frontier with France and his claims to the Spanish Succession,[30] was determined to make peace with the Sultan. Peter, in spite of his recent successes against the Turks, was thus forced to contemplate an armistice if he could only keep Azov, won by the navy he had built on the Don with the help of foreign shipwrights (many of them Danes).[31] The War of the Holy League had, however, been of immense advantage to Muscovy—or Russia, as it was increasingly called towards the end of the seventeenth century. Papal diplomacy had persuaded John Sobieski, king of the Polish-Lithuanian Commonwealth, that the crusade against the infidel merited Polish sacrifices: the truce of Andrusovo was converted into a permanent peace in 1686, and, as far as Poland was concerned, the ban on military and technological contacts between Russia and the West was lifted. The influx of Dutch, German, English, and Scottish merchants and army officers had, in any case, broken Russia's isolation from Western technological advances; and Peter himself, during his European travels of 1697 and 1698, had engaged naval architects and officers and purchased ships.[32]

Moreover, with the prospect of diminishing returns from the Turkish venture, the tsar became more willing to listen to Danish proposals for an offensive league to attack Sweden while Charles XI's successor was a young and untried lad of fourteen and the Swedish nobility restive after the introduction of absolutism in the 1680's.[33] The Livonian nobility was equally dissatisfied, and one of their leaders, Johann Reinhold von Patkul, was free with his promises to the newly elected king of Poland, Augustus (the Elector Frederick Augustus III of Saxony and from 1697 also Augustus II of Poland), as well as to Tsar Peter about the rewards that would come to those who freed the Livonians from the Swedish yoke. At Amsterdam, it was reported to Stockholm the tsar had broadly hinted that he aimed, "as soon as he had finished with the Turks,"[34] to get a foothold on the Baltic once more.

The treaties for a combined Dano-Saxon attack on Sweden of March, 1698, and September, 1699, were widened during the Rawa meeting of the summer of 1698 between Augustus and Tsar Peter; and by November, 1699, a treaty between the two was signed.[35] Augustus stipulated that Swedish Livonia should become his (to be used, he hoped, as a counter in negotiations with Poland to obtain hereditary kingship for his family in exchange for a "Polish Livonia" regained by his Saxon soldiers); Ingria was to be the share of Russia, in return for which Tsar Peter agreed to begin his offensive against Sweden's Baltic provinces as soon as news of his armistice with the Sultan reached Moscow.

The tsar, who was not the initiator of the anti-Swedish coalition,[36] entered wholeheartedly into its spirit once the die was cast. His ideas went further than those of his allies in one respect. Whereas they concentrated on plans for cutting the Swedish monarchy down to size, he looked beyond the mere acquisition of Ingria to a change in the Swedish form of government. Since the Russian hold on Ingria had proved so slippery, he urged, in the interests of all three allies, that the Swedish monarchy should be abolished, and the Swedish state, shorn of its conquests, be changed into a republic: "For Republics were less dangerous to their neighbors." [37]

Changing circumstances during the Great Northern War enlarged the acquisitional war aims of Tsar Peter. Modern Russian historians are apt to stress that the tsar fought alone and could not trust or rely on any of his allies, who left him in the lurch time and again.[38] Though the resourcefulness and persistence of Peter (and the burdens taken on by Russia) should not be minimized, it is clear that Peter and Russia benefited enormously from the coalition throughout the war, with the possible exception of the year 1708, and that he put Russian expanding war aims first, without regard for his allies or for his oral promises or treaty obligations.

The necessity under which Charles XII found himself to fight on Polish-Lithuanian soil after the Swedish defeat of the Russian army at Narva in November, 1700 (a necessity the tsar helped to engineer),[39] enabled the tsar to get a firm foothold in Ingria. His first victories in 1702 and 1703 permitted him to ravage the Estonian and Livonian countryside (though he could not touch the towns at this stage), to plunder and burn, to remove cattle and people so as to isolate Ingria. He took Nöteborg (October, 1702) and rechristened it Schlüsselburg, ignoring its old Russian name in favor of a German, Western word, to signal his program for the future: this was to be the key that opened the Swedish empire and the key that would keep the Russian gains safe. He razed Nyen and built a new town closer to the Finnish Gulf, St. Piterburch or St. Petersburg (after the first church raised), and a sea fortress which he named Cronschlott. In March, 1703, he took Nyenskans, the fort that had protected Nyen, and rechristened it Schlotbruch. Iama (rechristened Jamburg) and Koporje became his in May of the same year. He determined to stick to the whole of this area, come what may. "Rather a ten years' war," was his stock reply to Swedish offers of peace on the basis of a restoration of the status quo.

Augustus II's difficulties, both military, such as his defeat at Kliszów by Charles XII, and political, such as Polish opposition to his plans for political reform, encouraged Tsar Peter to negotiate directly with representatives of the Polish Diet and conclude a treaty in 1704 whereby the Commonwealth was promised Livonia, in contradiction of his treaty with Augustus of 1699 and of the Birsen treaty of 1701 whereby he had confirmed Livonia and added Estonia as well to Augustus' share. Meanwhile, as his men and money helped to keep Charles XII in the South, he proceeded to conquer Dorpat (July, 1704) and Narva (August, 1704), though he had to postpone until 1710 an attack planned on Kexholm. There is no doubt that he aimed to keep both towns. Narva, he argued, was not part of Estonia, but of Ingria; Dorpat, he held, was an old "Russian" town since his father had ruled it for five years and Ivan IV had held it for over twenty years. He did not publicize his intentions to Augustus or the Poles, but their uneasiness (already aroused by the systematic devastations in Estonia and Livonia) was not diminished when Peter, taking advantage of Augustus' need for larger Russian armies in the Commonwealth, occupied Courland between 1705 and 1706.[40]

The Russian hold on the Swedish Baltic provinces eased (as Charles XII had predicted) when the Swedish king began his invasion of Russia.[41] In 1707 and 1708 all Russian forces were withdrawn from the north (with the exception of the garrison at St. Petersburg): Ingria was devastated to make reconquest by the Swedes difficult; the German inhabitants of Dorpat were moved en masse in February, in long sledge caravans, to Vologda; the non-Germans were left to their own devices and the town mined; similar destruction and relocation of population were the order of the day all along the Russian border as well. The Swedish defeat at Poltava in the summer of 1709 became, however, the signal for a speedy reoccupation of Ingria, for sieges of Riga and Reval, which fell to the Russians in June and July, 1710, and for determined and successful attempts at Vyborg and Kexholm.

When the Swedish garrisons had departed in 1710, those Estonians and Livonians who had resented the introduction of Swedish absolutism were gratified by Peter's returning the liberties and privileges they had enjoyed before the 1680's.[42] In return he asked for the title of "Tsar and *Imperator*," but there was no question of the Russification of Estonia and Livonia. Here Tsar Peter showed originality and foresight. The Baltic provinces as a whole were to serve as the Russian window to the West. Its urban inhabitants would form an avant-garde through whose influence Russia itself would be transformed into a commercial and industrial state on the Western pattern. Policy decisions remained with the tsar; but post-1710 exploitation was lessened by a desire to keep the area as prosperous and contented as possible in the interests of Russia's future.

The tsar's plans went further afield than the eastern end of the Baltic. In the early war years he had established diplomatic relations with the duke of Mecklenburg, to whom he had offered an offensive alliance directed against Sweden, but Duke Frederick William had preferred to play a waiting game. When war flared up in the western Baltic after Charles XII's return from Turkey (November, 1714), and the anti-Swedish coalition was increased by the king of Prussia and the elector of Hanover, plans (which had been attempted with limited success between 1710 and 1714) [43] were put into effect to deprive Sweden permanently of its gains from the Thirty Years War: the Duchies of Pomerania, Bremen and Verden, and the town of Wismar. After Stralsund's fall (December, 1715) the success of the anti-Swedish coalition seemed certain, and the new duke of Mecklenburg (Charles Leopold, who had succeeded his brother in 1713) now accepted the Russian alliance and married the tsar's niece Catherine in April, 1716.

It used to be held that Peter valued the Mecklenburg alliance as a temporary prop for his participation in the Scanian descent plan of 1716. Recent research and examination of the treaty clauses within the context of all available material has, however, uncovered long-term plans: Mecklenburg was to serve as a Western commercial base for Russian trade, trade that would be facilitated if Tsar Peter were able, as he hoped, to bypass the Sound with a canal to be dug from Mecklenburg to the North Sea, and to gain a foothold in Wismar. The canal project may be regarded as typical of the many plans for canals mooted all over Europe at this time (stimulated by Louis XIV's Languedoc canal of 1684), and similar to projects proposed by other Baltic powers when they felt hemmed in by Denmark.[44] If few of the canal projects were carried out until much later, the specific regulations for Russian commercial privileges in Mecklenburg—and for Russian control of Charles Leopold's policy—had nothing chimerical about them.[45]

In the event, the quartering of a large Russian army in Mecklenburg on the abandonment of the Scanian invasion plan caused the greatest concern in the empire. Concerted pressure by German and non-German powers urged the tsar to remove his troops. Threats of military action were not wanting, but a sigh of relief that there was no need to carry them into effect went up when Peter, in the interests of Russia's standing with European powers outside the Northern alliance, and particularly with France, withdrew beyond the empire's borders in the summer of 1717. Suspicion remained, however, and was nurtured by the close hold which the tsar had already established over the Polish-Lithuanian Commonwealth. The marriage of his niece Anna to the duke of Courland in 1710, and the duke's death on the journey home from the marriage ceremony in Moscow, aroused fears of a permanent Russian vassal state inside the Commonwealth as Anna began to govern Courland in accordance with Tsar Peter's directions. Through intervention on the side of "Polish liberties" against King Augustus' reform plans to strengthen the central government, the tsar managed to weaken the Commonwealth: his treaty with it of April, 1716, severely limited the number of Saxon and Polish troops which could be stationed on its territory.

The harnessing of Russia's impressive resources in men and material to create a powerful sea-going navy, as well as a fleet of galleys particularly well suited to exert control in the Baltic archipelagoes, again gave rise to widespread concern. It was Charles XII's recognition of Tsar Peter's "penchant et génie pour la marine" that prevented the Swedish king from making peace in the years when the tsar was willing to give up all his conquests bar St. Petersburg. If Peter were once given a foothold on the Baltic, Charles argued, he would soon be able to dominate it with his navy: in conjunction with the fleet of Denmark-Norway he could crush Sweden's great power position.[46] Allies, as well as opponents, feared the build-up of the Russian fleet; particularly after Charles had been able to split his enemies by separate negotiations in 1717 and 1718 with Tsar Peter on the one hand and George I on the other. George I was at war with Sweden only in his capacity as the Elector Georg Ludwig of Hanover, but carried weight in the anti-Swedish coalition mainly because of his position as king of Great Britain with a fair amount of control over the use of its navy; he was haunted by the prospect that the tsar would carry out his threat to support, whether in conjunction with the Swedes or alone, James Francis Edward Stuart, pretender to the British throne. After the death of Charles XII in 1718, there were similar fears that the Russians might act with the Spanish prime minister, Giulio Alberoni, who could employ the rapidly growing Spanish fleet for the same purpose.[47]

This general European fear of Russian expansion brought forth plans to limit Tsar Peter's gains from the Great Northern War. Charles XII's successors (his sister Ulrika Eleonora until 1720 and her husband Frederick I, after her abdication) were persuaded to make peace with Hanover, Denmark, and Prussia (1719 to 1720) in the expectation that Great Britain, France, and the Holy Roman Emperor would actively help in restoring a balance of power within the Baltic region by reconquering for Sweden at least part of Estonia or Livonia, including the port of Reval or Riga. Various circumstances, the South Sea Bubble, Law's crash, the Emperor's change of mind, the war-weariness of the Polish-Lithuanian Commonwealth, and Prussia's desire not to take undue risks, brought the "Peace Plan of the North" to naught.[48] Sweden was left alone to face Russia's naval power, which was far superior to its own in galleys that could ravage the coast, burning and plundering as they slipped inside the islands where no deep-draught men-of-war could follow. At Nystad, in August, 1721, Sweden made peace at the cost of sacrificing all its Baltic possessions to Russia, and had to give up the greater part of Karelia, including Vyborg, and restore Kexholm.

It took time before Sweden accustomed itself to these losses. Various kinds of attempts at partial recovery were tried: by adopting an heir to the throne acceptable to Russia (this was tried in 1743, after earlier abortive attempts);[49] by cooperation with Russian rulers (as in the support given to the Tsarina Elizabeth in gaining the throne in 1741); by fighting on the side of Russia's enemies (as in the Seven Years War); by single-handed attack (as in the war of Gustavus III between 1788 and 1790) to make the rulers of St. Petersburg agree, if not to restore part of the Baltic provinces, then to permit and aid Sweden's obtaining an "equivalent" for its losses in Norway.[50] Even those Swedes who disagreed with the reconquest policy or the equivalent plans resented the tutelage Russia imposed on Sweden in the eighteenth century.

This tutelage and Russia's persistent refusal to consider any modification of the Nystad treaty arose from extreme sensitivity in respect of St. Petersburg, the capital from the later years of Tsar Peter's reign. (Indeed the Tsarina Elizabeth turned on her partner of the coup in 1741, declaring war on Sweden and inaugurating a most acute period of interference in Swedish affairs, instead of handing back, as agreed, part of Russia's gains of 1721.) Charles XII's fears that there was not room for both Sweden and Russia in the Baltic were repaid with interest by the Russians: only if Sweden-Finland was limited to the northern shore of the Gulf of Finland, and that shore kept under the strictest Russian supervision, did successive Russian governments feel that their Baltic position was safe. The navy of Tsar Peter was at times greatly neglected; and though the direct influence on Sweden's policies compensated to a large extent for such neglect, the time came, in 1808 and 1809, when Russia proceeded to the conquest of the whole of Finland.

The commercial, financial, and cultural rewards of generous access to the Baltic that Tsar Peter had anticipated were speedily realized, though Estonia and Lithuania had suffered much from serving as the battlefield for Swedes and Russians, to which were added the woes of the plague of 1710 and the concentration of new privileges in St. Petersburg.[51] Income from the export of naval stores and from the many kinds of raw materials drawn from the vast hinterland of the Russian and Lithuanian river basins swelled the coffers of the state. Already by the 1730's Russian iron competed successfully with that of Sweden on the European markets.[52] Great Britain became Russia's most important customer after the commercial treaty of 1734, and Great Britain's dependency on Russian naval stores until the late eighteenth century was such that it helps to explain the various ways in which Whitehall facilitated the sailing of the Russian fleet from Kronstadt (Peter's Cronschlott) via the Sound and the Straits of Gibraltar to attack the Turkish navy and obtain the favorable peace of Kuchuk Kainarji in 1774. In the partitions of Poland, Russia contracted its influence on the Commonwealth as a whole, but gained as a result of incorporating Lithuania (except for Galicia, which went to Austria) and Courland.

Finland had been granted favorable terms in 1809. It retained its Swedish constitution and became a grand duchy in dynastic union with Russia, although its foreign policy was subordinated to that of the dominating partner. Its merchant fleet was of great importance; its sailors helped to man the Russian navy, and Finnish officers served in considerable numbers in the Russian army and earned more speedy promotion than their Russian brother officers.[53] Not until the Russification attempts of the 1890's did Finland begin to experience Russian imperialism and gross interference in its domestic affairs.

Russia's conquest of Finland had, however, important international repercussions. The Åland Islands, the archipelago of islands in the Bothnian Sea, are situated so close to Stockholm that their fortifications, though directed, the Russians claimed, at Great Britain, Russia's enemy and rival for the greater part of the nineteenth century, were felt to be a threat to Sweden's security. Certainly the near presence of Russian troops and ships exercised some influence on Swedish foreign policy after 1815 and imposed some restraints.[54]

Russia possessed still another means of making its influence felt in the Baltic in the nineteenth century, in respect of Denmark. The Russian claim to the ducal portions of Holstein, which had been sacrificed by Catherine II on behalf of her son Paul in 1767 (and confirmed by him when he reached his majority in 1777), was specifically limited to the direct line of the reigning Danish dynasty (whereas the Danish incorporation of Sleswig of 1721 had been recognized "forever"). The threat of a revival of this Russian claim was useful (as was the cruising of the Russian navy in the western Baltic) in settling the Sleswig-Holstein crisis of 1848 to 1852 in the interests of the status quo and the preservation of the European order. There was no element of imperialism in Russian diplomacy over this issue, and indeed the tsar worked closely and well with Stockholm throughout the crisis.

The hope of a reconquest of Finland died slowly in some circles in Sweden and played a considerable role both during the Crimean War and in the second Sleswig-Holstein crisis of 1863 and 1864. Cooperation with Great Britain and France, within the letter of the Swedish declaration of neutrality of 1834 but outside its spirit, was rewarded at the Congress of Paris in 1856 when the Åland Islands, at Sweden's request, were demilitarized. Finland remained in dynastic union with Russia, however. No serious attempt was made to test its willingness to return to Sweden during the Crimean War, basically because the majority of the British cabinet was unwilling to give the formal guarantees that Oscar II of Sweden wanted for a future union.[55] Charles XV, who as crown prince had felt irritated by his father's slow progress towards the anti-Russian side in the Crimean War, failed in his own plans to conquer Finland by cooperation with Napoleon III over Poland in 1863.[56] Finland was, as many Swedes perceived, developing along lines that precluded reunion with Sweden after the Crimean War. A nationalist movement, which embraced both Swedish-speaking and Finnish-speaking Finns, emerged after the debacle of the Scandinavian Union movement in 1863 and 1864 and gained strength in the 1890's during the period of attempted Russification.

Russia was relieved at the collapse of the Scandinavian Union movement and at the setback for Charles XV of 1863 and 1864, since both the liberal and the dynastic aspects of the movement had been seen as a threat to Russian interests. Russia's resentment at the demilitarization of the Åland Islands remained great and activated its diplomacy. The unified Germany's power in the Baltic had not unduly worried Russia in the nineteenth century since Bismarck had been willing to exert pressure on Sweden to Russia's benefit,[57] though he proved unwilling to give more than good words in respect of successive Russian governments' efforts concerning the Åland Islands.

Only with a repeal of the "servitude clauses," Russia argued, could it exercise its rightful influence in the Baltic; and the political circumstances of 1905 to 1908 (when the dissolution of the Swedish-Norwegian Union begged the question of replacements for the Anglo-French guarantee of the territories of the United Kingdoms) favored German attention to Russia's wishes in the Åland issue in the hope of regaining the ally lost in the early years of Kaiser Wilhelm's reign. German diplomatic help was promised; but the efforts that followed were strongly opposed by Sweden and Great Britain. Germany climbed down and lost face with Russia, though both became partners in the Baltic treaty of 1908 for the retention of the status quo in that sea.[58] When the 1914 war broke out, Russia, an ally of the Western powers, restored the Åland Islands fortifications unilaterally.

Russia's military defeat in World War I lost it the Baltic gains of 1721 to 1809. The Russian revolutionaries approved in principle that Finland and the East Baltic states should be free to settle their own affairs, though they naturally wished that such freedom should not imperil the security of Russia proper. In respect of Poland the position was more complicated, since here more than control of the Baltic coastline was involved. Memories were vivid of the seventeenth-century struggles for the eastern half of Lithuania, of the eighteenth-century partitions, as well as of the Russification policy operative for the greater part of the existence of Congress Poland.

The steamship of the nineteenth century, as well as competition in respect of naval stores from North America from the late eighteenth century, had to some extent diminished the economic importance of the Baltic parts of the Russian empire.[59] The building of railways had certainly lessened dependence on the river and canal system leading to the Baltic. Murmansk, for instance, the ice-free port of the far North which had been of no use to Russia in the days of inland water traffic, since no great river linked the port to the heartland, became important in the age of rail.

That strategic considerations in respect of the Baltic still weighed (and weigh) heavily in times of European conflicts is, however, demonstrated by clauses of the Stalin-Hitler pact of August, 1939, and by the speed with which the U.S.S.R. gave them effect, by the two Finnish wars that followed, and by the Baltic policy of successive Soviet governments after 1945. "Gentlemen," one of the Soviet ministers is reputed to have told the Finns, "we can do nothing about geography."

The need, implied by Nikita Khrushchev, to protect border territory, and even the Russian heartland itself, against attack from outside forms one thread in the post-1485 history of Russia's relationship with its Baltic neighbors. To the Muscovite rulers their claim to expand to the farthest borders of the Novgorod trading empire was self-evident, and when Ivan III (for reasons of domestic security) destroyed the town of Novgorod, further expansion to include ports on the Baltic proper became a near-necessity.

Since Sweden proved the most powerful opponent of such expansion, the Swedes were, for centuries, the people most disliked and feared by Moscow. Their pride was particularly resented, but they were also (in the words of Ordyn-Nashchokin in 1668) "a well-known, old enemy" who "slyly provoked quarrels and awaits the time to attack and perpetrate all kinds of evil." [60]

Their place was taken by the Germans after 1919: the nation that encouraged Finnish independence in the hope, so it seemed to the Russians, of obtaining a base uncomfortably close to Petrograd (now

Leningrad). Had they not, during their expedition to help the white Finns, razed those fortifications on the Åland Islands which the Russians had rebuilt on the outbreak of war in 1914? [61] And were not some Germans, if not the government, clamoring for the annexation of those East Baltic states which, like Finland, were using the opportunity of the 1917 Revolution to free themselves from Russian control?

Such memories go part of the way to explain the Soviet decision to occupy and reabsorb Estonia, Latvia, and Lithuania in 1939 and 1940. On the one hand these smaller states might be held to have lost their hinterland for trade by their separation from the post-1917 Russia; on the other they would serve as a shield for a German attack on the U.S.S.R.[62]

The protection of what was thought of as legitimate Russian interests embraced economic and financial advantages: the income from tolls and dues on the naval stores exported to the West from Baltic and Gulf ports (deal and ship's masts and planks as well as pitch and tar, hemp and flax, all of which remained important even when the trade in furs and wax declined). A Saxon diplomat estimated in 1727 that Russia received 600,000 rubles annually from such tolls and dues, of which Riga alone contributed between 250,000 and 300,000.[63] His figures may not be reliable (and Riga, in any case, was soon to be eclipsed by St. Petersburg), but the increase in government income from the taxes levied on the vast export trade of the Baltic ports was astounding. The trade itself had always brought specie to the hinterland producers, and enriched many a noble landlord; the state could only profit directly once conquest made economic imperialism possible.

Tsar Peter modeled himself on the Swedes, reducing tolls in order to attract more trade and thus obtain more money in the long run. In this he achieved a great measure of success, as also in his canal building inside Russia to facilitate the exports of goods via the Baltic—by 1709 the river-canal route from Astrakhan to St. Petersburg was in use. In his wider economic and imperialist plans Peter achieved little. The failure of the Wismar and Mecklenburg plans has already been mentioned. Peter's alternative (via a Holstein-Gottorp alliance after 1718) of making Kiel a free port—again to bypass the Sound and get direct access to the oceans of the world—was not realized, and Peter's eighteenth-century successors remained satisfied with defending what he had built in the Baltic.

The dynastic union with Finland that followed the conquest of

1809 widened Russia's scope in world trade. The Finnish merchant fleet was an important one, and Russian goods were exported in ships which, though they belonged to the Grand Duchy of Finland, were thought of as Russian. Indeed, the complaints of other restive members of the Russian empire (the Poles, for example) were that the Finns held a privileged position and did not deserve European sympathy to the same extent as those who felt the full force of Russian economic and cultural control.[64] In time, however, many Finns began to think of themselves as suffering under Russian imperialism,[65] and the Russification program of the 1880's and 1890's brought about a resistance movement.

It would be wrong to assume that Russian imperialism in respect of the Baltic was principally economically motivated. Recent research has emphasized that the Moscow merchants, long thought to have pressed hard in the late seventeenth century for access to the Baltic,[66] did no such thing and that the initiative was that of Tsar Peter.[67] Peter the Great, like Ivan the Great and Ivan IV before him, was driven by political ambitions even more than by considerations of income for the state. The concern to have Russia recognized as a European great power and the concern for *gloire* in its widest sense [68] were powerful motives with all tsars who took the initiative in empire building on the Baltic. Since Tsar Peter was so strikingly successful he has become the very symbol of its achievement. His Russian contemporaries were well aware of this. "The two heroes of this century" ("ces deux héros de ce siècle"), is the phrase used by Fedor Golovin, Tsar Peter's statesman and diplomat, in a letter to the French diplomat the Marquis du Héron, to characterize Louis XIV and Peter (admittedly at a time when the tsar was courting the alliance of France).[69] Posterity has agreed with him. St. Petersburg, the capital for so many years, has always been connected in the popular imagination with the tsar rather than with the Apostle of the church of St. Peter and St. Paul, and Peter was clearly the hero in *Peter the Great,* the U.S.S.R. film of the 1930's.

WALTER LEITSCH

Russo-Polish Confrontation

"Dès leur apparition dans l'histoire, il s'agit de décider auquel des deux Etats appartiendra l'empire des races slavonnes réunies. Sans peut-être en avoir dès le principe la conscience, ils étaient poussés dans l'arène par le destin, pour débattre cette grande question. Telle est l'origine fatale des guerres entre la Russie et la Pologne, qui, dès le seizième siècle surtout, devinrent pour l'une des deux une question de vie ou de mort politique." [1]

However exaggerated this point of view may be, conditioned as it was by an age that attached Pan-Slavic significance to the struggle between Poland and Russia, Adam Gurowski, writing in 1834, nevertheless pointed to a fundamental fact in the mutual relations of the two nations. From the fourteenth or the sixteenth to the twentieth century the goal of Russian expansionist endeavors was not a Polish national state; rather, Polish imperialism stood in the way of Russian imperialism. It was not a fight between national states but between two empires. In the final analysis none of the notable opponents of Russia, namely the Kipchak, Sweden, Turkey, and lastly even Germany (before 1918) and Austria, was a national state. In their context, the concepts "imperium" and "imperialism" are somewhat magniloquent if one bears in mind the original meaning of the word, for only the Mongols and Turks had plans for world control.

Like other states which called themselves empires, Russia, particularly from the beginning of the eighteenth century was a great power, hungry for land and power within the framework of a system of theoretically anti-imperialistic European states, a system of partners enjoying essentially the same rights and thirsting equally for expansion.

How is it that Poland and Russia could be dangerous rivals? Were the two at all comparable as powers? In 1959 there were 3.7 times as many Russians as Poles. True, capable minorities often governed majorities, but the Poles never were so much more martial and better organized than the Russians as to make up for the large difference in their numbers. In the sixteenth century, at the height of the rivalry, the population ratio was quite different: Poland-Lithuania had slightly more than 6 million inhabitants, and the Muscovite state about 11 million. In physical extension Poland-Lithuania stood second to the Muscovite state among European countries.[2] The area within which the boundary shifts occurred embraced close to 700,000 square kilometers. It is not interrupted by mountain ranges or delineated by bodies of water. Only the rivers give it a certain definition. Since it is contained in the same climate zone, neither opponent had the advantage in military campaigns by reason of weather. With the exception of the fertile steppe area near the Dnieper, the soils are poor; moreover, they are very similar to those in the central areas of settlement of both peoples. Mineral resources within the disputed area are insignificant, except for the ore deposits of Krivoi Rog and Kursk (which were not worked until the nineteenth century), and therefore offered neither state the possibility of an essential economic gain.

Although the Poles joined the Western church and the Russians the Eastern church and although from the tenth century on they lived in two different cultural worlds, there was nothing special about their political relationship up to the fourteenth century. The ruling families of the Rus of Kiev and Poland occasionally intermarried (ten marriages up to 1138), and the rather rare conflicts did not change to any remarkable extent the borderline as it had developed around the year 1000. Both realms—the Kievan Rus after 1054 and Poland after 1138—were divided up by the ruling families into a number of principalities, but those along the border were of about equal size and strength and kept each other in check.

The situation changed in the fourteenth century. During the first two decades most of Poland united again into a kingdom of considerable strength, and in the years 1340 to 1387 the westernmost section of the lands of the Kievan state, Halich—better known by its

Latin name, Galicia—became part of Poland. Had this been the only loss of territory, a reunited Russia could have easily regained it. The most serious dispute between Russians and Poles that was to poison their relations for centuries was the consequence neither of Russian nor of Polish policies; it was the consequence of the expansion of Lithuania. The Lithuanian grand dukes separated Poland and Russia by conquering most of the western and southern parts of the once Kievan state during the fourteenth century. It was their ambition to reunite all Russia and liberate it from Mongol domination, but they were prevented from achieving this aim by the grand dukes of Moscow, who controlled most of the eastern part of the once Kievan state and who also wanted to reunite all of it under their rule. In the fourteenth century Poland was for the Muscovites a distant country of little concern to them; their Western neighbors and enemies were the Lithuanians. These controlled a much greater part of the lands of the former Kievan state than the Poles.[3]

Moscow's Ideology and First Successes

The union of Lithuania and Poland (Krewo, 1386) and the election of the grand duke of Lithuania, Jagiełło, as king of Poland might have brought Poland to the attention of the Muscovites, but the Polish-Lithuanian union is probably not mentioned in the early fifteenth-century *Troitskaia Letopis,* although in the report concerning the return of Vasilii I it was noted that Poles came to Moscow in his entourage.[4] Later chronicles contain the following information under the year 1486: Jagiełło went to Hungary to the king to be married, got married there and was baptized in the German faith, came to Vilna and baptized the Lithuanians also in the same faith.[5] The same error was repeated in the *Compilation* of the end of the fifteenth century.[6] In his reports concerning the later years the chronicler seldom mentioned Jagiełło and only in connection with Lithuania. Also, the Poles as a people were rarely mentioned in the chronicles and then always only in the same breath with the Lithuanians. Thus the Muscovites were well aware of the connection between Lithuania and Poland: in 1401 the inhabitants of Smolensk had to suffer from "the pagan Liakhs [Poles]," [7] and when the war with Witold of Lithuania began, they had as opponents "many Lithuanians and Liakhs." [8] Also when Witold advanced on Pskov in 1426, there were Poles in his army.[9] Inasmuch as it is noted for 1404 that Witold "placed Liakhs as his governors" in Smolensk, it is probable that Catholic Lithuanians rather than Poles are meant in the entries for 1406, 1408, and also 1426.

Muscovite reactions to the union between Lithuania and Poland appear early in the documents, but only sporadically, and they were rather weak: in 1396 the following proviso was inserted into a treaty between Moscow and Tver: "We should act, brother, as one against the Tatars, the Lithuanians, the Germans, and the Liakhs." The formula is repeated in later treaties (*c.* 1439, *c.* 1456, and 1462 to 1464);[10] however, this is peculiar to the treaties with Tver. In the corresponding treaties with Riazan, for example, only Tatars and Lithuanians are mentioned, although the situation later was very similar.[11] It can therefore be assumed that the peculiarity of the treaty of 1396 was copied in the later treaties for no special reason.

For the Muscovites, Poland was situated at the end of their world or rather in another world, in the domain of the hostile and alien Church of Rome.[12] Only occasionally did the Muscovites mention Poland as having any more than minor importance, and this was in connection with the Lithuanian problem. This problem soon became the central problem of the political activity of Moscow and was so to remain until the second half of the seventeenth century.

When Ivan III[13] acceded to the throne of Moscow in 1462, relations with Lithuania were regulated by the treaty of 1449, whereby the spheres of interest were neatly demarcated. Neither of the two signatories adhered strictly to the treaty. Casimir, king of Poland and grand duke of Lithuania, was involved in conflicts with the Teutonic Knights (1454 to 1466) and with Bohemia and Hungary (1471 to 1478), and for that reason had a strong interest in preserving a calm eastern frontier. Ivan utilized Casimir's multilateral obligations with great skill to enlarge and strengthen his sphere of power and to bring Muscovy into the arena of international politics; he wanted Moldavia, Hungary, the Emperor, and the Crimean Tatars, all to march off against Casimir, but only in the case of the Tatars were these efforts of lasting success.

While Casimir was occupied in a war against the Turks (1485 to 1489), Ivan turned slowly to the attack. An accomplished diplomatic tactician, Ivan wanted for the time being to avoid a large war, for which, as yet, he did not consider himself strong enough. At the end of 1486 he began with border raids, and these he gradually intensified.

Lithuanian princes who had small fiefs on the border were naturally no match for the Muscovites without the support of their own grand duke, even in a guerrilla war, for Ivan's most important measure within the framework of these unrelenting raids was to deport the population from the Lithuanian border principalities and settle them in the interior of the Muscovite state. As soon as their principalities were depopulated, there was nothing left for the princes to do but to defect to Ivan along with their hereditary principalities (*votchina*). They, so to speak, followed their subjects. Since Moscow, for propaganda purposes, portrayed the strife with Lithuania as a religious war, many of these economic fugitives designated themselves religious fugitives. Immigrants even at that time knew it best to find motives for their change that would sound good to those who were to receive them.

The objectives of Ivan were not known to the Lithuanians. In the negotiations in 1492 Ivan did not express himself clearly, but in the first letter he addressed to Alexander of Lithuania he applied to himself, for the first time in correspondence with Lithuania, the title "ruler of all the Rus." Yet in the peace negotiations Ivan showed himself to be very tractable, not insisting on the acquisition of all occupied border cities. Only Viazma, situated on the military road running from Moscow to Vilna, was an important gain.

One day before the instrument of peace that was formulated as a friendship agreement (February 7, 1494), a marriage between Alexander and Elena, a daughter of Ivan III, was concluded by proxies. Alexander and Ivan had contradictory aims in arranging this marriage. Whereas Alexander hoped to make an end to the disturbances launched by the Muscovites, Ivan wanted to extend the disturbances to the court in Vilna. Elena and her household had not only to gather information for Ivan. In the marriage agreement Ivan, contrary to the wish of Alexander, had laid down that Elena should not convert to Catholicism, even voluntarily. Ivan intended that an Orthodox opposition to the grand duke should be formed around Elena with the object of handing over to Moscow all the territories settled by the Orthodox.

Immediately after the conclusion of peace Ivan began diplomatic and military preparation for a major war against Lithuania. He established contact with the Sultan, ensured the friendship of the Danish king, and gained the khan of the Crimea as an ally. Ivan made great propagandistic efforts to make his war of conquest appear a religious war. In the years 1499 to 1501 negotiations proceeded in Lithuania—

for a long time the last such negotiations—concerning the union of the Orthodox with the Roman Catholic Church. Ivan pretended to be much disturbed; in reality it suited him well if stresses and strains arose between the Orthodox and Catholics in Lithuania. It is difficult to determine how much pressure was brought to bear against the Orthodox in Lithuania, but it is rather improbable that this exceedingly difficult and ticklish question was seriously pursued in Lithuania at a time when the danger from the southeast was particularly strong and when relations with Moscow were strained and the personal union with Poland temporarily suspended. But Ivan posed as the protector of the Orthodox and intervened because of Elena. When Lithuanian envoys presented a protest in Moscow because Prince Belskii had deserted to Ivan with his *votchina*—contrary to the treaty of 1494—Ivan answered that Belskii had been persecuted because of his Orthodox religion and that he, Ivan, could not but offer him protection. This was in effect a declaration of war. The war began three months later.

Ivan thus found a pretext for renewing the war of conquest, whereby he could expect an additional advantage. At the start of the campaign some of the border princes went over to Ivan, and as a result the Muscovites occupied Chernigov, Starodub, and Novgorod-Severskii without a battle, though the siege of Smolensk was unsuccessful. By 1502 the contenders were exhausted, and in March of 1503 they agreed to an armistice for six years. A vast territory now passed to the Muscovite state (Chernigov, Gomel, Starodub, and Rylsk, along with the areas lying to their rear; Dorogobuzh, Toropets, Nevel, and Sebezh). The entire frontier was pushed forward and Lithuania had to relinquish more than a quarter of its territory to the Muscovites. This was the most successful of all the Muscovite wars of conquest, and it was complemented by success in the sphere of diplomacy.

Ivan thus took a big step toward his goal in 1503. He also clearly and unmistakably defined this goal in the negotiations with the Lithuanians: acquisition of the entire territory of the Rus of Kiev. It could not have escaped him that he laid claim also to a portion of the Polish territory and that he thus contributed considerably to strengthening the community of interests between Poland and Lithuania. Earlier, in a treaty made with the Holy Roman Emperor in 1490 and 1491, Ivan III had withheld the Duchy of Kiev for himself as a share of the expected booty.[14] In 1499 he refused to cite Kiev in the Lithuanian sovereign title[15] and indirectly thereby indicated his claims. Then, at the negotiations in March, 1503, he openly stated his aims, declaring himself heir to all Russia.[16] Ivan enveloped his calculated plan of conquest in a cloak of international law. When Grand Duke Alexander in 1504 claimed the return of the conquered territories, Ivan answered: "the entire Russian land, Kiev, Smolensk, and other cities which he holds within the Lithuanian state, is by God's will our heritage from antiquity [and] from our ancestors." Ivan concluded that if Alexander desired to be on good terms with Muscovy he would have to relinquish these cities.[17]

The most important point of Muscovite foreign policy—the *otchina* theory or the theory of paternal legacy—was thereby clearly defined. Ivan in all probability did not appraise the difficulties realistically after the successes of 1500 to 1503. For the next one hundred and sixty years the Muscovites had to wage one war after another to attain this objective. Only in 1667 were they satisfied with partial success, and under Peter the Great the *otchina* theory lost its political significance.

The parts of Rus which belonged to Poland were for the time being not expressly mentioned. In 1504 Ivan III spoke only of Lithuania, and Vasilii III (1505 to 1533) did not extend his claims.[18] Only Ivan IV presented the demand for Halich [19] to Sigismund Augustus in a list of ninety-seven cities to which he had laid claim on the basis of the constructed hereditary right.[20]

The wars against Lithuania were a logical continuation of the unification of eastern and northern Russia. There the Muscovites could rely on the readiness of a part of the nobility for union. In the sixteenth century, however, the Lithuanian-Rus(sian) nobility demonstrated an astounding loyalty to the Lithuanian state that upset Ivan's calculations. Thus the Rus(sian) territories of Lithuania had to be conquered properly and the nobility subjugated. The other classes of the population remained passive; the occasional asseverations of Russian historians that the lower classes yearned for the harsh authority of Moscow finds no support in the sources. Much blood was spilled and much effort expended to win territories that contributed little to the wealth of the Muscovite state. But to the nationalistic Russian historians the *otchina* theory was a constant source of edification.

Once the program had been formulated, the successors of Ivan III had only to carry it out.[21] After the short third war (1507 to 1508) Vasilii III succeeded in concluding a peace treaty. Several cities of minor importance were returned to the Lithuanians, who militarily had been very successful; the extensive gains of 1503 were now guaranteed by treaty. Even during the "peace" the border raids did not stop, and four years later the fourth war (1512 to 1522) began, to the great disappointment of the Lithuanians, who in 1504, as before in 1449 and 1494, had hoped that the grand dukes of Moscow would be placated by concessions. After the third siege, Smolensk, the most important fortress on the military road from Moscow to Vilna, fell (1514). The war in the following years was uneventful; it ended with a truce (1522), which in 1526 was extended to 1532. The border raids went on and relations worsened; the truce was again extended but for only one year. Vasilii apparently intended to renew the war at the end of 1533, but he died three weeks before the end of the truce. His three-year-old son succeeded him as Ivan IV. The Lithuanians had already prepared themselves for a defensive war and now wanted to exploit the internal weakness of Moscow in order to gain the lost provinces. The fifth war (1534 to 1537) finally brought some gains to the Lithuanians (Gomel; the Muscovites acquired Sebezh and an area near Polotsk).

As in the previous wars, the military action showed that once the Lithuanians and Poles pulled themselves together for war on a large scale, they were superior on the battlefield. The central authority was, however, so weak that the formation of an army became a very difficult and drawn-out undertaking. Moreover, this army almost exclusively functioned defensively, and favorable opportunities for attack, as in the fifth war, could not really be utilized. The power of the grand duke of Moscow, by contrast, was almost absolute; he could at any time call up an army of considerable size and keep it in the field for years if necessary. This gave him a politico-tactical superiority that made territorial acquisitions possible. He could attack when the situation was most favorable; however, he could also keep the caldron of war at a slow simmer, as in the years 1515 to 1522.

In this period the kings of Poland, who were dependent on the nobility, could not pursue a resolute foreign policy and were forced to leave the initiative to their rivals. Sigismund I did not make use of the difficulties of the Muscovite state in the 1540's. He evidently had completely given up the idea of recovering the lost territories and restricted himself to the hope that the Muscovites would attack no more.

The armistice of 1537 was concluded for only five years but was extended first to 1549 and then to 1554.

One of the problems at the negotiations in 1549 arose from Ivan IV's assumption of the title of Tsar in 1547. The Muscovites argued that it was not an innovation (in their eyes something new could not be good), that Vladimir Monomakh of Kiev had already borne the title. In the negotiations of the following decades there was still much quibbling over this matter. The title appeared, for example, in the Russian version of the treaty of 1549, but not in the Lithuanian version. In the years 1551 and 1552 the Rada (Senate) and the Duma had to negotiate because negotiations between the sovereigns had become impossible as a result of Ivan's insistence on the title. This same situation recurred in later decades. The armistice was twice extended (1554 to 1556, 1556 to 1562). In these twenty-four peaceful years the border raids and the kidnappings in the Tatarian manner also ceased.

Disappointments and Reverses

In the 1560's the struggle between the Muscovite state and Poland-Lithuania became part of a greater conflict in which many countries were ultimately involved and which affected the interests of still more countries. Although Ivan III engaged intensively in diplomacy, neither he nor his successor succeeded in constructing an effective community of interest. Neither the Habsburgs nor the other neighbors of Poland had an interest in dividing up the Polish-Lithuanian Commonwealth. The Muscovite state had no allies, and therefore waged alone the great war of conquest. On the other hand, the Muscovites were not disturbed by any other neighboring power in their policy of territorial expansion. Ivan extended the scope of Muscovite expansionist policy considerably by conquering Kazan in 1552 and Astrakhan in 1556 and attacking Livonia in 1558.

His expansionist drive to the Baltic Sea corresponded to Muscovy's economic and cultural need for direct communication with trade partners and with the technologically more developed parts of Europe. It was precisely this, however, that Muscovy's Western neighbors wanted to prevent. Not only diplomatic contacts but also importations of weapons and technical experts were made difficult by Sweden, Livonia, and Lithuania so as to cut off the Muscovite state from the

Baltic Sea. Livonia was the most favorably situated to achieve this end but was the weakest. In the spring of 1558 Narva capitulated; in July, Dorpat (Tartu). The resistance was weak. In 1559 the Muscovites advanced to the gates of Riga and invaded Courland, but from May to November, 1559, a truce was kept, probably under the pressure of the diplomatic intervention of the Holy Roman Emperor and the kings of Sweden and Denmark. Ivan probably hoped that the Livonians would now sue for peace, but they first looked for allies and then for new masters: between 1559 and 1561 Estonia came under Danish, then Swedish rule; Ösel came under the rule of Denmark; and Livonia under that of Lithuania. The greater part of the country came under Polish-Lithuanian protection; by the treaty of November 28, 1561, Livonia became a Polish-Lithuanian province. In the summer of that year war broke out in Livonia between Poland-Lithuania and the Muscovite state, the sixth since 1487.

For a time calm prevailed at the old border, but in January, 1563, a large army appeared before the gates of Polotsk and the city capitulated the following month. The Lithuanians, completely at the mercy of the Muscovites, made a truce. Now Ivan IV stretched his demands too far by claiming for the first time Halich, the Polish part of the Rus of Kiev. Such a claim could only strengthen the Poles' interest in the war, and accordingly their resistance against the Muscovite state. As the war dragged on, Ivan's situation became noticably more critical. The Swedes had fought against Sigismund Augustus from 1561 to 1567; in 1569 they turned against Ivan. In 1569 the Turks and Crimean Tatars attacked. In 1570 the kings of Denmark and Sweden made peace. Ivan was now completely isolated and weakened, whereas the situation of Poland-Lithuania was strengthened. When negotiations were resumed between Ivan and Sigismund Augustus at the beginning of 1570, Ivan found himself face to face with two envoys, one representing Poland and the other Lithuania. The previously Lithuanian boundary had now become a Polish-Lithuanian one. The Union of Lublin substantially strengthened Poland-Lithuania.

Ivan IV managed to present himself to the world as a land-devouring monster, precipitating thereby the formation of an anti-Muscovite alliance. He lacked the wise reserve of his father and grandfather. His domestic policy (*oprichnina*) weakened the country and gained him the reputation of a cruel tyrant. Exploiting the unsavory reputation that Ivan had earned for himself, the Polish king made efforts to win over the kings of Denmark, England, and France to agree on a suspension of the Narva commerce; he appealed to their European conscience not to strengthen the dangerous enemy of the Christian "free nations." Thus Sigismund Augustus excluded the Muscovite state from the family of European nations and turned the realm of the Jagellonians into a barrier protecting the West. He made it clear that Europe could be safe from the barbaric hordes only as long as Poland-Lithuania checked them, which in view of the numerical superiority of the Muscovites was possible only as long as the Muscovites were technologically inferior.[22] Before him Casimir the Great had attempted to appeal to the solidarity of the West, and so had other Polish rulers and Lithuanians after the reign of Sigismund I. Always they bent their efforts to barring from Europe all peoples east of the Poles.

During the three-year armistice declared in 1570 King Sigismund Augustus died (July 7, 1572). He was the last of the Jagellonians. The Poles and Lithuanians now had to elect a king: Henri de Valois was elected in May, 1573, but returned to his native land in June, 1574. Then in December, 1575, they elected Stephen Báthory. In both elections members of the Habsburg family appeared as the most promising rival candidates. Ivan IV supported them at times, but he himself also came forward as a candidate. Since his father had sought the Lithuanian throne after the death of Alexander in 1506,[23] the idea of acquiring the *otchina* together with Lithuania by peaceful means was not new in Muscovy. Vasilii III probably had not thought of acquiring Poland as well, for in his thinking Poland was outside his world. But Ivan IV was willing to let himself be elected king of Poland. Even before the death of Sigismund Augustus, Ivan's envoys discussed the possibility of his candidacy (1570), and from 1572 to 1575 there were numerous negotiations. The Lithuanians and the Poles encouraged these discussions if only to prevent Ivan from attacking during the interregnum.

During the first interregnum the candidacy of Moscow was not at issue, but during the second the *szlachta* or nobility of Volynia, Mazovia, Greater Poland, and, to a lesser extent, Lithuania, was favorably disposed to a Moscow candidacy, whereas the senators, the aristocracy, and above all the clergy were opposed. Ivan spread the word privately in Poland-Lithuania that in the event of his election he would be ready to conclude a union between the Muscovite state and Poland-Lithuania similar to the union effected by Jagiełło. He further indicated that he would be willing to convert, if it could be proved to him that Roman

Catholicism was better than Orthodoxy. It is clear that Ivan only wanted to protract the interregnum and increase the confusion, for he set unacceptable terms (cession of Kiev and Volynia and coronation by the Metropolitan) and finally sent only a courier to the Sejm in May, 1575, with an insignificant message. His supporters were disappointed. They expected peace on the part of Moscow from a Danilovich on the throne, the return at least of Polotsk, less taxes, because the tsar was rich, and the suppression of the magnates or high aristocracy. At the electoral Sejm the number of supporters of the Muscovite candidacy had dwindled considerably. The one courier Ivan sent was to request passes for *minor* envoys. This the nobles could only take as an insult. There is good reason to assume that Ivan did not take the matter very seriously.[24]

Stephen Báthory proved himself to be an eminently capable king.[25] Ivan did not utilize the interregna to attack Poland-Lithuania, but from the end of 1572 he again expanded his position in Livonia more strongly. At the close of 1577, Báthory assumed the offensive, dislodged the Muscovites from Livonia, captured Polotsk in 1579, advanced in 1580 and 1581 into the old Novgorod territory and besieged Pskov. Ivan had completely exhausted the energies of his country. On January 15, 1582, he concluded a ten-year armistice: Polotsk, Vitebsk, and Velizh were returned to Lithuania, and Ivan renounced all claims to Livonia. What probably carried the most weight was that Báthory had broken the spell of the invincibility of the Muscovites.

The initiative for several decades now passed to Poland-Lithuania. Báthory conceived the great plan of winning back all the territories that had belonged to the Grand Duchy of Lithuania and, thus strengthened, to go to war against the Turks. Even after the conclusion of the armistice with Muscovy he did not give up this plan; however, he was frustrated by the unwillingness of the *szlachta* to wage a war of aggression. After the death of Ivan IV (1584) he extended the truce for only a short time. In Moscow the aggressive intentions of Báthory were known and feared, and every effort was made to avoid any conflict; concessions were even made in questions of ceremony. Thus the Muscovites gave up the haughty and defiant attitude they had displayed for a century.

The first era of Muscovite expansion at the expense of Poland-Lithuania was over. Ivan had wanted to achieve too much and had exhausted the country. His successor had to learn to fear Poland-

Lithuania once more. The death of Báthory (1586) freed the Muscovites from fear for only a short time. They learned lessons from the evil consequences of Ivan's passivity during the preceding interregna. The election of Báthory had in the final analysis been the prelude to the first great defeat of the Muscovite state in its struggle against Poland-Lithuania.

The propaganda for the election of Prince Sigismund of Sweden frightened the boiars of Moscow into activity. Whereas the danger of a Polish alliance with Turkey as a consequence of the election of Báthory had been rather vague, Sigismund, if he became king of Poland and later also of Sweden, would unite the two strongest rivals of the Muscovite state on the Baltic. To prevent this the Muscovites hastened to advance the candidacy of their own prince. To the electoral Sejm a large legation was this time promptly sent with the additional promise that Fedor would conquer Estonia for Poland-Lithuania and keep only Narva. The envoys were received well, but they could offer no union, only an alliance. The tsar, they said, would reside in Moscow, would remain Orthodox, would not unify the churches, and would not hinder the Pope in his dealings with the Polish clergy. The Muscovite state would have to appear first in the title. On the strength of this, the senators rejected the candidacy of Fedor.[26]

Again there was a double election: in August, 1587, Archduke Maximilian and Sigismund of Sweden were elected in short succession. Even before it was decided which of the two would prevail, the Lithuanians made a fifteen-year truce with the Muscovite envoys. The question might now be asked: why did they not make peace? The Lithuanians, who were now tired of war, wanted to tie the hands of their future ruler. This was particularly important in case Sigismund should succeed. The length of the armistice almost gives the impression that the Lithuanians hoped that the Muscovite state would disintegrate in that time. A few years more, and these hopes would almost have been fulfilled.

At first there was great fear of a close cooperation of Poland-Lithuania with Sweden, but it was soon discovered that King Sigismund was not popular in Poland and Lithuania, and therefore was weak. The danger once again became acute when Sigismund became king of Sweden after the death of his father (1592). Sigismund, however, was already having difficulties with his uncle Charles of Södermanland in 1593, and in 1599 a war broke out in Livonia between

Poland and Sweden. Now the situation that had appeared critical for the Muscovites in 1587 and 1592 and 1593 had reversed itself: for a long time the Muscovites could count on Poland-Lithuania and Sweden to be archenemies.

Fedor's successor, Boris Godunov (1598 to 1605), thus faced a situation that was better than ever before with respect to Poland-Lithuania and Sweden. He could afford to be haughty to the envoys of Sigismund who came to Moscow in 1600. Under the pretext that his big toe was hurting him, he had them wait forty-one days for the audience. But the Muscovites overestimated the weakness of the Lithuanians and underestimated the diplomatic skill of their chief envoy, Lew Sapieha. The latter did not take the threats of the Muscovites seriously, and proposed a close union between the two countries: a perpetual and firm defensive alliance should unite them. The subjects of both rulers were to be free to serve the other ruler, to travel to his country, to contract marriages with his subjects, to own land, and to go to school there. Furthermore, the two countries were to build up a common defense of the Ukraine against the Tatars and introduce common currency and free trade. Finally, provision was to be made for a future personal union of the two countries. Smolensk and the Severian land were to be returned to the Polish-Lithuanian state. Close alliance between the two countries was rejected by the Muscovites, but after difficult negotiations a twenty-year armistice (to 1622) was concluded. Calm now seemed assured for an unusually long period of time.[27]

The domestic situation in the Muscovite state became more and more critical, however. The rule of Godunov was not secured, and yet —or rather therefore—he did not give up the old plans for expansion and attempted to win over the Emperor to a partition of Poland-Lithuania (1604). Through a joint military campaign the Archduke Maximilian was to be placed on the Polish throne and Lithuania was to be incorporated into the Muscovite state.[28] Before the Emperor had an opportunity to express his opinion of these proposals, the Muscovite state was engulfed in a civil war and its neighbors were incited to plans for expansion.

The Poles and Lithuanians were most successful. In 1609 they attacked the Muscovite state and occupied Moscow; they then brought about the election as tsar of Władysław, the oldest son of Sigismund III, and finally, after a long siege, conquered Smolensk (1611). The whole undertaking was risky, for it was impossible for a Polish king to wage a war of aggression without getting into conflict with the nobility. At the decisive moment the Sejm did not provide Sigismund III with the means to pay the mercenaries, and the military enterprise collapsed. The king's political tactics were unfortunate. On the one hand, he had to win back Muscovite territory in order to gain the support of the nobility; on the other hand, he himself wanted to become tsar and therefore delayed his son's move to Moscow until it was too late. Since at the least Smolensk had to be restored to Lithuania, the Polish move was just as hopeless as had been the efforts of Ivan IV four decades earlier to be elected king of Poland with the stipulation that Kiev and Volynia should pass to the Muscovite state.

The Muscovites organized resistance, forced the Poles in Moscow to capitulate (1612), and elected Michael Romanov their tsar (1613). The war with Poland went on for another five years and was ended with an armistice (Deulino, December 24, 1618). The Muscovites lost approximately half of the territories they had acquired in the sixteenth century. The loss of Smolensk hurt them most severely: the sole strong bastion on the military road from Vilna to Moscow was now in the hands of the Lithuanians, who at any time could easily march to the gates of Moscow.

The Muscovites were acutely aware of their military inferiority, and therefore in the following decades they set themselves only one goal: to regain Smolensk. The great plans for the conquest of the *otchina* had to be postponed to a more distant future. The tsar tried to conclude alliances with the Sultan and the king of Sweden and, despite Muscovy's weakness from the preceding turmoils, thought to attack Poland as early as 1621. However, the Turkish campaign against Poland was a failure, and the Muscovites did not want to wage war given Sweden as their sole ally. Militarily and diplomatically they made arrangements for war and planned to attack after the expiration of the armistice. Shortly after the death of Sigismund III (1632), the well-equipped Muscovite army did attack, but the interregnum was brief and the Poles and Lithuanians remained united. Muscovy had no aid in this war, for neither the Sultan nor Sweden was ready to declare war on Poland-Lithuania. This time also the Muscovites by themselves were no match for the Poles and the Lithuanians. They lost their entire army before Smolensk, and in the peace that was concluded in 1634, the first since 1508, they acquired several rather small border strips, but in return for this gain they had to recognize the large losses of 1618 and 1619. It was now decided in Moscow that further offensive action must await the favorable moment when Poland should fall into a paroxysm of weakness. The wait was not very long.

In 1648 there erupted a great Ukrainian Cossack rebellion which the king of Poland, John Casimir (1648 to 1668), could not suppress. The Cossacks constituted an independent state and established relations with the enemies of Poland since they were aware that they could not survive as an independent entity without foreign help. The Muscovites did not at first let themselves be dragged into the conflict; they waited until the Cossacks and the Poles-Lithuanians had exhausted each other. By the year 1654 the Cossacks were in a desperate situation and were ready to recognize the supremacy of the Muscovites. When, by the treaties of 1654, the center of the territory of the Rus of Kiev passed to the tsar, the most important objective of the foreign policy of Moscow, as Ivan III had outlined it, seemed to have been achieved. In 1654 also the Muscovites conquered Smolensk, and in 1655 Minsk and Vilna; only Lvov withstood a siege.

But even as Moscow's early political objective of "gathering of the Russian land" seemed possible of attainment, it became obvious that changes in the general situation of Eastern and Northern Europe since the start of the sixteenth century had worked to the disadvantage of the Muscovites.

The Preponderance of Russia and Protectorate Politics

The times of unhindered expansion westward were past. Even in its heyday in the sixteenth century, the Polish-Lithuanian state was situated on the periphery of the European political scene, for its kings, being dependent financially on the nobility, could not carry on an active foreign policy; the nobility itself had no foreign political ambitions, but watched that the kings did not develop initiative in foreign politics. Poland was a stable and stabilizing power, strong enough to deter its Western neighbors from attacking its borders. It had no real foes in the West, but no real friends either. The Habsburgs and the French fought diplomatic battles for influence in Poland, but the European situation hardly changed whether, for example, Báthory, who was hostile to the Habsburgs, or Sigismund III, who was friendly to the Habsburgs, sat on the Polish throne. Hence neither the ones nor the others were interested in what was happening on the eastern Polish frontier, and the Muscovites could pursue unimpeded their policy of expansion.

The view that only the Poles and Lithuanians stood in the way of Muscovy's "gathering of the Russian land" persisted in Moscow to the middle of the seventeenth century, but it no longer corresponded to the facts. The Muscovite state was also indirectly a neighbor of Turkey. Therefore the Turks and the Crimean Tatars were vitally interested in preserving an equilibrium between Lithuania-Poland and the Muscovite state. The Muscovites were wary of coming into conflict with the Turks, and they skillfully used the then common slogan of the solidarity against the infidel of all Christian rulers; as a rule, however, they used it only when they hoped to gain some advantage in their struggle against Poland.

The third common neighbor was Sweden. In the sixteenth century the position of Sweden in European politics was still more marginal than that of Poland, but in the 1620's Gustavus Adolphus gained ascendancy in the Baltic, took possession of all of Livonia, and shut the Muscovite state off from the sea. In the 1630's he and his chancellor, Axel Oxenstierna, managed to maneuver Sweden into the center of European politics. From 1630 on it was of interest to every European state whether Sweden became stronger or weaker. Sweden's might depended essentially on the *dominium maris baltici,* and this, in turn, depended on Sweden's possessing Livonia and on the exclusion of the Muscovites from the Baltic Sea. Sweden as a military power, an important part of the European system in the middle of the seventeenth century, had a lively interest in preventing the Muscovite state from expanding westward. The conquest of Vilna was an alarm signal for Sweden. Swedish historians have offered many explanations as to why Charles X Gustavus did not attack the Muscovite state but devastated Poland and snatched it from under the very nose of the tsar, yet none could refute the commentary that Charles X Gustavus in the final analysis paved the way to the Baltic Sea for Peter the Great.[29]

Shortly after the Swedes invaded Poland (July 25, 1655), the Muscovites discontinued their military action against the Lithuanians and Poles. Muscovy's perspective now changed fundamentally for a limited time, for should the Swedes succeed in gaining a sure footing in Poland, the situation for the Muscovite state would become catastrophic. The struggle for the "paternal legacy" receded into the background for several years, and Sweden became the principal enemy. However, the war in Livonia against Sweden brought no success; by the peace treaty of Kardis (1661) the old boundary was restored. The chief objective in the invasion of Livonia was to acquire a Baltic seaport; the Swedish successes in Poland, however, provided the inducement. There were also plans to partition Poland-Lithuania (treaty of Radnot, December 6, 1656), but only Sweden, Brandenburg, the Cossacks, the prince of Transylvania, George II Rákóczi, and the mighty Lithuanian magnate Janusz Radziwiłł were to receive shares; the Muscovites were to leave emptyhanded.

That is why in the years after 1655 the Muscovites were keenly interested in preserving Poland-Lithuania. They negotiated with Polish-Lithuanian envoys in 1656, but as a precondition for cooperation against Sweden they demanded that Tsar Alexis or his son be nominated or elected as the successor of the childless John Casimir. To the horror of the Austrian mediators the Polish negotiators accepted the condition and concluded an agreement with the Muscovites on November 6, 1656. In that year the situation of Poland was still bad, and the help of the Muscovites against Sweden was extremely welcome. For the Lithuanians there was an additional motive born of their hope of regaining possession of their landed estates. But in 1657 the situation of Poland improved, and the help of the Muscovites proved less effective than had been expected. In 1658 the Sejm decided not to carry out the election as long as the king was alive. In the same year the Muscovites concluded an armistice with the Swedes.

The struggle for access to the Baltic was again postponed, whereas that for the Ukraine was resumed. In 1658 the armed conflict began again. In 1660 the Poles-Lithuanians won several victories over the Muscovites, thereby strengthening considerably their position in the Ukraine; at this point, however, both opponents were at the end of their strength. Only in the winter of 1663–64 did John Casimir attempt an offensive; it was to be the last undertaking of its kind. In 1665 a civil war broke out in Poland and by the time it ended in August, 1666, it had consumed whatever strength the Poles had left. Since the Muscovites were in similar case, they were obliged to negotiate without the backing of a strong army. The negotiations begun in 1660 had not been allowed to break off, and finally, on January 30, 1667, an armistice was concluded in Andrusovo for thirteen and a half years. Muscovy received the whole of the territory lost in 1618, and in addition the

Ukraine was divided along the Dnieper, Muscovy receiving the territory on the left bank. A Muscovite garrison was to remain in Kiev for only two years—but the city was never returned to Poland.[30]

Again the Muscovites had taken a step forward, but extensive lands of the Rus of Kiev still remained joined to Poland-Lithuania. It is difficult to determine how effective the *otchina* theory still was in the period 1654 to 1667, for in these years the old and the new were mingled in Moscow's policy toward Poland. Conquest and candidacy for the Polish throne had become essential aims in the sixteenth century, but it was not until 1656 that serious efforts were made to cooperate against third powers. Since the Crimean Tatars—the Polish king's most faithful allies during the whole course of the war—and the Swedes hindered the tsars from expanding further at the expense of Poland, it was logical that Moscow should try to win over the Poles as allies against Sweden and against the Crimean Tatars, who were backed by Turkey.

Afanasii Ordyn-Nashchokin, the tsar's adviser and director of foreign affairs, had long urged the tsar to make a settlement with Poland-Lithuania and to take concerted action against Sweden in order to gain access to the Baltic Sea. In a long memorandum in the spring of 1664 he cited a long series of additional advantages which could be obtained by a close alliance with Poland-Lithuania: among other things, the Orthodox subjects of the king would be better protected; the Orthodox Balkan nations would fight themselves free from Turkish rule and join the alliance.[31] Tsar Alexis, however, clung firmly to the old orientation of Moscow's foreign policy. True, he permitted Ordyn-Nashchokin to negotiate with the Poles about an alliance in 1663, and this minister also took an active part in the negotiations in Andrusovo and after the conclusion of the armistice. He worked, insofar as his instructions allowed, for an understanding between Poland-Lithuania and the Muscovite state.

The necessity of cooperating against the Crimean Tatars and the Turks gained an increasing importance during the negotiations before the treaty of Andrusovo (1667). The idea was not new. In 1493 the Emperor Maximilian I wanted to reconcile Ivan III with Poland-Lithuania in order to mount concerted military action against the Turks,[32] and this issue subsequently came up frequently in the negotiations between the Holy Roman Emperors and the rulers of Muscovy. In 1558 Alexis Adashev, the influential adviser of Ivan IV, suggested to the

Lithuanians that the old claims be buried and that there be unity for cooperation against the infidels.[33] Cooperation in the form of reconnaissance against the Tatar raids did prevail in the first half of the sixteenth century, and in 1551 an agreement about this was signed.[34] Sapieha proposed joint action against the Crimean Tatars, and after long negotiations Alexis and Władysław IV concluded a defensive alliance against the Crimean Tatars (September 5, 1647).[35]

Nonetheless, both sides also tried to obtain assistance from the Crimean Tatars in fighting each other. In 1655 John Casimir won them over and kept them as allies until the end of the war. There was, however, no doubt that they would attack Poland as soon as John Casimir made peace with the tsar. It was for this reason that the armistice treaty had to contain provisions binding the signatories to military cooperation against the Tatars.[36] The treaty partners did not, however, adhere to the provisions. When at first the Poles were exposed to the attacks of the Turks, they received no assistance; rather the Muscovites were content to have Poland weakened, as this could favorably influence their efforts to improve the treaty of 1667. When, however, in February, 1671, Ordyn-Nashchokin had to surrender the direction of foreign affairs to A. S. Matveev, the policy favoring a settlement with Poland-Lithuania was abandoned. In the Moscow treaty of April 9, 1672, the stipulation concerning cooperation against the Crimean Tatars was weakened. In the same year the Poles did not obtain the assistance they urgently required and had to cede an extensive territory to Turkey by the peace of Buczacz (October 18, 1672). The Moscow threats were not taken seriously by the Grand Vizir, and the Muscovites went on expecting that the Turks would finally compel the Poles to give up Kiev to them although they were fully aware of the dangers to be anticipated from the Turks, as the diplomatic actions in Europe in 1667 and 1672 show.[37] Since the Poles had received no aid[38] against the Tatars in 1674 and 1676, they did not help the Muscovites in 1677 and 1678. In these years Muscovy had to defend its outposts on the right bank of the Dnieper River against Turkish attack. Meantime, the Poles utilized the unfavorable situation of the Muscovite state to make a new treaty on August 17, 1678, according to which the Muscovites had to cede Nevel, Sebezh, and Velizh.[39]

In the end both drew lessons from these experiences, and from 1679 on, at the urgent request of imperial and papal diplomats, serious negotiations were again resumed concerning an alliance against the Turks. The foreign political program proposed by Ordyn-Nashchokin slowly became part and parcel of the official policy of the Muscovite state. The Muscovites negotiated tenaciously and with great skill; their change of policy was honored with a peace treaty which finally ensured their possession of all recent acquisitions, including Kiev. This peace treaty, signed in Moscow on May 6, 1686,[40] ended an epoch in the relations between Poland-Lithuania and the Muscovite state. The "gathering of the Russian land" was thereby ended only with partial success. It is possible that there were still supporters of the foreign policy of Ivan III, but Matveev was its last important representative. Such supporters perhaps attached just as much value to the peace of 1686 as their forefathers once had to the peace treaties of 1508 and 1634, but they and the *otchina* theory were to gain no more influence on the official policy.

What profit did the eleven wars with Poland-Lithuania between 1487 and 1667 bring the Muscovite state? Did perseverance in an anti-Polish foreign policy over the one hundred and eighty years strengthen the Muscovite state to an extent that justified the enormous sacrifices? With the exception of the southern parts, the acquired territory was, compared with the old, rather densely settled, but the soil, again except for the southern parts, is poor. Considered from the standpoint of climate and vegetation, the new territory did not supplement the old to advantage. The acquisition and defense of the new territory probably cost more than could be expected in crop yield within a reasonable period of time. Only the strategic advantage was considerable; the center of the Muscovite state was less exposed to attack.

When Ivan III made the *otchina* theory his official program, he had just ended the most successful of all eleven wars. He could not foresee that, even after nine more, in part much more difficult wars, the undertaking would have to be given up, the goal still far away. The successors of Ivan III held tenaciously to his program, even after it no longer was reasonable and useful, and the resources spent sometimes stood in an absurd relationship to the attainable gain. It was much more important for the economic development of the Muscovite state to obtain access to the Baltic and to protect the fertile area in the south from the Tatars and thus preserve it for cultivation. Ivan IV and

Ordyn-Nashchokin clearly saw the significance of acquiring Baltic seaports, but they were unable to realize their plans and to surmount the anti-Polish fixation in Muscovite foreign policy.

Simultaneously with the peace treaty of 1686, an alliance against Turks and Tatars was formed. Indirectly the Muscovite state now belonged to the Holy League formed in 1684. The military contribution of Poland in 1683 had been significant, but thereafter it was minimal. The partners, the Emperor and Venice, therefore forced John Sobieski to surrender Poland's eastern territories to buy the participation of the Muscovite state in the League. A substantial advantage was expected from the Muscovites, namely, their aid in restraining the Crimean Tatars, who had proved a strong enemy in the struggles in Hungary. Until 1695 the military contribution of the Muscovites to the common war was slight; the military campaigns against the Crimea in 1687 and 1689 were complete failures. Neither of the two partners benefited at first from the new alliance because both were militarily too weak. This was indeed to remain the case with Poland, whereas Russia under the leadership of Peter the Great soon became a European great power. At this juncture Poland became an object of international politics carrying little weight either as a foe or a friend.[41] It took some time, however, for contemporaries to become aware of this change.

Peter the Great had to take his first stand on Polish affairs during the royal election after the death of John Sobieski. He did so with determination and threatened (though not openly) military intervention should the Poles elect the French candidate. His primary reason was to avoid losing Poland as an ally against the Turks, although in fact the Poles contributed hardly anything to the joint war.[42] The election of Augustus of Saxony was acceptable to Peter, and the troops which stood at the border did not see action. In later years Peter was to interfere frequently in the internal affairs of Poland, but at first he hoped to make Poland an ally against Sweden. He came to an understanding with King Augustus II (verbally in 1698; by treaty, November 11, 1699),[43] and the war with Sweden began in 1700 (Peter declared war on August 19, 1700).

Only as elector of Saxony was Augustus his ally. The Poles refused at first to enter the war, but when Charles XII of Sweden attacked Augustus on Polish territory, capturing Warsaw and Cracow in 1702, the Polish nobility were forced to take sides. Two parties formed. Those loyal to the king were ready to enter the war against

Sweden and on August 19, 1704, formed an alliance with Russia against Sweden.[44] Those hostile to the king elected Stanisław Leszczyński as king on July 12, 1704, and formed an alliance with Sweden on November 18, 1705. Thus both Peter and Charles XII had Polish adherents, but no one pursued policies advantageous to Poland, for Leszczyński from the beginning was nothing more than a puppet who was powerless without the Swedish help.

When Charles XII forced Augustus to renounce the Polish crown in the treaty of Altranstädt (September 24, 1706), Peter held a large part of Poland. Now there were only Swedish and Russian Poles, with both groups dependent on their protectors. As guardian, Peter sought a new king for his orphaned minor. He negotiated with Prince Eugene of Savoy, with the sons of John Sobieski, with Francis Rákóczi, and in the end held in reserve a native candidate, the grand hetman of the crown, Adam Mikołaj Sieniawski. He also attempted to talk his Poles into accepting his son Alexis, but they showed so little enthusiasm that Peter did not force the plan. In all negotiations Peter acted in a very natural way, as if it behooved him to dispose of the Polish crown.[45]

The Swedes drove Peter out of Poland before he could find a new king. Augustus returned to Poland immediately after the battle at Poltava, and Peter again signed an alliance (October 20, 1709) with him, according to which, as in the case of the previous alliances, Livonia should pass to Poland or rather Augustus in the event of victory.[46] In 1711 Peter reiterated his promise—simultaneously to Poland and Augustus—but he no longer thought of honoring this pledge, and in 1718 he made this known publicly.[47] Augustus and the Poles were to leave emptyhanded, since they did not have the power to force surrender of their share of the booty.

After 1709 Peter behaved in Poland as if he were the real master of the country, and in a sense he was. The Turks felt alarmed about this. When they had surrounded him in Jassy in 1711 and could more or less dictate the terms of peace, they forced him to promise to withdraw his troops from Poland and to renounce all future intervention.[48] Peter did not think of keeping this promise, and for this reason a new Turkish war almost developed.[49] However, Peter's troops remained in Poland and levied contributions there,[50] and the population was ever less enthusiastic over their presence, particularly since the Saxon army was also stationed in Poland. In the end this led to a confederation of the nobility against the king. Since the Russian army was the strongest force in the country, Peter's attitude was to decide the quarrel between the nobility and the king. The agreement (signed November 3, 1716) negotiated by Peter's envoy, Prince Grigorii Dolgorukii, provided, among other things, for the reduction of the Polish army to 24,000 men (at the time it was even smaller than that); the king was permitted to have 1,200 men of the Saxon guard stationed in Poland. Dolgorukii signed the agreement; this, to be sure, did not correspond to a Russian guarantee, but an alteration was in practice impossible without the consent of Russia. From that time on the military impotence and the "liberties" of the nobility were under Russian protection.[51]

The massive intervention of the Russians and the constant presence of Russian troops evoked a wave of anti-Russian sentiment of which Augustus made good use: he publicly demanded the withdrawal of the Russian troops and made a pact with the Emperor Charles VI and George I of England concerning measures to be taken against Russia. Among other things Peter was to be compelled to end his intervention in Polish affairs and to withdraw his troops. The king and the nobility were in agreement for a brief period of time, but the unity was soon lost when Peter, under the pressure of the powers, withdrew his troops. A low point was reached when Peter disclosed to the Polish nobility that Augustus had been negotiating with the king of Prussia about a partition of Poland. Peter now posed as the protector of Poland and the "liberties." On February 6, 1720,[52] he had come to an agreement with the king of Prussia that they should jointly protect the Polish "liberties." This represented a kind of ancient monuments protection act and was designed to preserve Poland's political impotence.[53] Peter inserted a similar stipulation in 1724 into the alliance with Sweden, which the Emperor joined in 1726. Now all three of the later partitioning powers, the politically important neighbors of Poland, were united in the effort to keep Poland in its state of weakness. The political decisions that concerned Poland were from now on made outside Poland; only by distributing bribes to Polish dignitaries did the powers indirectly admit that the Poles also had some say.

In the years 1722 to 1724 Peter intervened vigorously in favor of the Orthodox and assigned himself the role of protector of his fellow believers under Polish rule.[54] He thus marked out the entire program of activity of Russian diplomacy with respect to Poland up to the final partition: intervention in the royal elections, meddling in the disputes between nobility and king, building up of a Russian party by means of bribery, military pressure by the stationing of Russian troops on Polish territory, negotiation with other powers to regulate joint intervention in the internal affairs of the country, and finally intercession on behalf of the Orthodox subjects of the Polish king. The great innovator of Russia also determined the policy towards Poland for the following decades, but he could not be persuaded to allow the partitioning of the country among its neighbors. It seems that the distant goal for which Peter strove was the incorporation of the entire country into the Russian empire. Until this should be achieved, Poland was to remain a Russian protectorate. Peter's successors continued his policy, although with less energy and readiness to act.

After Peter's death, Poland for the first time became an acute problem: a successor had to be found for Augustus II, who died February 1, 1733, for not one of the neighboring powers would think of exposing itself to the incalculable risks of a free royal election. There was a strong party in Poland which wanted to raise to the throne Stanisław Leszczyński, onetime puppet of Charles XII and now father-in-law of the king of France. The three neighbors, however, were determined not to open the path to the throne for a representative of French interests. Instead they used military force to obtain the election of the late king's son Augustus, although there had been serious doubts about him because his election could seem to set a precedent for the heritability of the throne. It is interesting that the Russians and Austrians wanted to talk each other into military intervention, although later the neighbors all too gladly sent their hungry soldiers out into Polish pastureland. There is one more unique phenomenon connected with these events: A European power took up arms in support of a freely elected candidate to the throne of Poland. The king of France supported Stanisław. Thus one of the many Austro-French wars was called the War of the Polish Succession. In the end the Russian army was successful and drove Stanisław out of the country.[55]

The might and influence of Russia grew by its military presence, but Tsarina Anna turned it to no further advantage. In the years that followed, Russo-Polish relations were uneventful. Elizabeth played the role of protectress of the Orthodox in Poland, undoubtedly out of inner conviction, with more zeal than did Anna; in return she showed more understanding than her predecessor for the political wishes of the Poles. These were, however, nuances, for in principle nothing important could be done or decided in Poland without Russian approval.

Small reforms were occasionally permitted, but an effective strengthening of Poland was hindered.[56] Russian troops frequently marched through Polish territory without requesting even formal permission. The ravages of Poland were still within tolerable bounds during the Turkish War with Austria and Russia (1736 to 1739) and during the Russian participation in the War of the Austrian Succession (1745 to 1748), but during the Seven Years War Russian troops inflicted immense damage on the country, to which were added the depredations of Austrian and Prussian troops. The reversal of alliances furthermore deprived Poland of its last protector. France left Poland to its fate.[57]

Russian diplomats, in their constant intervention in the domestic affairs of Poland, appealed more and more frequently to the agreement of 1716 and demanded insistently to be sole arbiter in the internal differences of the Poles.[58] Toward the end of the Seven Years War, Poland was completely ruined; occupied by Russian troops, deserted by its last protector, the country was now definitely treated with disrespect by the European powers.

The Partition of Poland

If European countries could choose their geographical position and their neighbors, not one would select the most uncomfortable of all possible locations: a territory wedged between the Germans and the Russians. Given the consistent deterioration of the Polish state, particularly from the middle of the seventeenth century, and the concurrent rise of Prussia and Russia, the future of politically impotent Poland, placed between these two states, was very dim. The Russian protectorate over Poland did not remain unchallenged; Russian control of what was still left of Polish politics had to be strengthened ever anew. Anti-Russian movements continued to ferment under the leadership of Polish magnates, who persisted in their efforts to gain support from other powers, in particular from France and Austria. The Polish crown was elective, and it probably would have been most advantageous for Russia, whose vote was decisive in the elections, to put the ruling tsar or a tsarevitch on the throne. However, since the Russians did not even have men for their own throne, they had to promote to the Polish throne weak candidates pliable to Russian wishes. The problem became acute after the death of Augustus III (October 5, 1763).

At this point the attitude of the court in St. Petersburg toward

Poland changed perceptibly. Those responsible for foreign policy under Tsarina Anna (Andrei Ostermann) and Tsarina Elizabeth (Bestuzhev Riumin) were satisfied with keeping Poland in the Russian sphere of influence, with preventing it from gaining strength, but they otherwise attached no special importance to the country. The chancellor, M. V. Vorontsov, expressed this quite clearly in January, 1762. Half a year later Catherine II, the new tsarina, appointed one of her most trusted advisers, Count Hermann Karl Kayserling, as envoy in Poland, and thereafter the tsarina and Nikita Ivanovich Panin (since 1763 also officially head of foreign policy) paid great attention to Polish affairs. Panin once stated: "We shall lose a third of our power and advantages if Poland is not dependent on us." Poland obviously occupied an important place in his system.[59] For a time nothing was changed in the objectives of Russian policy, except that the pressure on Poland became stronger, the tone increasingly domineering and the interference more massive. Catherine acted first against Polish interests when she forced Courland, which *de jure* was a Polish fief, into the Russian sphere of influence.[60] The tsarina plainly and simply informed the Polish court that it was her right (on the basis of the treaties of 1716) to see that the laws of the republic of Poland were obeyed and the "liberties" of the nobility respected.[61] What was meant by this solicitude became evident at the subsequent and last royal election.

Internally, Poland was badly torn by party strife. One of Kayserling's most important tasks was to form a Russian party, for this had been neglected in the preceding years. One of the two big parties of the Polish magnates, the "family" Czartoryski, had, it is true, repeatedly cooperated with Russia since the 1740's, but its goal was a strengthening of Poland by reforms, for which the "family" could not gain Russian consent. It nevertheless again made overtures of cooperation and averred its devotion to Russia. When the formation of a party which would exclusively serve Russian objectives was unsuccessful, Catherine II had to cooperate with the "family" at the royal election after the death of Augustus III; but she did not make the head of the "family" king of Poland, but rather Stanisław Augustus Poniatowski, her former lover, a less important man of the party. Later the tsarina provided her own commentary for her decision: "Stanisław Poniatowski was chosen by Russia for the Polish throne because of all the candidates he had the least prospects and consequently must feel most gratitude for Russia." [62] Russian troops drove away all the opponents of the "family" and forced the election of Stanisław Augustus. Catherine II had made a prior agreement with Prussia which gave her a free hand in Poland.[63] Austria and France let matters run their course, that is, they likewise left Poland to the Russians.

After the election Catherine II presented her king with the bill: he was "in the course of his entire reign to regard the interests of Our Empire as his own, to preserve them and further them will all his powers. . . ."[64] Since Stanisław Augustus knew that he could not maintain himself without Russian support, there was nothing for him to do but to do as he was told. He was intelligent but weak-willed, educated and extravagant; Catherine repeatedly paid his debts. That was the king whose neighbors divided up his kingdom among themselves.

During the interregnum the "family" had carried out some reforms and now hoped to continue the party's work with Russian help. But Catherine put an end to that and supported the opposition to the "family." Finally, because of Catherine's demand for complete equality of rights for the Orthodox, it came to a break with the "family." This demand is to be seen in the context of Catherine's domestic policy: the German-born Empress, who was reared as a Protestant, had to stress her devotion to Orthodoxy to please her Russian subjects. Furthermore, the Orthodox who gained political rights by the intervention of Russia were to form the nucleus of a purely Russian party and finally make Catherine independent of the assistance of the "family." The latter naturally resisted.[65] The Russian ambassador, Prince Nikolai Vasilevich Repnin, organized the opposition and arrested a deputy to the Sejm who spoke out against the presence of Russian troops in Warsaw during the session of the Sejm.[66] However, not all deputies and senators let themselves be intimidated. To crush the resistance, Repnin had Kajetan Sołtyk, the bishop of Cracow, and three other well-known persons arrested and deported to Russia.[67] Now the intimidation was successful; the Sejm appointed a delegation which, together with Repnin, was to draft an edict of tolerance, a catalogue of fundamental rights, and an alliance with Russia. Repnin treated the delegates like bad, stupid schoolboys; he ordered them to be silent or to sit down, bellowed and jeered at them, and finally threatened them with imprisonment. With Sołtyk's fate vivid in their minds, they had to swallow every insult. The Russian army controlled all streets leading out of Warsaw.[68] In February of 1768 the Sejm confirmed the results of the negotiations. Russia now guaranteed the constitution, and the real ruler in Poland was the Russian ambassador.

For most Poles this was too much. In the spring of 1768 the enraged nobility formed the confederation of Bar. For four years they struggled without the slightest prospect of success. Not only were the Russians superior militarily but the Poles squabbled among themselves, there being numerous groups with very diverse and mutually contradictory goals. France supported the confederates to a degree and Austria tolerated their institutions in Hungary and Silesia, but only the Turks took up arms. Their objective was to prevent a definitive incorporation of Poland into the Russian empire.[69] The Russo-Turkish War of 1768 to 1774 did not permit Catherine to deploy all her forces for the "pacification" of Poland. A struggle now began at the court of St. Petersburg between a protectorate party (Panin) and a partitioning party (Grigorii Orlov). In the end the latter prevailed.

The totality of the problems connected with the partition cannot be presented here. It is too vast and complex. Plans for the partitioning of Poland or Poland-Lithuania had arisen repeatedly since the Middle Ages.[70] Such plans were not foreign to the rulers of Moscow. One partition project was inspired by Sweden in the 1650's, but it was Augustus II of Poland who negotiated at least five projects with all those possibly interested, thus making partitioning a set ingredient of political imagination, since he preferred a portion of Poland under his absolute rule to the entire republic under his nominal control. The kings of Prussia, in particular, were ready partners when it came to plans of partition, for Polish territory separated their Prussian and Brandenburgian possessions. Also Austrians and, at the end, even the French were ready to barter portions of the helpless and defenseless republic. Peter the Great, though with some hesitation, took a position against the deals with Polish territory, and in the following years all plans for partitioning went aground on the resistance of Russia. And why should Russia give up the glacis that was strategically advantageous as long as it was possible to keep Poland in complete political impotence and dependence?[71]

What prompted Catherine II to give up the time-hallowed principles with respect to Poland? Several reasons can be adduced. The international situation in 1771 was not good. In addition to the two wars against Turkey and Poland, war threatened to erupt with Austria. If

Austria were permitted to participate in the partition, then war could be averted. Furthermore, Frederick II was becoming a more and more reluctant ally, for he was obliged to pay subsidies to Catherine so that she could enlarge her empire at the expense of the Turks, an action which shifted the balance of power to his disfavor. With the situation as bad as it was in 1771, it was very important to keep him in good spirits, and this could be done by allowing him to acquire the Polish areas situated between his possessions.[72]

There is nothing to indicate that Catherine had to give up the old principles under pressure and coercion. The situation was serious but in no way critical. The will was lacking to continue the protectorate policy. From the beginning of Catherine's rule there were plans of annexation, and if one compares the boundaries before and after 1772, one immediately recognizes that those responsible for the defense of the country must have wished to round off the territory of the empire; the first project (October 6, 1763) emanated from the president of the War College.[73] The idea of feeding Frederick II with Polish territory to keep him in line came up several times.[74] In the eyes of Russian statesmen the idea of the territorial integrity of the Polish state lost its validity after 1763, and annexation of the Polish territory became a feasible possibility. From 1768 on the protectorate policy was costly and was binding Russian forces needed elsewhere: accordingly, annexation became more attractive.

To this must be added a personal motive: Catherine was a usurper and a foreigner. Only by means of spectacular successes could she impress her subjects and strengthen her rule. The protectorate policy with its distant goal of acquisition of the entire Polish-Lithuanian state was certainly the better and more prudent policy, far-sighted and less dangerous; but out of the advantages of this undisputed old wisdom Catherine could not make the victory wreaths she so urgently needed and highly valued.

At the beginning of 1771 the negotiations began between Prussia and Russia; Austria joined the negotiations later. The partition treaty between the three powers was concluded on August 5, 1772. Poland-Lithuania lost 30 percent of its territory and 35 percent of its inhabitants. Any resistance on the part of Poland or an intervention by other powers did not figure prominently in the planning or execution of the partition. In England and France the opinion prevailed that the Poles themselves were responsible for their misfortune.[75] Catherine could be satisfied with the result: the boundary was straightened and what remained of the kingdom continued to be a Russian protectorate, being practically ruled by the Russian ambassador. The other partitioning powers showed little interest in hindering Catherine.

With Catherine's approval and under the guidance of the Russian ambassador the administration of Poland was improved, but it remained completely under Russian control.[76] In the two decades after the first partition of Poland, the attitude of many Poles to the traditional political order changed. The determination for thoroughgoing reforms gained in force, and finally the reformers gained the upper hand. They gave the country a modern constitution (May 3, 1791), blocking the sources of disorder and weakness. Poland seemed to reawaken from its agony. These reforms were possible because the international situation made it impossible for Russia to intervene. The king of Prussia endeavored to counteract Russia wherever possible. For this reason he protected the Polish reformers and supported their demand for the withdrawal of the Russian troops. Catherine yielded since she already had two wars to wage (against Turkey and Sweden) and did not wish to risk two more against Poland and Prussia. The Poles now gave free rein to the anger and hatred they had built up against the Russians in the decades of Russian occupation.[77] The reforms were quite plainly a challenge to the former protectress. Catherine had no alternative but to pretend that she no longer had any interest in Poland.[78] But the respite that fate afforded the Poles was short. Their situation worsened visibly: the king of Prussia progressively lost interest in cooperating with Poland; Catherine ended the Swedish war, and the Turkish war was drawing to a close.

Commencing in May, 1791, Catherine planned a new intervention in Poland, for it ran counter to all principles of Russian policy to tolerate a strengthening and renewal of Poland—and this in a mood openly anti-Russian. She skillfully maneuvered her two partners of 1772 into a war against France and formed a Polish opposition against the reforms. The confederation was formed in St. Petersburg, though officially in Targowica (May 14, 1792). Catherine ordered the handful of "patriots" to ask Russia for help in saving the "liberties" and had a large army march to Poland. The resistance lasted only two months; the opportunists, to which the king belonged, joined ranks with the confederation.[79]

From the beginning Catherine probably had her eye on two immediate aims: the restoration of the protectorate either throughout the state as it then existed or in that portion remaining after a new partition. Ceding a portion of Polish territory, Catherine finally bought off the Prussians' agreement to her suppression of the new constitution. She rewarded herself amply for her efforts, for the Russian share alone in the partition was greater than the entire territory still remaining to the Poles. This small remainder became more than ever a protectorate of Russia; the treaty of alliance of October 14, 1793, was really a capitulation.[80] Again the Poles resisted, staged a great rebellion, and chased the Russian troops from some parts of the country, but the result was only the final partitioning of Poland (1795).

The way Catherine solved the question is truly impressive. Not only did she manage the other powers and enlarge her own share but she finally represented her policy of expansion as a contribution to the struggle against the revolution in France. Her political achievement was considerable: even the name of the once dangerous foe of Russia was to be obliterated, according to the final partition treaties of 1795.

The moment the Poles made serious efforts to overcome their helplessness and to withdraw from the Russian protectorate, Catherine no doubt made her goal the final partitioning and subjugation of Poland. This danger was implicit in the first partition, for it could not be supposed that Polish society was so far corrupted that it would not try to defend itself against the Russian tutelage and against others desirous of disposing of its territory. A strengthened Poland would have made the restoration of the territories lost in 1772 a cardinal point of its foreign policy. Had Poland still existed at the beginning of the nineteenth century, it would have become, to the great displeasure of its neighbors, an ally of Napoleon. Furthermore Poland would also have been ready to take sides against Russia, be it with Prussia, as was the case in 1790 and 1791, or with Austria. After all the mistreatment and humiliations the Poles had had to suffer from the Russian envoys and generals and from the soldiery, the possibility of sincere cooperation with Russia was hardly possible. A Poland which in principle was hostile was bound to be a danger for Russia. The first partition had to be followed by a final one.

Did Catherine perform a service to Russia by partitioning Poland? Certainly not, as later developments were to show, but she could not foresee the great change in the political thinking of Europe. She could not foresee that her policy, brilliant when judged by eighteenth-century principles, would be regarded by the next generation as a crime committed against a nation, as one of the most despicable misdeeds of immoral power politics. What is really tragic about the partition is that the succeeding generations not only of Poles but also of the partitioning powers had to live with a political reality that they believed dishonorable and criminal, but they were unable to change it because reparation of any sort involved incalculable dangers. Thus Catherine's cabinet masterpiece, the acquisition of an extensive territory without noteworthy military effort, became a heavy burden for later generations.

The Russian nationalists of the second half of the nineteenth century—both the more conservative Slavophiles (for example, S. M. Solovev) and the liberals (for example, N. I. Kareev)—condemned only the Prussians and Austrians. Catherine, they said, had almost completed "the gathering of the Russian land," and she could only be reproached for having given up Galicia to the Austrians. Politically, however, it was coincidence that the territories acquired by Russia had been at one time part of the Kievan Rus. It did not occur to Catherine to rationalize her policy of expansion by arguments of national unity. All subsequent justifications in later times merely reveal a bad conscience about the crimes committed by ancestors who very neatly separated politics and conscience.

The Attempts at a Reestablishment of the Polish State, 1795 to 1918

In 1795 it was most surely believed that any future writing about Russian imperialism and Poland would have to end with 1795 since Poland had ceased to exist in that year. But it was only for twelve years that there was no Polish state, and even earlier Poland was restored in the political intention of Alexander, the successor to the Russian throne: as early as 1796 he revealed to Prince Adam J. Czartoryski that he abhorred the partitions.[81] Alexander had close ties of friendship with the prince and made him his foreign adviser in 1802 and foreign minister in 1804. In this function Czartoryski also pursued Polish politics, presenting to the tsar projects for a restructuring of Europe in which a reestablished Polish state would play an important role.

In the case of a man as enigmatic and complex as Alexander I it can hardly be ascertained how much his decision to reassure the Poles in 1805 was influenced by the anxiety that they might throw themselves

The Growth of Russia in Europe

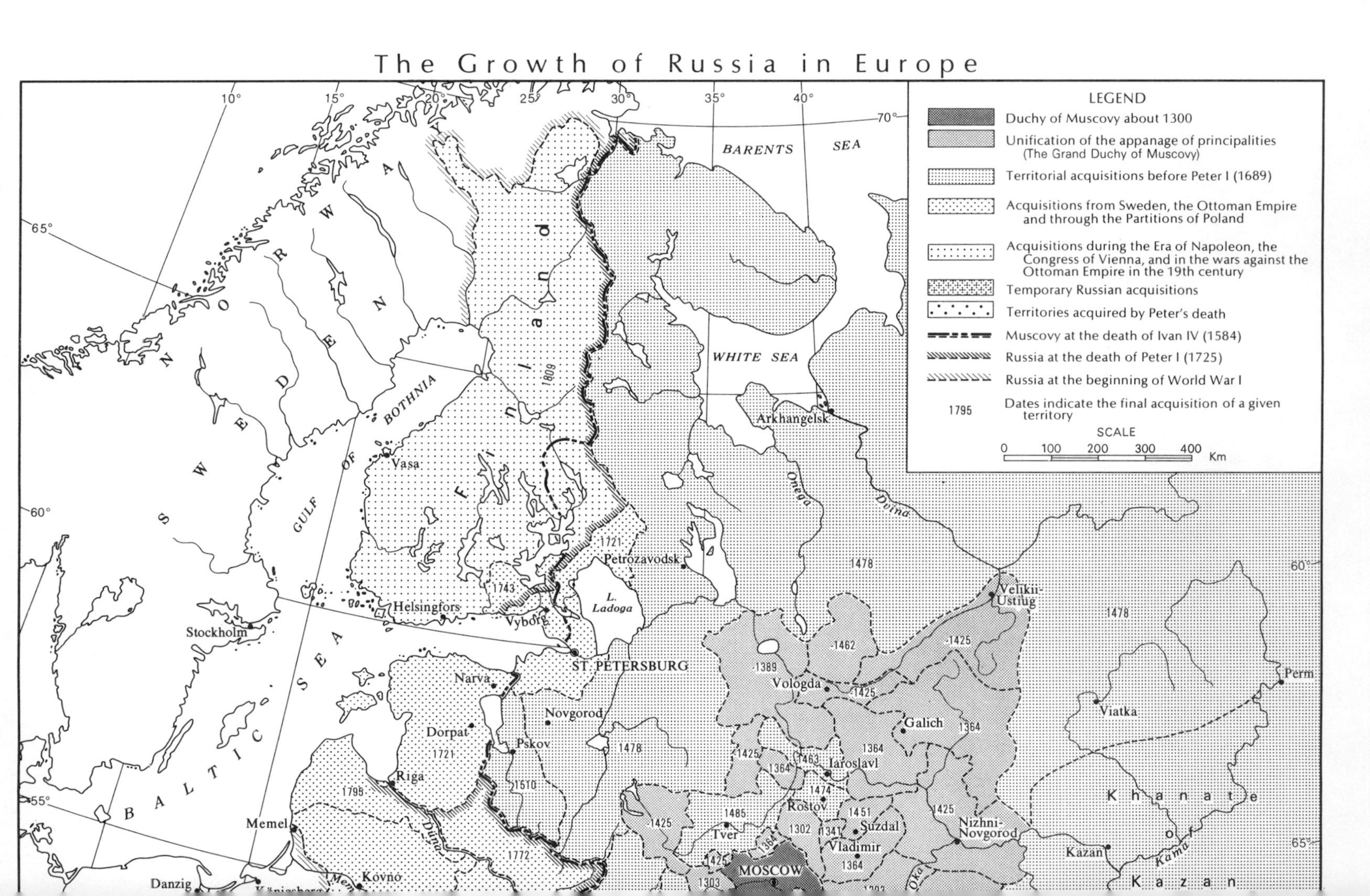

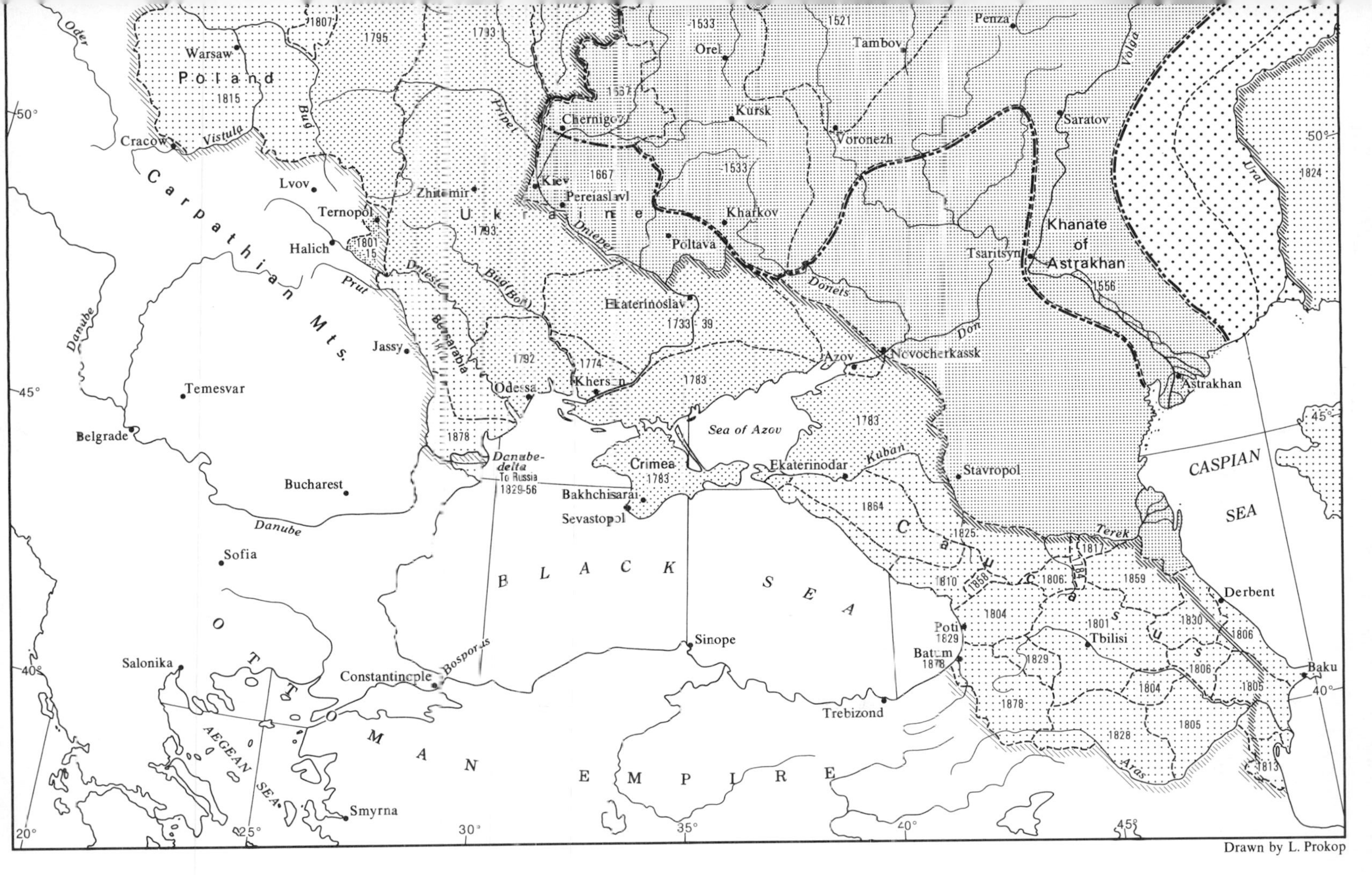

Poland
1815
Warsaw
Cracow
Vistula
Bug
Oder
Lvov
Ternopol
Halich
Carpathian Mts.
Prut
Jassy
Bessarabia
Danube
Temesvar
Belgrade
Bucharest
Sofia
Salonika
Constantinople
Bosporus
Smyrna
AEGEAN SEA
OTTOMAN EMPIRE
Ukraine
Zhitomir
Kiev
Pereiaslavl
1667
Chernigov
Pripet
Dnieper
Dniester
Bug(Bor)
Odessa
1792
1774
Kherson
Ekaterinoslav
1733–39
Poltava
Kharkov
Kursk
Orel
Voronezh
Tambov
Penza
Saratov
Volga
Ural
1824
Khanate of Astrakhan
Tsaritsyn
1556
Astrakhan
Donets
Don
Azov
Novocherkassk
1783
Sea of Azov
Crimea
1783
Bakhchisarai
Sevastopol
Danube delta
To Russia 1829–56
1878
BLACK SEA
Sinope
Trebizond
Ekaterinodar
Kuban
Stavropol
1864
Caucasus
1825
1817
1784
1806
1859
1810
1858
1804
1801
1830
1806
Derbent
Terek
Poti
1829
Batum
1878
Tbilisi
1829
1878
1806
1804
1805
1828
1805
1813
Aras
Baku
CASPIAN SEA
1795
1733
1793
1807
1801–15
1533
1521
1533
1533
50°
45°
40°
20°
25°
30°
35°
40°
45°
Drawn by L. Prokop

into Napoleon's arms, or how deep was his concern for Polish intentions of reestablishing the Polish state. It is, however, revealing that he resumed the Polish plans in 1811 and 1812, when the same danger threatened.[82] In the interim period, however, when Alexander half-heartedly cooperated with Napoleon, the Polish question was a constant disturbing factor. In 1807 Napoleon went so far as to offer the Polish crown to Alexander, but from these hands the gift carried a punishment.[83] Napoleon created the Grand Duchy of Warsaw out of the Prussian portion, but willingly left Bialystok (1807) and Ternopol (1809) to the Russians in order to make Alexander appear to the Poles as a man incessantly partitioning Poland.

After these unfortunate experiences it was only natural that Alexander I should strive for a more favorable settlement of the Polish question. After the defeat of Napoleon, to which Russia contributed the most, Alexander felt strong enough to demand at the Congress of Vienna the reestablishment of Poland in a personal union with Russia. Thus one of the old projects of Russian foreign policy reappeared in a new guise. Alexander pursued this objective with great zeal and determination, causing a considerable friction at the Congress.

He finally had to relinquish portions of Poland to Austria and Prussia. From the portion that was granted him from the territory of the Napoleonic Grand Duchy of Warsaw, Alexander I created a Kingdom of Poland with its own administration and army. He had himself crowned king of Poland and presided over the sessions of the Sejm. Why did Alexander, autocrat of the Russian empire, create this kingdom only out of the Austrian and Prussian shares? He originally must have had more far-reaching plans, for he had a vague passage referring to this inserted in the final agreement signed in Vienna: "S.M. Impériale se réserve de donner à cet Etat . . . l'extension intérieure qu'Elle jugera convenable." [84]

He reiterated this pledge until the end of his rule, even at sessions of the Sejm, but always in vague terms. Also he regulated the administration of Russia's western provinces (once the eastern sections of Poland-Lithuania) in such a way as to give the impression that he aimed to incorporate them into Poland.[85] He never took any steps to carry out such a plan and was very much aware of the real difficulty that was involved: the politically conscious Russians, namely the nobility, would not tolerate the loss of these territories.[86] This was the attitude not only of the conservatives of the older generation, who had grown up with hatred and contempt for the Poles, but also of the young liberals. A number of the Decembrists believed that the interests of Russia had to be safeguarded against the tsar, who wanted to give away parts of the empire to the Poles.[87]

Nicholas I, although he had no sympathy with Alexander's liberal experiments, had himself crowned king of Poland and presided over the Sejm. He, however, did not repeat the pledge,[88] and it was clear that he had not the slightest intention of incorporating the former eastern territories of Poland into the Polish kingdom. Political conditions in the kingdom were not quite as liberal as they should have been according to the constitution,[89] but they were more liberal than in the neighboring states and much more liberal than in Russia—a fact that could arouse the envy of the Russian liberals. In the 1820's Poland also took an economic upturn, but prosperity mattered less to the politically minded Poles than the honor and greatness of their nation. They wanted to be still less dependent on Russia, and above all they waited impatiently for the territorial extension of the kingdom.[90]

Nicholas was unwilling and unable to fulfill their wishes.[91] It was impossible to be at once a good tsar and a good king of Poland. The Poles helped the tsar out of the dilemma: in 1830 they rose against his rule and deposed him, but they were no match for the military might of Russia. As nationalism took possession of men's minds in this period, hatred grew between the nations, and even Pushkin wrote anti-Polish poems. These conditions enabled Nicholas to abrogate the liberal constitution. During the insurrection he thought for a while of partitioning Poland, that is, giving up portions of the kingdom to the Austrians and Prussians and turning what was left into a Russian province.[92] In 1846 he was in favor of incorporating Cracow into the Austrian empire. He did not want any more Polish subjects and treated them with deep mistrust, ruling the land with martial law and suppressing every political movement in the country.

The Polish émigrés took their revenge: they blackened his name all over Europe and provided generations of European liberals with a repulsive picture of the Russian nation. The damage to Russia, difficult though it is to measure, was certainly very great.

Nicholas' successor, Alexander II, again sought to find a *modus vivendi* by granting self-government to the Poles in the kingdom (1861 to 1863), but again a revolt broke out,[93] and again the hatred between the two nations flared up and made reasonable settlements impossible.

This time the penalties were still more severe: Poland was in effect reduced to a Russian province administered by Russians. The efforts at Russification started at this time were as onerous for the Poles as they were frustrating for the Russians.[94] The Russian statesmen wanted to ruin the restless nobility and base their rule on the peasants.[95] These plans likewise proved unsuccessful in the end.

The liberals of both nations were for a time convinced that a liberalization of political life in the Russian empire would ameliorate the wretched relationship between the nations and the intolerable conditions in the Polish kingdom; however, the Duma was no friendlier to the Poles than the tsar had been and it effected a further partitioning of Poland. Out of nationalist motives it sanctioned a reduction of the territory of the kingdom, which had no administration of its own anyhow.[96] Not even the measures aiming at Russification were revoked after 1905.

During World War I discussion was resumed concerning a rational solution of the Polish question, but only after the Russian army had been driven out of Poland by the Germans in December, 1916, did Russian statesmen suddenly develop a predilection for a united and free Poland. The conservatives even proposed the creation of a completely independent Polish state.[97] Two months later they had nothing more to propose. The Polish state arose without the help of Russia. There followed a brief period of weakness for both neighbors, and the Poles used the respite to begin rebuilding, at least partially, their old imperium. Being a small and weak empire between two much mightier ones, it was granted only a short life span.

The aversion fermented by the politically active penetrated the cultural life of both nations during the nineteenth century, and in the end the Poles and the Russians developed a national aversion for each other. In their nationalist exaggerations they went so far as to exclude each other from Slavdom. The Pan-Slavic Poles excluded the Russians from Europe on the grounds that they were Asiatics, and the Russians demanded purification from Latin contamination as a prior condition for admitting the Poles into the Slavic community.[98] The abyss ripped open at such great cost by the political quarrel will not be bridged without tremendous effort on both sides.

Translated by Otto J. Zitzelsberger

HENRY R. HUTTENBACH

The Ukraine and Muscovite Expansion

The relationship of the Ukraine to the Soviet Union has always been a cause of bitter dispute. Whether the membership of the Ukrainian Soviet Socialist Republic is voluntary or not is not only a question of academic interest to historians and political scientists but a profoundly personal matter to millions of Ukrainians at home and abroad who anguish over the degree of independence or at least autonomy they can legitimately claim as the largest national minority in the Soviet Union. Indicative of the dilemma are the various histories of the Ukraine [1] and of the Soviet Union which torturously strive to harmonize the all too obvious contradictions between the affirmation of a distinct Ukrainian history and its interpretation as an integral portion of Soviet history. Not only is the problem chronic and perennial but age old, dating back through imperial times to the period of Muscovite expansion in the sixteenth century when the history of the Russians became intertwined with that of Little Rus (as the Ukraine was then known) during its bloody struggle with Poland-Lithuania for supremacy in Eastern Europe, of which control of the southern steppe was the key.

If the relationship of the Ukraine to Russia is intellectually insoluble to the satisfaction of everyone (even to the uninvolved historian), the origins of the problem are readily discernible and identifiable and will serve as an introduction to the complexity of the controversy. Were it a simple matter of two distinct national groups, ethnically and culturally different, with two entirely separate historical antecedents, then the issue could be reduced to the conquest of one by the other. Unfortunately, as the history of the absorption of the Ukraine into the larger context of Muscovite and then into imperial Russia reveals, it is less the story of conquest and occupation than the meeting of two related peoples with a related past, each claiming to be the legitimate heir.

To understand the original historical causes of the Ukrainian-Russian problems, one must look back to the tenth, eleventh, and twelfth centuries, when a single civilization embraced the Dnieper and upper Volga valleys, an area approximately coinciding with Muscovy and the Orthodox provinces of Lithuania in the early fifteenth century (the time when Muscovy began to extend its influence into the Ukraine). Had the civilization of Kievan Rus maintained its political unity as a federation of principalities, it might have evolved into a modern nation state instead of suffering division into two segments as a result of foreign conquests.

Situated astride the forest and steppe regions from the Black Sea to the Gulf of Finland, Kievan Rus was vulnerable to nomadic assaults from the East sweeping across the wide plains of Siberia. In its rise to power, the Rus wrested control of the steppe from the Pecheneg tribes, only to be forced back again by the Polovtsi, whose persistent onslaughts brought on a major population shift westward and northeastward into the safety of the forests, almost splitting the people of Kievan Rus. The Mongol invasion that followed in the thirteenth century, even as it imposed a single political order on the Eastern Slavs, further aggravated this upheaval of the inhabitants in the Dnieper valley. Tens of thousands were killed or driven into slavery, while the survivors were left leaderless; the bulk of the upper classes who did not fall to the Mongols fled—princes, priests, and merchants. Before recovery could take place, the former Kievan territories were divided between two conquerors. Whereas the Rus princes of Galicia and Volynia failed to expel the Mongols in the second half of the thirteenth century,[2] the Lithuanians succeeded a century later. Under Grand Dukes Olgerd (1345 to 1377) and Vitovt (1392 to 1430), the Lithuanians won control of the Dnieper valley including the upper Donets basin,[3] leaving the rest of former Kievan Rus, the northeastern principalities, under Mongol rule. Thus did the Orthodox Slavs find themselves forced into two segments, the one Mongol and the other Lithuanian, under whose tutelage they were drawn on separate historical courses.

Over the course of the fifteenth century, Rus culture recovered. Kiev reemerged as a major economic center within Lithuania, and after 1458, with the appointment of a metropolitan, became the locus of the Orthodox Church in Lithuania. In the Northeast, Moscow became the capital of a rapidly expanding principality; and during the reign of Ivan III (1462 to 1505), Muscovy annexed and conquered all the remaining surrounding principalities. With equal aplomb, Ivan cast off the last vestiges of Mongol authority in 1480, declaring Muscovy to be an independent state. Then, turning to Lithuania, Ivan laid claim to its Orthodox territories as his rightful patrimony, and, before the end of his reign, effectively proved Muscovy's military superiority over Lithuania as a demonstration of the shifting balance of power.[4] Therewith began the slow but systematic advance of Muscovy westward and southward, a process that culminated three hundred years later in the reign of Catherine II (1762 to 1796) with the incorporation of virtually all of what had been Kievan Rus. This time, political power flowed out of the forest region of the North, where it was secure from the vicissitudes of the steppe.

During Muscovy's advance, however, the successors to the Rus in the South (east and west of Kiev) also evolved their own variants of political consciousness and cultural identity, which, although not entirely dissimilar from those emanating from Moscow, differed radically in that they focused upon Kiev, seeking to cast off Lithuanian and then Polish domination, even as Muscovy sought to become the unifying center of all the Orthodox. No wonder, then, that as these two movements converged (with Poland as a common enemy), each claiming to be the bearer of the heritage of Kievan Rus, the advance of Muscovy resembled either a conquest or a liberation depending on the vantage point. Even the Orthodox community in the Ukraine was divided in its opinion; for some, Muscovy spelled a guarantee against Polish landlordism and Catholicism, as well as protection against Tatar raids from the Crimea. For others, tsarist Muscovy loomed as a threat to their ecclesiastical autonomy, aristocratic status, and social traditions. Hence the complexity and the confusion over the interpretation of Muscovy's absorption of the Ukraine as Muscovy grew into a major European power. In fulfilling its national aspirations, did Muscovy violate the interests of the inhabitants of the Ukraine? A review of the sociopolitical evolution of the Orthodox peoples in Lithuania-Poland *vis-à-vis* Muscovite foreign policy may help to answer this question by explaining the contradictory and unbalanced forces that operated during the sixteenth, seventeenth, and eighteenth centuries between these two Slavic, Orthodox regions, which, but for the misfortunes of circumstance, might have shared a more harmonious past.

Muscovy and the Reawakening of the Ukraine

Though political independence came earlier in the Northeast, (thanks to the disintegration of the Mongol empire and the Golden Horde), desire for and attempts at political self-assertion were by no means lacking in the Orthodox part of Lithuania. The overlordship of the pagan Lithuanians was far less onerous than Muslim rule by the Mongols or, worse still, Catholic domination by Poland. Neither the princely aristocracy and church hierarchy (both of which proudly traced their lineage back to Kievan days) nor the fiercely independent peasantry felt threatened by their Lithuanian overlords. However, with the formation of a dynastic union between Lithuania and Poland in 1385 and the proclaiming of Catholicism as the only state religion in 1387, the rank and file of the Orthodox community became more and more anxious. Furthermore, princes and boiars (aristocrats) began to switch their allegiance to the grand duke of Muscovy, and, depending on their location, even transferred their entire estates to the principality of Muscovy in order to escape the political and religious prejudice that accompanied the incursion of Polish and Catholic influence into Lithuania.[5] Since this process could only fortify the belief in Moscow that the Orthodox in Lithuania preferred Muscovite rule over Lithuanian, it greatly affected the direction of Muscovite foreign policy, much of which was formulated with the advice of princes recently come from Lithuania.

Thanks primarily to these defections, Muscovy expanded southward into the crescent of the Desna River and the upper Donets, with the result that by the end of Ivan III's reign Muscovy's dominions protruded deep into the strategic steppe, allowing it to protect itself more readily from attacks out of the Crimea. Invasion from the Crimea was feared throughout the sixteenth century, compelling Muscovy to continue striving for control over the vast plains, if only because of security reasons.

Those Orthodox princes in Lithuania who were too far from Muscovy to profit from the mode of escape chosen by their peers near the border devised their own means of combating Catholic Lithuanian overlordship. The Catholic faction was increasingly determined to weaken Orthodox power. For example, in 1470, on the death of Prince Simon Olellkovich, no Orthodox prince was appointed to Kiev to replace Simon. Instead, the principality was dissolved in 1471 and replaced with a new administrative unit headed by an appointed *voevoda* (governor). In reaction, several Orthodox princes planned a rebellion to stamp out Polish influence in Lithuania and restore their aristocratic privileges. In 1481, three prominent Orthodox nobles, Princes Michael Olellkovich of Kiev, Ivan Iurievich Golshansky, and Fedor Ivanovich Belskii, plotted to assassinate King Casimir, replace him with Prince Michael,[6] and declare independence, while calling upon Muscovy to protect them against Polish interference.[7] But the conspiracy failed, forcing them to flee to Muscovy. Here Belskii became a leading voice in urging a drive against Lithuania and the conquest of all Orthodox territory, therewith adding their voices to those of their compatriots already joined with their estates to Muscovy.

Once again, in 1508, this time under the leadership of Prince Michael Glinsky, an Orthodox revolt broke out in Lithuania. Glinsky, who failed to protect his political status by converting to Catholicism, reconverted to Orthodoxy and rallied other princes to combat the Catholic oppression that was pushing them more and more to the political sidelines. On this occasion, no appeal was made to Muscovy; instead a call was made for the restoration of the old Kievan feudal federation. The autocratic Muscovite regime, so different from the Kievan institution, seemed less and less palatable as an alternative to the distasteful conditions forced on Lithuania by Catholic Poland. This insurrection also came to naught. Once again Muscovy received a wave of refugees, among them Prince Glinsky, whose family rapidly joined the inner circle of the court and agitated for a crusade against Lithuania and the reconstitution of Kievan Rus under Muscovite auspices. Politically, however, the future of this nobility rested on a fatal contradiction: on the one hand, they dreamed of a reconstituted Kievan Rus, a haven for their aristocratic privileges; on the other hand, the realization of their goal depended upon a centralized and autocratic Muscovy to expel Lithuania and Poland.

Throughout the sixteenth century, the Orthodox aristocratic secession movement in Lithuania gained little, despite occasional attempts to establish contact with antitsarist Muscovite boiars in the hope of winning support for the cause. For the most part, however, in the face of superior cultural forces, more and more Orthodox noblemen were attracted by the luster of Polish Renaissance society and, ultimately, by Catholicism itself in its Counter-Reformation form. Concurrently, discontent fermented in a new group, this time at the opposite end of the social spectrum, the peasantry.

Just as monarchy and Catholicism overwhelmed the Orthodox aristocracy, so did the institution of serfdom among the peasants. In the latter half of the fifteenth century Poland and Lithuania passed a series of regulations to safeguard the interests of landlords at the expense of the individual peasant and his lands. By 1500 the free *krestianin* (peasant) had officially become an *otchik* (a serf, or hereditary inhabitant of the estate).[8] Prompted to escape from the burdens of serfdom imposed by Catholic or Orthodox landlords, peasants by the hundreds and then by the thousands fled to the sparsely populated steppelands to the south and to the east bank of the Dnieper into the no man's land of the borderland—the Ukraine [9]—well beyond government control, there to mix with roaming Tatars or peasants. The most enterprising engaged in trade and developed a thriving though risky steppe economy, including farming, fishing, and cattle breeding, despite the threat of marauding Tatars and other brigands. Thus was born that phenomenon, the Cossack.[10]

The need for defense and the lure of booty encouraged the Cossacks to adopt a military organization led by an elected chieftain—the *otaman*. They fought Turk, Pole, and Muscovite with equal tenacity to maintain their semidemocratic existence in the rich farmlands of the steppe; and with similar lack of prejudice they fought for any one of the three powers if the reward was high enough. By the middle of the sixteenth century the Cossack had become an essential element in the balance of power in the Ukraine. And as Muscovy and Lithuania became locked in the long Livonian War, the security of their southern flank increasingly depended upon the role the Cossack played. Muscovy learned to respect the military prowess of the Cossack, but it also became increasingly suspicious of his reliability, recognizing the need to control him before reckoning on his assistance.

As early as the 1490's mercenary Cossack units under the command of Prince Bohdan Fedorovich Glinsky, *starosta* (military governor) of Cherkassy, fought on behalf of Lithuania against the Crimea to counteract Muscovite diplomacy [11] (whose bribes sought to direct the Crimean Tatars against Lithuania). The most successful of these expeditions took place in 1493.[12] Typically though, a generation later, Cossack mercenaries accepted the bribes of the khan of the Crimea and launched attacks upon Muscovy. Twice in the reign of Vasilii III (1505 to 1533), in 1515 and again in 1521,[13] large Cossack detachments led by one Ostap Dashkevich wreaked great damage on southern Muscovy.[14] So serious was Muscovy's concern over this growing menace along the southern frontier, a major foreign policy crisis was set off by the question of Cossack reliability in the reign of Ivan IV (1533 to 1584).

After conquering the Kazan khanate in 1552 and the Astrakhan khanate in 1554 (thereby gaining control of the Volga valley), Ivan IV decided on a war against Livonia to hammer out a Muscovite beachhead on the Baltic coast. His counselors favored first a war on the Crimean khanate in order to secure control of the steppelands and safeguard the vulnerable southern flank of Muscovy. Ivan, however, banked on the cooperation of the Cossacks. Under the leadership of Prince Dmytro Ivanovych Vyshnevetskyi, *starosta* of Cherkassy since 1551, these Cossacks had emerged as a potent force on the lower Dnieper. Vyshnevetskyi, recognizing the political potential of the Cossacks, had had himself elected *otaman*. Then he proceeded to exploit the fluidity prevailing in the steppeland to further his own vague ambitions. After failing to persuade the Sultan in Constantinople to accept his services, Vyshnevetskyi in true adventurous tradition offered his Cossack army to Muscovy in 1555 at the very moment of its foreign policy dispute. For large payments, Vyshnevetskyi agreed to harass the Crimean khanate and thereby free Ivan to launch his Baltic campaign. Ivan IV did begin this campaign in 1558, after Vyshnevetskyi had proved that Cossack expeditions could indeed curb Crimean interference.

The Muscovite-Cossack alliance lasted until 1561. During this time Vyshnevetskyi and his Cossacks fought side by side with Muscovite contingents. In 1556 he sailed down the Dnieper (over the objections of the Lithuanians, who sought to befriend the Crimeans);[15] in 1558 he set off down the Don where Ivan hoped to station Vyshnevetskyi permanently.[16] Vyshnevetskyi, however, did not wish to remain a mercenary indefinitely and decided to renew his services to Ivan on an annual basis, fighting in individual campaigns on the Livonian front until Ivan again began to insist that Vyshnevetskyi settle in Muscovy and swear allegiance to the tsar. Despite the promise of generous rewards, Vyshnevetskyi preferred his independence and returned to the steppe in 1561 to seek new adventures.[17] To strengthen his bargaining power, Vyshnevetskyi established his base camp on a large island beyond the cataracts in the lower Dnieper—hence the term Zaporozhian Cossacks as distinct from other Cossacks.

The construction of a permanent Cossack fortification radically altered the significance of the Cossacks in the steppeland. Since they controlled access and egress to the Dnieper River and were assured of a constant flow of supplies as well as abundant manpower, they were able to develop a flourishing economic base as a result of trade with Kiev. Moreover, the Sich, as the river stronghold became to be known, acquired political importance beyond its actual size (the Cossack force rarely numbered more than 6,000 men in the sixteenth century).[18] Given the precarious balance of power in the Ukraine due to the protracted war in the North between Muscovy and Lithuania, the Cossacks force could easily tip the balance of the war by either enhancing or curbing the Crimean khanate's ability to launch major attacks. It is not surprising that the farsighted Ivan IV tried to absorb the Cossacks into the Muscovite armies and that later Muscovite foreign policy constantly anticipated the necessity of taming the Cossacks to keep peace along the southern frontier. Cossackdom's dramatic growth and increasing independence from the time of Vyshnevetskyi to that of Khmelnytskyi a hundred years later, within the context of a weakening Poland, could only lead to collision between these two irreconcilable forces.

Despite Vyshnevetskyi's untimely death in 1563, the idea of the Sich survived to become the nucleus of a Cossack state with a peculiar social and political structure comprised of Polish and Rus ingredients and toughened by nomadic customs borrowed from the Tatars. Cossackdom was truly a steppe phenomenon, and its people were just as savage, warlike, and hardy as the nomads who had laid claim to the same steppelands in earlier centuries. The Sich became not only a trade center but a refuge for thousands of peasants in search of the rich soil and the freedom of the "Ukraina." The word steadily evolved from a descriptive term (borderland) to the proper name of a region (even though its boundaries were vague and undefined). As the population swelled and the coffers of the Sich filled, it became increasingly necessary to protect the community from Polish attempts to extend estates and reclaim run-away serfs as well as from bloody Tatar raids for booty.

By the turn of the century, the Sich had developed recognizable organizational features and traditions. Elections were held frequently, and the post of *kish otaman* (senior chieftain) or *koshovyi* fell more and more to the richest—more often than not to a man with education and an aristocratic background. Membership in the ranks of a Cossack *polk* (regiment) became restricted to a small number of experienced fighting men. Enriching themselves with booty after successful battles, these men purchased large tracts of land, and thus there arose a landowning Cossack class on whose holdings labored peasant Cossacks who had fled serfdom in Poland-Lithuania and whose safety increasingly depended upon this Cossack upper class. Only occasionally, in emergencies when the existence of the Sich was threatened, were additional regiments mustered; these were composed of peasant Cossacks but their officer cadre came from the landowning class—the *starshyna* (elders).

By 1594 a standing army of 6,000 handpicked men with a naval contingent of about sixty ships and the latest artillery weapons made up the heart of the Cossack army of the Sich, an army whose primary purpose was to preserve the independence of the Sich and to engage in whichever battles the Rada (Council of Elders) determined; in other words, the Cossack state's loyalty was to itself first, and to the highest bidder, whether Poland, the Crimea, or Muscovy, second. In the latter half of the sixteenth century, Poland had actively tried to harness the Cossack Sich to its purposes as a means of checking the Ottoman Empire in Moldavia and keeping Muscovy off balance with a second front in the South. To win the loyalty of some Cossacks, Poland offered permanent recognition to the richest by giving them legal status as "registered" Cossacks, as against the thousands of other Cossacks it looked upon as runaways and renegades.[19] Thus began a calculated policy to divide the Cossacks along socioeconomic lines in the hope of gaining greater control over them.

Severe tensions, however, developed between Poland and the Cossacks. Systematically, Poland extended its influence into the steppe by annexing large tracts of land and granting them to Polish landlords. This triple encroachment of the Polish aristocracy, Catholicism, and serfdom was bound to lead to a major confrontation since all three were antithetical to the various strata of the Cossack community. In 1591 the first anti-Polish uprising exploded in the steppe.[20] Its immediate cause was Poland's failure to pay its Cossack mercenaries; deeper causes, however, soon became apparent. Under the leadership of Kristof Kosinsky, a bankrupt Polish landowner, Cossack units marauded at will through Poland's southern provinces as far as Volynia, gathering plunder and triggering mass peasant uprisings. The rebellions spread the Cossack movement into new regions and led to the formation of new Cossack nuclei. For a year and a half Kosinsky wreaked havoc and threatened to keep southern Poland in chaos.[21] He was stopped by a Polish-sponsored army which, ironically, was recruited and led by Prince Constantine Ostrozhskyi, a leader in the revival of Orthodoxy in the Ukraine and elsewhere in Lithuania. Muscovy, while officially remaining neutral, nevertheless secretly sent supplies to keep the rebellion alive, hoping to kill two birds with one stone—weakening both the Cossacks and Poland.[22]

In 1594 the expanding Cossack movement rose in rebellion once again. This time it spread deep into the west bank as far as the province of Podolia. The uprising was led by Severyn Nalyvaiko, who, in alliance with the Zaporozhian Cossacks, launched an expedition against Moldavia. Here Orthodox peasants met them with enthusiasm and flocked back to the steppe in droves.[23] For almost two years Nalyvaiko roamed at will, setting off a social rebellion wherever he chose. In 1597, after careful preparation, a Polish army moved to suppress and eradicate the Cossack phenomenon, but the more ruthlessly it fought the more widespread became the peasant response to Cossackdom. Countless numbers migrated to the steppe, moving ever deeper, out of range of the Polish authorities.

By this time, yet another element of dissent had awakened in the Orthodox population, and eventually it forged strong links with the Cossack movement. Over the decades, Catholicism had become a serious threat to the existence of Orthodoxy. Poland, acting as the Eastern spearhead of the Counter-Reformation and assisted by the Jesuits, camouflaged its expansionist ambitions with an all-out crusade against Orthodoxy; the campaign challenged not only the Orthodox citizenry in Lithuania but the Cossacks and Muscovy as well. Partly at issue was the right of the monarchy to appoint the Orthodox hierarchy. More often than not, appointments went to loyal noblemen who coveted the rich revenues from church fiefs, with the result that the Orthodox hierarchy slowly became estranged from the communicants.[24] The bulk of the Orthodox population thus began to look increasingly for new spiritual and political leadership (large numbers of the Orthodox upper classes having taken the radical step of converting to Catholicism).

Threatened by this cultural decline, several devout Orthodox princes joined many wealthy merchants to spark an Orthodox renaissance by forming *bratstva* (brotherhoods), one in each of the leading Orthodox towns, where the numbers of Uniates and converts grew alarmingly.[25] The *bratstva* quickly multiplied as laymen enthusiastically joined in order to strengthen their religious identity. Led by Princes Ostrozhskyi and Khodkevych, the *bratstvo* movement spread from Lvov to Kiev.[26]

The *bratstva*, however, were politically too weak to curb both the direct advances of Catholicism and its indirect ones in the form of the Uniate Church. The Union of Brest in 1596 gave legal sanction to Uniate Orthodoxy but formally condemned independent Orthodoxy, thereby creating a profound cleavage in the Orthodox ranks.[27] Thereafter, the divided Orthodox community in the Ukraine turned into two warring camps; some thought of turning to Muscovy for aid, whereas others looked to the Cossacks.[28] Both sources were questionable. Muscovy, weakened by the long Livonian War, could only offer token assistance, and in the long run represented a social threat to the aristocracy. More important, from the point of view of the Orthodox hierarchy, Muscovy had been ideologically unreliable ever since the reforms of 1551. As for the Cossacks, their lack of political discrimination throughout the rebellions against Catholics and Orthodox diluted the enthusiasm for them.

In the ensuing half century, Cossackdom and Muscovite foreign policy matured sufficiently to bring them face to face. The Cossack movement, as it became more and more a separatist movement, was a threat to both Poland and Muscovy. During the Time of Troubles (1605 to 1613), Cossack forces from the Dnieper participated in the Polish invasion of Muscovy in support of the second false Dmitrii, whose forces invaded Muscovy in 1608. A second Cossack attack came in 1610 when Cossack regiments assisted the Polish army to invade Muscovy and occupy Moscow. Although Muscovy managed to arrange an accommodation between itself and the Don Cossacks, it could not do so with Cossacks in the Polish sphere. Pressure to solve the Polish problem mounted, not only because Poland was an age-old enemy but because a defeat of Poland would permit control of the Cossacks to the southwest. After the trauma of the Time of Troubles Muscovy never again trusted the Cossacks.

Meanwhile, the Cossacks hoped to wrest major concessions from the Poles in return for military assistance, namely, an increase in the number of registered Cossacks, more autonomy for the Sich, curtailment of Polish landlordism in the steppe, and greater freedom for the Orthodox Church. To attain these ends, Koshovyi Petro Konashevych Sahaidachnyi in 1618 joined the Polish army with a Cossack army of 20,000 highly disciplined men in an attack on Muscovy. Poland, however, refused to increase the ranks of the registered Cossacks, whereupon Sahaidachnyi raised the banner of rebellion in 1620. Aware of his limitations, he negotiated with Muscovy, but it wisely ignored his offer to swear allegiance to Tsar Michael Romanov (1613 to 1645), being unwilling to wage a war against a stronger Poland solely in Cossack interests.[29] However, Muscovy did send some supplies in the hope of keeping the rebellion alive. Sahaidachnyi continued his rebellion and entered Kiev in company with the visiting Patriarch of Constantinople in order to win support from the city population by giving his uprising the aura of a liberation movement.[30] The city, however, only gave him a mixed and cautious welcome: the Uniate congregation saw in him a threat to their newly won status, and the Orthodox were uncertain whether they should cast their lot with the Cossacks or with Muscovy, even though Sahaidachnyi helped restore to power the Orthodox hierarchy in Kiev. More important, the Orthodox aristocracy had severe reservations about the political impact of the Cossacks, especially the *starshyna,* whom they saw as a challenge to their landowning status. Many of the *starshyna* were minor aristocrats who had gained considerable power and prestige as Cossacks, especially if they were registered Cossacks.

In the following years, the various elements that made up the anti-Polish movement in the Orthodox ranks became even more divergent and complex. In 1624 the Orthodox hierarchy, fearing that it would soon be overwhelmed by the Uniate Church, finally sent a delegation to Moscow, thus appealing for help from the only independent Orthodox capital.[31] Muscovy, although, sympathetic to these requests, was helpless; not only was it unable to risk a war but it needed every year of the peace provided by the fourteen-year truce of Deulino

(1618) to revamp and modernize its armies. A year later, in 1625, the Cossacks once again burst into rebellion, but were severely repressed at enormous expense by the superior Polish army. Thus, Orthodoxy and Cossackdom, lacking outside help, suffered severe setbacks and were hard pressed to find ways of survival.

Luckily, Poland's increasing involvement in the Thirty Years War saved both from the might of Poland. Within the ranks of Orthodoxy, the *bratstvo* movement spawned a second stage of cultural revival led by Petro Mohyla (Movila in its original Moldavian form). Mohyla, as *arkhimandryt* of the influential Crypt Monastery in Kiev since 1627, envisioned a restoration of Orthodoxy in Poland through the development of a body of monks fortified with a superior education obtained in schools such as the one he founded in 1631—the future Kievan Theological Academy. Its learned monks not only aroused the envy of the Jesuits but later attracted the attention of Muscovy, to which several of its best graduates were sent.[32] As early as 1632, with the crowning of Władysław IV, the new Polish monarch, the conditions for Mohyla's dreams seemed to come true with the announcement of the recognition of Orthodoxy as an acceptable religion in Poland (a concession to keep harmony within the troubled Polish kingdom). Some of the Orthodox Polish hierarchy preferred this solution to the alternative of subordinating itself to the Moscow patriarchy, whose Orthodoxy it looked upon as less cultured and semiheretical.[33]

That same year, Muscovy and Poland again engaged in a war in which the Cossacks participated in considerable numbers on the side of Poland. Finally several regiments of registered Cossacks under the command of Hetman (general) Orandarenko tipped the battle in Poland's favor at Smolensk. On their own, however, in the south in Severia, the Cossacks were unable to defeat the Muscovite forces. This was a clear indication of the balance of power that would dictate events in the middle of the century.

For the next two decades, Muscovy carefully enlarged its armies and reformed them along European lines with the aid of hundreds of foreign officers. During the same years, Poland pressed deeper into the steppe, imposing serfdom on the peasants on the left bank of the Dnieper and at the same time building fortifications in the cataract region of the Dnieper River to contain the restless Zaporozhian Cossacks. To conduct its wars against Sweden, Poland registered more Cossacks and granted them privileged status as landlords, thereby aggravating the social ills that divided the Cossacks into landlords and peasants, each with his own sociopolitical orientation. Increasing numbers of these registered Cossacks were stationed along the frontier to protect Poland in the event of peasant uprisings and Cossack rebellions (by those who had been refused registered status) and to guard against Crimean and Turkish attacks. Their most important achievement was in curbing the many Cossack uprisings of the late 1620's and early 1630's; the generous reward they received for their services tended to tie them closely to Poland.

In 1637 a major Cossack uprising led by Pavlo (known popularly as Pavliuk) sought to push back Polish control, but his forces were put down by a combination of Polish contingents and registered Cossack units, who, since 1600, had grown from six to sixteen regiments of 6,000 men each. On the left bank of the Dnieper, thousands of peasants rose in rebellion in response to Pavliuk's call,[34] only to face brutal punishment from the Polish authorities. The Polish victory triggered an eastward migration into Don Cossack territory, and the Sich issued a call for an alliance with the Don Cossacks to the east. Hundreds and then thousands of Cossacks and their families moved to the Don and even into southern Muscovy seeking protection from the hated Poles. Otaman Iatsko Ostrianyn was one of those who chose Muscovy and was immediately recruited into the Muscovite border defense system.[35] Here he and his men were under strict order not to engage in independent action for fear of inciting the Turks. The necessity of placing the Cossacks under tsarist rule became more pressing with Turkish demands that the Cossacks be controlled (in the Sultan's mind the Cossacks, whether from the Don or from the Dnieper area, were merely an extension of Muscovy). Thus, any autonomy exercised by the Cossacks against the Turks could not be tolerated either by Poland or by Muscovy. As Muscovite power increased in relation to Poland's the greater became Muscovy's fear of jeopardizing a carefully developed foreign policy which rested on Turkish neutrality.

Muscovy and the Cossack State

It was in the middle of the seventeenth century that the balance of power between Muscovy and Poland altered radically. By this time Cossackdom had grown into a fully matured separatist movement that threatened to break up the Polish kingdom. Within its ranks were members of the upper and lower aristocracy who had not yet converted to Catholicism. Besides, strong support came from the city-based merchants, a class which looked increasingly to the Cossacks for its economic prosperity, since the bulk of its trade was with the Cossack-controlled steppe. Thus, as soon as the Cossacks had recovered from their failures in 1637 and 1638, they began to look for a new occasion to force Poland to grant them further concessions. Bolstered by their allies in the towns, the Cossacks sensed that the tide was turning in their favor, especially since increasing unrest among the oppressed peasantry signaled the possibility of another major rebellion.[36] As rumors spread that Poland would register more Cossacks in preparation for war against Turkey, the Cossacks felt that the time was ripe to extract a high price for their military services to Poland. All that was lacking was a charismatic personality around whom the disparate Cossack ranks could rally. In 1647, such a man appeared, the newly elected *koshovyi* of the Sich, Bohdan Khmelnytskyi. It was Khmelnytskyi who linked Cossack separatism to Muscovy and, thereby, provided Muscovy with the fateful opportunity to involve itself officially in the political affairs of the Ukraine.

Impatient with Polish promises, suspicious of Poland's real intentions, and disillusioned by Polish intrigue among the various strata of the Cossacks, Khmelnytskyi adopted forceful measures, beginning with the fortification of the Sich and calling for an alliance with the Don Cossacks. Khmelnytskyi successfully approached the Crimean khanate [37] for assistance against the Poles. The following year, Khmelnytskyi launched the expected uprising and managed to bring the majority of the registered Cossacks over to his side. Within two months, exploiting the death of Poland's king, Khmelnytskyi proved himself master of Poland's southern provinces. He lost no time in demanding negotiations with Poland to recognize the autonomy of the Cossack territories, although these were to remain within the framework of the Polish kingdom.

He was compelled to caution because of the extreme social tensions within his own domain which pitted peasant Cossacks against the registered and landowning Cossacks. Khmelnytskyi's power rested upon the élite Cossack group, and he could ill afford to sacrifice their services in exchange for the loyalty of the Cossack masses, since their armies alone were no match for Polish strength. Here, in a nutshell was the dilemma of the Cossack movement: profound sociopolitical conflicts doomed its homogeneity as a protonational movement. Furthermore, severe religious divisions wracked both the Cossack and the non-Cossack population in the Ukraine, setting Orthodox against Uniate, and this dissension was later compounded by disagreement over the need to turn to Muscovy.

In the flush of victory on November 17, 1648, as Khmelnytskyi marched into Kiev, there to be hailed by the entire population as its liberator, none of these problems seemed insoluble; but within a few days, as Khmelnytskyi tried to stabilize his position, he was forced to recognize the inherent contradictions in Cossackdom: the registered Cossacks desired a Cossack state based on landownership, whereas the rank-and-file Cossacks looked more to the democratic Cossack society in the Don as their ideal. Confronted with a breakdown of negotiations with the Poles, Khmelnytskyi sought assistance from Muscovy[38] (which had just codified its serf laws) and called upon the peasant Cossacks to assist him in fending off the Polish armies, even though he had discussed only the interests of the registered landowning Cossacks in his talks with the Poles. His proclamation of 1649 gathered most Cossacks to his banner, persuading them that a satisfactory future state could be established under his rule. By the end of the year, a compromise treaty (satisfactory to no one) had been signed with the Poles, with the result that new tensions broke out over religious matters. The Polish had refused to dissolve the Uniate Church, but some of the Uniate membership feared reprisals if forced to return to the Orthodox fold in areas where, according to the treaty provisions, Polish authority would be meager.

In preparation for a renewed struggle, Khmelnytskyi recruited a new army in which he permitted considerably larger numbers of Cossacks than agreed upon in the treaty with Poland (this satisfied the demands from his lower ranks). Khmelnytskyi triggered more trouble when he sought the help of Muscovy, for the Orthodox hierarchy feared that a transfer to the patriarchy of Moscow would cause it to lose the autonomy it presently enjoyed as part of the patriarchy of Constantinople.[39] Furthermore, it abhorred the ritual and textual deviations that prevailed in the Muscovite Church (the corrective Nikon Reforms had not yet begun). Yet Khmelnytskyi was thrown into Muscovy's arms when the khan of the Crimea demanded that the Cossacks attack Muscovy as a price for his support against Poland. Such was the situation when war broke out between Poland and the Cossacks in 1651; the Crimea provided only token help and then only upon the prodding of the Sultan. A year later, a military stalemate forced Khmelnytskyi to approach Tsar Alexis and to begin negotiations with Muscovy.

In 1653, the Muscovite assembly, the Zemsky Sobor, agreed to open talks with Khmelnytskyi. The debate revealed how great was the concern of Muscovite authorities over opening official negotiations with the Cossacks, despite Muscovy's territorial ambitions westward towards Smolensk and southward into the steppe. It was clear that Muscovy would not favor Cossack independence but merely autonomy under Muscovite supervision; an independent Cossack state would run counter to Muscovy's interests. Thus, extreme caution guided Muscovy from the start: although determined to pry the Cossack provinces away from Poland, it was equally determined not to let them remain independent to become a new enemy for Muscovy.

Point by point, Cossack-Muscovite relations had to be hammered out before the tsar agreed to become the protector of the Cossack territories and the Cossacks to swear allegiance to him.[40] Suspicion existed on both sides. When Khmelnytskyi demanded that the tsar first promise not to violate Cossack privileges, he was told vaguely that the tsar never broke his word. Forced to ensure the survival of Cossackdom against the Poles, whatever the cost, Khmelnytskyi's negotiators in 1654 signed the treaty of Pereiaslav, swearing allegiance to Tsar Alexis, without having received satisfactory assurances from Moscow as to the status of their autonomy.

Thus the uneven balance of power was already perceptible in the Cossack-Muscovite agreement; but whatever the written terms, Muscovite power was overwhelmingly superior and ultimately imposed its will. Take, for example, the eleven *Articles* issued by Tsar Alexis to appease the Cossacks.[11] For the Cossacks, the *Articles* served as a Bill of Rights which they frequently cited in their appeals to Moscow about breaches of tradition and organization perpetrated by Muscovite authorities. In fact, the *Articles* clearly denied the Cossacks any freedom in foreign policy, and thus placed them legally within the Muscovite empire. It was to be expected that the Cossacks would violate this clause as Muscovy replaced Poland as their foremost enemy. In the final analysis, the union with Muscovy, though technically between equals, was really between a large, well-organized, and dynamic state and an internally divided and much weaker political entity. In signing of the treaty of Pereiaslav, the Cossacks invited Muscovite penetration, by the military and by officialdom. And Muscovy did not hesitate to enter the region to secure its southwestern borders, to impose its will upon the Cossacks, and to curb the peasant rebellions originating in the steppe.

Equally important, the 1654 agreement was a betrayal of the interests of the peasant Cossacks. Once autonomy seemed assured, Khmelnytskyi began to give shape to the new Cossack society. Although he favored a flexible policy with respect to the number permitted into the ranks of the military Cossacks in order to appease the peasant masses and to guarantee himself a large army, the landowning Cossacks demanded a freezing of the ranks in order to entrench themselves as the new aristocracy in the new Cossack state.[42] For the lower classes this meant nothing other than the imposition of serfdom.

With respect to Muscovite-Polish relations, the treaty of Pereiaslav upset the balance of power and set the stage for the decline of Poland as a major East European power, leaving Muscovy as the major power in the region. Only the young Cossack state stood between Muscovy and control of the vast riches of the Ukraine.

Internally, the Cossack state immediately suffered from its social contradictions: whereas peasants exercised their "right" to seize former estates, including church lands (both Catholic and Orthodox), the Cossack élite tried to establish their claim over these lands as their "rightful" inheritance.[43] Thus revolutionary energies clashed with conservative interests. Khmelnytskyi's task was to preside over this confrontation of contrary forces. Wary of losing his popularity, Khmelnytskyi claimed that the tsar had given him the power to set the numbers of the *starshyna,* but he was contradicted by senior Cossacks who claimed that the tsar had fixed their numbers. Both sides regarded Moscow as the final arbiter and guarantor of Cossack internal tranquillity.

For the first few years, however, a Cossack administration managed to rule its Ukrainian provinces successfully, with much of the sociopolitical discontent subdued by the granting of considerable self-rule on the local and village level. It was immediately apparent that the natural wealth of the Ukraine benefited people in all walks of life, so that even the Poles began to make overtures for a reconciliation, especially when the war with Muscovy swung against them in Belorussia. The mood of the upper-class Cossacks as well as the negotiations with other states conducted sub rosa by Khmelnytskyi (in obvious defiance of his agreement with Muscovy) suggested to Poland that the Cossack leadership was by no means permanently bound to Moscow. The campaign mounted against the Poles by Khmelnytskyi in 1655 lacked conviction, and by 1657, when Muscovy and Poland discussed peace in the face of a common enemy (Sweden) without consulting Khmelnytskyi, the first signs of discontent between Moscow and Kiev became visible.

News of the impending Muscovite-Polish agreement met with divided response. To simplify an immensely complicated situation, Khmelnytskyi decided to pursue the war against Poland independently of Moscow. He allied himself with Cossack forces that sprang up in Podolia and planned to join the armies of Sweden and Prince Rákóczi of Transylvania (a Swedish-backed candidate for the Polish throne) in the hope of expanding his control over adjacent Polish territory.[44] As soon as the peasant Cossacks in the army heard that they were engaged in a war against Poland rather than against the Tatars (as Khmelnytskyi had falsely led them to believe), a mutiny broke out in the Cossack ranks, in part because of their consternation at having unwittingly broken their oath to the tsar, and they began to look upon their officers with great suspicion and antagonism. As Khmelnytskyi's prestige sank and his state threatened to disintegrate, this first great Cossack leader died, leaving behind a civil war rather than a united state. Poland took the opportunity to reestablish its influence in the Ukraine by offering guarantees to the *starshyna* in return for their services. Faced with the threat of revolutionary overthrow, the *starshyna* complied, recognizing that the post-Khmelnytskyi period was against them.

Out of the political vacuum following Khmelnytskyi's death emerged a new leader, Ivan Vyhovskyi, a vocal anti Muscovite who had himself elected at a meeting of the Rada at which neither the pro-Muscovite Cossacks nor representatives from the Zaporozhian Sich were present. The latter rallied around Iakiv Barabash, in opposition to Vyhovskyi. Immediately, Vyhovskyi sought a Tatar alliance to counteract the Sich, a move the Dnieper Cossacks promptly communicated to the tsar.[45] At the same time, Vyhovskyi purged his ranks of any *starshyna* who were opposed to an alliance with Poland. In the meanwhile he ignored the claims of Khmelnytskyi's son Iurii, around whom rallied the bulk of the unregistered Cossacks. Others, near Poltava, rallied around Colonel M. Pushkar, who remained pro-Moscow. The Sich Cossacks, together with Pushkar's Cossacks, fended off Vyhovskyi's efforts to suppress them and thereby maneuvered to offset the alliance with Poland by forcing him to swear allegiance to Moscow (though this did not stop his secret negotiations with Poland). At the same time, Vyhovskyi plotted with the Crimean khan to attack Muscovy in order to remove the Muscovite garrisons established in the Ukraine since the treaty of Pereiaslav. Unable to quell the uprising of the peasants, Vyhovskyi attacked the rebels, whose base was Poltava, and, with the help of the Tatars, inflicted dreadful punishment upon the peasants.[46] Survivors fled by the thousands into the interior, eastward, while Vyhovskyi consolidated his position by signing the treaty of Hadiach with Poland in 1658, according to which Russia (the Cossack area) would be an equal partner in the revamped Kingdom of Poland.[47] For Muscovy, this new move to reestablish Poland in the Ukraine was intolerable.

Muscovy did not have to wait long to seize the initiative in rectifying matters, for Poland provoked a second war with Muscovy, this time bolstered by a sizable Cossack army. Vyhovskyi took the opportunity to reconquer the left bank of the Dnieper and, along with the Tatars, again decimated the rebellious peasant population of the Ukraine steppelands; however, the contagion of rebellion spread into his own ranks and forced him to flee. As for Muscovy, the episode had cost it severe losses.

In Vyhovskyi's place appeared a compromise leader, Iurii Khmelnytskyi, who was elected with Muscovite supervision; he briefly reconciled the pro- and anti-Muscovite factions among the Cossacks (who tended to be situated on the left and right banks of the Dnieper, respectively). The resulting treaty, though it did not resolve the problem of disunity within the ranks of the Cossacks, strongly entrenched the Muscovite military presence throughout the Cossack provinces. Upon Muscovy's insistence, peasant rights were protected, whereas the authority of the registered Cossacks was curbed.[48] By the time the war with Poland ended with the treaty of Andrusovo in 1667,[49] Muscovy had not only firmly established itself on the left bank of the Dnieper but, to boot, captured the prize city, Kiev, as well as gained ironclad assurance from Poland that it would never again challenge Muscovy's ambitions on the left bank. Thus, Cossack independence had been abolished, and the Muscovite supremacy was assured.

Muscovy's Absorption of the Ukraine

After the peace of Andrusovo, half the Ukraine found itself officially under Muscovite control. So began an era of rapid consolidation of Muscovite authority designed to eradicate the separatist tendencies that had arisen in the Ukraine over the past one hundred and fifty years. The policy of Iurii Khmelnytskyi (who had risen against Muscovy in 1663) and the Muscovite victory over the Poles on the left bank of the Dnieper in 1664 suggested the future course. Stability in the newly conquered regions, it was reasoned, would only come with the complete absorption of the Cossacks into the Muscovite administrative and defensive systems. The Cossacks, in Moscow's view, were neither reliable nor capable of maintaining order within their ranks. Whatever its territorial ambitions, Muscovy saw no alternative but to oversee the life of the Ukraine. The Ukrainian revolt against its *voevoda* in 1666 gave Moscow all the more reason to plant itself firmly in the Ukraine. At the same time, apprehension that the Stenka Razin peasant revolt would spread to the Ukraine prompted Muscovy to consolidate its power as soon as the partition of the Ukraine had been agreed upon with Poland.

The guiding mind of Muscovite policy towards the Ukraine was Afanasii Ordyn-Nashchokin, and he was succeeded in 1671 by Artamon Sergeevich Matveev. In their estimation, the left bank had to be sealed off from the separatist influences coming from the right bank, among them those that had encouraged Hetman Ivan Brukhovetskyi to lead an anti-Muscovite rebellion in 1668. To begin with, according to the Hlukhiv agreement of 1669, Muscovy increased its large military garrisons in the towns of the Ukraine, and, correspondingly, it limited the number of registered Cossacks to 30,000.[50] The reasoning behind this (apart from securing the internal stability of the Ukraine) was that the threat of war with Turkey called for a strong defense line and a reliable military force in the South. At the same time, tsarist officials weeded out disloyal elements among the Cossacks who might engineer future rebellions. One such was Hetman Demian Mnohohrishnyi, who, through the cooperation of Cossacks loyal to the tsar, was arrested and sent to Moscow; here he was tried and exiled to Siberia in 1672. The same year, Cossacks on the left bank were again ordered not to engage in any foreign relations and warned not to shelter any runaway serfs from Muscovy.[51]

While the military secured Muscovy's position along the left bank, diplomats sought to win over the Cossacks on the right bank. In Ivan Mazepa they found a loyal agent who kept Muscovy informed of the many anti-Muscovite plots hatched by Hetman Peter Doroshenko, the flamboyant head Cossack on the right bank. Furthermore, Muscovy tried to cultivate the sympathies of the Zaporozhian Cossacks, some of whom anticipated incursions of the Turks, for Muscovy calculated that the Turks would soon become their mutual enemy. By 1675 plans had been laid for a major campaign against the Crimea in which troops from Muscovy were aided by the entire Cossack world, including those from the Don region. After much delay and hesitation, the expedition ended with a show of force that extracted a pledge of loyalty from Doroshenko in 1676. This interference in what the Turks considered their sphere of influence greatly increased the danger of war with Turkey, and in 1677, even as the Turks sought to restore their influence on the right bank with the assistance of the Zaporozhian Cossacks (who feared Doroshenko), a Muscovite army consisting primarily of loyal Cossacks inflicted its first defeat upon a Turkish army, thereby demonstrating the dramatic rise of Muscovite military power in the Ukraine. It was now only a question of time before Muscovy would become the undisputed master of the entire Ukraine. For the time being though, neither Muscovy nor Turkey was interested in a showdown over the right bank, each having concerns elsewhere, Turkey in the Balkans and Muscovy in the Baltic (where its goal of reaching the coast was still unfulfilled). For the moment, both sides were content to let small Cossack units conduct raiding parties and continue the internecine struggle that devastated the region but weakened the Cossack movement considerably.[52]

Although the peasantry suffered terribly, the bulk of the *starshyna* who served Muscovy loyally emerged rather quickly as a wealthy and privileged class. By the end of the century, in the reign of Peter the Great, this group had become a hereditary class profiting immensely from huge land grants acquired from the state. Instead of discouraging them, Muscovy saw fit to support this élite group as a logical extension of its own social system to achieve effective control of the peasantry. As for the aristocracy in the Ukrainian cities, they too received privileged treatment and administrative assignments (though these were largely in central Muscovy where they soon exerted considerable cultural influence).

Similarly, numerous churchmen who graduated from the respected Kievan Academy were given high appointments in the Orthodox hierarchy, and all became staunch spokesmen for the rule of Muscovy. Eminent theologians, such as Epifany Slavinetsky, Dmitry Rostovsky, and Simeon Polotsky, brought superior scholarship into the Muscovite hierarchy. Polotsky, a product of Mohyla's Academy, had come to Moscow as early as 1644 and founded the school of the Zaikonospassky Monastery; its graduates became distinguished servants of the Muscovite government bureaucracy. All these men encouraged the Ukrainian Orthodoxy to find shelter under a Muscovite roof (though later in life Polotsky expressed some qualms). The most eloquent contributor to Muscovite expansionist theory was Archbishop Theofan Prokopovych. Though he had been a Uniate, he became a fervent apologist for Peter the Great. As an unofficial Ukrainian spokesman, however, Prokopovych hoped to preserve Kiev's significance within the empire by proposing the Second Jerusalem theory as a counterweight to the Third Rome theory; Muscovy, the political center and protector of Orthodoxy, would not attain its fulfillment until it had incorporated Kiev, the Second Jerusalem, the eternal capital in which Orthodoxy was first given to the Rus. Muscovy was the state, but Kiev was its soul, its spiritual center.[53] The two, however, were an organic indivisible whole.

In general, Muscovy did not hesitate to recruit into its service the better educated Ukrainians, rewarding them generously and assimilating them into the framework of the empire. Craftsmen, artisans, and technicians of all sorts entered the service of Tsar Alexis. Indeed, Alexis openly favored Ukrainians over Muscovites, not without causing considerable envy and resentment. Hundreds of Ukrainians became tutors and teachers, visibly accelerating the process of intellectual and cultural modernization in Muscovy. On the whole, these first Ukrainians came as eager immigrants, not as strangers but as men with a similar language and religion.[54]

Naturally, the official hospitality extended to the Ukrainians aroused envy and distrust in the Muscovites. As for the Ukrainians, they disdained the coarse manners and poor education of the Russians. These tensions produced a reaction in the next reign, that of Tsar Fedor (1676 to 1682).[55] Not only were many Ukrainians removed from high posts but Muscovite authorities questioned the loyalty of all Ukrainians. In a very short time, the cultural pendulum swung in favor of traditionalists who opposed the inclusion of a Latin curriculum and called for a return to traditional Muscovite Greek learning. The Latinists defended themselves from the schools of the Zaikonospassky and Andreev monasteries, while the Grecophiles made their centers the Greco-Latin School and the school of the Chudov Monastery. There was little doubt that a real anti-Ukrainian bias lay behind the theoretical debate.[56]

During the Regency of Sophia (1682 to 1689) Muscovy once again favored the progressives; but whereas the Russian faction regained its influence, its Ukrainian counterpart did not—it had served its purpose. Henceforth, the fruits of the Ukrainian labors would be reaped by Russians who had profited from the cultural tutelage supplied by the Ukrainians. The next step was economic integration to open up the wealth of the Ukraine to Russian markets. In 1687, Sophia removed the customs barriers, henceforth systematically linking the economy of the Ukraine to that of Muscovy. Within a few years their markets and industries had become interdependent and inextricably intertwined;[57] and such has been the case to this day. Once in 1687 and again in 1689, major expeditions were sent into the Crimea to discourage its attacks on the steppe and to assure the tranquil economic evolution of the region. By the end of the century, Muscovy was well prepared for the Petrine reforms that converted the Ukraine into an integral part of the Russian empire.

Like all other regions in the Russian empire, the Ukraine felt the strength of Peter the Great. His reign began traditionally; that is, in his preparations for war against Sweden, he integrated Cossack forces into his army along the frontier, among them the troops of Hetman Ivan Mazepa, who had been rewarded with the hetmanship of the Ukraine ever since his loyal services for Muscovy along the right bank. In this capacity, however, Mazepa was exceedingly sensitive to the ferment of anti-Muscovite attitudes among the masses, the bulk of which now consisted of runaway serfs from Muscovite estates. Counting on the possibility that Peter might lose the war against King Charles XII of Sweden, Mazepa elected to fight on Sweden's side. The famous battle of Poltava in 1709 proved him tragically wrong on two counts: not only was Sweden utterly defeated but only a handful of landowning Cossacks rallied to his side in the name of an independent Cossack state. A mere 2,000 soldiers joined him in 1707, and none had even the consolation of having participated in the classic battle that made Russia a major European power: the rebellion was put down even before it could contribute towards Charles' invasion of the Ukraine, giving Peter an excuse to impose an even stricter rule upon the Cossack world.

From then on, two senior Muscovite officials were appointed alongside the hetman. They acted as viceroys with veto powers and equal jurisdictional rights. Henceforth, no decision could be made from the hetman's office without the counter-signature of one of the tsar's representatives. They, however, could initiate appointments and regulations without the hetman's consent. Furthermore, these officials from the capital (now moved to St. Petersburg) had a large personal staff that kept a sharp eye on all Ukrainian officials suspected of fostering foreign contacts. And large numbers of tsarist troops were stationed in strategic places to suppress any signs of rebellion. Other agents infiltrated the lower ranks of the population and encouraged them to report misdemeanors of the *starshyna* in order to aggravate and exploit the tensions between the two groups and thus erode respect for the hetmanate and inspire a preference for Petrine authority. Most of this took place during the tenure of Hetman Ivan Skoropadskyi, himself a tsarist puppet chosen to succeed Mazepa.

In 1722, as part of a general government reform, the Ukraine was placed under the jurisdiction of a new government bureau, the Malorossiiskaia Kollegia, headed by General S. Veliaminov, who presided over a committee made up entirely of Russian army officers. All administrative, financial, judicial, and police affairs fell under their jurisdiction. The following year, every Cossack regiment received a Russian as its superior officer, despite the brave but vain protests of a new hetman, Pavlo Polubotok. In response to this act of defiance, Peter abolished the elected post of hetman and made it an appointed office in 1723, arresting all those who dared continue to appeal for a return of Cossack autonomy.

Only Peter's death saved the Ukraine from extreme oppression. His successors for a variety of reasons (none of them because they personally favored the Ukraine *per se*) countermanded many of Peter's decrees for the region. Fear of Turkey and a desire for Cossack support led to the restoration of the hetmanate. The Malorossiiskaia Kollegia was closed down and many of the taxes levied by Peter were abolished. Nevertheless, the future hetmans were always government-approved candidates. The reprieve was short for under Empress Anna (1730 to 1740) there was a return to the Petrine order; no new hetman was elected and rule by the Kollegia was restored. Another era of relaxation followed in the reign of Empress Elizabeth (1740 to 1762), who, under the influence of her Ukrainian lover, Prince Alexis Rozumovskyi, brought back the office of hetman and had his brother Cyril installed, after what amounted to a mock election. He, however, was thoroughly Russified and chose to live in the capital, leaving administration of the hetmanate to the Rada, whose members were exclusively Russians.

The final chapter in the absorption of the Ukraine into the Russian empire was written in the reign of Catherine the Great (1762 to 1796), who took pride in fulfilling Peter's vision of a unified empire and finally outperformed him in many areas. In the Ukraine, Catherine acted more vigorously than elsewhere to bring about cultural uniformity. "Russification," as her policy became known, was adopted in 1764 as the means of assimilating the Cossack into the population and bringing him up to acceptable cultural standards; for in her view the Cossack, be he Zaporozhian or Siberian, lacked social discipline and intellectual sophistication. In a sense, Catherine looked upon the Cossack as a barbarian. Russification was to strengthen the similarities between the Cossack and the Russian and bind the Cossack more closely to the state. Not until he had been tamed and civilized could he be counted upon as a full-fledged citizen.

By the time Catherine ascended the throne, however, the process of assimilation was already well under way in the Ukraine. The troubles of past decades had decimated the population time and time again. If Central Europe, particularly Germany, suffered horribly from the ravages of the Thirty Years War, the Ukraine suffered immeasurably more. Not only were millions of people deported in Tatar raids but others, who sought to settle in the steppe, were repeatedly uprooted by Cossack internecine strife. And with the constant upheavals created by international wars, it was impossible for any developing society to achieve stability and plant firm roots. No wonder then that by the middle of the eighteenth century the Muscovite Petrine system was already the most powerful socializing factor among the peoples in the plain. The introduction of Russian estates with Russian serfs, the Russification of *starshyna,* and the imposition of Russian garrisons and Russian administrative techniques had combined to erode the Ukrainian elements.

Most affected, of course, was the Cossack community, for its oldest segment, the Zaporozhian Sich, had lost much of its virility and dynamism. Established on the very battleground of the Russian and Ottoman empires, it was doomed to be crushed by their combined weight.

A Cossack Ukraine could offer little resistance to Catherine's Russification decree, one purpose of which was to increase the productivity of the steppe in order to allow the empire to maintain its costly stance in Europe. Only the cities of the Ukraine preserved some measure of identity, but these declined in consequence of the more rapid Europeanization of St. Petersburg. The magnificence of the imperial seat attracted the élite of the South, and as the Ukrainian towns were abandoned, Kiev, especially, suffered from provincialism and was rapidly reduced to a shadow of its former self.

In 1764, Catherine announced that she had instructed Prince A. Viazemskii of her intention to integrate culturally and administratively those regions in the empire that still enjoyed some autonomy. Besides Finland and the Baltic states, Catherine had the Ukraine uppermost in mind. With the abruptness that only autocracy can afford, Catherine removed Hetman Cyril Rozumovskyi and replaced the hetmanate with an eight-man state council headed by P. A. Rumiantsev-Zadunaisky. It was his assignment to oversee the transition to a fully Russified Ukraine, a program that included the requirement of Russian as the official administrative and instructional language, and the encouragement to print books only in Russian.[58] In this period the educated élite was more fluent in French and/or German than Russian, and Ukrainian had all but disappeared as the language of the upper classes and become the sole property of the peasantry.

A few years later, in 1775, Catherine ordered the abolition of the Sich, that is, of what remained of it. In her eyes, the Sich was a primitive organization and an obstruction to progress, having of itself no governmental capacity to control the behavior of its adherents. More often than not, it bowed to the unpredictable rebellious demands of its membership, instead of containing their restlessness and imposing upon them a degree of discipline. Whatever control was exercised in the Zaporozhian region originated from Russian advisers who supervised many of the Sich's functions. Furthermore, fearing that the contagion of the Pugachev rebellion (1773 to 1774) would spread to the rank and file of the Sich, Catherine was eager to bring it under full government supervision. In erasing the Sich from the political map, Catherine merely terminated the life of an already moribund commu-

VKRANIA
quæ et
TERRA COSACCORUM
cum vicinis
WALACHIÆ, MOLDAVIÆ, MINORISq;
TARTARIÆ PROVINCIIS
exhibita
à IOH. BAPTISTA HOMANNO
Noribergæ.
VOLHYNIA SUPERIOR
VOLHYNIA
VOLHYNIA INFERIOR
RUSSIA RUBRA
KIOVIENSIS
PALAT.
POKUTIA
PODOLIA
UKRAINA
PODOLIA INFERIOR
BRACLAVIENSIS
WALACHIA
TRANSYLVANIA
MOLDAVIA
TRANSALPINA
SANGIACATUS
TARTARIA BUDZIACENSIS
BULGARIÆ PARS
NICOPOLIENSIS
PONT
Occidens

MOSCOVITICA
DUCAT MOSKOU
DUCAT RESANIENS
Moskou
Colomna
Murom
Kadom
TARTARIÆ
MOSCOVITICÆ PARS
Tambof
Koslof
Bolgovoi
Biel gorod
Oskol Vetus
Oskol Novi
Czuguief
Deserta sine aqua
CAMPI DESERTI
Ubi nulla hominum habitatio, nec planta reperienda est.
COSACCI CIRCASSI
DESERTUM ASOVIENSE
Aras Alexandri Magni
KIOVIA
TARTARIA
NAGAJENSIS
Petruschina tuba
SINUS ASOVIENSIS
MARE DEL
ZARACHE
PALUS MÆOTIS
KABARDINKI
CIRCASSI TARTARI
Kuban
EUXINUS
hodie
RE NIGRUM.
Milliaria Germanica.
Milliaria Polonica.
Anagria
Sebastopoli
Oriens

nity.[59] The community had been so wracked by internal dissension, so deranged by migrations to the Ottoman Empire and then by the return of the same Cossacks, that it had lost its cohesiveness and succumbed to the turmoil of the steppe and the brutal contest for its control.

The Zaporozhian Cossacks were tragically impoverished, exploited by the Russified *starshyna,* who were none other than agents of the Russian state who abused their power. Totally alienated and pauperized the Zaporozhian Cossacks attempted one last stand which amounted to a death tremor by trying to join the Pugachev movement. In failing, they lost all hope of survival as a society with a distinct personality. With the loss of the Sich, they were powerless against the forces of Russification. The more resolute among them cherished memories of golden days and of epic heroes, echoes of the past that were resurrected by Ukrainian poets in the late eighteenth and early nineteenth centuries during the rise of a new Ukrainian nationalism.

In 1781, Catherine, in the context of reorganizing the entire empire, divided the central Ukraine into three provinces (Poltava, Chernigov, and Kharkov), each governed according to the provincial system devised in 1775; later she added three more (Kiev, Podolia, and Volynia). Throughout the 1780's, Catherine encouraged the colonization of the Ukraine to promote its agricultural potential. In 1783 serfdom was officially extended to the left bank, even though in fact it had been there for decades.[60] Simultaneously Catherine encouraged the aristocracy to move their serfs to their new estates in the South, often stimulating this process by handing out generous grants to favorites. Thus, hundreds of thousands of serfs from central Russia were settled in the Ukraine, there to upset the Ukrainian majority in fulfillment of the official conscious effort to Russify the region ethnically. Furthermore, all peasants, whether serf or not, were subject to the infamous poll tax, which made no distinctions among the peasantry according to official status or ethnic identity. Meanwhile, Ukrainian and Cossack estate owners became absentee landlords, taking up careers in the civil service; as they moved up, they won high government posts. Their extravagant social life entailed lavish expense and forced them to extract the last drop of profit from their estates, with the result that serfdom in the Ukraine was very onerous.

By 1796 when Catherine died, the Ukraine had been stamped with the seal of the empire.[61] The Turkish Wars and the Partitions of Poland had brought the Russian empire the entire west bank of the Dnieper River, except for Galicia (which became part of the Habsburg empire). By the end of the century, the Ukraine had been completely absorbed, economically and administratively. Culturally, Russia had seized the initiative in the process of modernization and Europeanization that Peter the Great had set as a national goal. Whereas Kiev was a major cultural center as long as it remained in the Polish fold, it rapidly lost ground once all resources were channeled to St. Petersburg.

The brave and repeated attempts to preserve a Cossack society in the Ukraine came to naught, leaving the Ukraine without a political alternative except that imposed by St. Petersburg. Only the peasant masses preserved a sense of separate identity, clinging to tales and legends, practicing their peasant crafts, and speaking a language that was distinctly their own. Thanks to the gulf that separated official Russia from the masses, they were able to perpetuate their Ukrainian tradition and were saved from cultural extinction, even though they lacked the means of throwing off the bonds of serfdom and defying the Russian political system. Whereas the agrarian Ukraine retained its ethnic character, the urban Ukraine was rapidly assimilated. Cities and ports such as Ekaterinoslav, Kharkov, and Odessa were Russian;[62] even Kiev had the air of a small city of the Russian empire and less that of a provincial capital of a non-Russian province.

Muscovy, once transformed into the Russian empire, with superior military, political, cultural, and economic forces, steadily imposed its order upon the Ukraine. Yet it must be stressed that the Muscovite system and the yoke of empire weighed just as heavily upon the Russian masses as upon their Orthodox Ukrainian cousins. Furthermore, even though the ultimate responsibility for the Russification of the Ukraine rests with Moscow and with St. Petersburg, the enserfment and cultural Russification were carried out just as much by Ukrainians as by Russians. The landowning Cossacks on the whole welcomed Muscovite support of their status as soon as the hetmanate proved too weak to suppress peasant opposition. Moreover, as Muscovy demonstrated its superiority, the Ukrainian Church hierarchy, after much fluctuation and hesitation prior to the imposition of Catherine's Ukrainian policy, finally gave its enthusiastic, unqualified endorsement of Muscovite expansionism. As for the aristocracy, they enthusiastically joined the Europeanized society of St. Petersburg and rarely showed any concern for the plight of the Ukrainian masses. The rural Ukraine was deserted by every group that might have assumed Ukrainian leadership. The lure of Muscovy and the temptations of the empire were too great, and what triumphed in the end was less the force of alien power exerted upon a weaker subordinate than the superiority (political, social, economic, and military) of a mightier state whose ambitions included possession of the legendary riches of the Ukraine.

Men of many kinds had cast covetous eyes on the steppeland. Wave upon wave of invaders settled and tried to defend the plains and win possession of the left and right banks of the Dnieper, the backbone of the Ukraine. As if by mischievous design, topography assisted in guiding conquerors to the Dnieper valley: not only was the valley accessible from all points of the compass but it was devoid of natural features that might have isolated and protected it. Both nomads and agriculturists competed for the riches to be derived from pastoral pursuits or farming. Time and again the agriculturist established himself in the area only to fall prey to nomadic invasions. Finally, with the expulsion of the Mongols, the last of the nomadic conquerors, a struggle began among sedentary peoples for control of the steppe. In the end, strategic and economic factors called for control of the Ukraine; without it Muscovy and Poland would have been perpetually plagued by the instability and turmoil it generated.

A successful Cossack state might have brought equilibrium, but it rose to prominence too late. On the one hand, it lacked social cohesion and was therefore continually subject to internal conflict; on the other hand, it lacked the quantitative strength to fend off its rivals. A weak Cossack state had to rely on foreign guarantees of protection that entangled it in the fateful duel between Muscovy and Poland. And as the already divided Cossack ranks became hopelessly split into pro-Muscovite and pro-Polish factions, they invested more energies in contending with this schism than in searching for a principle of cohesion. In the end, the Cossack state became a victim of the struggle for the steppe, and a triumphant Muscovy dictated its terms, discouraging any degree of Ukrainian autonomy.

Given the makeup of the Ukrainian population, this was not very difficult, despite the occasional intense opposition of the masses, but the Russian empire paid a heavy price as it imprisoned the Ukrainian peasantry in serfdom. Though it finally possessed the treasures of the

Ukraine and controlled the trade routes to the Black Sea, it was master of an alienated population which harbored little loyalty for official Moscow. The tighter its rule, the more intense became the determination to resist. Such is the historical background for the disturbing relations between the central government of the Soviet Union and the citizens of the Ukraine.

TRAIAN STOIANOVICH

Russian Domination in the Balkans*

Russian involvement in the Balkans raises once more the question of what imperialism is and how it works. My own proclivity is to regard it in part as a particular form of the more general human longing to flee the constraints of space and achieve the kind of "boundlessness" described by Nicholas Gogol in his novel *Dead Souls:* "Russia! Russia! . . . Thou art wretched, disjointed, and comfortless . . . , yet an incomprehensible secret force draws me to thee . . . and my thought is numb before thy vast expanse. What forsooth does this boundless space presage? Does it not foretell that here in thee will be born an idea as infinite as thyself? . . . And that thou too, O Russia, will then dash on like a fleeting troika that nothing can overtake, the road asmoke, the bridges rumbling, beneath [thy wheels] . . . !" [1]

Modernity: A Hunger for the World

In their larger aspects, discovery, exploration, colonization, and imperialism are manifestations of what Fernand Braudel fittingly calls "a hunger for the world." [2] Initially a prelude and later a response to the development of a visual stress, the craving for an El Dorado and for unknown horizons is characteristically strong in periods of "modernity," when old laws and customs are eroded and men strive to run on wheels, to fly with wings, to elude the law of gravity. The journey

* I am grateful to Barbara and Charles Jelavich, Daniel C. Matuszewski, and Herbert H. Rowen for their valuable comments on an earlier draft of this essay.

from parochialism to modernity has been long, arduous, and often interrupted. Discoveries and explorations have had to be made over and over again. For Russia the journey was harder than for Western Europe, but Russia too was on its way by 1550.

Russia rediscovered the world in many ways, partly through the revival and intensification of cultural influences from the Southwest, the territories of Cossackdom and onetime Kievan Rus. The Cossacks have not always been regarded as agents of modernization, and in many respects they were traditionalists; but by their maritime forays against Ottoman Istanbul, so similar to those of the Rus, their predecessors, against Byzantine Constantinople more than half a millennium earlier, they ultimately drew Russia's attention to the Mediterranean. A Soviet historian has taken note of Cossack incursions into the Bosporus in 1624,[3] during the great Ottoman and indeed European and worldwide political, social, and economic disorders that started in the 1580's and lasted into the 1660's. In the worst of the 1620's the Turks daily predicted their own necessary early and crushing defeat.[4]

A seventeenth-century English historian and consul at Smyrna, Paul Rycaut, has left a vivid description and careful analysis of the long, light raiding boats in which, in 1626, Cossack corsairs executed a daring razzia in the Bosporus:

"During these Troubles the Cosacks taking advantage of the Captain-Pasha's absence in *Tartary,* entred the *Bosphorus* with about an hundred and fifty Sail of Saicks [caiques] and Boats; these Boats and Vessels which the Cosacks use are built long and light with ten Oars of a side, and two men to an Oar; the Head and Stern are not unlike, so that they hang the Rudder sometimes at one end, and sometimes at the other, being not obliged to turn their Vessel, but without loss of time to proceed with that end which happens to be foremost. Each Boat carries fifty select men armed with Fire-arms and Cemiter, in the management of which they are very expert; and are a People sober, enduring labour and hard diet, and so speedy in their Incursions, that they forestal the advices, and commonly strike before they threaten. With these Boats and people (as we have said) they entred the *Bosphorus,* where they burnt several Villages and Houses of Pleasure; on the Grecian side they burnt *Boyuc-deri* [Büyük Dere] and *Yenichioi* [Yeni Köy], on the Asian side *Stenia* [İsteniye]. The appearance of this Enemy so near the Imperial City caused a general consternation, not unlike that at *London,* when the Dutch entred the River of *Chatham.* To oppose this Force there was not one Gally in readiness, so that Saicks, Chimbers, and small Boats were armed to the number of four or five hundred, and man'd with such people as the present haste and expedition offered; the great Chain was then brought forth to cross the *Bosphorus*, which the Grecian Emperours used at the siege of Constantinople: and ten thousand men were issued from the City to defend the shoar from depredation and further mischief. The Turkish Fleet faced the Cosacks to give them a stop, whilst they hovered about the middle of the Chanel in form of a Half-Moon, and so continued the whole day until Sunset; when with the night they returned into the Sea, carrying with them, besides their Booty, glory sufficient to have entred the Chanel, and without blows or opposition to have braved the Capital Seat of the Ottoman Monarchy, and the most formidable City of the whole World. Not many days after they returned again with greater Force than before, which put the City into the like consternation; and having hovered about three or four days at the Mouth of the Black Sea, they burnt the Pharos or Lantern with certain Villages thereabouts, and being laden with Spoils and Glory, they again returned into their own Country." [5]

Benedict H. Sumner, author of one of the most equitable estimates of the reign of Peter the Great, concludes that only four changes wrought by Peter "had either nothing leading towards them in the immediate past or so very little that it scarcely counts." One of these was the creation of a navy.[6] But if pre-Petrine Russia lacked a navy, the Cossacks of the Ukraine had already built one by the early part of the seventeenth century. Even as an architect of a navy, therefore, Peter was not an absolute innovator. Russia succeeded in creating a navy, at least in part, as it acquired the maritime propensities of the peoples and cultures in the new territories it absorbed.

Expansion with a Purpose

Joseph A. Schumpeter defines imperialism as "the objectless disposition on the part of a state to unlimited forcible expansion" and explains it as a consequence of the hammering of certain "peoples and classes into warriors" and of the fact that "psychological dispositions and social structures acquired in the dim past in such situations, once firmly established, tend to maintain themselves and to continue in effect long after they have lost their life-preserving function." Imperialism is consequently an atavistic social and psychological structure, a survival of past rather than an indicator of current relations of production.

I should be among the last to quarrel with the view that certain archaic cultural traits, and perhaps even structures, are embodied discreetly in modern civilizations. Schumpeter errs wholly, however, in identifying one of these traits as the absence of militancy or aggressiveness on the part of "the Slavic masses" and in ascribing the militancy of "triumphant czarism" entirely to soldierly Germanic and Mongol elements with whom the Slavs were fatefully joined.

War, he maintains, was part of the "settled order of life" of Russia's great lords, "an element of sovereign splendor, almost a fashion." They waged it "whenever the occasion was offered, not so much from considerations of advantage as from personal whim. To look for deep-laid plans, broad perspectives, consistent trends is to miss the whole point." [7] I have long pondered upon these fundamental statements, and my research has led neither to an affirmation nor to a negation but to a unifying conclusion. War and expansion, in the Russian case if not generally, were a question of whim and fashion. They were also conducted, and often simultaneously, with a conscious or unconscious purpose.

The objects of domination have varied, moreover, in accordance with variations in the relations and ways of production, social organization, distribution of space and resources, demography, and communication of goods and ideas. The goal of nomadic conquerors, for example, was traditionally the levying of tribute and the seizure of slaves (especially women, skilled craftsmen, and other specialists), sheep, cattle, horses, and other chattel. In retaliation, precapitalist settled societies attempted to augment the arable land, achieve a demographic superiority, and establish greater security in local and long-distance trade, without wholly abandoning an interest in the objects of primary concern to the nomads. Capitalist societies in turn developed a national economy and a technological advantage which has allowed them to produce an ever greater quantity of manufactured goods, whereas the increases in the production of agricultural societies stay in line more or less with world demographic growth.

As a result of the unequal distribution of political power and economic goods, societies and economies tend to become—directly or indirectly, voluntarily or involuntarily—dominant or dominated in their relationships to each other.[8] A politically or economically dominant society is said furthermore to be imperialist. In fact, however, a country may be dominant in one political or economic sector, or in one region, and dismally overshadowed in other geographical areas, and in other spheres of life endeavor. It may dominate in old ways or new, or in different combinations of the two. A clear ability to command in every realm, including ideas, takes long to achieve but is rarely of long duration. Competence of imperium shifts in fact from one ethnic and political group to another, and from nomadic to agricultural, from agricultural to industrial, societies.

Geography, Demography, and Technology

Subject for a time to the domination of nomads, the Russians developed ways of dominance characteristic of agricultural societies. Through their relations with the Crimean Tatars, they were drawn ever further southward, into the *okraina* or new Frontier and old Metropolis (*Mala Rus*). The motives of the new conquerors were sometimes ambiguous, but a meaning emerges even from a seeming meaninglessness.

The southward expansion of Russia was an act of modernization. If Russia had remained sullenly passive, if its lords and priests and peasants had been content with the old territorial limits, it could hardly have augmented and improved its farmlands, and nomads and seminomads might have continued to prevail in the *okraina*. Tatar horsemen and auxiliary infantry troops might have persisted in taking their customary toll of Russian labor (slaves) and capital (cattle)—several thousand prisoners (not counting persons who were sold into slavery) and tens of thousands of head of stock each year.[9] If Russia ransomed the prisoners who fell into the hands of the Tatars, it lost one scarce commodity: money. If it failed to ransom them, it lost another: labor. In any case, until the 1620's or 1630's, Russia was always a loser of capital, a commodity no less rare.

As nomads and seminomads, the Tatars had to strive to prevent a rise of population on their prairie lands. Their raids were generally remunerative, but even if a market for slaves had been nonexistent, they would no doubt have been obliged to organize periodic man hunts in order to maintain, from the point of view of nomads, a satisfactory relationship between people and cattle, namely a denser distribution of herds.

By cultivating wheat and other cereals, men can obtain a caloric value three, five, or ten times that of the meat which can be produced when the same plot of land is given over to grazing.[10] The population of a given area can be thus quickly tripled, and even increased tenfold, simply by a change from a grazing to a farming economy. The Poles and Russians of the sixteenth and seventeenth centuries were perhaps unaware, or only dimly aware, of the operation of this principle. They nevertheless acted *as if* they knew, for their goal was colonization. Pastoral habits were less common among them than among the Tatars, and by doing no more than pursue their customary way of life—that is, by being traditionalists—they became agents of modernization, or of the transformation of a pastoral and nomadic into an agricultural economy.

Europe has long been divided into four concentric zones of population density. In 1500, the density in the core area, which then included Italy, Greece, Aegean Macedonia, several other portions of the Mediterranean, northern and eastern France, southern England, the Netherlands, and the Rhineland, was 20 persons or more per square kilometer. Around this core was a large ring, within which were included the bulk of the Iberian and portions of the Balkan peninsula, southwestern and central France, most of Ireland, the rest of England, perhaps the Scottish Highlands, and Central Europe as far east as Mazovia (Warsaw region), with a density of 10 to 20 persons per square kilometer. In southern Sweden and east of Mazovia and north of the line Halich-Chernigov-Kazan and south and west of the line Tikhvin-Beloozero-Kazan, the density fell to 2 to 10 persons. North, south, and east of this area, it declined to less than 2 persons per square kilometer until the outer limits of Persian and Chinese civilization were reached, whereupon new rings of demographic concentration were laid out, this time with a Persian or Chinese orientation.[11]

Around the middle of the sixteenth century, the population density of the Dnieper Ukraine was approximately a fifth of Little Poland's and not much over a tenth of Mazovia's. But in the century after 1570, as a result of repeated wars, of famine and plague, and of the flight of people eastward from Poland and southward from Muscovy in order to escape the growing harshness of serfdom in the countries of settled agriculture, the population of Poland and Russia declined and that of Volynia and of the right-bank Ukraine began to rise.[12] In the eighteenth century, the process was extended to the left-bank Ukraine, where the demographic growth between 1724 and 1795 was in the order of 86 percent on the basis of official statistics. In the second half of the century, Russia undertook a vast program of colonizing the southern Ukraine.[13]

The plow won the steppe,[14] but it was able to win it because of the support of a vast military organization. In the Russian as in the Austrian agricultural advance, writes William H. McNeill, "the army carried state power into the empty lands ahead of settlement, thus giving officials the opportunity to superintend the establishment of new cultivators and set up rules to which the pioneers had more or less to conform." Moreover, "a great many of the new settlers were military men, either discharged veterans or colonists assigned militia duty and thus subject to military rather than civilian official control." [15] To stave off and stop the rapid thrusts of the nomads, the Russian military, beginning in the 1570's but more especially in the seventeenth century, built across their southern marches a series of carefully patrolled defensive networks of newly planted woods and log and earthen fortifications,[16] thus simulating in the steppe the forest milieu of the North.

Other aids to the conquest of the steppe were the cannon and the musket. In the first half of the fourteenth century, a certain "Boris the Roman" went apparently from Tver to cast bells in Moscow and Novgorod, and by the end of the century the Russians may have been manufacturing both cannon and church bells. But in the latter part of the fifteenth century the Florentine Rodolfo Fioraventi again had to instruct the Russians in the art of founding cannon and clocks. A Russian metallurgical industry capable of supporting a "modern" war economy was of a still later date, however, going back to the establishment of gun foundries and other ironworks at Tula, south of Moscow, by Dutch, Swedish, and other foreign artisans during and after the 1620's.[17] After Peter the Great's consolidation and further development of the metallurgical industry,[18] Russia was finally in a position to match Ottoman technology, which had stagnated during the seventeenth and retrogressed in the eighteenth century.[19]

The geography of the steppe—"those Desart Plains, which do so far resemble the Sea, that the Mariners Compass may be useful for Direction in the one, as well as the other" [20]—more or less dictated that the plain should succumb to that neighboring power which could prove its demographic and technological superiority. The Cossack threat to Tatar and Ottoman power lacked a modern technological base, but the

Cossacks and their sea-like steppes drew Russia ever farther southward into the Ukraine and toward the sea. By the quick action of their mobile field and naval artillery and by their modest but nonetheless real technological superiority in other respects, the Russians prevailed over the Ottoman cavalry and navy during the second half of the eighteenth century.[21]

The Limits of Universal Monarchy

From the reign of Peter the Great to 1853, according to Karl Marx, Russia's frontier advanced a thousand miles in the direction of Persia, seven hundred miles in the direction of Berlin, Dresden, and Vienna, and six hundred and thirty miles in the direction of Stockholm, but only (the "but only" is my own thought) five hundred miles toward Istanbul and the Balkans.[22] The obstacles to Russian southwestward expansion beyond the steppe were more formidable than the hindrances to aggrandizement in other directions.

In Europe or the region west of the Scythian steppe, moreover, Russia encountered a force that was inimical to the very principle of universal monarchy, namely a strong tradition of opposition to territorial bigness, and to power without limits. Eighteenth-century political science acted to reinforce this tradition. Montesquieu stipulated in his *L'Esprit des lois* (1748) that a state should be "mediocre" in size and that it should confine itself to "the [territorial] limits natural to its government" and maintain the laws, customs, tribunals, and privileges of the territories and peoples that it conquered.[23]

In his *Institutions politiques* (1760), Baron Jacob Friedrich von Bielfeld, scion of a Hamburg merchant family and privy councilor to Frederick the Great, reached a similar conclusion. The ambitions of kings and ministers should be "proportionate to their states and their situation." Wisdom dictates that the political system of France should limit itself "to making the seas, the Alps, the Pyrenees, and the Rhine as the frontiers of its states. . . ." If, on the other hand, it "aims at Universal Monarchy, if it engages in far-flung conquests in Europe, it becomes foul, blameful, dangerous, chimerical. The same applies to the other powers."[24]

Finally, Jean-Jacques Rousseau, who is generally considered to have been an advocate of the small state but who in fact argued that there is no wholly satisfactory way of defining the size most appropriate to states, believed that there were then some states in Europe that were too big to be well governed and others that were too small to be able to preserve their independence.[25]

Montesquieu's *Esprit des lois* was probably of some import in persuading official Russia, which was eager to form an integral part of prestigious European civilization, of the value of a policy of balance of power and of its corollary, territorial partition and spheres of influence. Such, in any event, was the policy that Russia pursued under Catherine in regard to Poland, and such also was the policy of the "Grand Plan," which she sought to apply to the Ottoman Empire.

The "Grand Plan" called for a division of the Balkans into a Russian-controlled Dacian state in the northeast, an Austrian zone in the west and north center, and a Greek or neo-Byzantine state in the central and eastern Balkans, with its capital at Constantinople. Provision was also made for a zone of the maritime powers, particularly France and Britain, in the Mediterranean. The agreement between Russia and Austria in 1782 to implement a portion of this project met with unexpected failure, but Russia never entirely abandoned the basic vision of a separation of the Balkans and other segments of the vast Ottoman Empire into several distinct spheres of influence and domination.

Known as *le système copartageant,* this policy was based on the premise that new territorial acquisitions by the great European powers ought to be equal. A redistribution of territories should therefore be made only on careful consideration of comparative soil fertility, the quality and size of each territory's population, and the political value of its situation. Casuistry in all this there doubtless was, but *le système copartageant* did assure the maintenance of a precarious equilibrium in Europe, and it hindered the assertion of universal monarchy. Not until the French Revolution and the Continental System was there a temporary challenge to the politics of balance of power, and even Napoleon had to pursue a course of spheres of influence for a few years in his relations with Russia.[26]

Population growth, agricultural development, and improvements in military technology enabled Russia to occupy a large part of the steppe, namely the plains at some distance from Austria. But a set of new social, mental, and geographical structures then stymied further Russian westward expansion.

One of these impediments, as we have seen, was the underlying

European hostility to the idea of universal monarchy, which one may usefully regard as an Asiatic principle and institution translated to the Mediterranean and then to Europe. But Europe—and this includes the Balkans—has found it very hard to accommodate to this principle, for geography and history have combined to make of Europe a land of multifarious liberties, franchises, and autonomies—rural, urban, and territorial.[27]

On reaching the Black Sea and the Danubian principalities, Russia attained at last a region that was in less need of colonization. Further obstacles to Russian expansion were the mountain and the forest; these were of advantage to the Balkan peoples, just as the Russian forests had benefited the Russians. Limits were also posed by the fact that Russia was now in immediate physical contact with two other empires, the Habsburg and the Ottoman, and by the existence of a medieval Western European tradition of colonialism in the eastern Mediterranean and Balkan periphery.[28] When colonizing Genoa and Venice were eclipsed as dominant political entities, other European states—France, England, Holland, Austria, Belgium, Italy, and Germany—asserted their interest in the area.

Equally inimical to universal monarchy were the forces that nurtured Europeanization and nationalism. Long before Russia achieved a common border with the Balkans toward the close of the eighteenth century, the peninsula's inhabitants—Christians and Muslims alike, though in unlike ways and with different goals in mind—had made a habit of resistance to inefficient Ottoman absolutism and were therefore consciously or unconsciously moving toward the cultural restoration of the Balkans to Europe. A further step in this direction, and perhaps the most important step, was the restatement of the principle of autonomy through the creation of new Balkan states and the diffusion of the revolutionary principle of nationality.

Lands of Peace and Lands of War

Before the triumph of nationalism, religious notions defined, and sometimes seemingly governed, relations between states and peoples. Not only the territorially minor faiths but even such major ecumenical religions as Buddhism, Islam, and Christianity have acted in certain periods of their history to deny to members of their culture the right to enter or reside in areas of divergent religious beliefs.[29] The historian

Jacques Le Goff thus aptly characterizes the policy of medieval Christianity as one of "religious racism" and exclusion.[30] To have acted contrarily would have been tantamount to acquiescing to contamination, and equivalent perhaps to a disturbing acknowledgment that truth is essentially relative.

In Sunni Islam, a specific distinction was made between the "land of peace," or the orthodox Muslim world, and the "land of war." The "land of war" comprised the peoples of the world whose faith orthodox Muslims were obliged to regard as inferior. Whenever practicable, it was the duty of good Muslims to extend the frontiers of the "land of peace" and diminish the dominions of the "land of war." [31] The jihad, or Muslim crusade, was the chief instrument to the achievement of this end.

Conquest was not always feasible, however, and a "land of war" sometimes possessed goods for which there was a demand in a "land of peace." It therefore became customary to grant special privileges to foreign merchants, or at least to the most eminent among them, for it was preferable that foreigners should leave themselves open to defilement than that one's coreligionists should expose themselves to such a fate.

Eminent foreign merchants were recognized in Muscovy as the *gosti,* or "guests," of the prince. But "guests" or unknown travelers and wanderers have been regarded traditionally as gods, saints, or demons: powerful doers of good and evil. As such, they have been esteemed and feared simultaneously,[32] and the prince's *gosti* were treated in like fashion. Privileged in normal times, the *gosti* were in fact scapegoats and the victims of contempt and reprisal in periods of war between the host country and their own or in a time of social strife in the host country.[33] Attitudes toward diplomatic envoys and missionaries were very similar.

The institution of the merchant and foreign guest assumed a somewhat different form in the Ottoman Empire, where an even greater need was felt for foreign traders. To assure their continuing presence, the Ottoman government developed the practice of granting capitulations, or charters of privilege, to one foreign power after another, on the basis of which the merchants and other visiting subjects of these countries obtained what were in effect rights of extraterritoriality.

The first of the capitulations proper was concluded in 1535 by Suleiman the Magnificent's grand vizier, Ibrahim, and Francis I's envoy to Istanbul, a knight of the order of Saint John of Jerusalem, the abbé Jean de la Forest. Among the numerous guarantees extended to French subjects by this agreement, writes a modern scholar, were "freedom of trade, security against extraordinary duties, immunity from Ottoman law, release from imprisonment or slavery, and the right to practise their own religion and to protect the Holy Places of Palestine." [34] Later capitulations were even more comprehensive, and those of 1604 not only augmented the privileges of French merchants, and made their trade more secure, but alluded for the first time to the protection of Christian pilgrims in the Holy Land and of priests and churches in all Ottoman territories.[35] Other European powers acquired similar advantages, especially during the seventeenth and eighteenth centuries.

Russia, however, was not assimilated into the system of capitulations until it had demonstrated that it was both a great European power and able to challenge the Ottoman Empire on the seas. Commercial agreements between the two states had existed since the latter part of the fifteenth century, but not until the treaty of Kuchuk Kainarji of July 21, 1774, which terminated the Russo-Turkish War of 1768 to 1774, was Russia granted rights of extraterritoriality. The Ottoman government promised by this treaty to give "a constant protection to the Christian religion and its churches." It also guaranteed to Russian subjects the right to trade without hindrance in the Ottoman dominions, whether by land or by sea, to enter any port, including Istanbul, and lay anchor at any shore, to navigate freely even on the Danube, and to have access from the Black Sea to the Aegean and from the Aegean to the Black, a privilege that had been denied to foreign powers since the 1590's.[36] The two countries also agreed to apply "most favored nation" treatment to each other, and Russia was further to benefit from the capitulations that the Turks had accorded to France and Britain, subject only to paying the low customs duties and import and export charges exacted of the most favored nations.

A Russo-Turkish commercial treaty of June 21, 1783, authorized Russian subjects to engage in trade anywhere in the Ottoman Empire, wear the dress of their own country, and remain in Ottoman territories under Russian protection for an unlimited period of time. By permitting Russian traders to sell their merchandise to any Ottoman buyer, it divested Ottoman subjects of monopoly rights to the purchase of certain raw materials. By authorizing Russians to buy rice, coffee, olive oil, and silk anywhere in the Ottoman Empire except Istanbul, and to ship grains of non-Ottoman origin through the Straits, it undermined the rights of monopoly of Istanbul to the products of the Black Sea and reduced its rights of special access to those of the Aegean. The treaty, moreover, lowered Ottoman import and export duties to 3 percent *ad valorem* and freed the Russians from the obligation to pay transit duties and exceptional import and export taxes and excises. Similar rights were granted between 1784 and 1806 to Austria, the United Kingdom, France, and Prussia.[37]

The object of the capitulations from an Ottoman viewpoint was to allow Ottoman subjects to acquire those goods that they wanted, dispose profitably of goods that were wanted in Europe, and in the process shrewdly avoid their own profanation. From an overall Ottoman and Muslim cultural position, a policy of extraterritoriality was thus expedient. In the eighteenth and nineteenth centuries, however, the European powers took advantage of their capitulatory rights to discourage Ottoman manufactures,[38] and in the nineteenth century they reduced the successor Balkan states to similar capitulatory terms in an effort to preserve the Balkans as a reservoir of raw materials.

Russia sought to use the religious clause in the treaty of Kuchuk Kainarji to exalt itself to the rank of custodian not merely of the Orthodox but of all the Christian populations in the Ottoman realm. Partly in the hope of implementing this aim, it began to question the desirability of a policy of partition. In any event, shortly before news of the treaty of Adrianople reached St. Petersburg, a special secret committee on Turkish affairs—made up of members of the imperial council—advised Tsar Nicholas that it might be to Russia's advantage to maintain the integrity of a weak Ottoman Empire.[39] Russia was still more firmly opposed to partition during the early 1830's, when it seemed that the benefits might accrue to one of the great powers only (France) and that a powerful new state (Egypt) and dynasty (that of Muhammad 'Alī) might emerge from the Ottoman ruins. Unable to agree on a division of the tottering Ottoman state into separate spheres of influence, the European powers ultimately experimented with transforming it into a joint protectorate.

The ways in which Russia sought to dominate in the Balkans and the eastern Mediterranean differed somewhat from those of the other European powers. Religious, ethnic, and geographical factors account in part for this distinction. Even more basic in taking Russia along a path all its own in its relations with this region were its technological and economic structures and the way in which these were enmeshed in the complex web of the European, Balkan, and world economies, and in the total culture of Western Europe and the Balkan and Mediterranean peoples.

Current Relations of Production

In Western and Central Europe, the Russian fur trade began to decline before 1700.[40] In the Ottoman Empire, on the other hand, pelisses continued to be highly valued as symbols of wealth and station,[41] and furs were to be Russia's chief export to this area until well after the middle of the eighteenth century. However, it was not Russians who normally brought this merchandise to the Ottoman consumers but rather Constantinopolitan Greeks and Jews, or Greeks and Vlachs from Epirus, Thessaly, and Macedonia. From the southern and eastern Balkans, fur traders journeyed to Galaţi, Jassy, Khotin or Kamenets, Vasilkov, Kiev, and Nezhin, and Central European traders often joined them at Khotin. At Nezhin, Russian merchants met the Southern and Central Europeans and exchanged their expensive furs for the Hungarian sequins or other hard currency in the latter group's possession. Upon reentering Khotin, the Central European traders—now without the great European demand for Russian furs that had existed before 1650 or 1700—often diverted their furs to Greek and Vlach merchants in return for silk belts, embroideries, fabrics, cotton carpets, cotton yarn dyed in red, incense, and other Ottoman articles then in demand in Germany, Poland, and Hungary.[42] In 1776, however, a brief two years after Kuchuk Kainarji, a French consular official noted the arrival at Nauplion by way of Istanbul of two so-called "Russian merchants" carrying "30 *bourses de pelleteries,*" whose seeming object was the purchase of Moreot silks.[43]

The Ottoman demand for Russian furs remained at a high level during most of the second half of the century,[44] but another Russian export, namely grain, was to acquire an ascendancy in the Aegean which even furs had never enjoyed. The two products, or the structures of which they were components, tended to orient Russian policy toward the Greek much more than toward the Southern Slavic world.

It is true that Peter the Great had been particularly eager to recruit qualified South Slavic and Italian sailors from the Adriatic when he strove to build an Azov fleet. He had also sought out Greek sailors,[45] but the emphasis could hardly have been Greek then, in view of the fact that a revived Greek merchant marine did not even come into being until the middle of the century.[46] On the other hand, he entered into diplomatic relations not only with the nearby Rumanians but with the more distant Southern Slavs, especially with Montenegro; and Ragusan (Dubrovnik) poets vied with each other to compose dithyrambs in his honor.[47]

Under Catherine II, the methods were modified even though the goals may have remained the same. One reason for this change was the appearance in Montenegro of a mysterious charismatic stranger, generally known as Šćepan Mali (Stephen the Little), who succeeded in enforcing his rule on the credulous people of that land. When the story spread that he might be Peter III of Russia, the husband Catherine had sacrificed to an aristocratic conspiracy, Catherine sought to have the pretender removed. Her failure may have persuaded her to beware of the Southern Slavs.

Much more basic in molding Russia's policy, however, was the fact that its economic relations with the Southern Slavs were almost nonexistent,[48] whereas trade with the Greeks had a very long history behind it. Moreover, as a result of the creation of a Greek merchant marine, and of Russia's occupation, colonization, and agricultural development of the Ukraine, Russo-Greek commercial relations were to reach heights never previously attained.

Partly in response to the economic structure, partly because of a generally growing craving for the world, and partly in imitation of Western and Central Europe, the élites of St. Petersburg were to make the second half of the eighteenth century a time of "Grecomania." Their philhellenism and cult of antiquity took the form of an expanding interest in classical Greek literature, the adoption of a women's fashion called the *grechanka* or "Grecian," the establishment of a "Greek Cadet Corps," and the christening of many new towns in the South with Greek names.[49] A further manifestation of this Greek perspective was Catherine's project of a neo-Greek state.

The economic links between Russia's southern territories and the Greeks were steadily strengthened in the half century between 1770 and 1820. Thus, in 1785, the wine imports from the Greek or Aegean Archipelago to the Russian port of Kherson amounted to 3,926,800 piasters, or 90 percent of Kherson's total imports.[50] Greek wine exports to Russia appear to have antedated the establishment of Russian power and commerce on the Black Sea, but there is every indication that they grew in importance after the Russo-Turkish War of 1768 to 1774 and the treaty of Kuchuk Kainarji. By the time of the Napoleonic Wars, the greater part of the wine surplus of the Greek Archipelago, especially of such islands as Samos, Rhodes, Naxos, Santorin, Tinos, and Syros, went to the ports of southern Russia.[51]

Of the 700,000 rubles' worth of merchandise exported from Kherson in 1785, an amount set at 200,000 rubles consisted of grains,[52] a good portion of which may have originated in Poland.[53] As the steppe was occupied and nomadic habits were partly repressed, more Ukrainian grains were made available for export, and the chief market for Russia's grains was to be the very archipelago which supplied the main import needs of the southern Russian territories. After 1783, in effect, Black-Sea Russia and the Aegean islands were to become economically complementary areas.

Many of the Greek islands, especially the smaller ones, ordinarily were obliged to import two thirds of their annual grain requirements.[54] But during the second half of the eighteenth century, particularly after the Russo-Turkish War of 1768 to 1774, when Greeks and Orthodox Albanians from the Morea and the Greek mainland fled there to escape Muslim Albanian pressures, their population—and hence their cereal needs—increased very rapidly.[55] This demographic growth could occur for two reasons only. Once Turkey fully and formally recognized Russia's right to send merchant ships through the Dardanelles in 1783,[56] the Russians and Ukrainians were at last in a position to market their grains in the Aegean. Second, the Russians were able to stimulate Aegean demographic growth by furnishing the emerging Greek or Greco-Albanian merchant marine with an abundance of freight, allowing Greek merchant ships to fly the Russian flag, and authorizing their own merchant marine to be manned by Greek crews.[57]

The Russo-Turkish Wars of the latter part of the eighteenth and early part of the nineteenth century were partly a consequence of the Russian ambition to export a portion of the Russian grain production beyond the western confines of the Black Sea to regions in which a higher price normally prevailed, and of the desire of many of the Turkish and perhaps some of the other inhabitants of Istanbul to preserve their ancient right to preempt the cereals and other food products of the Black Sea. All Ottoman governments lived in fear of urban disturbances and public remonstrances against high prices and food scarcity and thus had to strive to weaken or nullify those treaty provisions which empowered Russian merchant ships to pass through the Turkish Straits in either direction. War against Russia therefore could be popular among the little people of Muslim faith in the Ottoman capital, who no more desired boats charged with grains to pass from Istanbul to the Aegean than did their governments. The Turkish wars against Russia could easily assume the guise of resistance to the high cost of living.[58]

Under the threat of French political and economic aggrandizement in the eastern Mediterranean, however, Russia and Turkey signed a convention on August 20, 1798, whereby a Russian fleet of thirteen vessels was admitted through the Bosporus and Dardanelles so that it might join the Turks in a concerted naval action against France. Armed with an encyclical from the Patriarch of Constantinople inviting the Greeks of the Ionian Islands to cooperate with the two new allies in shaking off French revolutionary tyranny, the combined fleets quickly seized the meagerly garrisoned islands of Cerigo, Zante, Cephalonia, Ithaca, and Santa Maura; after a siege of several months they took Corfu. A year later, on March 21, 1800, the Russians and Turks consented to the union of the islands as an autonomous republic which, like the republic of Ragusa, was required to acknowledge Ottoman suzerainty and pay a regular tribute. It was also agreed that Russian troops should remain in occupation of the fortresses and ports of the new republic until the restoration of peace in Europe.

On July 9, 1807, on the heels of the Tilsit meeting between Alexander I of Russia and Napoleon, a secret Franco-Russian convention was signed by which, in violation of the Russo-Turkish accord, Russia returned the Ionian Islands to Napoleon.[59] In exchange, Alexander obtained Napoleon's acquiescence, in the event that peace could not be mediated between Russia and Turkey, to the statement that France and Russia would "come to an arrangement with each other to detach from the yoke and vexations of the Turks all the provinces of the Ottoman Empire in Europe, the city of Constantinople and the [vast] province of Rumelia excepted."[60] A year later, Napoleon reluctantly acceded to Russia's occupation of Moldavia and Wallachia.

Mutual distrust between the two powers did not abate. Early in 1812, in preparation for the increasingly inevitable conflict with Napoleon, Russia reluctantly concluded peace with Turkey, restoring Moldavia and Wallachia to Ottoman suzerainty. But a Corfiot Greek in Tsar Alexander's service, Count John Capo d'Istria (Capodistrias), proposed to the Russian sovereign in 1816 that he order mobilization again in order to persuade Turkey to agree to a confederation of Moldavia, Wallachia, and recently insurgent Serbia.

In Capo d'Istria's scheme, the three Danubian territories were to remain under Ottoman suzerainty. In slightly modified form, Turkey was to retain its right to preempt food products needed for the capital. Capo d'Istria's proposal further specified that each of the three Danubian lands should be governed by a ruler drawn from a German princely family and that the three provinces should be placed under joint Russian and Austrian protection, or perhaps even under the protection of Russia, Austria, Britain, and France.

Alexander had learned, however, that war waged on the Danube against traditionalist Turkey was a vehicle of revolution. His answer was clear: "All that is fine thought, but to make it work would require the firing of cannon, and that I do not want. There has been enough of wars on the Danube; they demoralize armies, as you yourself can bear witness. Peace, moreover, has not yet been consolidated in Europe, and the makers of revolutions would like nothing better than to see me at odds with the Turks." [61]

The antirevolutionary obsession of Russian governments led them on occasion to forsake or minimize Russian economic interests. In the short run, a discordance between political ideology and economic advantage was frequent, and the two approaches were sometimes almost irreconcilable. In the long run economic interests were not neglected.

Aided by notions of Slavic unity and by a sense of mission to liberate the Orthodox world, Russia ultimately turned its attention to the defense of its Black Sea trade. Countries are perhaps drawn to war periodically by contradictory, semirational, almost inexplicable forces, so that in the history of human societies periods of peace and war alternate and peace culminates dialectically in war. Russia too may have been lured again into war by impulses of this kind. But rational explanations are not wanting, and Vernon John Puryear may be correct in his conclusion that "one of the outstanding reasons" for the Russo-Turkish War of 1828 to 1829 was the "Turkish interference with the export trade of Odessa and the other Black Sea ports of Russia."

During the Greek War of Independence (1821 to 1829), Turkey adopted a policy of "visiting" or searching Russian merchant vessels and confiscating the wheat and tallow aboard. Turkish officials not only delayed the departure of vessels until they obtained a firman authorizing their passage through the Straits but allowed them to leave only after their captains had ingratiated themselves by distributing bribes or gifts. Such abuses were finally corrected by the treaty of Adrianople (September 14, 1829), which deprived Turkey of the right of preemption to Russian and other Black Sea (Moldavian, Wallachian, and Bulgarian) goods, established complete freedom of trade on the Black Sea and the Danube, and guaranteed to merchant ships a clear right of transit through the Straits.[62]

Russia secured these rights for itself (and others), however, only by resorting to war. The outcome of the conflict was an unprecedented blow to Ottoman forces of tradition. Resulting in the creation of an independent Greek state and of an autonomous Serbia, in the loss of Turkish rights of priority to the products of the Black Sea, and in the issuance by Russia of organic statutes or charters to the Rumanian principalities, the war had the even more radical effect of introducing into the Ottoman Empire the very notion of fashion and fashionableness[63] and in other ways undermining the Ottoman conception of a society of statuses.[64] No previous war or act of diplomacy had ever quite so emphatically served the cause of Balkan modernization as the Russo-Turkish War of 1828 to 1829 and the treaty of Adrianople. In effect, though not in purpose, they were symbolic acts of the long, splendid, disturbing drama to which Robert R. Palmer has given the name "Western Revolution."

Shortly after its founding in 1794 at the site of the fisherman's village of Hajibey, the port of Odessa took over Kherson's function as the chief Black Sea emporium for the export of grains and other agricultural produce from the estates of the landlords of Podolia, Volynia, and the Ukraine.[65] In fact, Odessa quickly became Russia's principal wheat export center. But on each occasion of war between Russia and Turkey (1806 to 1812, 1828 to 1829) or of civil and national war in Turkey (the Greek War of Independence of 1821 to 1829), the wheat exports of Odessa suddenly declined. In 1808, for example, it exported 104,000 chetverts * (217,880 hectoliters) of wheat; in 1809 and 1810 its wheat exports were still more negligible, and in 1811 they amounted to 145,000 chetverts (303,775 hectoliters). In 1817, a year of relative calm and peace, they rose to 1,100,000

* 100 chetverts equal 72 British imperial quarters, 576 imperial bushels, 594.5 U.S. bushels, or 209.5 hectoliters.

(2,304,500 hectoliters). After 1821 Odessa's wheat exports fell again, with an annual average of 685,000 chetverts (1,435,075 hectoliters) for the period 1815 to 1826.[66]

Between 1793 and 1830, the export of grains from Russia as a whole—both northern and southern—constituted a similar pattern of ups and downs:

	Average Annual Export of Russian Grains	
Years	(in chetverts)	(in hectoliters)
1793–1795	400,000	838,000
1800–1805	2,218,307	4,647,353
1806–1810	595,953	1,248,522
1811–1815	549,620	1,151,454
1800–1813	1,719,820	3,603,023
1816–1820	2,770,869	5,804,971
1815–1824	2,115,000	4,430,925
1826–1830	1,323,907	2,773,585

Grain exports from Black Sea and Sea of Azov ports at times declined precipitously in consequence of Russia's recurrent difficulties with Turkey between 1783 and 1829. A rising trend in grain (mostly wheat) exports from this region was nevertheless evident. From 68,731 chetverts (143,991 hectoliters) in 1786, Black Sea and Sea of Azov grain exports rose to 162,000 chetverts (339,390 hectoliters) in 1793; 666,093 (1,395,465 hectoliters) in 1824; 928,391 (1,944,979 hectoliters) in 1825; 1,016,160 (2,128,855 hectoliters) in 1826; 1,746,528 (3,658,976 hectoliters) in 1827; fell to 100,697 chetverts (210,960 hectoliters) in 1828; and attained 373,229 chetverts (781,915 hectoliters) in 1829; 2,247,942 (4,709,438 hectoliters) in 1830; 1,185,109 (2,482,803 hectoliters) in 1831; and 1,688,307 (3,537,003 hectoliters) in 1832.

In compensation for the decline in Black Sea exports during the war years 1828 and 1829, there was a sharp rise in 1830, followed by normal peacetime exports in 1831 and 1832. But the Russian harvests of 1833, 1834, and 1835 were very poor, and grain exports from Russia's Black Sea and Sea of Azov ports fell to 619,457 chetverts (1,297,762 hectoliters) in 1833, and 132,396 (277,370 hectoliters) and 712,264 chetverts (1,492,193 hectoliters) in 1834 and 1835. Nature's interference with Russia's export trade was thus sometimes as grave in its effects as an involvement in war with Turkey. Despite nature and politics, however, a rise in grain exports from Russia's southern areas was bolstered. The yearly average export of Russian grains from Black Sea and Azov ports was 1,096,911 chetverts (2,298,029 hectoliters) for 1826 to 1830; 806,507 (1,689,632 hectoliters) for 1831 to 1835; 2,092,689 (4,384,183 hectoliters) for 1836 to 1840; and 2,100,529 (4,400,608 hectoliters) for 1841 to 1845.

Between 1827 and 1846, a yearly average of 508,992 chetverts (1,066,338 hectoliters) was dispatched from Russia's Black Sea and Azov ports to Turkey and Greece. Before 1845, Russia's Black Sea areas were linked primarily with the eastern and central Mediterranean. A third of their cereal exports went to Istanbul, other parts of Turkey, Greece, and the Ionian Islands. Another third was destined for Trieste, Genoa, Livorno, and Marseille.

Russia's grain exports achieved another spurt—more important than the one based on its earlier emergence as a Mediterranean power—as a result of the Northern European potato blight of the mid-forties and of the repeal in 1846 of the English corn laws. Large quantities of grain were thereafter shipped to Great Britain. Between 1860 and 1905, in response to Europe's urbanization, shipments grew still more considerably. Continuing to follow the Mediterranean route, they grew in quantity as their destination ceased to be primarily Mediterranean.

If one can give credence to official statistics and estimates, Russia's grain exports expanded as follows between 1831 and 1910:[67]

	Average Annual Export of Russian Grains	
Years	(in millions of chetverts)	(in millions of hectoliters)
1831–1835	1.1	2.3
1824–1846	1.6	3.4
1847	5.9	12.4
1844–1853	5.5	11.5
1856–1860	4.0	8.4
1861–1865	8.4	17.6
1866–1870	14.8	31.0
1871–1875	20.4	42.7
1881–1885	31.8	66.6
1891–1895	46.4	97.2
1896–1900	46.6	97.6
1901–1905	60.1	125.9
1906–1910	61.1	128.0

The transformation of the southern Russian areas into a source of supply for Britain of wheat, maize, and other cereals prompted a sharp British reaction. To reduce its dependence on Russia, Britain strove to increase its cereal imports from the Ottoman principalities of Wallachia and Moldavia. Between 1837 and 1847, the export of wheat and maize from the ports of Galaţi and Brăila grew as follows, much of the produce going to Britain: [68]

Grain Exports

	Wheat		*Maize*	
Year	(in chetverts)	(in hectoliters)	(in chetverts)	(in hectoliters)
1837	350,000	733,250	213,000	446,235
1838	494,000	1,034,930	157,000	328,915
1839	499,866	1,047,219	248,000	519,560
1840	509,014	1,066,384	354,959	743,639
1845	645,894	1,353,148	372,001	779,342
1846	513,644	1,076,084	623,815	1,306,892
1847	807,440	1,691,587	1,200,013	2,514,027

The export of all varieties of grains from these ports amounted to 612,500 chetverts (1,283,188 hectoliters) in 1837; 662,500 (1,387,938 hectoliters) in 1838; 838,750 (1,757,181 hectoliters) in 1839; and 930,000 (1,948,350 hectoliters) in 1840.[69] Another estimate sets the exportation of grains from Brăila at 1,419,700 hectoliters in 1850 and 2,959,011 in 1851. Grain exports from Galaţi amounted to 865,516 hectoliters in 1850 and 1,536,328 in 1851. A third of the two ports' cereal trade went to Britain.[70]

From a British standpoint, it was imperative that no great power should obtain control of the grains of the whole northern and western Black Sea littoral. Since the Ukraine and Bessarabia were politically already Russian, the logic of the case called for a British denial to Russia of the right to occupy or control Moldavia, Wallachia, and Bulgaria, in all of which cereal production was to augment constantly during the nineteenth century. According to one estimate, grain cultivation in Bessarabia increased by nine times between 1814 and 1861, while the average per capita product rose from 1.7 chetverts (3.56 hectoliters) between 1812 and 1825 to 3.6 chetverts (7.54 hectoliters) between 1860 and 1868. In other words, Bessarabia's per capita cereal output was doubled. By the 1860's Bessarabians were able to market 35 percent of their cereal crops.[71]

In a New York *Tribune* article of April 27, 1855, Karl Marx emphasized the importance of the grain question in bringing on the Crimean War: "The growing value of the Danubian countries as granaries forbids England to allow their gradual absorption into Russia, and the closing of the navigation of the Danube by the same power. Russian grains form already a too important item in British consumption, and an annexation of the corn-producing frontier countries by Russia could make Great Britain entirely dependent upon her and the United States, while it would establish these two countries as the regulators of the corn-market of the world." [72]

Britain sought at the same time to place an ever greater portion of its manufactures in eastern Mediterranean, Near Eastern, and maritime Balkan markets. Its conquest of Ottoman markets occurred in three stages. Although its share in Ottoman trade appears to have declined during the first half of the eighteenth century, it was subsequently slowly restored.[73] By curbing French commerce during the French Revolution and Napoleonic Wars, Britain further improved its position. The third stage was ushered in at Russia's expense, after 1840, and proceeded from Britain's assertion as the world's foremost industrial power.

In 1825, Britain sold 2.5 percent of its production of cottons to Turkey; in 1855, when its output was much greater, it sent 11 percent to Turkey. Other major British exports to Turkey were refined sugar, hardware, cutlery, other iron and steel products, unwrought tin, woolens, and woolen yarn. By 1850, Turkey was the third most important outlet for British manufactures, after the Hanse towns and the Netherlands;[74] and most of Wallachia's supplies of hardware, cottons, muslins, and imported woolen cloth were of British origin.[75] About a quarter of Turkey's trade was with Britain and almost 15 percent with Russia in 1853. By 1861, 40 percent was with Britain and only 5 percent with Russia.[76]

In the early decades of the nineteenth century, the Russians held a virtual monopoly of trade in foreign manufactures in Trebizond. After 1840, British goods flowed into Western Asia from two directions, by way of the Indus and through the Straits; and Russian trade at Trebizond was put on the defensive.[77] The number of British ships passing through the Dardanelles grew from 250 in 1842 to 1,397 in 1848, and to 1,741 in 1852.[78]

Many different personal and public logics explain the Crimean

War, and in some ways the war was illogical. While noting the lack of logic or the multiplicity of logics, however, one should also observe that the logic of existing economic relations seemed to demand that Britain uphold Turkey against Russia. In responding to this logic, Britain extended its interest from the southern to the eastern maritime zone of the Balkans and became a formidable obstacle to Russian economic expansion.

Britain had ranked first in the Russian import and export market throughout the period 1827 to 1853, but the comparative relations of production were soon to change on the European continent. Even before the Crimean War, conditions had begun to prevail which would eventually make rivalry between Russia and Britain somewhat less relevant, and Russian rivalry with Prussia, and subsequently Germany, more serious. From eighth place among Russia's trade partners in 1827, Prussia jumped by 1853 to second place.[79] As Russia succeeded in putting increasingly larger amounts of its farm crops on Europe's markets, it became a threat to eastern German agriculture.

After the Franco-Prussian War, the world price of wheat fell and remained at a low level until World War I. In Russia, the agricultural crisis was particularly acute after 1885. The fall in wheat prices resulted in part from the reduction in transportation costs (from which the highly industrialized regions benefited most), made possible by the rapid diffusion of the steamship and railroad. The price of wheat was further depressed, however, as areas with low labor costs, such as India, or with a capital-intensive agriculture, such as parts of the United States, put more and more grains on the world market.[80] Occupying an intermediate position between the countries with very low labor costs and those with a capital-intensive agriculture, Russia had to export ever greater quantities of wheat in order to realize an equivalent profit. The tripling of Russian land prices between 1863 and 1897 [81] undermined still more the competitive position of Russian producers.

Official Russia reacted to the agricultural crisis by instituting a program of systematic industrial development. To the Russo-German misunderstandings in agriculture was thus added a new misunderstanding in the realm of industry. Bismarck's foreign policy of alliance with Russia was subverted, and power shifted in the new Germany to great functionaries and businessmen who knew statistics and to a new Emperor, William II, who promoted their ambitions. Precisely because the new men were economists and businessmen of acumen, commercial relations between Germany and Russia suffered only during a brief transitional period, namely, 1891 to 1894.[82]

Although Russia tripled its grain exports between 1881 and 1901 it was reduced by 1880 to second place as a world exporter of grains.[83] With the expansion of its own urban economy, the amount of wheat directed to export markets declined from almost one half the total harvest in the 1880's to a quarter between 1901 and 1905 and 15 to 16 percent in 1912 and 1913, and this despite the growth in the value of grain exports from 31 percent of Russia's total export trade between 1861 and 1865 to two fifths or more in the period 1880 to 1904.[84] At the same time, Russian Black Sea exports to Europe increased from 28 percent of Russia's total exports to Europe between 1842 and 1846 [85] to 43.3 percent in 1910.[86] Instead of diminishing, Russia's need for uninterrupted access to the Mediterranean was enhanced.

The Straits were denied to Russia approximately one year out of ten during the nineteenth century, namely, during part of the period 1806 to 1812 and in 1828 and 1829, 1853 to 1855, and 1877. Even during the Italo-Turkish War of 1911 to 1912, when Russia and Turkey were not embroiled in war with each other, Russian exports by way of the Straits declined. In the first six months of 1912, for example, Russian Black Sea exports of cereals and cereal products were 45 percent less than those of the corresponding 1911 period.[87] As the Black Sea gained in commercial importance to Russia, however, Russia needed more assurance than ever that the two narrow channels connecting the Black and Aegean seas would not be suddenly closed to its ships.

Russia's interest in the Balkans did not derive from the greatness of trade between the two regions. Their trade relations might have grown if Russia had industrialized more rapidly, but because of the industrial and commercial power of Western and Central Europe it was impossible to establish in the Balkans the kind of trading pattern Russia had with the Far East and Central Asia. Between 1842 and 1846, for example, 60 percent of Russia's exports to Asia comprised manufactured articles; its exports to Asiatic Turkey and Persia included metal manufactures, leather, porcelain, and woven goods. During the same years, 96 percent of Russia's exports to Europe consisted of raw materials and semifinished goods.[88]

Russian economic relations with the Balkans were of a third type, that is, relatively negligible after the mid-nineteenth century. The nature of trade between the two areas depended on political decisions and on their respective factor endowments. But Russian and Balkan factor endowments were similar. Where differences existed, it was generally more advantageous for each area unit to export elsewhere. Since the two had very little but raw materials to export to each other and since Russian manufactures were in a weaker competitive posture than those of geographically closer and technologically superior Western and Central Europe, they traded very little with each other.

The importance of cereals in the export economy of Moldavia and Wallachia has already been noted. Much the same held true in Bulgaria and Serbia, especially after 1860. By the period 1906 to 1912 cereals formed 56 percent of Bulgaria's export trade, and by 1910 they were valued at about half of Serbia's exports.[89] The senior adviser in the Russian foreign ministry from 1856 to 1887, A. G. Jomini, wrote to his superior on October 9, 1878, concerning the Balkan Slavs: "They have nothing to sell to us and nothing to buy from us, nor do we have anything to sell or buy there." [90] Russia's share in the trade of the Balkan countries continued to remain low even after its program of industrialization. Between 1909 and 1912, it broke down as follows: [91]

	Russia's Percentage Share in Total Trade	
Country	*Imports*	*Exports*
Rumania	2.7	1.0
Bulgaria	3.9	0.2
Serbia	2.4	0.0

Over the longer period 1884 to 1911, Serbian imports from Russia varied from a low of 0.5 percent of its total imports in 1907 to a high of 4.8 percent in 1895, with a general tendency to level off at 2 percent. Serbian imports from Russia grew significantly after 1904, but imports from other countries grew proportionately, and there was therefore no perceptible increase in the scale of imports from Russia. Exports to Russia averaged well under 1 percent of Serbia's total export trade throughout the period 1899 to 1909.[92] Poor roads and distances were a key factor in limiting trade between the two countries.[93]

As for capital investments, Russia's role in the Balkans was again negligible except for loans that were made for what were primarily political purposes. Private investments in the Balkans were not particularly encouraged by the Russian government. Investment capital thus flowed into the Balkans mainly from Western and Central Europe, while Russian capital investments, like Russian manufactures, were destined primarily for the home market or for various parts of Asia.[94]

Trade Routes and War Routes

Russia traded principally with Europe and with the Black Sea and Aegean areas. Its trade with the latter, moreover, was proportionately greater in the two decades before 1840 than in the subsequent half century. Finally, in an effort to bypass the narrow sea lane of the Straits, which it could not control, Russia began to show a greater interest in the Balkans proper. Russia was consequently drawn to the Balkans for essentially political reasons.

From Odessa, Taganrog, and other Russian Black Sea ports extended a system of sea routes which converged at the Bosporus to become one route, controlled on both sides by enemy artillery and fortifications until a second strait—the Dardanelles—was passed. Russia's interest in the Balkans was at least partly one of finding other routes. Had it been able to do this, it might have been able to stimulate its commerce with the Balkans. But even if Russia had discovered another route, it could not have used it to place its chief export product—grain—on the European and Mediterranean markets simply because the land routes were so much dearer than the sea routes.

Russia had built a Black Sea navy in the reign of Catherine II, but the Russian navy's inferiority to the British and French navies remained always in evidence, even in the eastern Mediterranean, where Britain could resort to "gunboat diplomacy," especially in relations with Greece. On learning of the Greek military coup d'état of September 15, 1843, as a consequence of which King Othon had to grant the Greeks a *syntagma,* or constitution, the French and British quickly dispatched several warships and other boats to Piraeus. But as late as October 10, the Bavarian minister to Athens, Karl von Gasser, was able to inform his government: "Russia is not represented by a single bark." [95]

After its occupation of Bessarabia at the beginning of the century, Russia had acquired control of the Sulina channel of the Danube delta. The efficient quarantine regulations it instituted on the Sulina in 1829 kept the plague out of Moldavia and Wallachia in 1835. But the other powers, especially Austria and Britain, claimed that Russia's quarantine regulations were designed to hinder non-Russian and promote Russian trade. Why else should the normal quarantine period at the Sulina channel be twenty-eight days as against merely six at Odessa? Moreover, despite the Austro-Russian commercial treaty of 1840 binding the Russian government to improve navigation facilities on the Sulina, Russia neglected to deepen the channel.

Commenting on his trip from Galaţi to Istanbul on the Austrian steamship *Metternich* (Lloyd Line) during the mid-1840's, the Russian diplomat Nicholas K. Giers, then on assignment in Moldavia, frankly admitted in his unfinished memoirs (written while he was minister to Stockholm, 1873 to 1875): "The estuary of the Danube along which we sailed divides into three arms, the Kilia, the Sulina, and the St. George. All of them were then in our possession. We directed our course along the Sulina arm, the only navigable one at that time, but with great difficulty because of the shallow water. Like the estuary of the Nile, which forms a delta, the estuary of the Danube has sand bars, so navigation over it was often impossible. It was Russia's responsibility to clean the estuary, but we did this for the sake of appearances only, because it was not to our advantage to make this route easier for foreign trade with the Black Sea region to the detriment of Odessa, whose development was rapidly proceeding at that time. I recall that at the beginning of my service in the Asiatic Department [which, among other things, was concerned with Ottoman and Balkan affairs] complaints from foreign powers with respect to this became so insistent that in order to pacify them the Ministry of Foreign Affairs decided to send to Sulina Active State Counselor Rodofinikin (the son of the famous K. K. Rodofinikin who directed our Eastern policy for many years) to investigate the question on the spot. This pacified the foreign governments, but not for long, because they soon were convinced that the Danubian commission headed by Rodofinikin would achieve nothing. The question was important particularly to Austria. It is not surprising, therefore, that following the unfortunate Crimean campaign Austria succeeded in setting up in 1856 a European commission which is also active today in the estuaries of the Danube. The work of this commission, which costs tens of millions, was crowned with success, and navigation in this region no longer presents difficulties."[96]

Because of the obstacles to navigation before the Crimean War, lighters had to carry grains and other merchandise from the Sulina to the open sea, where the goods were reloaded on ocean freighters. Since such transshipment was unnecessary for boats calling at Odessa, freight rates from Odessa were lower than those from the Danubian ports. Being generally inferior to the wheat of Odessa, the wheat of the Rumanian principalities had to be sold more cheaply. But the high freight rates were sometimes a deterrent to sales.[97]

At the conclusion of the Crimean War, the treaty of Paris (1856) provided for the creation of a riverain commission, which was made up of one representative each from Württemberg, Bavaria, Austria, Turkey, Serbia, Wallachia, and Moldavia, and was charged with the removal of impediments to navigation on the Danube. The treaty likewise called into being the European commission mentioned by Giers, which was made up of one delegate each from Great Britain, Austria, France, Russia, Sardinia, and Turkey, and whose function it was to superintend the proper initiation of the previous provision. While supposed to transfer its powers to the riverain commission after two years, it refused to surrender control. The lower Danube thus remained under its authority until World War I, to the detriment sometimes of the riparian states.[98]

The treaty of Paris further required the dismantling of the Russian Black Sea fleet, and by depriving Russia of Bessarabia it disqualified it as a riparian power and member of the riverain commission. Having lost the partial control of the mouth of the Danube it had exercised earlier, Russia began to show an interest in alternative routes.

In 1850 and 1851, the Serbian government had sought international approval for an Adriatic route which would extend across Serbia to Ottoman Novi Pazar, Peć (Ipek), Djakovica, Prizren, and Alessio (Lesh), along the valleys of the Ibar, White Drin, and Drin. Fearful that the road might facilitate and encourage Serbian aggrandizement, Turkey opposed the project. Austria pursued a similar course in order to prevent Serbian economic emancipation and the emergence of a possible rival to Trieste. Prior to the Crimean War, even Russia had been hostile to the project, in evident fear that Moldavia and Wallachia might make use of the new route and in that way narrow Bessarabia's commercial role.[99]

Russia's opposition to a transversal road linking Serbia and Wallachia to the southern Adriatic may have been based on the belief that it would eventually acquire the Straits. The Crimean War momentarily dashed such expectations.

Official Russia nevertheless objected to the joining of the Ottoman and European railways even in the 1860's. Apprehensive of its ability to prevent this, however, Russian diplomacy was ready by 1869 to assent to the connection of the Ottoman and Austro-Hungarian railways by way of Bosnia, where the difficulties of the terrain made construction possible only at a great cost in time and money. For military and political reasons alike, Russia continued to oppose the junction of Balkan and Austro-Hungarian railways by way of Serbia. In any event, the Russian ambassador to Istanbul, General Nicholas Pavlovich Ignatiev, appears to have taken action in 1873 to bar a solution of the Ottoman railway question in Serbia's favor.[100] Toward 1875, however, a portion of the Russian press started to agitate in favor of a railway line that should extend southward from the Danube to Bar (Antivari), Ulcinj (Dulcingno), or San Giovanni di Medua (Shëngjin) on the Adriatic, and continue northward by way of the Rumanian railway system to Odessa.[101]

After the war of 1877 to 1878, the Russian government threw its support to a line that was supposed to run from Ruse (Rusçuk) or Svishtov (Sistova) to the Maritsa valley, thus corresponding to the line of advance of the Russian army during the 1877 campaign. The chief advantage of this route was its convenience for the movement of Russian troops toward the Straits in case of war with Turkey or Britain. But the treaty of Berlin had put Bulgaria under obligation to construct an international line that should run from the Serbian frontier to Sofia and thence to the Turkish frontier. Bulgaria could not afford to build two lines simultaneously, and since the proposed Russian line was of slight economic value, whereas the Sofia-Niš-Belgrade line could serve to bring Bulgarian goods to Central European markets, it opted for the second solution.[102]

In 1886, a Russian railroad contractor and financier, Samuel Poliakov, tried to persuade the Russian government to aid his company and affiliates to form a syndicate in the Netherlands to buy up existing shares in Balkan railroads, including the Ruse-Razgrad-Shumen-Varna line, which had been built with British capital and opened to traffic at the end of 1866.[103] Early in 1887, however, Britain, Italy, and Austria-Hungary signed an agreement to maintain the status quo in the Mediterranean, Adriatic, and Aegean seas. The Russian government's Mediterranean policy was thereby further circumscribed, and Russia lost interest in the promotion of schemes such as Poliakov's.[104]

The economic historian David S. Landes defines "imperialist exploitation" as the "employment of labor at wages lower than would obtain in a free bargaining situation" or as "the appropriation of goods at prices lower than would obtain in a free market. Imperialist exploitation, in other words, implies nonmarket constraint."[105] The great powers forced the Balkan states to build railroads, improve the Danube, and create the kind of transportation system that at least initially was of primary advantage to the dominant countries. The underdeveloped Balkan nations were thus constrained to pay for part of the continued economic expansion of the economically most highly developed European countries.

Of all the European powers, Russia shared least in the program of aid to the *developed* countries that had been imposed on the underdeveloped Balkan nations by the great powers and their bourgeoisies. Although Russia's limited economic power (rather than selflessness) accounts for this peculiarity, it is certain that "imperialist exploitation" by Russia was of less significance than that by any other European power.

Russian industrialization entailed, moreover, the importation of an ever greater quantity of tools and other industrial commodities for the development of an industrial economy. As a result, Russian trade was diverted increasingly to Germany. By 1900, Germany had replaced Britain as Russia's chief trading partner, and Germany's position continued to improve between 1900 and 1913. Imports to Russia from Germany grew from an average of 35.8 percent of Russia's total import trade between 1901 and 1905 to 52.7 percent in 1913, while Russian exports to Germany increased from 23.5 to 31.7 percent of Russia's total export trade.[106]

At the same time, German commercial expansion hurt Russia's position in the Near East. After 1895, flour and beet sugar were the only Russian products able to compete on the Istanbul market with German goods.[107] German exports to Turkey, and imports therefrom, grew on the other hand, as shown in the following table.

From fifteenth on the list of exporters to Turkey in 1886, Germany jumped by 1910 to the rank of second or third. Germany, Italy, and Austria-Hungary were also elbowing France out of the Turkish market, and they were in the process of overtaking Britain.[108] German capital, moreover, was being invested in Rumania and Bulgaria, and Russia was concerned lest Germany and Austria-Hungary—both by that time important capital investors in the Balkans and the Near East

Year	*German Exports to Turkey* (in marks)	*German Imports from Turkey* (in marks)
1882	5.9	1.2
1888	11.7	2.3
1890	34.1	9.6
1893	40.9	16.5
1895	39.0	22.0
1900	34.4	30.5 (or 30.2)
1904	75.3	43.4
1905	71.1	51.5
1906	68.6	55.1
1910	104.9	67.4 (or 67.5)
1911	112.8	77.6
1913	98.4	74.0

—should combine forces and exercise still greater control over the economic and political life of the Balkans and Asia Minor.[109]

A major factor in the growth of Germany's share in Ottoman commerce may have been the direct and relatively rapid flow of goods from Germany, Austria, and Hungary to Istanbul, which was made possible by the joining of the European and Ottoman railway systems in the summer of 1888. The German aim of a northwest-southeast trans-Balkan railway was realized, whereas the Russian goal of a north-south railroad in the eastern Balkans or of a northeast-southwest Balkan railroad was frustrated.

As late as 1887, no German capital was invested in Ottoman railways. Germany quickly took advantage of the new Balkan railway system, however, to become the dominant power in Turkey. By 1892, the Deutsche Bank and its collaborators controlled the railways of Turkey from the Austro-Hungarian border to Istanbul and began to sponsor a project that was soon known as the Berlin-to-Baghdad railway scheme.[110]

Turkey meanwhile had become indebted to European investors, and in 1881 the great powers had set up an Ottoman public debt administration, with an executive body known as the Council, comprising one representative each from the United Kingdom, France, Germany, Austria-Hungary, Italy, and Turkey. The Council exercised control over the assessment and collection of revenues earmarked for Turkey's creditors.

With its finances and indirectly its entire economy under *five-*

power control, the Ottoman Empire was one of the two regions of the world—China was the other—on which was imposed the principle of the "Open Door." In Egypt, the principle of *dual control* had been operative since 1876, when the profligate khedive Ismail, unable to meet his growing debts to European creditors, had transferred Egyptian finances to the control of French and British agents. If, however, there was a dual financial control, there was but one military control. The latter had been established in 1882, when, without French assistance because of strong opposition to colonialism in the Chamber of Deputies, Britain had suppressed an Egyptian revolt fanned by xenophobia and led by militant nationalists.[111]

At the close of the nineteenth and the opening of the twentieth century, the danger of a world conflagration was greatest perhaps in the areas under multiple-power control—the countries of the "Open Door"—and along their peripheries, where one of the powers normally exercised exceptional privileges, namely in such countries as Egypt, Bosnia-Hercegovina, Indo-China, Serbia, and Manchuria. In Serbia, Bosnia-Hercegovina, and the Ottoman Empire, however, Russian financial control was even more negligible than Russian commerce.

But following defeat by Japan in 1904 and 1905, Russia shifted its attention to obtaining French and British consent to Russian annexation of the Straits.[112] Increasingly worried over what would happen to its Mediterranean line of communications if the Ottoman Empire suddenly collapsed and another power replaced it at the Bosporus,[113] Russia clung to a policy of spheres of influence. As Germany became a greater threat to their trade, Britain and France grew less reluctant to yield to Russia's ambition to rule the Straits. They agreed to this, however, only in 1915, during the turmoil of the Great War.

Before official Russia and Russian commercial and agrarian interests could realize their aspirations, the Russian Revolution fatefully intervened. Condemning the tsarist policy of spheres of influence, the new Soviet government formally renounced Russian rights to the Straits.

Noneconomic Dimensions

Russian domination in the Balkans was primarily ideological. Even in this respect, however, Russia was less successful than many other European countries. Moreover, the appeal of Russian ideas and idcals, whether in the realm of religion, of literature, or of politics, was not equally alluring to all parts of the Balkans.

In Greece, the early links with Russia had been both religious and economic. Following its War of Independence, however, Greece created an autocephalous or national church, which failed for a time to obtain the recognition and approval of the patriarchate of Constantinople; the patriarchate, on the other hand, was the recipient of Russian support. The economic links between Russia and Greece similarly grew proportionately weaker after 1830.

Bulgarian connections with Russia were primarily of a geographical and mythical character. The geographical relationship is self-evident. The mythopoeic link took the form of belief in the return of a legendary savior called *diado* or "ancestor" Ivan and may have had a factual basis in the deeds of Ivan III (1462 to 1505),[114] who liberated Muscovy from its dependence on the Tatars, laid claim to all the lands of former Kievan Rus, married a Byzantine princess, and assumed the Southern Slavic title of Tsar, or Caesar. Legends about the might of Moscow and its ruler spread during his reign to all Russian lands, and the myth of *diado* Ivan may have been fashioned in Bulgaria in the latter part of the fifteenth century, when expectations of a savior and of the millennium were widely current in the Ottoman-dominated Balkans. In the millennial dreams of the Slavic and Orthodox world, the year 1492—known to them as 7000—was regarded as the end of the cosmic "week" of seven cosmic "days" each a thousand ordinary years long, and therefore as the occasion for the day of judgment and the abolition of historical time.[115] As historical time continued to oppress the Balkan peoples, however, legends foretelling the coming of a savior gathered force. The legend of *diado* Ivan may have benefited from this general inclination, particularly since Ivan was also one of the magical names of the Southern Slavs of Hungary for the mythical savior who was supposed to liberate them.[116]

The Muscovite state of the fifteenth and sixteenth centuries, however, was more concerned with promoting regular trade relations with the Ottoman Empire and securing Ottoman protection against the intrigues of the khanate of Crimea than with protecting the Balkan Christians or liberating the Southern Slavs. Not until the reign of Fedor I Ivanovich at the end of the sixteenth century did a vague Russian ideology of delivering Moldavia, Wallachia, Bosnia, Serbia, and Hungary from bondage start to take shape.[117]

This liberation ideology had its basis in community of religion or/ and similarity of language and ethnic origin, and Russia propagated it in the eighteenth century by furnishing the Pannonian Serbs with teachers and with grammars and other printed books.[118] Russian influence also spread among the Serbs of Hungary through the flow of a small number of Serbian students—at least sixty-five in the eighteenth century—to Russian theological, civil, and military schools.[119]

Except for the odysseys of Orthodox priests, however, such links were rare with the Southern Slavs south of the Danube and the Sava until 1840, when a program of scholarships for Bulgarian students was instituted at the Odessa seminary.[120] The program of Russian scholarships was accelerated soon thereafter, and about five hundred Bulgarian students were awarded such grants between 1856 and 1876. The Slavic Benevolent Society of Moscow, which was founded in 1858, was particularly active in enabling Bulgarian students to go to Russia.[121]

A similar influence was felt in the principality of Serbia at about the same time, although Russian influence in education became important there only after the Revolution of 1848. In 1839, the Serbian government had established a program of stipends which made it possible for a few Serbian students to obtain a higher education abroad at the expense of the state, and in that year all ten recipients of state stipends were sent to Austria and Saxony.[122] A few students were later sent to the University of Paris, but for a time there were no state scholarships for study in Russia.

In 1847, the Russian agent Colonel Danilevskii tried to persuade the Serbian government to recall its students from the German states and France and divert them to Russia. Although Danilevskii does not appear to have had much immediate success, Russian influence rose in Serbia after Russia's intervention in 1849 against the Hungarian Revolution. In January, 1850, the French consul in Belgrade advised his government of the Serbian senate's refusal to name state scholars to Western Europe but of its authorization of six state grants for study in Russia.[123] Perhaps under the influence of the Russian consulate, an article appeared a few days later in the official Serbian newspaper castigating those Serbian functionaries who had chosen to study in Western Europe and denouncing their "French ideas" as contrary alike to human nature and to divine law.[124] The Russian consul general in Belgrade, General Dmitrii Sergeevich Levshin, sought to dominate the Serbian government by overseeing the nomination of public officials and intervening in other domestic affairs. The tiny group of young Serbians who had been educated in France and held a few administrative posts tended to give their support to the Serbian minister of the interior, Ilija Garašanin, who had come to be identified as an opponent of the Russian "party." [125]

As in the rest of Europe, however, the forces of reaction were then strong. Early in 1852, under Levshin's influence, the Serbian government appointed an émigré Serb and graduate of the schools of Odessa and Kiev, Aleksa Vukomanović, to the chair of national history, language, and literature at the Lyceum (the future University) of Belgrade. One of Vukomanović's Odessa professors, the émigré Serb Simon Platonović, was summoned the following year to reorganize the Lyceum and assume the function of chief inspector of schools. But the sharp reaction of Serbian teachers against his attempts to regulate all aspects of their lives, from the way to lecture to the way to shave, persuaded the government in 1855 to dismiss him.[126]

If influence can be measured in terms of the flow of Serbian students to Russian schools, however, it continued to grow in importance. In 1863, when nineteen Serbian students were holders of state scholarships in various European schools, six of the nineteen held appointments in St. Petersburg and Kiev.[127] As of 1865, moreover, the number of scholarships extended to Serbia by the Russian government and various Pan-Slav organizations increased substantially. In 1866, among the recipients of Serbian state stipends made available through the offices of the Russian ministry of foreign affairs was the future Serbian socialist leader Svetozar Marković. The increase in scholarships for study in Russia seems to have been in part the fruit of efforts exerted by the anti-Ottoman and anti-Habsburg Pan-Slavist Nicholas Pavlovich Ignatiev, who between 1868 and 1877 served as Russian envoy and ambassador to Istanbul.

Between 1868 and 1888, the St. Petersburg Slavic Committee enabled one hundred and four men and sixteen women students to study in Russia; of this number, fifty-eight men and six women, or 53 percent, were from Serbia.[128] The chief sponsor of Bulgarian students, on the other hand, was the Moscow Committee. Serbian students were thus drawn to Russian schools where Western or European influences were strong, whereas Bulgarian students were drawn to schools with a more purely Russian orientation. Moreover, more Bulgarians than Serbians, perhaps four times as many, were recipients of Russian-sponsored stipends. On a per capita basis, however, the proportion in favor of Bulgaria was less great. What made the Russian impact stronger in Bulgaria than in Serbia was the scarcity of Western European outlets for Bulgarian students until Bulgaria was made an autonomous principality in 1878.

Russia's endeavors between 1840 and 1880 to accomplish in belief and ideology what it could not achieve in the material and economic spheres were subverted by a variety of forces. Until 1848, and even until 1860, a program of Slavism might have won the support of many Balkan Slavs, but the Russian government failed to demonstrate such an interest until after the Crimean War. When it was finally ready to take advantage of the ideology of Slavism, there were only two peoples —the Bulgarians and the Montenegrins—who were still attentive to the call. In Serbia and Vojvodina, on the other hand, liberals and radicals denounced the hegemonistic aims of Russian Pan-Slavism.[129] After 1860, regional nationalisms replaced Slavism as a force of attraction to the Slavs of Serbia and Austria-Hungary. Slavism obviously could never win the support of the non-Slavic peoples of the Balkans, such as the Greeks, Rumanians, Albanians, and Turks.

Another ideology to which the Russian government appealed was Orthodoxy. Orthodoxy had been weakened, however, by the formation in Greece and Serbia of autocephalous churches, which were only spiritually and nominally under the direction of the patriarchate of Constantinople. Russia later encouraged the creation of a Bulgarian exarchate, but Greeks, Serbs, Rumanians, and the patriarchate of Constantinople regarded the exarchate as an agent of Bulgarian nationalism in religious garb. Among the non-Bulgarian Slavs of the Balkans, moreover, Orthodoxy had been enfeebled by the diffusion of secularism, and it could not appeal to Southern Slavs of Roman Catholic and Muslim faith.[130]

There was consequently a time gap or cultural lag between the value systems of the Russian Pan-Slavists and Russian government and the ideologies of the Balkan élites. The ideologies of the new Balkan élites were nationalism, secularism, modernism, liberalism, radicalism, and socialism, all suspect to the Russian government. Russian Pan-Slavists and volunteers who went to Serbia in 1875 and 1876 to fight in the war against Turkey discovered to their dismay that Serbia was, in comparison to Russia, a Western country, with a social structure and habits of mind quite different from those prevalent in Russia.[131]

A further complication in the relations between Russia and the Balkan Slavs was the Russian government's expectation of greater loyalty from the Southern Slavic countries than from its own subjects. As the Russian envoy, Colonel Prince Vasilii Andreevich Dolgorukii, seems to have said in 1838: "Serbia's comportment toward Russia should be like that of a Turkish woman toward her husband. Not only should she be faithful, but she should neither show her face nor talk to any other man." [132] Suspecting their Russian advisers of a similar attitude toward Bulgaria, sensitive Bulgarian nationalists forced the Russians to leave their country in the 1880's, almost oblivious to Russia's crucial contribution to the achievement of Bulgarian autonomy and constitutional government.

The Russian government, moreover, pursued in general a policy of maintaining the Ottoman and Habsburg empires at least partially intact as a barrier against the "empire" of Revolution. Russian agents sometimes misinterpreted, reinterpreted, and exceeded their government's aims, thus misleading both the Balkan peoples and other countries as to official Russia's real intentions. Official Russia might occasionally entertain the notion of giving succor to a rising of the Balkan Christians in defense of Christianity; it could not tolerate national and social insurrection. Even the Pan-Slav ideal could succeed in appealing momentarily to official Russian circles only after Russia's defeat in the Crimean War, which Russia waged in part as a religious crusade.[133] But if there was one idea around which Balkan liberals and radicals could rally, it was the belief in the need to destroy the Ottoman and Habsburg empires.

Cultural Mission of the Small Fry

What an illusion, however, to assume that only great powers strive to dominate and establish an economic, political, or ideological imperium! Did not Russia and Rumania both lay claim to the province of Bessarabia? Further south, as early as 1832, soon after the institution of a nominally independent Greek state, Russia and Greece similarly found themselves at odds, divided by rival claims to Constantinople and the Byzantine heritage. Against the various Russian visions of the future emerged the "Great Idea" of the Greeks, namely, a revived Byzantium under Greek hegemony.[134]

As early as 1843 or 1844, at the suggestion of Polish leaders who were envious of Russian power and sought to bring the Southern Slavs under their own influence, Serbian leaders began to embrace the notion of expansion to the Adriatic as a means of freeing the Serbs from their economic dependence on Austria.[135] By the end of the century, thinking in terms of an outlet to the sea was more or less general among Serbian commercial, professional, military, and bureaucratic elements. In 1912, the famous Serbian geographer Jovan Cvijić vigorously defended Serbia's claim to Albanian-inhabited territories and to communications rights across northern Albania to the southern Adriatic as an "anti-ethnographical necessity." [136] In a letter of November 30, 1912, the British minister to Belgrade complained to his government that the Serbians were "quite off their heads" in their "visions of blue seas and Servian ships in the offing bringing home the wealth of the Indies." [137]

Among the Bulgarians, the policy of an "anti-ethnographical necessity" took the form of claims to the whole of the ethnically very mixed region of Macedonia and to eastern Serbia and of a search for access to the Aegean. After 1878, their aspirations were codified in the form of demands that the "Great Bulgaria" provided for by the Russian-sponsored treaty of San Stefano be made a reality.

Under the influence of bourgeois values, even peasant leaders began to advocate a policy of "anti-ethnographical necessity." In a book published in 1904 under a title that would translate as *Modern Colonization and the Slavs,* for example, the Croatian Peasant party leader Stjepan Radić embraced a Slavophile and Dostoevskian mood in his assertion of the destiny of the Slavs to become the "cultural nucleus and psychic mirror of the whole of humanity." Radić further contended that "we Danubian Slavs are far more able than the Germans to revitalize the Danubian region and colonize and awaken Asia Minor to a new life. The Germans nevertheless trample over us and the Rumanians and Magyars, not to mention the peoples of Asia Minor, as if we were in the swaddling clothes of civilization and only on the first rung of national consciousness."

One of the reasons for Russia's failure to expel the Turks from the Balkans, he claimed, was its reliance on religion (Orthodoxy) and the unprogressive Orthodox Slavic peoples. If, instead, Russia had put its trust in the progressive Czechs, Croatians, and Hungarians, that is, the Danubian peoples, the results might have been quite different.

Radić looked forward to the total destruction of Ottoman power.

But espousing the view that the region between the Danube and the Bosporus prospered only when regular and frequent commercial intercourse existed from one end to the other and when it was organized as a single political entity, he envisaged the need to establish another political unit to take its place, this time under the leadership of the Danubian Slavs. On the premise that such a state could not long endure unless it controlled both shores of the Bosporus, he proposed that Asia Minor be converted into a colonial area under the domination of the Danubian Slavs. By their ties of religion, he thought, the Muslim Slavs of Bosnia-Hercegovina were suited to play an especially important role in promoting Danubian commerce with the Near East.[138]

Against the policy of "anti-ethnographical necessity" were raised the voices of Balkan socialists, chief among them Serbia's Dimitrije Tucović. At the First Balkan Social Democratic Congress in Belgrade, February 7–9, 1910, Tucović and other Balkan socialists harshly condemned the narrowly nationalist and hegemonistic programs of the Balkan bourgeoisies. Simultaneously, they chastised the great powers for their intervention in Balkan affairs. In the eyes of Balkan socialists, the Balkan and Yugoslav questions could be understood properly only in the framework of the larger problem of relations between dominant and dominated peoples or between colonizing and colonial countries. By pursuing a policy of self-determination, they intended to abolish the colonial status of the Balkan peoples.[139]

Balkan bourgeois nationalists, peasant leaders, and socialists had at least one goal in common: to limit the authority of the great powers and extend that of their own ideal states and social systems. Aspiring to become "eagles," "bears," and "lions," the small fry of the Balkans sought to augment their own ability to dominate by winning adherents to their own conceptions of self-determination and necessity. This orientation was anti-Russian only occasionally. In practice, it worked sometimes to Russia's advantage. In either case, however, the main aim was to promote, not the goals of official Russia, but rather those of one or more individual Balkan nations, or of the Balkans as a whole, or of some large or small Balkan social group.

In this study of the evolving and yet almost stable makeup of Russo-Balkan relations over several centuries, attention has been drawn to some general as well as to particular aspects of domination and imperialism. The object of focusing on both the *goals* and the *limits* of Russian dominance in the Balkans has been to show how the political, economic, and other forms of dominance were a direct function in part of particular spatial and cultural relationships, and how the temper and degree of dominance tended to acquire a long-term character. Thus, from the rise of Russian might to World War I and the 1917 Revolution, a broad variety of structures—geographical, economic, psychological, ideological, international, and specifically national and social—conspired to make Russia's ability to dominate in the Balkans less emphatic than that of the other European states. The study of Russian imperialism in the special local environment of the Balkans has put into relief the enduring features of Russo-Balkan relations. In a more indirect way, it may have cast some light on the general importance of the long view in history.

FIRUZ KAZEMZADEH

Russian Penetration of the Caucasus

Though the Caucasus is topographically, climatically, ethnologically, and linguistically one of the most varied regions on earth, it possesses a historical unity imposed by its very position as a mountain fastness between two seas.

The Caucasus has always been a battleground of peoples, cultures, and religions. The Persians, the Greeks, the Romans, the Arabs, the Turks, the Russians, have been involved in the Caucasus and fought over it. The Russians were latecomers, the last of a long series of invaders and foreign rulers.

Russia's contacts with the Caucasus go far back. Russian historians point out that as early as the second half of the fifteenth century Russian travelers and merchants visited the Caucasus, while Russian goods made their way beyond, to Tabriz, Delhi, and Baghdad. S. A. Belokurov found in the Moscow archive of the ministry of foreign affairs documents relating to early embassies from Shirvan and Georgia. Afanasii Nikitin, author of a famous book of travels in the East and India, was in the party of merchants who accompanied a return embassy to Shirvan in 1466.[1]

At first these contacts were occasional and relatively insignificant. It was the fall of the Tatar khanates of Kazan and Astrakhan, both successor states of the Golden Horde, that opened to Russia the road to the East and the South. Once established on the northern shore of the Caspian Sea, Russia inevitably became a Caspian power whose interests spread to Tarqu, Darband, Kabarda, and, beyond the Great Caucasus, to Georgia, Armenia, and northern Persia.

The acquisition of Astrakhan made it necessary for Russia to participate in the affairs of the North Caucasian peoples, such as the Avars and the Kumyks of Daghestan, the Ossetians, the Kabardians, and the Circassians (Cherkes). These were warlike tribes, independent, unruly, and virtually unconquerable before the day of modern military power. Year after year the Mountaineers of the Northern Caucasus formed intricate alliances, involving not only themselves but, frequently, the Crimeans, the Turks, and sometimes the Persians as well. As successors of the khanate of Astrakhan, the Russians inherited the latter's conflicts with the shamkhal (ruler) of Tarqu, a Daghestani state. The loose confederation of Kabardian chieftains, enemies of Tarqu, almost automatically became Russia's ally.[2]

The Kabardians, like the Cherkes a branch of the Adighe people, were Sunni Muslims. They lived in clans under petty chieftains, many of whom had only a few horsemen at their command and none of whom recognized any supreme authority. There were no towns in Kabarda, very little commerce, and no sense of national unity.

A few contacts had been made between Kabarda and Russia even before the latter conquered Astrakhan. As early as 1552 two Kabardian chieftains appeared in Moscow. Russian sources claim that they pledged allegiance to the tsar in the name of all their people. Claims to sovereignty over all sorts of states and principalities were typical of Muscovite Russia. Such claims seldom had any foundation in fact. Thus in 1554 the Russian envoy in Poland, Fedor Voksherin, stated that "The Cherkasy [the Russian name for the Kabardians] are ancient serfs of our Sovereigns. They had fled from Riazan; but two years ago . . . Cherkas princes came . . . to supplicate the Sovereign, who received them graciously. Today they are all in the service of our Sovereign and execute his orders." [3]

For one reason or another the "annexation" of 1552 must have seemed insufficient to the Muscovite government. Perhaps most of the Kabardians were not even aware of it. Be that as it may, in 1557 Prince Temriuk, a powerful chieftain, came to Astrakhan seeking Russian aid against the shamkhal of Tarqu. In the same year he and another chief, Tazriut, sent envoys to Moscow with a request for protection. This was interpreted by the Russians as Kabardian submission.

"Thus the year 1557 must be regarded as the date of the voluntary adherence of Kabarda to the Russian State," writes the Soviet historian, N. A. Smirnov:[4]

"The adherence of Kabarda to Russia, which had a voluntary character, corresponded to the interests of the Kabardian people, protected it from hostile attempts on the part of Crimean khans and Turkish sultans. It was an event of great and progressive significance that played a tremendous positive role in the historical destiny not only of the Kabardian but of other North Caucasian peoples as well."[5]

The political alliance between Temriuk and Ivan the Terrible was cemented in 1561 by the marriage of the tsar to the chieftain's daughter. Temriuk exploited his illustrious connection both against the shamkhal of Tarqu and against domestic enemies and rivals. He invited the tsar to build forts and station troops on the Terek River, hoping to maintain and expand his own unstable authority. Other Kabardian princes followed the same policy of relying upon Muscovite support. In 1577 Temriuk's brother, Kanbulat, persuaded Ivan to erect another Russian fort on the Terek, this one at the mouth of the Sunzha. Like Temriuk, he used Russians to destroy his private enemies. The Russians were happy to support and subsidize such princes, thereby making of them moderately reliable clients. By 1590 several Kabardian princes were in the pay of Moscow. The "voluntary adherence" of Kabarda to Russia, emphasized by N. A. Smirnov and other Soviet historians who see the expansion of the Russian state as a "progressive" phenomenon, did not go beyond a loose alliance of a number of primitive tribal chiefs with the increasingly aggressive Russian power.

In July, 1588, a number of princes signed a *Shert'* (treaty or charter) which stated that the tsar, Fedor I Ivanovich, extended his protection to them, that he would, as his father had before him, aid them against all enemies, while they would remain faithful to him and his successors.[6] To the Russians the meaning of such a pledge of allegiance, embodied in an official document signed under oath, was altogether different from its meaning to the Kabardians. The former had a centralized state, an autocratic tsar, a formal system of written law, a functioning bureaucracy, and an ideology that sustained the station, power, and prerogatives of tsar and nation. The latter were a wild people, relatively recently Muslimized and largely untouched by Islamic civilization, without a state, without written law, even without a firm notion of sovereignty. To the Russians a Temriuk was the Kabardian tsar; to the Kabardians he was only another chieftain. No charter signed by him or anyone else was considered binding by his peers and rivals. Thus an act that to the Russians signified submission was, in the eyes of the Kabardians, an insignificant semiprivate event.

East of Kabarda in Daghestan the Russians pushed into the domain of the shamkhal of Tarqu, a state, or rather an agglomeration of Turkic-speaking tribes wherein the Kumyks were dominant. The Kumyks (Ghumuq), like the Kabardians, were Sunni Muslims, but the proximity of the Caspian and easier access to Astrakhan and Persia produced among them a more highly organized society and a rudimentary state. Russian attempts to induce the shamkhal to accept a protectorate such as the one nominally established in Kabarda were rejected. As a result the Russians tried to conquer Tarqu.

In 1591 the governor of Astrakhan, Prince Sitskii, was provided with funds for an expedition against the shamkhal. Two years later Prince Aleksander Fedorovich Zasekin opened hostilities supported by 5,000 Russian troops and 10,000 Kabardian allies.[7] Russian troops captured several villages and began to move against the shamkhal's capital, the town of Tarqu. In 1594 Tsar Fedor I Ivanovich appointed Prince Ivan Andreevich Khvorostinin to take Zasekin's place. The new commander fought a disastrous battle with the Kumyks. Some 3,000 Russians were killed. The rest fled in disorder. Thus ended Russia's first Caucasian war.

Aware of Russia's power and its ability to resume hostilities, the shamkhal appealed to Shah Abbas the Great of Persia for help and protection. The shah, through the Russian envoy Prince Zvenigorodskii, suggested that the Russians leave the shamkhal alone. Military defeat and Persian pressure led Moscow to adopt a more cautious policy.

When a new Perso-Turkish War (1602 to 1612) created an unstable situation throughout the Caucasus, Georgian princes, hoping for help from their coreligionist to the north, sent envoys (1603) to Boris Godunov with the request that he build a fortress on the river Terek to prevent the shamkhal of Tarqu from raiding Georgia. Tsar Boris dispatched Voevoda Ivan Buturlin to the Caucasus, and Russia was soon deeply involved in Georgian and Daghestani affairs. In Georgia a series of conspiracies resulted in the murder of King Alexander and of one of his sons, George, by another son, Constantine, who called himself "a slave of the Shah." Before being overthrown in his turn, Constantine refused to swear allegiance to Russia and caused Russian envoys to leave the country in May, 1605.[8]

Buturlin's first steps in the Caucasus were seemingly successful. He attacked and captured the town of Tarqu. However, in a relatively primitive society such as that of Daghestan, the loss of the capital meant very little. The shamkhal, aided by some Turkish troops, continued the struggle. Soon Buturlin found himself under siege in Tarqu. He negotiated with the Turks, who promised him a safe retreat to the Russian lines on the river Terek. When his troops left the town, the Kumyks and the Turks attacked and wiped out the entire Russian force of 7,000 men. Buturlin perished with his troops.[9]

The onset of the Time of Troubles put a stop to further Russian activity in the Caucasus for almost a century. The energies of the Russian state were expended in struggles against Poland, Sweden, and Turkey, the annexation of the Ukraine, and the suppression of domestic anarchy. Russia maintained tenuous connections with Kabarda and occasionally sent agents to Georgia, but did not resume expansion in the Causasus until the reign of Peter the Great.

Peter's initial interest in the Caucasus was to a considerable extent a result of his wars against the Turks. Russia's acquisition of the fortress of Azov in 1696 was a threat to the Crimea and a challenge to Turkish hegemony in the Black Sea. To strengthen its positions on the eastern shore of that sea, Turkey supported the attempts of the Crimea to subdue Circassia and Kabarda. The Crimean khan, Devlet Girey, urged the Sultan not to permit Russia to retain Azov and the mouth of the Don.

Russia's brilliant victory at Poltava further alarmed the Sublime Porte. While the defeated Charles XII of Sweden pressed the Sultan to resist the Russians, Peter assumed a belligerent tone in his relations with Constantinople, demanding such impossible concessions as the extradition of the Swedish king, who was in Turkish territory, and threatening war in case of noncompliance. As a result the Turkish government decided on December 1, 1710, to go to war. The new conflict led to the defeat of the Russians, the loss of Azov, and the exclusion of Russia from the Black Sea.

Since the Black Sea was now out of his reach, Peter turned his attention to the Caspian and beyond. B. H. Sumner has written of Peter: "For all the concentration of his main energies on Europe, he had from his earliest years taken a lively interest in Asia. The enthusiasm of the explorer was allied with the gold-dazzled phantasy of the prospector and the merchant."[10] Central Asia and India fascinated him as possible objects of commerce and conquest. A Russian expedition against Khiva in 1717, which ended in disaster and the loss of 3,500 men, failed to discourage the tsar. Two years earlier he had dispatched Artemii Volynskii, a young and ambitious officer, to Persia. Volynskii was to gather economic, political, and military intelligence, and, specifically, to ascertain whether there were in Persia rivers that could be navigated to the borders of India. Volynskii found Persia on the brink of anarchy. The Safavid dynasty had degenerated. Only traditional awe of the shah prevented the component parts of the great empire from flying apart. Volynskii perceived Persia's weakness and advised Peter to conquer that rich country before it recovered its strength under some new and energetic ruler.[11] Though Peter agreed with Volynskii's reasoning, he did not act on his proposals until the war with Sweden had been brought to its conclusion by the treaty of Nystad.

In August, 1721, Lezghian tribesmen, nominally subjects of the shah, attacked the town of Shemakha, causing much loss to Russian merchants and providing Peter with a pretext for military intervention. He could not have chosen a more propitious moment. The Persian empire was undergoing a deep crisis. The Afghans had revolted and were marching on Isfahan virtually unopposed. King Wakhtang of Georgia, a powerful vassal of the shah, refused to come to his sovereign's aid, and the proud capital of Iran fell to the Afghan tribesmen who sacked the city and eventually put to death the hapless Shah Soltan Hoseyn Safavi. His heir and the future shah, Tahmasb, who had eluded the Afghans and maintained a semblance of government in the north, was confronted with the Russians invading Persia along the western shore of the Caspian.

In his official proclamation of June, 1722, Peter had declared that his campaign would not be directed against the Persians. However, the fall of Isfahan and the total collapse of the Persian government made an invasion of Iran irresistible. Russian troops passed Shemakha and pushed on into Gilan. Soon Mazanderan and Astarabad were occupied as well. There was scarcely any resistance from the Persians.[12] In September, 1723, Shah Tahmasb, whose Afghan and Russian antagonists were now joined by the Turks who invaded the country from the west, signed a treaty by which Darband, Baku, Talesh, Gilan, Mazanderan, and Astarabad were ceded to Russia.

On their way to Persia, Russian troops had to pass through a number of Caucasian khanates, the most important of which was Tarqu. The shamkhal, fully aware of Persia's collapse, tried his best to cooperate with the Russians, but when the latter failed to keep to the seashore and began to penetrate the mountains, he was alarmed. The Russians built forts and behaved as though they planned to stay indefinitely. The shamkhal's reaction was violent. He called upon the tribes of Daghestan to resist Russian encroachments and fight the infidel. To the Russians, who had received the shamkhal's "submission," this was treason.

The newly built Russian fort of the Holy Cross was the first object of the shamkhal's attack. The Mountaineers were inexperienced in the art of reducing fortresses and their attack was repulsed. The shamkhal then turned to guerrilla tactics, but in 1726 he was tricked by a compatriot in Russia's pay to enter into personal negotiations with the Russians at the fort of the Holy Cross. Here he was arrested, in violation of a formal pledge of safety, and exiled to Arkhangelsk on the White Sea.

The Russian occupation of the Caucasus and of Persia's Caspian provinces did not last long. Diseases killed off more than half of the Russian force. Peter's immediate successors had little or no interest in the area and were deeply absorbed elsewhere. Persia revived under the leadership of Nader Khan Afshar, the future Nader Shah, and swept away the Afghans. Russia was not prepared for a trial of strength. The Empress Anna Ivannovna evacuated the Caspian provinces as well as Darband and Baku. In March, 1735, at Ganjeh a treaty was signed confirming the return to Persia of all the territories annexed by Peter the Great. An article of the treaty specified that "Daghestan and other places under the Shamkhal . . . will remain as before, on the side of the State of Iran." [13]

Withdrawal from Iran and Daghestan did not mean that Russia was abandoning the entire Caucasus. The government of Anna Ivannovna had great territorial ambitions, which, as Count B. C. von Münnich wrote during the war with Turkey, included the annexation of the Crimea, of Kabarda, and, ultimately, of Constantinople.[14] The mention of Kabarda with the Crimea and Constantinople shows, of course, that the so-called union of Kabarda and Russia in the sixteenth century had been only a fiction.

Münnich's dream of capturing Constantinople remained only a dream. The war with Turkey came to an end, and the treaty of Belgrade, signed in September, 1739, largely restored the status quo ante bellum. Russia even sustained minor losses, abandoning some of her claims in the Caucasus, agreeing in Article 6 that Kabarda would remain free "and will not be subject to either of the two empires but will serve as a barrier between them." [15] Moreover, the Turks were permitted to take hostages in Kabarda, thus acquiring legal status equal to that of Russia. However, nothing had really changed. Kabardian princes continued their interminable quarrels, siding with this or that neighbor and paying no attention to international agreements signed by others or even by themselves.

In 1762 Peter III inaugurated vigorous action in the Caucasus, pushing forward Cossack settlements and ordering the construction of new fortresses. One of these—Mozdok (1763)—was located on Kabardian pasturelands. Kabardian princes in 1764 sent a deputation to Catherine II with the request that the fortress be demolished. Since the Russian government refused to comply with this request, the Kabardians sought support in the Crimea and at Constantinople, thereby turning a local affair into an international dispute.[16]

When in 1768 war broke out again between Russia and Turkey, both empires tried to enlist Kabardian support. As usual, Kabardian chieftains had no common policy: Some responded to the call of Sultan Mustafa III, who, as Caliph, was their spiritual leader; others accepted Russian subsidies and allegiances. The decisive battles of the war were fought elsewhere. Under P. A. Rumiantsev and A. V. Suvorov Russian troops won several battles in Moldavia and crossed the Danube. The Turks, fearing for the fate of Constantinople, sued for peace. In July, 1774, a peace treaty was signed at Kuchuk Kainarji. Article 21 stated that Kabarda had close relations with the Crimea and that therefore the issue of Russia's possession of Kabarda must be left to the decision of the khan of the Crimea. Since the Crimea had already been transformed into a Russian protectorate, there could be no doubt what the khan's decision would be. In fact the decision had already been rendered by the Russo-Crimean treaty of 1772, which accepted Russia's annexation of Kabarda. However, these international agreements had no more validity in the eyes of the Kabardians themselves than all the other documents of the previous two centuries.

The steady growth of Russian Cossack settlements along the Terek and Kuban rivers and the multiplication of forts in the Caucasian foothills alarmed and angered the Mountaineers. Together with the Cherkeses and the Nogais, the Kabardians began to attack Russian fortresses of the so-called Mozdok line (Mariinskaia, Pavlovskaia, Georgievskaia, and Stavropolskaia). In July, 1779, Catherine II ordered Prince G. A. Potemkin to punish the raiders and pacify the area by military force.[17] However, neither occasional military expeditions nor negotiations could turn the unruly Kabardians into obedient subjects of the empress.

Relations between the Russians and the Muslim peoples of the Northern Caucasus deteriorated further in the closing decades of the eighteenth century. The outright annexation of the Crimea in April, 1783, was only one of the many steps in the rapid process of Russian empire building. The shamkhal of Tarqu and the petty rulers of Qaraqaytaq, Darband, and Bunaq one by one acknowledged the sovereignty of the empress, fearing that otherwise their lands would be conquered by force of arms. Others, however, preferred to resist.

In 1785, after an earthquake, there arose among the Chechens a religious leader, Shaykh Mansur (Ushurma), who appealed to the masses to resist Russian encroachments. Russian troops, sent to capture the shaykh, sacked the village which had sheltered him but were ambushed on their return march. Over 300 Russians, including a colonel and eight other officers, were killed; 200 were captured. Encouraged by this success, Shaykh Mansur attacked the Russian fortress at Kizliar. However, his cavalry was impotent in the face of Russian artillery that inflicted heavy losses on his followers and forced them to retreat.

Through the autumn of 1785 Shaykh Mansur's agents agitated among the Kabardians and the Kumyks, inviting them to join the struggle. The "rebellion" was spreading in spite of Russian attempts to stifle it as quickly as possible. General P. S. Potemkin, governor of the Caucasus, personally led an army of 5,698 men into Kabarda and defeated Shaykh Mansur. The father fled to Daghestan, where he continued his struggle.

The ferocity of Russian reprisals against the "predatory" tribesmen only increased the latter's determination to resist. Massacres of the local population and large-scale destruction of crops became the usual means of dealing with rebellious natives. "Such actions of the representatives of the tsarist command," writes a Soviet historian, "served only to set the Mountaineers against Russia and interfered with the liquidation of the uprising."[18]

In spite of his inability to defeat large Russian forces or capture

Russian forts, Shaykh Mansur kept the rebellion alive. The Russo-Turkish War of 1787 to 1791 helped the Mountaineers, for the Turks found it advantageous to supply them with moderate amounts of money, whereas the Russians were compelled to reduce the number of their troops in the Caucasus and even to abandon some fortresses. The Turks tried but failed to help the Mountaineers with troops. A Turkish detachment on its way to Kabarda crossed the Kuban River but was defeated by the Russians before reaching its objective.

Shaykh Mansur finally joined the Turks at the well-fortified Black Sea port of Anapa, defended by a garrison consisting of 10,000 Turks and 15,000 Crimean Tatars and Caucasian Mountaineers. On July 3, 1791, the Russians took Anapa by assault, killing and wounding over 8,000 men, and capturing 5,900 men and 7,588 women. Among the captives was Shaykh Mansur. He was treated as a criminal, sent to St. Petersburg in chains, and confined in the Schlüsselburg fortress, where he died in the spring of 1794.

Shaykh Mansur's movement in many ways presaged the wars of the peoples of the Caucasus in the next century under the leadership of Ghazi Mulla and Shaykh Shamil (Shamuil). It was the first native movement to cross tribal lines, bringing together at least a portion of the Chechens, Tatars, Kabardians, Kumyks, and others. It was the first native movement whose leadership stood above tribes and was not subservient to the interests of the chieftains. In fact the movement began among the poorest members of society and attracted some of the most backward tribes. The unifying spirit was, of course, provided by Islam, though the religious organization was not nearly as thorough as it was later with Shamil's murids. Even the tactics of Shaykh Mansur's warriors were to be used two generations later. Both movements were destined to defeat.

Russia's determination to control the Muslim peoples of Kabarda and Daghestan was itself a consequence of Catherine's decision to extend her protection to Erekle II of Georgia. In the years of anarchy following the assassination of Nader Shah, Erekle emerged as the outstanding Georgian leader. He succeeded in winning the favor of the uncrowned ruler of Persia, Karim Khan Zand, making it possible for himself to exercise royal authority in his own country, though it remained at least nominally a province of Iran. However, Karim Khan never succeeded in restoring the unity of the Persian empire and had neither the inclination nor the resources to protect Georgia against the

Turks. Erekle was compelled to seek support from Russia. From 1768 to 1774 he was Catherine's ally in the war against the Turks. Once the war had ended, Catherine abandoned Erekle. Russian troops were withdrawn from Georgia in spite of Erekle's pleas and of his offer to become a vassal of Russia.

The temporary withdrawal of Russia from Georgia and the diminution of Russian activity throughout the Caucasus was due partly to the threat posed to the ruling class by the peasant uprising of Emelian Pugachev. Once the movement of peasants, Cossacks, Old Believers, Bashkirs, and Volga Tatars had been defeated, Catherine's interest in southward expansion revived. Erekle was ready with more petitions for a Russian protectorate on condition that royal dignity be forever preserved to his descendants, that the Georgian Church remain autocephalous, that his army be subsidized, and that a Russian force be stationed in Georgia. This time Catherine was willing to negotiate.

In July, 1783, Russia and Georgia signed a treaty at Georgievsk in which Erekle renounced his allegiance to Persia and gave up his right to conduct foreign relations without Russian supervision and consent. In return Russia promised to recognize Erekle's heirs as kings, to maintain troops in Georgia, and not to interfere in her internal affairs. Moreover, the catholicos (head of the Georgian Church) was made a member of the Holy Synod and given eighth place among Russian prelates. The Georgian nobility, a relatively numerous class, were accorded the privileges and status of Russian *dvorianstvo* (serving nobility).[19]

Erekle's hopes of Russian protection were dashed once more when at the beginning of Catherine's second Turkish war Russian troops withdrew from Georgia and even from some of the fortified positions farther north. Though the Turks did not invade the Caucasus, a new threat appeared in the person of Agha Mohammad Khan Qajar, who had founded a new dynasty and unified Persia through cunning and terror.

In the summer of 1795 Agha Mohammad Khan invaded Georgia. On September 11 the Persians stormed Tiflis, entered the capital, massacred thousands of inhabitants, and led away to Persia thousands more. In vain did Erekle invoke the treaty of 1783. The Russians made no move. The French consul in Baghdad observed that certain well-informed Persian and Georgian notables, seeing that "the Russians do not take any overt action, either diplomatic or military, to aid the

Georgians, their former allies, think and assume with justification that this is a barbarous policy on the part of the Russian court, that it desires Erekle and Georgia to be crushed by Agha Mohammed Khan, and that it will subsequently deploy its strength to come and retake all Georgia to be retained forever by the right of conquest." [20]

Russia had no such sinister plans. It simply had failed to appreciate the relative power of a united Persia in the Caucasus and throughout the Middle East. The news of the sack of Tiflis spurred the Russians to action. They recognized that Iran's victory was a blow to Russia's prestige and that the more or less pacified peoples of the Northern Caucasus would rise again if they lost their fear of the armies of the tsar. To rectify the initial mistake of not helping Erekle defend Georgia, the Russian government now determined to conduct a major campaign to reoccupy Georgia, reconquer Persia's Caspian provinces, and annex Azerbaijan. In March, 1796, Catherine II published a manifesto justifying her forthcoming action, and in April an army commanded by Count Valerian Zubov marched down the Caspian coast, capturing Darband and Baku.

Agha Mohammad Khan was conducting a campaign of his own in Central Asia, and Persian resistance was slight. After Shemakha and Ganjeh had been occupied, Zubov was in a position to march on Tabriz, but the death of Catherine II in November, 1796, led to an abrupt change in policy. Tsar Paul ordered an immediate withdrawal of Russian troops from the territories they had recently secured, including Georgia.[21] Next summer the Persians began a new invasion, which, however, came to a halt as suddenly as had the Russian campaign and for a similar reason: the death of the ruler.

The Persians threatened Georgia again in 1798. Erekle too had died, and his successor, Giorgi XII, had no hope of resisting the new shah. Once again he begged the tsar for protection, offering to bring his country into the Russian empire. In September, 1799, he instructed his envoys in St. Petersburg:

> Surrender my Kingdom and domains immutably and according to Christian truth, and place them not under the protection of the Imperial Russian throne, but give them into its full authority and complete care, so that henceforth the Kingdom of Georgia may be within the Russian Empire on the same footing as the other provinces of Russia.
>
> Then humbly request the Emperor . . . that, while taking the Kingdom of Georgia under his complete authority, he will furnish me with his most gracious

written undertaking that the royal dignity will not be removed from my house, but be transmitted from generation to generation as in the time of my ancestors.[22]

A year later another Georgian embassy was sent to St. Petersburg to repeat Giorgi's offer of submission on condition that royal dignity be retained by Giorgi and his heirs. Negotiations lasted for months. In the end Paul proclaimed the annexation of Georgia but said nothing about the fate of the Georgian monarchy. King Giorgi XII died before receiving the news of the annexation. Paul was murdered soon after, leaving to Alexander I the task of resolving all the issues of the incorporation of new territories. After some vacillation Alexander decided to turn Georgia into a Russian province, abolishing the kingdom and the monarchy.

Persia might have acquiesced in the loss of Georgia had Russia refrained from advancing into Armenia and Azerbaijan. The capture of Ganjeh (Gandzha) in January, 1804, by P. D. Tsitsianov and his penetration of Armenia the following summer compelled the shah to make war. His allies, first the British, then the French, and again the British, proved unreliable and incapable of giving him effective support. The European powers were interested in using Persia in their own struggles, not in helping it recover lost provinces. After years of intermittent warfare Persia was defeated. The peace treaty of Golestan confirmed Russia's acquisition of Georgia and of the khanates of Darband, Ganjeh, Qarabagh (Karabakh), Shirvan, Baku, Kubeh, and Talesh. A second war, provoked by further Russian encroachments and Persia's desire to regain lost territories, resulted in more defeats for the shah and additional territorial gains for Russia (the khanates of Nakhjavan—Russian Nakhichevan—and Erivan). Thus by 1828 Persia was finally excluded from Transcaucasia.[23]

No sooner had the peace treaty been concluded with Persia than Russia declared war on Turkey. The main causes of this new conflict lay in the Balkans. However, Russia had certain territorial ambitions still unsatisfied in Transcaucasia. Russian troops won a number of victories, capturing Anapa, Sukhum, and Poti on the Black Sea. General I. F. Paskevich, hero of the recent Persian war, took Qars (Kars) and Erzerum. Having been defeated in the Balkans, the main theater, the Sultan sued for peace, which was signed in September, 1829. In addition to territories in Europe, Russia annexed a portion of the eastern coast of the Black Sea and the districts of Akhaltsikhe and Akhalkalaki. This essentially completed Russia's expansion in Transcaucasia. The frontier with Turkey was pushed further south as a result of the war of 1877 to 1878 but most of the area acquired was lost to Turkey in 1918 at Brest-Litovsk. The border with Persia has remained essentially unchanged since 1828.

Though Russia now had a fixed frontier in Transcaucasia, it was not in full control of the area behind it. Even as wars went on with Persia and Turkey, the peoples of the Caucasus rebelled against the Russian presence. The mountains south of the Kuban-Terek line had never come under Russian control. Though annexed to Russia on paper several times since the sixteenth century, much of Kabarda was as free as ever. Ossetian chieftains maintained their independence, and so did the various khans of Daghestan.

The resistance of the peoples of the Caucasus had many causes, the most obvious of which was the fear and dislike of intruders common to all societies and especially strong among the isolated, self-reliant, and independent Mountaineers. Russian treatment of local rulers confirmed their suspicions and fears. Russian military commanders were usually arbitrary and brutal. They believed and not without reason that gentleness or even plain decency would be interpreted by the native population as weakness. Neither the Persian shahs nor the Turkish sultans ever gained respect through mildness. In the Caucasus the Russians became worthy heirs of Agha Mohammad Khan Qajar. During his term as commander in Georgia, Prince P. D. Tsitsianov, himself a Georgian, was not above telling a Muslim chieftain: "You have the soul of a dog and the mind of an ass. . . . So long as you do not become a faithful tributary of my great Sovereign, the Emperor, so long will I desire to wash my boots in your blood." [24] Later General A. P. Ermolov gained fame for the intemperance of his language and the cruelty with which he suppressed resistance.

The establishment of new fortified settlements was another common cause of uprisings. The construction of Kislovodsk and of the Military Georgian Highway provoked both the Ossets and the Kabardians. The latter attacked Russian outposts in the valley of the Podkumok, and soon Russian garrisons in the triangle Kislovodsk-Georgievsk-Vladikavkaz were under siege.[25] After peace was restored in Kabarda, the Chechens erupted and received help from the khan of Avaria. Ermolov attacked, burned towns and villages, and conducted indiscriminate massacres hoping to intimidate the tribes. Instead they joined the movement, until in 1819 all the chieftains of Daghestan, except the shamkhal of Tarqu, were united against the Russians. They sent appeals to Abbas Mirza, heir to the throne of Persia and governor of Azerbaijan, who, according to Russian sources, sent them 20,000 rubles.[26] Ermolov's army of 48,000 was neither large enough nor strong enough to subdue and hold the mountains. Mass terror was a standard means of subjugating the tribes. A Cossack commander, Ataman Vlasov, wishing to punish disobedient Cherkes, "began his activities by crossing the Kuban into Circassian lands, where he felled forests, burnt crops, and finally, attacking their *auls* (villages), gave everything over to extermination."[27] An aristocratic officer commented on another occasion: "Our actions in the Caucasus are reminiscent of all the miseries of the original conquest of America by the Spanish."[28] And the greatest Russian poet, Pushkin, upon observing the actions of his compatriots, wrote in his *Journey to Erzerum:* "The Cherkes hate us. We have forced them out of their wide open pastures; their *auls* are ruined, whole tribes are exterminated." Lieutenant General A. A. Veliaminov elevated mass starvation to the rank of military doctrine. According to him, "the means of accelerating the subjection of the mountaineers [should] consist of depriving them of the plains and the settling of the latter with Cossack villages. The destruction of their fields five years in a row will make it possible to disarm them and will thereby facilitate all other actions."[29] Since the tsar himself shared such attitudes, they turned into official policy. When the treaty of Adrianople gave Russia the Black Sea coast almost up to Batum, Nicholas I wrote to Count I. F. Paskevich: "Having thus completed one glorious enterprise, another, equally glorious in my eyes, and a much more important one in regard to direct advantages, awaits you: The pacification forever of the Mountaineer peoples or the extermination of the unsubmissive."[30]

Pacification was the sine qua non of Russian domination. If left unsubdued, the Cherkes, Chechens, Kabardians, Ossetians, Avars, Kumyks, and dozens of other peoples and tribes would keep the Caucasus in turmoil. They would raid and loot the valleys of Georgia, disrupt Russian settlements along the Terek and the Kuban, and prevent the flow of Russian commerce. Though in absolute figures the volume of trade with or via the Caucasus was not very large, the Russian government paid it much attention. Already Peter the Great valued the Caucasus as a commercial highway to Persia and India. It was

Peter's hope eventually to divert European trade with the East from the Mediterranean and direct it through the Causasus and the Caspian. In the eighteenth century Russian merchants were to be found in every important town in the Caucasus. They sold wool jackets, shoes, writing paper, mirrors, locks, needles, soap, crystal, china, as well as products of foreign manufacture such as woolen cloth and velvet. They bought mostly silk and silk products.[31] Peter's hopes for the diversion of the Mediterranean trade persisted for more than a century. In 1821 Alexander I published a decree setting the maximum tariff on goods entering Transcaucasia at a low 5 percent and entirely exempting from dues all goods going to Persia across the Black Sea and Georgia. His minister of foreign affairs, Count K. V. Nesselrode, in a secret instruction to A. S. Griboedov, mentioned the existence of "an old plan of our government . . . promising us considerable profits by directing the Indian trade to the shores of the Caspian Sea." The Soviet historian A. V. Fadeev comments: "Precisely in this should be sought one of the reasons tsarism so persistently aspired to expand its Transcaucasian possessions." [32]

The Russian government was, of course, aware that trade with Asia was not an end but rather a means to political domination. The economic motive may have been important for a number of individual merchants, but they exercised almost no influence on government policy. A resolution of the State Council's department of state economy on the issue of the Asiatic tariff stated: "Having considered the substantial difference not only between the trade conducted by Russia with Asia and the trade with Europe but also Russia's political relations with these parts of the world, the Department has become convinced that the former, of itself and in its strong influence on the latter, is incomparably more important for us. . . . Our trade with Asia must not be accepted only as a usual exchange of mutual popular needs and usual commercial speculation but rather as the most reliable and even the unique tool for the achievement of the important aim of the protection of our frontiers and their complete tranquilization." [33]

The Caucasus itself was regarded as a colony by the Russian government. Count E. F. Kankrin, minister of finance, wrote in 1827: "The Transcaucasian provinces not without reason could be termed our colony which should bring the state rather significant profits from the products of southern climes." [34] Such opinions were expressed by many others, including Count I. F. Paskevich, who opposed the development of industry in Transcaucasia and asked: "Should we not regard Georgia as a colony which should provide us with raw materials (silk, cotton cloth, etc.) for our factories, receiving from Russia the products of manufacture?"[35]

Settlement did not play an important part in Russia's Caucasian policy in the eighteenth century or the early part of the nineteenth. The Russian government made a number of land grants, some very large, most of which went to the military. In 1765 V. V. Viazemskii was given 282,104 acres in the Kizliar area. Ten years later a certain Ustinov received 16,200 acres; and in 1778 General Savelev received 59,400 acres.[36] However, large holdings did not make up more than a small fraction of cultivated lands in the Caucasian piedmont. On the eve of the peasant reform of 1861, nobles owned no more than 2 percent of that region's land, producing on it 2 percent of the grain crops and raising 2.8 percent of the cattle. Serfs accounted for 2 percent of the population. Large-scale colonization of the area north of the rivers Kuban and Terek began after 1860 when waves of Russian peasants joined the sparse Cossack settlements of the old Caucasian "lines."[37]

The mountains themselves were not fit for Russian colonization, but the Cherkes, Chechens, and Kabardians were disturbed by the loss of winter pastures on the plains from which they were gradually being excluded by Cossack and military settlements. Nor did Transcaucasia, with the exception of large towns, attract a Russian population until the latter part of the nineteenth century. In spite of the relative immunity from Russian colonization, the peoples of the Caucasus, and especially the Mountaineers, were afraid of being displaced by infidels. This fear played no small part in the development of a movement of resistance.

Resistance to Russia could be organized only under the banner of Islam, the one bond between the Mountaineers, for they belonged to dozens of tribes, which spoke many languages and did not share a common political tradition. Since a unified Islamic institution did not exist in the Caucasus, the task of arousing the masses and leading them had to be assumed by some organized body. A Sufi brotherhood provided the ideology and the structure for anticolonialist resistance.

Russian writers have named this brotherhood, and the movement it led, muridism, but its members referred to it simply as "the path." The brotherhood was devoted to the practice of a mystic doctrine, a way leading to union with God. In this respect it was no different from

Russian Expansio

NORTH SEA
BALTIC SEA
BARENTS SEA
KARA SEA
ARCTIC
Franz Josef Land
Novaia Zemlia
Finland 1809
Kola
Helsingfors
ST. PETERSBURG
Riga
Poland
Vilna
Warsaw
Novgorod
Minsk
Arkhangelsk 1584
Pustozersk 1499
Ust-Tsilma 1555
Dvina
Vologda
Ural Mts.
MOSCOW
Kiev
Dnieper
Vladimir
Nizhni-Novgorod
1595 Obdorsk
Berezovo 1593
Mangazeia 1601
Enisei
Turukhan 1607
Odessa
Kharkov
Voronezh 1587
Kazan
Perm
Kama
Obskii-Gorodok 1585
Surgut 1594
West Siberi
Penza
Saratov 1590
Samara 1586
Ufa 1586
Tiumen 1586
Tobolsk 1587
Ob
Azov
Don
Volga
Tsaritsyn 1589
Tobol
Ishim 1670
Tara 1594
Narym 1596
Orenburg 1743
Petropavlovsk 1792
Eniseisk 1619
Ural
Omsk 1716
Astrakhan
Batum
Georgia 1801
1878
Gurev 1645
Tomsk 1604
Krasno 1628
Turgai 1845
Akmolinsk 1830
Irtysh
Tbilisi 1806
Fort Aleksandrovsk 1846
CASPIAN SEA
Aralsk
Barnaul 1738
Kuznetsk 1618
Baku
Aral Sea
Syr Daria
Semipalatinsk 1718
Tannu Tu
Tabriz
Perovsk
L. Balkhash
Krasnovodsk 1869
Khiva
Khiva 1873
Turkestan
Transcaspia
Teheran
Gök-Tépe
Ashkhabad 1881
Amu Daria
Bukhara
Tashkent
Verny 1854
Ili
Ili District To Russia 1871-1881
M 1871-19
Samarkand
Urumchi
Meshed
Merv 1884
Kokand
Sinkiang
PERSIA
Pamir
Kashgar
Tarim
Herat
Yarkand
AFGHANISTAN
Kabul
Kashmir
Indus
Tibet
ARABIAN SEA
INDIA
60°
80°
40°
20°
0°

Asia before 1914

CHUKCHI SEA
Alaska
To U.S.A. 1867
BERING SEA
Aleutian Islands
U.S.A. 1867
OCEAN
LAPTEV SEA
New Siberian Is.
EAST SIBERIAN SEA
Anadyr
Anadyrsk
1649
Nizhne-Kolymsk
1679
Sredne-Kolymsk
1634
Verkhne-Kolymsk
1647
Indigirka
Kolyma
Lena
Verkhoiansk
1638
East Siberia
Kamchatka
Nizhne-Kamchatsk
1703
Verkhne-Kamchatsk
1703
Petropavlovsk
1740
Bolsheretsk
1703
Zhigansk
1632
Ust-Viliuiskoe
1630
Viliuisk
1634
Yakutsk
1632
Okhotsk
1649
SEA OF OKHOTSK
PACIFIC OCEAN
Olekminsk
1635
Aldan
Udsk
1679
Nikolaevsk
Sakhalin
To Russia 1875
Alexandrovsk
1853
Kurile Islands
To Japan 1875
Karafuto
To Japan 1905
Kirensk
1631
Bratsk
1630
Amur Province
1858
Amur
Maritime Prov.
1858
1648
Barguzin
L. Baikal
Nerchinsk
1654
Blagoveshchensk
Khabarovsk
Verkhne-Udinsk
1647
Chita
1900
Argunsk
1681
Kiakhta
1727
Manchuria
To Russia 1900-1905
Harbin
JAPAN
SEA OF JAPAN
Vladivostok
1860
Karakorum
Inner Mongolia
influence
Mukden
Korea
Peking
Dairen
Port Arthur
1898 Russ.
1905 Jap.
Seoul
Nagasaki
Hwang Ho
CHINA
Yangtze
EAST CHINA SEA
80°
160°
140°
60°
180°
40°
120°

LEGEND

- Russian lands ca. 1581
- Conquests 1581-1619
- Conquests 1619-1689
- Conquests 1689-1855
- Conquests 1855-1904
- Russia 1904

Tobolsk 1587 — Places with dates indicate the establishment of bases or acquisition of cities

SCALE
0 250 500 750 1000 Km

Drawn by L. Prokop

other dervish orders of the Muslim world. Like all such orders, this particular brotherhood had its *murshid* (*pir, shaykh,* elder) and *murids* (disciples) sworn to obey him. The first *murshid* of the brotherhood in the Caucasus seems to have been Mulla Muhammad Yaraqi, who was converted to "the path" in Shirvan in 1824. Upon his conversion Mulla Muhammad Yaraqi began to preach holy war. Four years later he proclaimed one of his disciples, also named Muhammad (Ghazi Muhammad, Ghazi Mulla), imam of Daghestan and Chechnia, where the brotherhood had already won popular support and moral authority.

Ghazi Muhammad was born in 1794. He received an unusually good Islamic education, learning Arabic, absorbing the teaching of the Koran, and mastering complicated Sufi doctrines. Acquisition of knowledge went hand in hand with spiritual development through prayer, meditation, fasting, and ascetic practices. Having joined the mystic brotherhood, Ghazi Muhammad began to preach to the people, urging them to live according to the Shariat (Muslim law) rather than the ancient customs of their tribes, abstain from alcohol, and refrain from smoking. His sermons had a strong effect, and the circle of his followers expanded rapidly. One of his earliest disciples was Shamil, the future hero of the long war against the Russians.

All activities of the brotherhood under the leadership of Ghazi Muhammad were devoted to the imposition of his authority on the tribes, the welding of a single community of believers, and resistance to the conquering infidel.

"Ghazi Muhammad," writes a Soviet historian, "was one of the first leaders of the murids to turn the Shariat into a tool of the struggle for independence. He did not walk the path of "gentleness," "patience," and "submission," as was desired by the lackeys of Russian tsarism among the local feudal nobility, but rather resorted to daggers and sabers whose mighty blows weakened the power of tsarist Russia, prison of nationalities and gendarme of European revolutions." [38]

Ghazi Muhammad's sermons constantly repeated the doctrine of holy war as a means of salvation. A Muslim, he said, cannot be a slave or subject to anyone, nor can he pay tribute to anyone, not even to another Muslim: "He who is a Muslim must be a free man, and there must be equality among all Muslims. For him who considers himself a Muslim, the first thing is *qazavat* (war against infidels) and then performance of the Shariat. For a Muslim, performance of the Shariat without the *qazavat* is not salvation. He who holds to the Shariat must arm no matter what the cost, must abandon his family, his house, his land, and not spare his very life. Him who follows my counsel God will reward in the future life." [39]

Where persuasion failed, intimidation and terror were used to overcome the apathy of the masses and the misgivings of the chieftains intent upon compromises with the Russians. Attacks on Russian forces led to savage reprisals against the population, which would flock to the murids seeking protection and revenge. The brutality of Generals A. P. Ermolov and I. F. Paskevich probably contributed as much, if not more, to the rise of the anti-Russian movement as the activity of Ghazi Muhammad.

His forces grew rapidly and began to pose a threat to Russian garrisons and to "tame" native princes such as the shamkhal of Tarqu. The imam led them into the shamkhal's domain, whose population welcomed the murids and swelled their ranks. In 1831 Ghazi Muhammad defeated a Russian force at Andreevskoe, captured Tarqu, attacked Darband, and took Kizliar, the fortress that almost half a century earlier had successfully withstood the assault of Shaykh Mansur. In 1832, Chechen lands and northern Daghestan were the principal theater of operations.[40] Russian troops devastated the land, burning sixty villages. Ghazi Muhammad was surrounded in a mountain village. He fought to the end and died sword in hand, pierced by Russian bayonets. The murids recovered their *murshid's* body, displayed it to the people, and called for renewed resistance. One of the murids, Shamil, who had fought at his master's side, received a near-fatal bayonet wound but miraculously broke out of encirclement and lived to become an even greater leader than Ghazi Muhammad.

Ghazi Muhammad's successor, Hamzat Bek, had to overcome divisions within his own camp before he could challenge the foreign invader. He made great efforts to strengthen his position and to weaken that of the various tribal chieftains by enforcing the Shariat. He continued to agitate throughout the Northern Caucasus and to recruit fighting men for his forces. Many of the chieftains felt threatened by the brotherhood, which was rapidly transforming itself into a militantly puritanical state. A plot was hatched among Avar khans. In September, 1834, Hamzat Bek was murdered in a mosque.

Hamzat's successor, Shaykh Shamil (Shamuil), gained world renown for his military exploits. For nineteenth-century Europe he was a romantic figure. Englishmen, Frenchmen, Germans, saw in him a noble savage or a Byronic hero. The Russians themselves felt the exotic appeal of the shaykh. Even in our age Shamil continues to fascinate the West, where sentimentalized biographies of the great warrior are read no matter what their quality.

Shamil was undoubtedly a great man. His life is too well known to need outlining here. However, it may be pointed out that he combined considerable Islamic learning with military and political abilities of the highest order. Having been a friend and close collaborator of Ghazi Muhammad, he was acquainted with every aspect of the movement, while his personal qualities—courage, intelligence, devotion to the cause, horsemanship and swordmanship—made him the obvious choice to lead the struggle of his people. Shamil imposed upon himself and others a strict code of behavior and did not tolerate any deviation from it. His rule was harsh, even brutal, though not by choice. In a primitive and disunited society fighting for its life, in a culture in which unconcealed force was universally regarded as a legitimate means of government, among people who habitually exterminated their enemies, Shamil was a model of generosity and restraint. His purpose was not to destroy tribes other than his own, not to establish the rule of his own Avars over the Chechens, Kabardians, or Ossetians. His purpose was to unite them all in a large Muslim state strong enough militarily and morally to withstand Russian imperialism. In this he succeeded brilliantly. That he was defeated in the end was the result of the disparity between the potentials of his society and of Russia in wealth, population, and technology. Shamil's ultimate failure was an episode in the long confrontation of the Eastern world with the West, a confrontation that will regularly result in victory for the West until the other societies acquire Western techniques and use them against their inventors. Russia itself accomplished this under Peter the Great, Japan did it in the opening years of the twentieth century. Shamil could not have performed such a feat. His society was too primitive, the state he was desperately trying to build was too insecure, the material resources at his command were pitifully small, time was short, and above all the enemy was too formidable.

The Caucasian war lasted half a century. It cost Russia an enormous amount of money and tens of thousands of lives. Russian military historians and Western writers, John Baddeley for instance, have studied the military operations in minute detail. However, few writers have summarized the reasons for the vitality of the anti-Russian guerrilla as well as an officer of the Russian staff, Mochulskii, to whose unpublished manuscript on "The War in the Caucasus and Daghestan" the historian S. K. Bushuev devotes several pages of his book on Shamil: "He who saw the hardships and privations suffered by our troops in the Caucasus, who took part in the courageous brave undertakings of our fighters, must be horrified at the sight of the many sacrifices we have made during decades for the taming of the Mountaineers." [41]

Mochulskii points out the numerical superiority of the Russian army, which grew from the 4,000 men with whom General I. P. Lazarev entered Tiflis in 1800 to 60,000 men under A. P. Ermolov in 1818, 155,000 men in 1838, and over 200,000 men in the 1840's. The length of the Mountaineers' resistance Mochulskii attributes to fifteen factors:

(1) Natural obstacles to Russian offensive movements. High mountains where the Caucasians were at home were ideal fortifications. Lack of medicaments and rampant disease killed large numbers of Russians.

(2) Insufficient knowledge on the part of the Russians of the mountain areas and occasionally total lack of topographical information.

(3) The poor quality of leadership in the Russian army. Of the younger officers, Mochulskii writes: "Inactivity and boredom disposes them to vice and depravity, and the last sparks of military education disappear."

(4) Insufficient tactical training of Russian troops for mountain warfare where men must be able to climb, ride, throw, wrestle, shoot, swim, run, disperse quickly to avoid falling rocks and regroup just as quickly to meet enemy attacks, select the right places for ambushes, etc. (Bushuev comments that the murids had these abilities, as did their leaders Ghazi Muhammad, Hamzat Bek, and especially Shamil.)

(5) The Russian army's poor equipment. Heavy artillery was often useless, and the command tended to rely on "the bayonet and the breast," taking enormous human losses in consequence.

(6) The unfitness of Russian uniforms for the climate.

(7) The absence of roads, which made the supply of Russian troops extremely difficult.

(8) The scattering of Russian forces everywhere in the Caucasus and particularly in Daghestan and Chechnia.

(9) The location of the headquarters in Tiflis, out of contact with the troops in the field.

(10) The absence of a unified plan of operations. Officers hungry for medals and promotion habitually condemned everything done by their predecessors and changed their plans.

(11) The superior morale of the murids up to the late 1840's. Mochulskii noted that the superior morale of the Mountaineers was to some extent the result of "political events that have occurred in Russia since the beginning of the war in the Caucasus." [42]

(12) The successes of the Mountaineers as a result of "the notable example of the union of spiritual and military power." Islam and the charisma of the leaders whose authority was based on personal heroism played a most important role in the resistance to the infidel.

(13) The sympathy of the local population for the murids.

(14) The contribution of defectors from the Russian army to the strength of the Mountaineers. "Since the time large groups of recruits have begun to be sent to the Caucasus from the Western provinces and the Polish Kingdom, these renegades have frequently appeared in the mountains and undoubtedly helped in the operations of the Daghestanis and the Circassians. Ghazi Mulla was guided in his operations by a fugitive Pole."

(15) "External circumstances." These were the various international complications that stemmed from the involvement of England, France, and Turkey, whose interest lay in keeping Russia "mired in the war with the Mountaineers."

Though the war in the Caucasus lasted for almost two generations, its outcome was never in serious doubt. Only a major disaster resulting from defeat in the West could have stopped the Russians from conquering the Mountaineers. During the Crimean War, Britain, France, and Turkey might have been able to expel Russia from the Caucasus. The military writer R. Fadeev has stated that "if, at the time, of the 200,000 allied troops which sat on the ruins of Sevastopol, some help had been sent to Omar Pasha [a Turkish commander who had invaded the Caucasus with a small force], the issue of the war would not have been in any doubt . . . the Caucasus would have been irrevocably lost to Russia." [43]

After the treaty of Paris terminated the Crimean War, Russia returned to the Caucasus in force. While at home the government conducted far-reaching reforms, including the emancipation of serfs,

Alexander II, the tsar-liberator, was as determined as his father had been before him to pacify or exterminate the Mountaineers. Prince A. I. Bariatinskii worked out a detailed plan for military strangulation of Shamil. Step by step the murids were pushed deeper and higher into the mountains. Disease and starvation took their toll. Excessive suffering shook the faith of the weaker chieftains, who were constantly being tempted to surrender to Russia and receive pardon and pensions. In August, 1859, Shamil and a small number of devoted followers were pinned down in the mountain village of Gunib. This time there was no escape. The imam was captured and sent to St. Petersburg. Unlike Shaykh Mansur, Shamil was treated well, even generously, by his captors, eventually being permitted to leave for Mecca.

The struggle continued a few years longer. In the Cherkes lands by the Black Sea the Russian aim was depopulation. Prince Bariatinskii, supreme commander in the Caucasus from 1856 to 1860, was determined either to expel or to exterminate the Adighe tribes. The military justified this by their fear of anti-Russian uprisings in the future: "We had to turn the eastern shore of the Black Sea into a Russian land and therefore to purge the entire coast of Mountaineers. For the realization of such a plan, other masses of the Trans-Kuban population that barred access to the coastal Mountaineers had to be broken and moved . . . it was necessary to exterminate a considerable portion of the Trans-Kuban population in order to force the other part unconditionally to lay down its arms. . . ."[44]

The last phase of the Caucasian war can only be described as genocide. Under the new commander, Grand Duke Mikhail Nikolaevich, Russian troops systematically combed the mountains, valleys, and forests of Circassia, flushing out Cherkes tribesmen, driving them into the plains and to the seashore, or killing masses of them. Death, emigration to Turkey, or settlement in the plains under the guns of Russian forts in a ring of Cossack villages was the fate of the Mountaineers. We know from Grand Duke Mikhail's description that they fought desperately: "just as a single man in the field did not surrender before an entire army but died killing, so the people, after the sacking of their villages for the tenth time, clung to the old places. We could not retreat from the task that had been initiated and abandon the subjugation of the Caucasus just because the Mountaineers did not want to submit. It was necessary to exterminate half of the Mountaineers to compel the other half to lay down its arms. But no more than a tenth of those who perished died in battle; the others fell from privation and severe winters spent in snowstorms in forests and on mountain rocks. The weaker part of the population, women and children, suffered especially." [45]

On May 21, 1864, Grand Duke Mikhail reported to the tsar that the Caucasian war was over. The Cherkes tribes, their numbers cut by years of fighting, had been expelled from their homes. Demoralized, starving, and broken, the survivors huddled along the coast waiting for ships that would take them to Turkey, whose government consented to accept Cherkes refugees just as it had accepted Crimean refugees in the eighteenth century and Nogai refugees from the Piatigorsk area in 1860. Only 70,000 chose to settle in the Kuban plains. A vast majority, 250,000, left the country. A. P. Berzhe (Berger) has estimated that between 1858 and 1865 over 493,000 people emigrated to Turkey.[46] As a Russian officer put it, "this was the funeral of a people that was disappearing. . . . At the abandoned hearths of the doomed Cherkes people there now stood the great Russian people. . . . The weeds have been uprooted, wheat will sprout." [47]

In 1864 Circassia almost ceased to exist. Many Cherkes tribes (the Shapsug, the Natukhai, the Ubykh) had been either exterminated or uprooted. Others were overwhelmed by Russian settlers. Further to the southeast the Karachais, Balkars, Kabardians, Ossetians, Ingushes, Chechens, and Kumyks and the tribes of Daghestan lived under military rule. To the end of the tsarist regime they remained unreconciled and bitter, withdrawn and resentful of the Russians. During the Russo-Turkish War of 1877 to 1878 uprisings occurred in Daghestan and Chechnia. These were put down by bloody punitive expeditions which resulted in a new wave of flights abroad. As late as 1899 the Russian government worried about large-scale migration of the Mountaineers to Turkey. A portion of the tribal nobility made its peace with the conquerors, serving in the Russian army and adding color to the guards' regiments of the tsar. Many continued to resist in small guerrilla groups (the *abreks*) sometimes indistinguishable from bandits.

Time was on the side of the conquerors. Gradually the Caucasian piedmont lost its non-Russian character. Hundreds of thousands of Russians moved into growing towns such as Piatigorsk, Mozdok, Vladikavkaz, and Grozny. The disparity between the resources of the Mountaineers and the Russians was further demonstrated during the Revolutions of 1917 and the civil war when the peoples of the Caucasus tried but failed to reestablish their independence. Other and heavier blows were to come. Worst of all, the Soviet government in 1943 and 1944 deported several North Caucasian peoples (such as the Karachay, the Balkar, and the Ingush) to Siberia and northern Kazakhstan. Again, as in the years 1859 to 1864, hundreds of thousands were uprooted and their very names erased from the map. Though the survivors returned after 1956, their national existence was further weakened. Most Mountaineers have already become national minorities in their ancestral lands.

GEOFFREY WHEELER

Russian Conquest and Colonization of Central Asia*

From the beginning of the sixteenth to the end of the seventeenth centuries, Russia's Asian expansion had been due east along the line of least resistance. The area lying to the north of what is now the Trans-Siberian Railway was very sparsely inhabited by primitive peoples whose resistance was quickly overcome. To the south between the northeastern shore of the Caspian Sea and the frontier of China lay the vast expanse of the Kazakh steppe peopled by nomads and entirely lacking in urban culture and development. Further south lay the khanates of Khiva, Bukhara, and Kokand, successor states of the Timurid empire. Their territories were ill-defined and consisted mainly of desert interspersed with oases in which were many cities, some of them important centers of trade and Muslim culture. The khanates' relations with each other, with Iran and China, and with independent chieftains in Afghanistan were for the most part hostile.

The appearance of the Russians on the shores of the Caspian in the middle of the sixteenth century had brought Russia in touch with the khanates, and envoys from Bukhara and Samarkand began to arrive in Moscow. Trade concessions were agreed upon, but regular diplomatic relations were not established until nearly a century later.

* For the purposes of the present chapter the term Central Asia is taken as including the pre-Revolution *guberniias* of Turkestan and the Steppe Region (Stepnoi Krai), the oblasts of Turgai and Uralsk, and the khanates of Bukhara and Khiva, an area now occupied by the Uzbek, Kirghiz, Tadzhik, and Turkmen SSR's of Soviet Central Asia and the separate Kazakh SSR.

What is now the Bashkir Autonomous Soviet Socialist Republic was annexed to Russia late in the sixteenth century, and in 1584 a Russian fortress was established at Ufa, the present capital. Russian expansion southward into the Kazakh steppe began with the dispatch in 1731 of a mission to the Kazakh leaders of the Lesser Horde. During the next one hundred and twenty-five years the submission of the entire Kazakh steppe was brought about by gradual encroachment in which both negotiation and the use of military force played a part. During the second half of the nineteenth century the process of southward conquest and annexation was resumed and the whole region was brought under direct Russian rule, except for the khanates of Bukhara and Khiva, which were allowed to retain a semi-independent status similar to that of the princely states in British India.

As a bare chronicle of the events marking the establishment of Russian imperial rule over Central Asia, the foregoing outline does not differ in any important respect from that to be found in tsarist, Western, or Soviet historiography. When, however, it comes to the assessment of the motivation and ethics of the Russian conquest, the reactions of the indigenous population to Russian rule, and the nature and effects of Russian administration, the would-be impartial historian is confronted with peculiar difficulties: neither in tsarist nor in Soviet times has there been free access to state archives; during the tsarist period there was never any free expression of opinion on the part either of the conquered peoples or of liberal elements in the metropolitan country; and history of that period written under the Soviet regime, whether by Russians or natives of the region, has been and still is strongly influenced, if not entirely conditioned, by current political considerations. This is the exact opposite of the position confronting the student of an analogous subject—India under British rule up to 1947. On this there is a vast mass of material written from every conceivable angle—official, nationalist, socialist, literal, religious, and economic—and freely expressing every shade of opinion.[1]

Nevertheless the proper assessment of the tsarist period in Central Asia is slowly becoming easier. This is due to two circumstances: changing political requirements evoke corresponding changes in Soviet interpretation of Central Asian history and thus the release of previously suppressed archive material; and Soviet scholarship is developing beyond the stage when it could be constantly and effectively subjected to Marxist-Leninist methodology.

Although Soviet ethnographical, sociological, and other studies can make an increasingly important contribution to knowledge of the nature and effects of the imposition of Russian imperial rule on Central Asia, it should be borne in mind that all Soviet writing on the region is still conditioned by certain assumptions which have not so far been supported by any evidence acceptable to Western historians. The principal of these assumptions is that ever since the arrival of Russian troops and settlers, a great mutual love and friendship has subsisted between the Russian and Central Asian peoples. A corollary of this notion is that any resistance offered to the Russians during or after the conquest was not an expression of the peoples' will but the result of incitement brought about either directly by religious reactionaries, or indirectly by foreign powers such as Britain and Turkey. Finally, it is constantly asserted as a foregone conclusion that for the Russian presence to have been anticipated or supplanted by another power would have been an unparalleled disaster for the Central Asian peoples.

What follows represents an attempt to describe the circumstances and assess the effects of the Russian imperial presence in Central Asia up to 1917 in the light of material available from all sources—tsarist, Western, and Soviet.

The Peoples of Central Asia

The ethnography and culture of the Central Asian peoples who came under Russian rule and vassalage during the nineteenth century are complicated subjects of which only a very brief account is possible here. At the time of the conquest the total population of the region was probably not more than 8 million. Ethnically speaking, about 90 percent of these were Turkic and 10 percent Iranian, but the distinction of the peoples was not as between Turkic and Iranian groups but as between nomad and sedentary peoples. The nomads were exclusively Turkic, mainly Kazakhs with some smaller Turkmen and Kirghiz elements. The sedentary peoples included both Turkic (Uzbeks, Karakalpaks, etc.) and Iranian (Tajik) elements. Since the Muslim Arabo-Persian conquests of the seventh and eighth centuries Islamic culture had spread more or less over the whole region, becoming firmly established among the sedentary, but lying only lightly on the nomad peoples. Islam was a cultural bond of union, and the various Turkic languages in use were closely interrelated and mutually intelligible. But the idea of the nation, or even of nationality, was absent. Loyalties were tribal or clannish; allegiance to the rulers of the khanates was confined to their immediate entourage. This lack of cohesion, coupled with the generally unwarlike character of the people (an exception was the Turkmen people), accounted for the feeble and uncoordinated resistance offered to the Russian invaders.

Physical Conquest

By the end of the seventeenth century, Russian forces had gained control of the Bashkir country and Cossack colonies had been established along the Yaik (now Ural) River at Yaik (now Uralsk) and Gurev. In both of these areas contact had been established with the Kazakhs (or Kirghiz, as the Russians called them at this stage). Russian intentions with regard to the Kazakh steppe do not seem to have been clearly formulated; insofar as they existed at all they were probably initiated by local commanders.

According to one of the last statements on tsarist Central Asian policy made before World War I the immediate object of the mission under I. Kirilov and A. Tevkelev which set out from Ufa in 1731 was to establish a town on the river Or. Such an outpost, it was considered, would be necessary "not only to keep the Kazakhs in subjection and to seal off Bashkiriia but also in order to open the way for trade to Bukhara and India." [2] It is improbable that at this stage the Russians had any plans for the eventual subjection of the Central Asian khanates, which they seem at first to have regarded as "properly constituted states." What they had in mind was more likely on the lines of Peter the Great's plans for the development of Central Asian trade by the establishment of a defended line of communications reaching to the frontiers of India.

Looked at from the Russian point of view, that is to say, from the point of view of an expanding nation which, in Lord Curzon's words, "was as much compelled to go forward as the earth is to go round the sun," there is not much difference between tsarist and subsequent Soviet accounts of what the Russian motivation was and of what actually happened between 1731 and the final stages of Kazakh resistance in the middle of the nineteenth century.

Of the two accounts the tsarist is the more critical of Russian policy, mainly on the ground that the Russians allowed themselves to be duped into believing that repeated Kazakh declarations of submission and loyalty actually meant something. Professor V. Grigorev, writing in the 1870's, took the Russian government to task for failing to understand that "swearing allegiance is regarded by nomads as a bargain which binds to nothing, but in which they expect to gain four to one, and that for a mistake in their calculations they revenge themselves by pillage and incursions." The professor went on to criticize the conduct of Russian pacification operations in the Kazakh steppe from almost every conceivable point of view.

Given the great trading possibilities which lay beyond the Kazakh steppe, tsarist historians regarded the subjection of the Kazakhs as a perfectly legitimate undertaking which was fully in accord with the Russian sense of civilizing mission. The Soviet version of relations between the Russians and the Kazakhs in the eighteenth and nineteenth centuries has undergone a complete change in the past twenty-five years.[3] The first official history of the Kazakh people, published in 1943, while conceding that the submission of the Kazakhs to Russia conferred on them certain material benefits, warmly applauded Kazakh resistance to the Russian advance as a genuine movement of national liberation. Kenesary Kasymov, the most formidable opponent of Russian colonization, was styled "a hero of the Kazakh people." During the period of Russian chauvinism which ensued after World War II this line was strongly criticized as "incorrect" and a new official history, published in 1957, developed an entirely different version without, however, producing any evidence to support it.

This new version claimed that the Kazakh people as a whole were from the beginning perfectly ready to exchange the arbitrary rule of their tribal leaders for that of the Russians and that they were merely induced to participate in resistance movements by such leaders as Kasymov and Batyr Srym, who were actuated not by patriotism but by "feudal-monarchical considerations." Kasymov in particular, so far from being described as "a hero of the people" enjoying considerable authority and popularity, a talented statesman and general, was now depicted as rapacious and "barbarously cruel to the peaceable population." This theory with some slight modifications has been retained ever since and figures in the current *Sovetskaia Istoricheskaia Entsiklopediia* (1964).

Faced with these widely divergent interpretations in which Russian nationalist as well as Soviet ideological considerations clearly play an important part, the Western historian is hard put to it to decide the real character and significance of this initial stage in the establishment of what is today the last remaining European presence in Asia. Before attempting a more objective analysis of this initial stage, some notice must be taken of the essential difference between the Russian acquisition of Central Asia and the acquisition of parts of Asia by other European powers.

Of recent years several Western historians have found one of the main reasons why Russia has to a large extent escaped the charge of imperialism in the fact that it acquired its empire by overland rather than by overseas expansion. Acceptance of the notions of "the moving frontier" and "manifest destiny" by a dynamic state situated on the edge of vast, sparsely inhabited territories must inevitably result in that state's territorial expansion, especially when it is not confronted by any geographical barriers. This was certainly the case of the state of Muscovy after it had broken free from the Mongol yoke at the end of the fifteenth century.

One other circumstance is less often noticed: since the middle of the sixteenth century the Tatar khanates of Kazan and Astrakhan, relics of the Golden Horde which had ruled Russia for over two centuries, became integral parts of the Russian state. To the Russians, the Bashkirs, whose territory adjoined that of Kazan, did not seem very different from the Tatars, nor the Kazakhs very different from the Bashkirs. Russian encroachment on the Kazakh steppe, which in itself offered little material inducement in the way of trade, was regarded as a process of enfolding in the Russian embrace turbulent elements which, if left to themselves, would not only threaten the security of Russian trading operations further north but would block the extension of those operations towards the more profitable markets offered by the khanates lying to the south.

The real attitude of the Kazakhs towards the Russians is much less easy to establish. Internecine warfare resulting from the constant struggle for pastureland was a regular feature of life in the Kazakh steppe, and this naturally prevented any united resistance against the Russians. The strength of the Kazakhs had been further weakened by repeated attacks from the khanate of Dzungaria located in what is now the Kuldja district of the Sinkiang-Uygur Autonomous Region of China. Many of the Kazakh leaders naturally thought that Russian rule was preferable to extermination by the Dzungarians. Others sought to gain Russian support in their internal struggle against their own tribal rivals. The Dzungarian menace was removed by the complete destruction of the khanate by the Chinese in 1758, and it is after that date that the most serious resistance to Russian encroachment was offered. Before 1950 no evidence was produced by tsarist or Soviet writers that the Kazakh people, as distinct from their leaders, were eager to become incorporated in the Russian empire. Such an idea is deliberately discounted by M. P. Viatkin in his book published in 1941,[4] which gives by far the most credible description of the Russian conquest of Kazakhstan. It is noteworthy that whereas Viatkin was a prominent collaborator in the official history published in 1943, he apparently took no part in the compilation of the 1957 history.

With the defeat and death of Kenesary Kasymov in 1846, Kazakh resistance was virtually at an end, and by 1868, all the Kazakh lands had been annexed by Russia. Russian forces now occupied the so-called Syr-Daria line stretching from the north of the Aral Sea to Lake Issyk Kul. Earlier, in 1851, Cossacks had founded a town at Kopal, some twenty miles from the Chinese frontier. "The Steppe had been crossed and the Russians were now firmly established in a very rich and fruitful region. The time was now past when expeditions had to be provisioned down to the last crust from Orenburg." [5] Thus, the Russian government now had to face the problem presented by the much closer proximity of the khanates. "Incited from outside, they plundered our merchants, attacked small detachments, and detained not only our traders but our ambassadors, and incited the native population of the towns captured by us to start a *ghazavat,* or Holy War, against the infidels." [6]

By nineteenth-century standards the Russian advance against the Central Asian khanates was a much more high-handed operation than the absorption of the Kazakh steppe. In Kokand and Bukhara the rule of the khans was arbitrary and cruel, but backed as it was by the influence of the Muslim clergy, it hardly appeared so to the people. There were well understood systems of administration, land tenure, and taxation; there was a flourishing economy, and a brisk trade was carried on with Russia and other countries. Exports consisted mainly of raw cotton, cotton textiles, silks, dyes, and fruit; while from Russia were imported pottery, hardware, sugar, paper, tin, fur, mercury, candles, and, later, kerosene and manufactured goods and textiles. Khiva differed from Bukhara and Kokand in the sense that it was more compact and did not contain principalities with strong local traditions and a tendency towards separatism. Some of the towns, however, developed a kind of local patriotism which at times almost amounted to autonomy.

A great deal has been written about the considerations that moved the Russians to continue their advance until they gained control of the whole area enclosed on the east by the frontier of China and on the south by the frontiers of Afghanistan and Persia. There were evidently dissentient voices in St. Petersburg and Orenburg which expressed doubt about the expediency of Russia's involving itself in the unpredictable complexity of Central Asian affairs and thus risking a clash with Britain. The fact is, however, that having advanced thus far, the Russians had no course left to them but to go on.

Some Western historians have maintained that the central government was powerless to curb the initiative of local military commanders. In any event they seem never to have been disciplined for advancing without orders. Indeed, a Soviet historian writing of General Michael G. Cherniaev's decision to attack and capture Tashkent in contravention of existing orders claims that he took action "which in fact fully corresponded with the ideas both of the government and the military-feudal aristocracy of the Russian empire, and of commercial and industrial circles. He understood perfectly well that the repeated appeals by the diplomatic department for the cessation of further advance in Central Asia were a special kind of maneuver, a smoke screen, resulting from fears of undesirable protests from Britain. . . . He knew that not only would he not be taken to task for his 'independent' action, but that, on the contrary, he could count on receiving decorations and promotion." [7]

Whether or not the capture of Tashkent in 1865 was intended by the Russian government, it forced it to come to a decision about future policy in Central Asia. Since 1861 the military appreciation had left no doubt of what this should be; "With Tashkent in our hands," wrote General A. P. Bezak, governor-general of Orenburg, "we shall not only dominate completely the Kokand khanate but we shall strengthen our influence on Bukhara, which will greatly increase our trade with those countries [Kokand, Bukhara, and China] and particularly with the populous Chinese towns of Kashgar and Yarkand." Immediately after the capture a plan was put forward by Bezak's successor, General N. A. Kryzhanovskii, that Tashkent should be created an independent khanate under Russian control. This was opposed by Cherniaev, who favored outright annexation. In the event, the plan was rejected by the people of Tashkent themselves, at the instigation, it was said, of Cherniaev. In 1867, Tashkent was constituted the capital of a new province of Russia with General C. P. von Kaufman as its first governor-general.

The Russian government was now committed to the conquest of the whole region. Bukhara was invaded in 1868 and reduced to a status of vassalage, Samarkand being annexed to the new Russian province now called Turkestan. The same procedure was followed with the khanate of Khiva in 1873, and in 1876 the khanate of Kokand was overrun and annexed. Military operations were concluded with the battle of Geok-Tepe (1881), which brought Transcaspia under Russian control.

From a military point of view the Russian conquest of Central Asia was unremarkable. In duration, extent of the resistance encountered, and in climatic conditions it bore no comparison with the British conquest of India. Russian troops certainly performed some notable feats of endurance and were usually outnumbered; but apart from the guerrilla tactics of the Kazakhs and Turkmens they were opposed only by the so-called armies of the khanates, which were little more than undisciplined rabble with only a few antiquated firearms. Between 1847 and 1873 Russian casualties only amounted to 400 killed and about 1,600 wounded. Casualties in the fighting against the warlike Turkmens were much higher, amounting to 290 killed and 833 wounded during 1880 and 1881.

Administrative Structure

In the opening sentence of his *Short History of Turkestan,* the great Oriental historian V. V. Barthold described Turkestan as "the southernmost region of Russia." [8] This description sums up the way in which the Russian state regarded its Central Asian acquisitions: they were simply an extension of Russia, whose inhabitants, although temporarily called *inorodtsy* (people of other races), would eventually become merged with the Russians. This attitude was in great part due to the geographical contiguity of the area, and it involved an assumption that the extension to Central Asia of Russian administrative methods, coupled with an almost total disregard of traditional methods and susceptibilities, was both natural and necessary.

In the mid-nineteenth century, when the Russian dominion over the Steppe Region and Turkestan began to take permanent shape, the administrative system of Russia itself had hardly emerged from the semimilitary system of government, and particularly of provincial government, inaugurated by Peter the Great. The acquisition of Central Asia was essentially a military operation: it was not preceded as in the case of India by the establishment of trading centers. In the absence of any commercial network like that of the East India Company or of any cadre of civil administrators, the invading forces simply became an army of occupation and established a system of military government which remained in force until the Revolution of 1917. The governors-general, the oblast governors, and the *uezd* commandants were all serving army officers. With a few exceptions, of whom the most notable was probably General Gerasima Kolpakovskii, governor of Semirechie oblast in 1867, these officers were not selected for any administrative or even military ability which they might possess, and as late as 1908 and 1909, during the visit of the Pahlen Commission,[9] were found to be bywords of inefficiency and rapacity.

That the Russians, even with this unpromising administrative apparatus, were able to achieve as much as they did in the fields of internal security, agrarian reform, justice, public works, and economic expansion was due to several factors. In the first place, the local inhabitants were as a whole unwarlike. And they were cowed by the vigor of the Russian invasion; even the warlike Turkmens never recovered from the battle of Geok-Tepe, in which they lost, on General M. D. Skobelev's own admission, 8,000 killed. Second, the strength of the Russian military garrison never fell below 40,000 men among a native population which as late as 1911 did not exceed 10 million, including that of the khanates. Third, the immigration of Russian and Ukrainian settlers had begun in the 1840's and by 1914 had reached a total of 2 million. It was to the presence of these settlers that the economic expansion of the region was largely due. They provided not only technical ability for the railways and small but growing industry but actual labor. Finally, the Russian administration, although inefficient and corrupt in many ways, was very much less so than that of the innumerable chieftains and their entourage of sycophants. It was, moreover, headed for its first fifteen years by General Constantine von Kaufman, a man of outstanding ability and integrity.[10]

The problem facing the Russian government of arriving at a workable political division of the new territory was a serious one, and the arrangement reached was probably neither more nor less arbitrary than those taken by other imperial powers elsewhere in Asia and in Africa. The whole of the north of the territory was inhabited by nomads owing allegiance to khans and sultans whose property consisted not of land but of livestock. The delegation of responsibility to all or any of the three Hordes in which the various tribes and clans were loosely grouped was soon found to be totally impracticable. Direct rule was therefore the only course open to the new paramount power, and by 1864 this had been established over most of the territory lying to the north of a line extending from the Aral Sea to the Ala-tau Range.[11] In what was probably the last officially published tsarist justification[12] of the conquest of Central Asia, the advance from this line to the frontiers of Iran and Afghanistan was represented as a kind of punitive expedition against the khanates of Bukhara, Khiva, and Kokand, which, "in their half-brigandish existence, did not appreciate the significance of the events which had taken place, nor had they a proper understanding of the power of Russia."

As a result of the campaigns launched against the khanates, the territories over which Bukhara and Khiva claimed sovereignty were greatly reduced and confined to frontiers defined by treaty, while Kokand disappeared altogether. The semi-independent status of Bukhara and Khiva was preserved mainly to placate Britain, which regarded the extent of Russia's advance with considerable apprehension. The abolition of Kokand was found necessary partly because of its chronic turbulence but much more because it bordered directly on China.

The territorial division of Turkestan at which General von Kaufman tried to arrive was one by which the province should be divided into two zones, the northern nomadic and the southern settled. He never succeeded in achieving this aim, and at the time of his death in 1882 Turkestan consisted of four oblasts, of which two, Semirechie and Syr-Daria contained a mixed nomad and settled population. Transcaspia, which was created an oblast after its pacification in 1881, was administered from the Caucasus until 1890, when it became a separate unit under the direct jurisdiction of the ministry of war. It was not embodied in Turkestan until 1898.

The steppe oblasts peopled entirely by Kazakh nomads were at first administered partly (Akmolinsk and Semipalatinsk) by Western Siberia and partly (Uralsk and Turgai) directly by the ministry of the interior. The governorate-general of the Steppe Region consisting of Akmolinsk and Semipalatinsk was not created until 1882, largely to accommodate General Kolpakovskii, who had been passed over for the governor-generalship of Turkestan to make way for General Cherniaev. The latter proved to be quite unfitted for the post of successor to von Kaufman.

Although it is true that adjustments like the two just noted were not unconnected with personal ambitions, there is no foundation for the Soviet charge that territorial division of Central Asia was contrived with the express purpose of breaking down national formations. In his report to the tsar published after his death, von Kaufman wrote: "The administrative division of the Governorate-General should now, without prejudicing the business of government, correspond not so much with external and temporary conditions determined by military and political conditions of the past period of conquest and annexation as with the requirements of the civil administration of the territory we now occupy. This division, with obvious advantage to the business of internal administration, should be based on actual ethnographic, territorial, administrative, economic, financial, and living conditions." [13] The government did not take national groupings into consideration because the idea of the nation had not yet penetrated the region. In the interests of internal security it did aim at breaking up tribal confederations on lines since advocated and practiced by the Soviet government; but this process did not in any way disturb the integrity of the only peoples who showed any signs of national cohesion—the Kazakhs and the Turkmens.

Russian attempts at agrarian, fiscal, and judicial reform were affected by two circumstances. In the first place, the contiguity of the newly acquired territory with metropolitan Russia made it necessary to aim at bringing practice in all these matters in line with that current in the rest of the empire. Second, the internal situation in Russia itself was crying out for reform in various spheres and hardly provided a useful model.

Agrarian and Fiscal Reforms

The agrarian and fiscal reforms, although arbitrary, aimed at simplification and were on balance to the advantage of the poorer classes. In accordance with what was recognized as normal procedure by the local population, the Russian government declared itself the prescriptive owner of all lands outside the newly circumscribed limits of the khanates of Bukhara and Khiva. In addition, it expropriated all land except that owned by the *waqfs* (religious foundations) and made it the property of, or rather loaned it to, the existing tenants, that is, to those who actually worked it as distinct from absentee landlords. This measure had the political advantage of reducing the hold that the local aristocracy had over the peasantry and thus of minimizing the chances of organized revolt. The time-honored tax system dating back to the Arabo-Persian conquest was also reformed, some taxes being abolished, but a new levy, the *kibitka* tax, was instituted on nomad households.

However beneficial these reforms might have been, they were strongly criticized on the ground that they were new and therefore suspect. In time they would no doubt have been accepted and made to work had it not been for the disastrous policy of colonization that resulted among other things in large tracts of the steppelands being declared "surplus" to native requirements and handed over to Russian settlers.

The Judicial System

In attempting to reform the Central Asian judicial systems the Russians soon found themselves out of their depth. Even more than other colonial powers they were victims of the delusion that notions of justice and judicial procedure which have been accepted and made to work in one society can be applied to another with entirely different social and moral standards. The declared Russian aim was "the preservation of the native courts with the changes necessary for the good of the people and the lessening of their fanaticism, a process which would lead to the removal of barriers to their drawing closer (*sblizheniye*) to the Russians." [14]

In his official report written in 1909, Count K. I. Pahlen declared that absolutely no progress had been made towards this goal and that the measures taken had merely led to a completely alien type of juridical procedure without achieving any positive good. Such an uncompromising admission of failure could have augured well for the future, and it is reasonable to suppose that in time the tsarist administration could have arrived at an acceptable and workable system. In the event, however, the tsarist regime collapsed only eight years after Pahlen had submitted his report and before effect had been given to any of his recommendations.

Attempts have sometimes been made—by Count Pahlen himself among others [15]—to compare the judicial system set up by the tsarist regime in Central Asia with that instituted by the British in India. Various circumstances make such a comparison impossible: there was nothing in Central Asia remotely resembling the Hindu-Muslim communal problem; in Britain itself there was a thoroughly stable judicial system, whereas a modernized system had only been introduced into Russia in 1864; finally, the purely military Central Asian administration contained no element comparable with the Indian Civil Service with its intimate knowledge both of local conditions and English law. Nevertheless, the fact that two centuries of judicial reforms in India by the British did result in a system which, after over twenty years of independence, has remained substantially intact in both successor states shows that, given stable conditions at home, the grafting of one judicial system onto another by an imperial overlord is within the bounds of possibility.

The judicial reforms that the Russian administrations proposed to introduce were supposed to be embodied in three statutes—the Turkestan Statutes of 1865 and 1886 and the Steppe Statute of 1868. Broadly speaking, two kinds of procedure were recognized, that according to the Muslim canon law (Shariat), administered in the settled districts by the *kazis,* and that according to customary law among the nomads. The various articles in the statutes relating to the courts were extremely vague, unclear, and, in some instances, contradictory. Russian attempts to systematize and simplify something whose complexities and ramifications they did not themselves understand merely made for further confusion and corruption, and the situation confronting Pahlen in 1909 seemed to him little short of chaotic, particularly in Transcaspia.

When, however, he came to write his memoirs in 1921, he took a much more favorable view of the judicial structure than that expressed in his official report. He praised, for example, the chief Russian innovation of elected judges, whereas it was common knowledge that this was the source of greater corruption than before. "Natives who fell into the hands of the Russian judicial authorities," wrote Richard A. Pierce, "received no better treatment than in their own courts. Instead of having a normal trial, their cases were often disposed of by 'administrative procedure.' [Russian officials] could jail a native by verbal order without trial, and release him when it suited them."[16] However, the rough justice meted out, for example, by A. N. Kuropatkin during his eight-year governorship of the Transcaspian oblast, could and did sometimes earn popular acceptance and appreciation.

Public Works

When it is recalled that only thirty-six years elapsed between the final pacification of Central Asia in 1881 and the Revolution of 1917, and that during this period Russia was involved in a major war with Japan and the Revolution of 1905, the tsarist achievement in public works in the region must be seen as remarkable by any standard. In spite of persistent Soviet attempts to belittle this achievement, it is comparable with and in some respects more notable than their own. The tsarist government was confronted with a vast, largely desert area with a sparse but resentful population, no railways or even roads, where building, agriculture, and irrigation were carried on with techniques over a thousand years old, and where industry was confined to silk, cotton, and carpet weaving, and a few domestic handicrafts. The Soviet regime, on the other hand, inherited a good road network and the beginnings of a railway system; there were modern port facilities on the Caspian and Aral Seas and on the Amu Daria River; there were well-built modern towns all over the region; and there were already some 2 million Russian and Ukrainian settlers to supplement and keep in check the still sparse and resentful population.

The main tsarist achievements were in respect of communications. A system of post roads with fifty-five post houses already existed in the Kazakh steppe by 1866, and after 1867 this was extended to connect the main centers of Turkestan. These roads were intended primarily for the conveyance of mail and passengers, goods being carried by camel. The first railway was built in 1881 from the Caspian to Kizyl-Arvat. This was gradually extended until it reached Tashkent in 1898; but Tashkent was not connected with Orenburg and thus with European Russia until 1906. In 1898 and 1899 branch lines were built from Merv (now Mary) to Kushka on the Afghan frontier and to Andizhan, the former causing considerable alarm to Britain. The famous Turkestan-Siberia line linking the Central Asian system with the trans-Siberian line was planned during the tsarist regime, and work was begun at both ends in 1912 and 1913; but it was abandoned in 1914 and not resumed until 1927. It was completed in 1930.

Russian achievement in the replacement of the age-old and highly inefficient native irrigation system fell far short of expectation. This was due to faulty planning, insufficient technical expertise, and inadequate financial backing. Only two major projects of the Hungry (Golodnaia) steppe were successfully completed; but many smaller irrigation schemes were carried through on native initiative, which was a tribute to the improved security resulting from the Russian presence. Russian backwardness in irrigation was fully recognized by the authorities: an article in the official gazette *Turkestanskie Vedomosti* of January, 1906, describing the development of irrigation in the Panjab stated: "In comparison with what British engineers have done, our weak and largely unsuccessful attempts to irrigate a small area of land in Central Asia appear positively pitiful and insignificant." [17] With the improvement of technology there is no reason to suppose that the ambitious scheme for the irrigation of 12,500 square miles of new land put forward by the Agricultural Administration in 1912 could not have been carried out.

The Economy

It may be an exaggeration to say that the invasion of Central Asia was initiated by the trading community in Russia; but the merchants certainly welcomed it when it became a *fait accompli*. Direct Russian rule over the greater part of the region and the trade agreements imposed on the nominally independent khanates would, they assumed, ensure much better conditions for Russian trade than it had enjoyed previously. "The tycoons, the bankers and indeed the world of learning were vocal in their demand that the Government should secure conditions of trade . . . so that Russian goods might creep forward over the Asian landmass as far south and as far east as possible."[18] The government certainly did what was expected of it: pressure on the khanates resulted in the removal of restrictions on non-Muslim merchants, and Central Asia in general became a profitable market for Russian manufactured goods, which were not up to the quality required by Western Europe. "Bukhara's inclusion in the Russian customs system in 1895 led to both a sharp rise in trade with Russia and a corresponding fall in the import of British goods from India."[19]

During the first few years after the conquest of Turkestan the economic future does not seem to have been regarded with much optimism. After his Central Asian tour of 1873, Eugene Schuyler, then American consul general at St. Petersburg and presumably in close touch with the world of commerce, wrote: "Central Asia has no stores of wealth and no economical resources; neither by its agricultural nor by its mineral wealth, nor by its commerce, nor by the revenue to be derived from it, can it ever repay the Russians for what it has already cost, and for the rapidly increasing expenditure bestowed upon it."[20] This gloomy forecast was hardly justified even in tsarist times, much less later. The official view expressed in 1914 was still that for a long time, until in fact Central Asia could produce a trained labor force, it would remain "a purveyor of raw material for the metropolis and a consumer of its manufactures."[21]

During the tsarist period there was a general improvement in the state of agriculture and more particularly in the cultivation of cotton. Russian efforts in improving agricultural methods were mainly with an eye to the Russian advantage, but they also contributed to the well-being of the local population except in two important respects—the deliberate expansion of cotton growing increased the region's dependence on other parts of the empire for its staple diet, wheat; and the handing over of pastureland to Russian settlers struck a severe blow at the stockbreeding industry of the steppe.

Colonization

By far the most striking—and the most lasting—manifestation of Russian imperialism in Central Asia was white colonization. Richard A. Pierce, after describing the economic, cultural, and administrative effect of "the urban communities which grew up beside the native cities," finds that "the immediate interests of military strategy, the long-term interests of state policy, and the consolidation of the newly conquered region all required colonization by a more representative cross section of Russian society, particularly by the preponderant peasant class."[22] By the exercise of greater restraint and better organization these interests could have been served without inflicting serious harm on the local population, which was admittedly too small for the effective exploitation of the region's resources. In fact, however, colonization was carried out with a complete and cynical disregard for the people's interests.

The first settlement was of Cossacks, first along the Ural River, then south of Orenburg, and finally in Semirechie consisting of what are now the Alma-Ata oblast and the eastern half of the Kirghiz Soviet Socialist Republic. By 1881 some 30,000 peasants (as distinct from Cossacks) had been established in the last district, thus implanting a permanent Russian population on the Chinese border. Meanwhile, after their pacification had been completed, intensive and largely uncontrolled colonization began in the steppe oblasts. The Resettlement Act of 1889 did little to help matters, and by the 1890's the influx of peasants was completely out of hand, with disastrous results not only for the local population but for the settlers themselves, thousands of whom were soon destitute and out of work. The creation in 1896 of the Resettlement Administration did not improve matters, and its operations were roundly condemned by Count Pahlen.[23] No official notice of this was taken, and after 1910 plans were made for greatly increased settlement not only in the steppe but in the settled oblasts, where Russian peasant colonization had hitherto been prohibited by the 1891 statute for the government of Turkestan.

The last pre-Revolution figures available, those of 1911, showed that in the Uralsk, Turgai, Akmolinsk, and Semipalatinsk oblasts Russian settlers made up 40 percent of the population with a total of 1,544,000 persons. In Turkestan, they made up 6 percent of the population, with 204,000 in Semirechie and just over 200,000 in the remaining oblasts.[24]

No Muslim land under imperial rule has ever been subjected to white colonization to the same extent as Russian Central Asia. This phenomenon must be attributed partly to geographical propinquity and the relatively temperate climate, but also to deliberate policy coupled with inefficiency, ignorance, and neglect of humane considerations on the part of the imperial Russian government. In retrospect, Soviet historians have severely criticized the "plundering colonization policy of Tsarism" [25] and point with pride to the restitution of land to the Muslim peasants after 1920. This restitution was, however, quickly followed by the equally if not more oppressive collectivization policy and by the trebling of the Russian settler population.

The hostility towards the Russians engendered in the Muslim population by the colonization policy was the underlying cause of the 1916 revolt. It also resulted in their temporarily welcoming the overthrow of the tsarist regime in the mistaken belief that henceforward they would not be ruled by Russians. But it was the presence of 2 million Russians in 1917 which made the eventual extension of the Revolution to Central Asia possible. It was the seizure of power by the settlers which ensured the perpetuation of Russian domination until such time as regular contact could be reestablished with the center, where the idea of according independence to the Muslims had early been abandoned.

The Cultural and Social Impact

The Russian conquest of Central Asia began just when the Russians were beginning to feel the effect of Peter the Great's modernizing reforms. The invading armies were therefore more struck by what seemed to them the backward and effete nature of the predominantly Muslim culture that confronted them than they would have been twenty years earlier. The conventional Russian attitude towards Islam in general was influenced by several circumstances: during the greater part of their two hundred and fifty-year domination of Russia the Mongol rulers had been Muslims; and after their conquest by the Russians in the middle of the sixteenth century the Muslim Tatar khanates of Kazan and Astrakhan had become and remained integral parts of Russia as distinct from the Russian empire. These two circumstances had brought the Russians into closer contact with Islam than any other Christian nation. Whereas the Russians were inclined to regard their acquisition of the Muslim lands of the Volga region and later of the Caucasus and Central Asia as an act of retribution for the Mongol domination of Muscovy, they also looked upon Islam as a respectable religion and deserving of greater toleration than Jewry and the non-Orthodox Christian sects. Thus, during the early years of the annexation of the Kazakh steppe Catherine II ordered the building of mosques and the importation of *mullahs* from Kazan to act as a stabilizing influence on the Kazakhs, whose practice of Islam was found to be reprehensibly lax.[26]

As the physical conquest of the region proceeded, the Russian administration developed an attitude that can be broadly described as one of tolerance interrupted by occasional accessions of suspicion and alarm. Throughout his fifteen-year governor-generalship Kaufman held to the view that the best way to treat Islam was to ignore it: left to itself, and confronted with the superior Russian culture, it would gradually die of inanition. In accordance with this view he refrained from any interference in the conduct of education either in the mosque schools (*mektebs*) or the seminaries (*medresehs*). He saw to it, however, that the temporal power and dignity of Muslim rulers and officials should, as far as possible, be circumscribed. During the period of his office, the khanate of Kokand was abolished and the territory and jurisdiction of the khans of Khiva and Bukhara greatly reduced, as well as their prestige as Muslim potentates. Kaufman also abolished the office of *kazi kalan,* or chief judicial administrator of the Shariat (canon law), resident in Tashkent. But the operation of both the Shariat and *adat* or customary law was only partially invalidated.

The policy advocated by Kaufman generally speaking persisted in until the so-called Andizhan uprising of 1898 (to which reference will be made later). Appointed governor-general shortly after this event, General Sergei M. Dukhovskoi commented in a report that "our continued absolute interference in this sphere of native life and our widespread lack of interest in Islam, which is a very stable and certainly hostile force, should be considered harmful to Russian interests in the Muslim area." [27] Investigations into the prevalence of Islamic influence soon disclosed a situation that astonished and alarmed the Russian administration. No steps adequate to cope with this situation were taken until the appointment in 1908 of the Pahlen Commission, some of whose recommendations related to cultural matters; but these together with the rest of the report were not acted upon by the central government.

Soviet historians accuse the tsarist regime of pursuing a policy of Russification. There is no evidence to support this charge. There were, of course, Russian advocates of such a policy, the most notable being N. A. Ilminskii, who was, in the words of Richard Pierce, "a gifted orientalist with a combination of missionary zeal, ardent Russian nationalism, bigotry, and ultra-conservatism." [28] Attempts made by Ilminskii and others to Russianize the Muslim system of education were doomed to failure from the start owing to the government's unwillingness to introduce any element of compulsion that might result in a clash with the Muslim hierarchy either inside Russia or in the adjoining Muslim countries. There were other contributory factors: although Russian educationalists gained the support of a few enlightened Muslims, this was more than counterbalanced by the opposition of the reactionary clergy; and the Russian military authorities opposed the extension of any kind of education on the ground that it would merely "put ideas into the heads of the natives."

The first Russian experience of educational problems in the newly acquired dominion was during the penetration of the Steppe Region. The only nominally Muslim nomad Kazakhs had no towns and no mosques; there were consequently no schools of any kind. The first school established in 1850 by the Russians and run on Russian lines was one in Orenburg for the training of interpreters. But since the government had from the first encouraged the spread of Islam and had facilitated the introduction of Tatar *mullahs* for the purpose, a number of mosque schools under Tatar control were gradually established in the northern part of the Kazakh steppe. This led to what the Russians now regarded as the undesirable growth of Tatar and Muslim influence among the Kazakhs. This view coincided to a considerable extent with that of a group of Kazakh intellectual reformers who emerged in the middle of the nineteenth century and aimed at the introduction of culture to the Kazakh people on Russian rather than on Turkic or Muslim lines.[29] Russian attempts to make common cause with this group were successful for a time and resulted in the creation of a number of Russo-Kazakh schools and a kind of Russo-Kazakh cultural cooperation. But when the great influx of Russian settlers into the Kazakh steppe began in 1891, "the generous and sincerely held concept of co-operation between Russians and Muslims was shattered by economic and demographic realities." [30]

Whereas before the coming of the Russians education of any kind was unknown in the Kazakh steppe, the situation was quite different in the oasis regions of Turkestan. Here education on Muslim lines had been more or less firmly established for many centuries. From the middle of the eighteenth century onwards the economic situation of the khanates had greatly improved and the mosque schools and higher educational establishments were in a fairly flourishing condition. By Western standards the education imparted in these institutions was limited in scope and had little practical application. Most of the learning was by rote, and literacy in the Western sense was confined to about 1 percent of the population. Nevertheless, school and religious instruction formed an important part of life.

Unlike that followed at first in the Steppe Region, Russian cultural policy in Turkestan tended to side with the conservative hierarchy and to discourage any inclination towards modernization of the existing system. General Kaufman advocated the creation of Russian schools to which a certain number of Muslim children would be admitted. It was thought that the effect of these schools would be gradually to break down the Muslim system of education. In fact, however, their success was minimal, the average number of Muslim entrants being not more than 4 or 5 percent. The unpopularity of the schools was mainly due to the absence of religious instruction, the Muslim view being that Islam was not only a part of education but its essential basis.

After the end of Kaufman's administration, another type of school, the *Russko-Tuzemnaya shkola* or Russo-native school, was introduced. The medium of instruction in these schools was the appropriate local language, and their object was to acquaint Muslim children with the elements of Russian civilization and culture. The Russian language was also taught. The first school of this type was opened in Tashkent in 1884, and by 1911 there were eighty-nine in Turkestan. The system was extended to the Steppe Region, where there were one hundred and fifty-seven schools by 1913. These Russo-native schools certainly achieved some success, but in the early years of the twentieth century they encountered serious competition from the New Method (*usul-i-jadid*) schools established by the so-called Jadid movement.

Like a somewhat similar movement started by Sir Sayyid Ahmad among the Muslims of India in the second half of the nineteenth century, the Jadid movement was an inevitable consequence of imperial rule. Struck by the more practical and realistic approach to the problems of modern life adopted by their Western conquerors and alarmed by the threat that it carried to the very foundations of Islamic culture, the Jadid reformers proposed to improve the defensive position of Islam by shedding some of its archaic and less essential features and by acquiring what they conceived to be the intellectual armor of the West.

Originated by Ismail Bey Gasprinskii, a Crimean Tatar, the movement soon spread from the Crimea and Kazan to Turkestan, to a minor extent to the Steppe Region, and eventually to the khanate of Bukhara. Its aims were cultural rather than political, defensive rather than aggressive; and its main instruments were education on modern lines and the introduction of a lingua franca for use by all the Turkish peoples of Russia. The latter instrument never took effective shape, largely owing to the wide dispersal of the various Turkic nationalities. But the New Method schools achieved a considerable success.

It is incorrect to regard Jadidism as a nationalist movement. Although it proposed to defend Islamic culture with the weapons whose use Muslim intellectuals had learnt at Russian hands, it voiced no demands for separation or even for self-government. For this reason it was not until the last few years of the tsarist regime that the movement began to excite official apprehension.

Aware that the New Method school was making much more headway than the Russo-native school, the Russian authorities elected to form what V. V. Barthold has described as "an alliance with old-style Islam." Having studiously ignored the traditional Muslim educational establishments, the Russians decided in 1907 that the Muslim *mekteb* bore comparison with the ancient Russian Christian school. "The *medreseh* curriculum was recognized as 'a very serious one' compatible with the real requirements of the people's life, and as susceptible only of gradual and cautious extension in the sense of the introduction into it of elements of modern knowledge, and not of radical dismemberment." [31]

It has been said with justice that the Jadid movement was activated to a considerable extent by the liberal ideas that were beginning to have currency in Russia at the beginning of the twentieth century. By 1908 these ideas had borne fruit to the extent of the Pahlen Commission. But they were not reciprocated in any important degree either in the imperial court or in the colonial administration of Central Asia.

When the governorate-general became aware of the growing influence of the Jadid movement, it made no attempt to come to terms with it, as the British did with the Aligarh School, the Brahmo Samaj, and other similar cultural movements in India. Instead of playing up to the evident trend towards Westernization by creating European-style universities (Bombay, Calcutta, and Madras Universities were founded in 1857), the Russians veered towards the reactionaries and the *medresehs.* This policy paid few dividends: in the uprising of 1916, it was the *mullahs* who exercised the greatest subversive influence: the Jadids, with a few exceptions, remained on the side of law and order.

In the Kazakh steppe the impact of Russian culture had the same effect as in Turkestan of whetting the intellectuals' appetite for modern education; but here there was no reactionary clerical element with whom the authorities could make common cause. Although culturally less advanced than the peoples of the southern oases, the Kazakhs, being more homogeneous, were more susceptible to the idea of the nation. They therefore started producing what might be called national newspapers before the more sophisticated Uzbeks and Tajiks. The savage hatred of the Russians bred in the Kazakhs by the vast inflow of Russian settlers into the Steppe Region was clearly expressed in the Kazakhs' writing after the Revolution of 1905. "We are dominated by the Russians," wrote Zhandybaev in 1907. "They play with us as a fox plays with his prey. We see the Russian peasants established in our midst taking away our land before our eyes." [32]

The creative arts—literature, music, and architecture—were much more advanced in Turkestan than in the Steppe Region. It was in the former therefore that the impact of Russian cultural influence was more noticeable. Since, however, this Russian influence was largely transmitted to literature by Jadid writers, it tended to be confined to political writing and to satirical drama, the latter being directed mainly against the Muslim reactionaries. Edward Allworth has pointed out that "the European systems brought by the Russians had not replaced the older educational tradition before outstanding members of the new generations born under czarist occupation or protection were able to reach their prime and influence the course of modern intellectual development there." [33] It was this fact, coupled with the absence throughout the tsarist period of Central Asian universities or even of anything approaching Aligarh College, founded in India in 1875, which prevented the emergence in Central Asia of Westernized Muslim thinkers and writers of the caliber of Indian Muslims such as Sayyid Ahmad, Amir Ali, or Muhammad Iqbal. On the other hand, the influence of Western music was greater in Central Asia than in India, where it was negligible.

The main result of the Russian conquest on Central Asian Muslim architecture was in the creation of modern cities adjacent to but separate from existing Muslim cities centered round a citadel. This system was quite different from the British-Indian system of cantonments, which were merely military settlements built a short distance from native cities and containing no public buildings. The modernization of Central Asian cities was begun in 1866, and already in 1876 Tashkent reminded Schuyler of the American city of Denver.[34]

The impact of Russian culture on the peoples of Central Asia met with much the same mixture of resistance and acceptance as a similar impact in other colonial situations: resistance sprang from a built-in love of tradition and from objection to alien innovation; and acceptance partly from genuine appreciation and partly from a sense of expediency.[35]

Russia's impact on Central Asian society was much less complex than its cultural impact. The Muslim population tolerated the Russian presence simply because they had no choice in the matter, far less choice than the peoples of India in a comparable situation. There is no evidence whatever of the contention frequently advanced by Soviet writers that the Muslims of Central Asia welcomed their Russian conquerors with open arms and greatly preferred Russian rule to that of their own khans.

Tsarist writers were under no illusions in this matter: Schuyler quotes from an article by N. Petrovskii in *Vestnik Evropy* of October, 1875, to the effect that the Russian system of government "creates among the natives a general discontent with the Russians, which is not diminishing, but on the contrary is increasing, and is being propagated in the neighbouring Khanates, exciting vain hopes for the return of what they have lost, and encouraging them to such acts as a constant demand for the return of Samarkand, and even to the invasion of our territories."[36]

Schuyler himself noted that "cruel and tyrannical as they [the Muslim Khans and beks] were in many respects, there were certain bounds which custom forbade them to overstep. . . . But for the Russians there seem to be no limits. They are of an alien faith, they seem to know little and care less about the old customs and traditions of the country, and to a man of Tashkent or Hodjent, who knows nothing of the intricacies of Russian law . . . honour and prosperity seem to be at the mercy or whim of the Russian official."[37]

The impressions formed by Count Pahlen over thirty years later when he visited Turkestan as head of a Russian Senate commission were much the same as the foregoing. There is, however, a good deal to be said in extenuation of the Russian attitude. To begin with the administration was essentially a military one, and close contacts with the local population were not encouraged. There were no "covenanted services" in which administrative officials served permanently. Moreover, the treatment of the Muslim peasants was not greatly different from that to which the Russian peasants had been accustomed for generations.

Although the Russians considered themselves culturally superior to the Muslims, their social attitude was much more egalitarian than that of the British in India: they did not expect to keep up a standard of living far higher than that of natives of equivalent social status. Count Pahlen noted the fact that the railway porters in Turkestan were Russians, a phenomenon quite impossible in India. Genuine intermingling between the Russians and the Muslims, and, in particular, intermarriage were—and are still today—extremely rare. As Schuyler noted, this was due to the fact that "the natives hold aloof from the Russians rather than the Russians from the natives."

Resistance to Russian Rule

Once the conquest was complete, this is to say, after 1868 in the Kazakh steppe and after 1881 in Turkestan, physical resistance to the Russian presence was slight until the revolt of 1916. The people were not bellicose; their loyalties were restricted to their tribal leaders; and they had never learnt the use of modern weapons or had access to them. There was no military power like that of the Sikhs, who continued to threaten the presence of the British in India long after the establishment of British paramountcy, or of the Pathans, who continued to tie down a considerable British field army until the transfer of power in 1947. Minor disturbances occurred occasionally, such as the disorders incident on the outbreak of cholera in Tashkent in 1892, when the government tried to introduce sanitary measures which took no account of local custom regarding the seclusion of women and the washing of the dead. This had no political significance and was badly mishandled by the authorities.

Of greater importance was an outbreak of religious fanaticism in the Andizhan *uezd* in 1898.[38] This was described as "an uprising," but from the fact that the leaders' following did not exceed 2,000 and that the disturbance was completely put down in two days it can be assumed that its importance was greatly exaggerated. In order to sustain the illusion that there must be some underlying reason for any sign of dissatisfaction with Russian rule Soviet historians have attributed this "revolt" to British and Turkish machinations. Similar rumors were current at the time, but the tsarist authorities did not take them seriously.

Soviet historians constantly try to make out that the Muslim population of Central Asia was actively involved in the Revolution of 1905. Khalfin, for example, speaks of "joint action" against tsarism by Russians and Muslims. In fact, however, the mutinies, the strikes, and the disturbances of 1905 were confined to Russian troops and workers. Russian political affairs were beyond the comprehension of all but a few Muslim intellectuals, who were interested in the growth of liberal rather than revolutionary ideas, and who were disposed to support rather than oppose the tsarist regime. They were certainly interested in the inclusion of Central Asian Muslim deputies in the First and Second Dumas and disillusioned with their exclusion from the Third. But it is important to emphasize a point often obscured by Soviet writers, namely, that at this stage the demands, and even the aspirations, of the Central Asian Muslims were confined to such matters as the cessation of peasant colonization, freedom of religious teaching, freedom to publish books and newspapers, and the right to elect deputies. Nor did violence ever accompany such demands which, apart from the first, had no connection whatever with the only serious challenge to tsarist rule on the part of Asians, the great revolt of 1916.

The immediate cause of the revolt of 1916 was an imperial decree calling up a total of nearly 500,000 workers from Turkestan and the steppe oblasts for labor duties in the rear of the Russian forces engaged in World War I. This was regarded as an outrage by the Muslims, who had hitherto been exempt from any kind of military service. It was nevertheless only the final puff of wind which fanned into a blaze the smoldering embers of resentment at the Russian presence and at the widespread inefficiency and maladministration. The revolt quickly spread to all parts of the region and involved heavy loss of life and destruction of property. Russian civilian losses amounted to 2,325 killed and 1,384 missing presumed killed. In addition, 24 Russian and 55 native officials were killed. Russian losses in the steppe oblasts were never reported, but they were probably much smaller. There is no reliable estimate of native losses but they were without doubt enormous, resulting more from massacres organized by the Russian peasants than from military operations. A Soviet demographer quoted by Frank Lorimer [39] estimated an absolute loss of 1,230,000 or 17 percent in the population of Turkestan between 1914 and 1918, most of which he attributed to the revolt. Another Soviet source estimated that during 1916 some 300,000 persons fled to Chinese territory.

Soviet historians have greatly exercised themselves in trying to reconcile the facts of the revolt with their steady insistence on the great love and sympathy which have always subsisted between the Central Asian Muslims and the Russian people. Many hundreds of thousands of words have been written on the subject. Broadly speaking, two contradictory trends are observable in this writing: until 1953 the tendency was to find the revolt "progressive" in the sense that it was anti-tsarist and antifeudal. Since then, however, a certain wariness has crept into Soviet writing on the subject of resistance to any kind of Russian rule.

To take but one example of this change: Yu. Tarasov, a Russian (not Muslim) writer, stated in 1951: "the peasants who rebelled [in Transcaspia in 1916] had no revolutionary programme. They had no quarrel with their own khans or with the feudal and patriarchal Turkmen nobility. They had no revolutionary leaders and no contact with the Bolsheviks. All the hatred that the peasants cherished for the colonial regime was directed against the Russians as a whole; it did not distinguish between the Tsarist administrators and the remainder of the Russian population. . . . The 1916 movement in Turkmenistan prevented the establishment of a single front between the toilers of Turkmenistan and the Russian working class; the movement was anti-Russian." [40] Two years later, the publication of a frank and factual assessment of this kind had become impossible.

With some occasional minor qualifications, the Soviet assessment of the 1916 revolt has crystallized into the following taken from the most recent book devoted to the subject: "The heroic struggle for liberation by the peoples of Central Asia and Kazakhstan in the revolt of 1916 was one of the most important of the revolutionary events that took place on the eve of the February Revolution and evokes legitimate pride among all Soviet peoples. By the historic experience thus gained the peoples of Central Asia became convinced that their revolutionary struggle for freedom could only achieve success under the direct leadership of the working class of Russia." [41] The author of this preposterous statement is, it should be noted, a Soviet Muslim and therefore likely to be "plus royaliste que le roi."

No serious student of the available facts, whether Russian, Muslim, or Western, could disagree with Richard Pierce's summing up of his lucid and objective account of the revolt: "Desirable as it may be from the Soviet standpoint to explain the uprisings of 1916 away, they indicate clearly the failure not only of the Imperial Government but of the Russian people to win the friendship and trust of the peoples of Central Asia."

Relations with the Khanates and Foreign Powers

Russia's advance into Central Asia complicated its relations not only with the khanates of Kokand, Bukhara, and Khiva but also with China and Iran and, above all, with Britain, for whom the creation and maintenance of Afghanistan as a buffer state was a vital factor in the defense of India. The governments of all these states were naturally in doubt about the eventual extent of Russia's imperial aspirations.

At the time of Prince Alexander Gorchakov's famous note [42] to the powers in which he spoke of Russia's intention to advance only to the frontiers of "properly organized states" the Russian government had probably not made up its mind whether the khanates were any less properly organized than, for example, Afghanistan. The decision was taken for them by local military commanders: the capture of Tashkent sealed the doom of Kokand, and it was soon apparent that Russia could not sustain its position in Central Asia without reducing Bukhara and Khiva to a state of vassalage. That they were not incorporated outright in the Russian empire was due, as we know, to Russian disinclination to risk a clash with Britain. This consideration continued to overrule repeated proposals for incorporation, the last being put forward in 1910.

Although the status of the khanates *vis-à-vis* the Russian government resembled in a general way that of the princely states of India, a good deal more latitude was permitted to the khanates, and particularly to Bukhara, in the conduct of their internal affairs. Various barbarous practices were allowed to continue, including slavery, which, although nominally abolished in Bukhara, continued very much as before. In Khiva, torture was not even nominally abolished until 1888. In other respects, Khiva was kept under much closer Russian control, particularly in respect of trade.

Relations between the emir of Bukhara and the governor-general were complicated by the former's skill in playing off the latter against the tsar, to whom as a fellow monarch he claimed the right of direct access. The emir toadied himself into favor both with the court and with officials in Russian-administered territory by the donation of decorations and valuable presents. He in turn was given the rank of lieutenant general and other pretentious titles. As time went on, the nominally independent status of Bukhara was reduced by the building of railways and by the treaty of 1888, which established Russian railway "settlements." In addition, the Customs Union, which was extended to Bukhara in 1894, resulted in Russian garrisons' being stationed along the southern frontier of the khanate. But the position of the Russian representative in Bukhara was more that of a high commissioner than of a political agent in an Indian State.

"To what extent," wrote Barthold in 1927, "the despotic government reflected on the well-being of the khanate, and whether the material and cultural level of its population was lower or higher than that which could be observed at the same time in other areas of Central Asia is a matter which has never been made the subject of impartial investigation." [43] Barthold also quoted a number of Russian officials and foreign travelers as testifying to the prosperous state of agriculture in the khanate. Commenting on reports of fugitives from Bukharan tyranny into Russian and Afghan territory, he mentioned the migration of Kirghiz into Bukharan territory, "from which it appears that the Kirghiz at least did not always prefer Russian to Bukharan rule." [44]

The first clash of Russian and British interests on what might be called the southern periphery of Central Asia took place in Iran and Afghanistan in the 1830's. Fath Ali, shah of Persia, was leaning heavily on Russian advisers in Tehran, and Russian and British agents were competing for influence with Dost Muhammed Khan in Afghanistan. Territorially, the two empires were as yet far apart: the Russians were still engaged in annexing and pacifying the Kazakh steppe; while in India, Britain had not yet annexed either Sind or the Panjab. During the next half century the gap was narrowed: Russia advanced to the northern frontiers of Afghanistan, while British rule was established over the whole of northern and northwestern India.

During this half century much was done on both sides which was calculated to foster mutual suspicion of each other's intentions, apart from the actual increase of territory. The Crimean War took place;

Britain fought two wars with Afghanistan; British agents appeared in Khiva and Bukhara; and Britain established friendly relations with Yaqub Beg, a native of Kokand who had constituted himself ruler of the so-called khanate of Kashgar in Chinese territory bordering on Russian Turkestan. Russia for its part had interfered actively in the affairs of Afghanistan; as a riposte to Britain's negotiations with Yaqub Beg, Russia had occupied a large area of Chinese territory; and, in spite of an express undertaking to do no such thing, it had occupied the Merv oasis, firmly established itself at the junction of the Afghan and Iranian frontiers, and built a railway from Merv to Kushka on the Afghan frontier. The last-named development brought Britain and Russia to the brink of war.

In retrospect it is clear that there were no real grounds either for Russian fears that Britain intended to advance into Turkestan or for British fears of a Russian invasion of India. There is, however, no doubt that Russia aimed at securing in Turkestan a position strong enough to keep England in check by the threat of intervention in India, and was not averse to Britain's believing that such a threat could be translated into action. No British government ever contemplated advancing into Russian-held territory: British plans for preventing a Russian advance never extended beyond the occupation of advanced military positions in Afghanistan, and even these plans were in fact never realized. But whereas British belief in Russian designs on India was, although unfounded, for a time quite serious, the tsarist government never seriously supposed that Britain had designs on Russian possessions in Central Asia. Before the signing of the Anglo-Russian Convention of 1907, the British government had perceived that the Russian threat to India had no substance, and Russia, for various reasons most of them internal, had decided to confine itself to opposing British policy in Iran.

Although the above situation is amply confirmed from British and tsarist sources, Soviet historians have painted an entirely different picture. They insist that Britain was always intent on overrunning Russian Central Asia and enslaving its peoples, and that it was only the presence of the Russians that prevented this. Their reason for persisting in this extraordinary fabrication is the desire to distract attention from the essentially imperialist and colonialist nature of the Russian presence. "Soviet historians are of the definite opinion," writes Khalfin, "that for Central Asia to have become part of the British colonial dominions would have been the greatest disaster for its peoples."[45] That this disaster would eventually have resulted in the Central Asian peoples' gaining their independence along with India and Pakistan is never mentioned.

But if tsarist Russia's designs on India and Afghanistan can be discounted, its designs on China and Iran can not. Russia had occupied the whole of the Kuldja district of Sinkiang from 1871 to 1881, and it is significant that in the map published with Schuyler's *Turkistan* this is shown as Russian territory, Schuyler having the clear impression that the Russians had come to stay. Russian influence was strong in Sinkiang until the Revolution of 1917, and indeed until 1942; and after the Chinese revolution of 1911 Russian troops were again introduced into Sinkiang, and the Russian consul general in Kashgar conducted an active campaign to enroll local Muslims as Russian subjects. During the Iranian revolution which began in 1906, Russian troops occupied parts of Iranian Azerbaijan in 1909 and remained there until 1917. Mashhad was occupied for a time in 1912 and the holy shrine of Imam Reza bombarded.

Great importance should not perhaps be attached to the recommendations for further Russian expansion in Asia addressed by General Kuropatkin (then governor-general of Turkestan) to the tsar in February, 1917. He advocated not only the annexation to Russia of the Iranian provinces of Mazanderan, Gilan, and Astarabad (now Gorgan) and the establishment by agreement with Britain of a Russian protectorate over the northern part of Iran, with Tabriz, Tehran, and Mashhad, but "a change in our border with China . . . by drawing it in a direct line from the Khan Tengri Range and the Tien Shan to Vladivostok." Thus, "Kuldja, northern Mongolia, and northern Manchuria will become part of the Russian Empire."[46] It is possible, even probable, that these ideas were or would have been totally rejected by the Russian government, but that they could be put forward at all shows that, at least in the minds of the military leaders, Russian imperial expansion was far from over.

Conclusion

Consideration of the causes, course, and consequences of the Russian conquest and colonization of Central Asia has been much affected by hindsight, by modern views on economics and ethics, and most of all by the Soviet need "to explain why the vast and valuable territories acquired by the Tsarist Government by a process of naked aggression still remain an integral part of what is simply the Tsarist empire under its new name of the Soviet Union." [47]

As regards causes, it may be interesting, and perhaps even instructive, to analyze and explain in modern economic and ideological jargon the subconscious urges that brought about the fifteenth and sixteenth centuries' Russian *Drang nach Osten* from the Urals to the Pacific and the subsequent southern drive to the frontiers of China, Afghanistan, and Iran. The Crimean War, the British presence in India, British trade rivalry, and Russian messianism all played their part. But most of the time the Russians were simply following their noses, or rather the noses of local military commanders, who never worried about natural laws, *zakonnomernost,* productive forces, and the like, and who never for a moment supposed that they or the Russian settlers who followed them were loved by the people whose land they had come to seize and exploit to their own advantage. "In the nineteenth century," writes Professor Hugh Seton-Watson, "the governments of the Great Powers did not think it wrong to make conquests: they were ashamed only when their efforts were defeated. Disapproval of imperialism was not yet part of the common fund of respectable opinions." [48]

As the ruler and arbiter over the destinies of a vast region populated with peoples of different race and culture, Russia was on balance probably no better and no worse than other imperial powers. The creation and administration of all colonial empires "has been accompanied by a bewildering mixture of altruism and cupidity, of accident and design, of indulgence and oppression, of sincerity and hypocrisy, of satiety and expansionism, of the selfless devotion and tireless energy of individuals, and of the neglect and obtuseness of governments." [49] All these conflicting phenomena were observable in Russian Central Asia; and when due consideration is given to the immensity of Russia's internal problems, the impermanence of its own social, administrative, and judicial structure and the shortness of the time at its disposal, its achievement must be seen as by no means discreditable. Apart from the excessive colonization of the Kazakh steppe, Russian treatment of the local inhabitants was humane by nineteenth-century standards: in spite of the military system of government and the disproportionate size of the permanent military garrison,[50] the administration was not oppressive or intolerant.

Where it failed to come up to the standard of other contemporary imperial administrations was in provision for eventual self-government: nothing whatever was done on the lines of the Indianization ushered in by the Morley-Minto Reforms of 1909 in India. This was simply because the tsarist regime never entertained the idea of self-determination for its subject peoples. No Russian statesman could ever have said what Mountstuart Elphinstone said at the beginning of the nineteenth century about British rule in Asia, that "for it the desirable death to die would be that the peoples themselves should reach such a standard that the retention of government by foreigners would be impossible." [51] Neither before nor after the Revolution of 1917 have the Russians ever seriously considered abdicating their right to rule over the Central Asian territory which they acquired by force of arms in the eighteenth and nineteenth centuries.

It has been said of imperialism that it not only retards the natural growth of colonial peoples but may postpone it indefinitely. For this reason, even long after a colonial territory has gained or been granted complete independence it is difficult to say to what extent it has profited or suffered from its former association with a materially superior power. Today, twenty years after India and Pakistan became independent, it is impossible to say with complete assurance whether their peoples as a whole are better or worse off both materially and spiritually than they would have been if the British or any other Western power had never gone there. Both countries inherited from the British trained civil services and police, a workable judicial system, disciplined armed forces trained in the use of modern weapons, and the elements of parliamentary democracy, all of which enabled them to take their place as independent powers without any great internal upheaval.

Russia endowed the peoples of Central Asia with none of these things; Russia had, moreover, dismantled the existing traditional fiscal, judicial, and administrative systems, except in the khanates, where they had been deliberately frozen at a medieval level. The result was that, on the collapse of the tsarist regime in 1917, the people were totally unfitted to take charge of their own affairs. After a brief period of anarchy they once again found themselves wholly dependent on Russia for the restoration and future maintenance of law and order and without any status recognizable as independent either inside or outside the Soviet Union.

The main consequence of the Russian annexation of Central Asia was that it conditioned the region for a complete take-over by a new regime which has not so far displayed any intention of relaxing the central political, economic, and military control exercised by its predecessor. But this second phase of Russian imperialism in Central Asia differs markedly from the first in the sense that it has already seen the creation of native élites which never existed in tsarist times and which year by year become more capable of assuming complete control of their own affairs. "The storm which will burst when the Muslim intelligentsia claims real independence is still beyond the horizon." [52]

SUNG-HWAN CHANG

Russian Designs on the Far East

Russia's eastward expansion had two distinct phases. The first was the conquest of Siberia, a huge, largely unpopulated territory the greater portion of which was claimed for the tsar in the seventeenth century. In contrast, the second phase, which began in mid-nineteenth century, saw Russian interest turned toward the populated areas of the neighboring countries. During this period the Russians were successful in gradually extending their power into China and Korea, the pace of their activities quickening as the end of the century approached. By the time the Russo-Japanese War was over in 1905, however, it was clear that their influence had already started to recede from that part of the world.

The ebb and flow of Russia's fortunes in Asia during this half century has been sufficiently treated in diplomatic history, and it is the intention here to analyze the Russian performance with reference to four major questions: in what name, by whom, under what circumstances, and in what manner was the penetration of the region carried out? We may start with a chronicle of events marking the vicissitudes of Russian imperialism in the Far East.

Russia on the March

Russian expansionism in Asia had its beginning in the overthrow of the Mongol domination and the emergence of the tsardom of Muscovy. After a slow start, this movement gained momentum late in the sixteenth century. Once Ermak Timofeevich and his Cossacks had thrust deep into the trans-Ural region, they were followed by explorers, fur trappers, seekers of fortune, and assorted adventurers who rather quickly pushed farther east. Jumping from one river system to another, these men trekked over the vast expanses of Siberia, reaching the Pacific coast by 1649. It was inevitable that they should eventually find themselves on the borders of the Chinese empire. Given the fact that the Ch'ing dynasty (1644 to 1912) was then young and powerful and that Manchuria happened to be its zealously guarded home territory, the small bands of Russians were a poor match for the Chinese. In the treaties of Nerchinsk (1689) and Kiakhta (1727)—the first treaties China was to sign with a Western power—the Russians were kept well out of the Amur watershed and away from the frontiers of Mongolia.[1]

For the next century or so, the Chinese rebuff had the effect of diverting Russian expansion to other parts of Asia and beyond: Kamchatka, Sakhalin, northern Japan, the Aleutians, Alaska, and California. Not until the middle of the nineteenth century did the Russians find their way back into the Chinese border region. While China was having difficulties with domestic rebels in the south and foreign intruders along the coast, they began sending flotillas and barges down the Amur valley in 1854, building outposts all the way down to the confluence of the Ussuri and the Amur rivers. There Russian troops and settlers soon created a position of strength with which the local Chinese could not cope, as they were now left to their own devices by the embattled government in Peking. The Russians could with impunity occupy sparsely populated frontier areas to achieve a *fait accompli.* The northern bank of the Amur and the area which later came to be called the Maritime Province fell into Russian hands, the transfer of the territories becoming formal in the treaties signed at Aigun (1858) and Peking (1860).[2] The founding of Vladivostok (literally, the Ruler of the East) in 1860 signaled that Russia meant to become an Asian power.

Yet for over three decades after its eastern border had been pushed to the Amur and the Sea of Japan, Russia remained more or less inactive in the region. This was in part due to a general westward shift in Russia's imperial orientation. A wholesale retrenchment of Russian positions in the easternmost reaches of the empire took place in this period: the sale of Alaska in 1867 and territorial adjustments with

Japan (involving Sakhalin and the Kuriles) in 1875. On the contrary, the Russians became deeply entangled in the West, the Near East, and Central Asia. Their activities in the last region led to military incursions into western China; and Ili in Sinkiang—the Kuldja district of Chinese Turkestan—remained under Russian occupation for ten years, between 1871 and 1881.[3] Soon, however, Russian expansionism underwent another reversal in direction. The decision to build a trans-Siberian railway (work on the road started in 1891) rekindled Russia's interest in Asia, and the imperial government began to foster more active participation in the affairs of the area. The conjunction of events also made Russia more venturesome. China was going through an accelerated phase of decline; and in the wake of the Sino-Japanese War (1894 to 1895), in which China was defeated, Russia could very easily establish a wide range of rights in Manchuria, where "peaceful penetration" proceeded apace.[4]

In adjacent Korea the Russians followed a similar course. Initially, between the 1850's and the 1890's, they showed little interest in the country. As early as 1854 they surveyed the waters off the northeastern tip of Korea but took no further action until the 1860's, after the Maritime Province had been acquired and Russia and Korea began to share a common border. At that time the Russians made several attempts to open trade relations with the Koreans in the border region, but when repulsed by the isolationist Korean authorities, the Russians did not persist. The contact during this period produced one tangible result: the migration of several thousand Korean farmers—refugees from hard times and harsh government—who settled in the Maritime Province. At first, the Russians were not averse to having the Koreans open up the land, but soon they began to curtail the influx, forcing it to stop by the late 1880's. Russian indifference toward Korea continued even after the Hermit Kingdom had been opened to the outside world, and it was not until 1884 that Russia signed a treaty with Korea—eight years behind Japan and only after such faraway countries as the United States, Great Britain, and Germany had done so. Immediately upon the conclusion of the treaty, Russia found itself in the center of political upheavals and international complications in Korea but quickly extricated itself from the sticky situation and for the next ten years refrained from getting involved in the affairs of the peninsula.[5]

In the last years of the nineteenth century, however, Russia's trend toward a more energetic foreign policy and the advance of its power to southern Manchuria were to have an immediate impact on Russian relations with Korea. No longer pretending diffidence, Russia was now willing to step into political entanglements in Seoul; and when the Koreans, powerless before a rampant Japan, sought outside help, the Russians were ready and accommodating. During this period (1896 to 1898) the Russians enjoyed great favor at the Korean court and their influence in the country was at its zenith. For a short while Russian activities in Korea seemed to be subsiding, but after 1900 they were renewed. With troops in China ostensibly to help subdue the Boxer Rebellion, the Russians were in virtual control of Manchuria, where their expanded operations were wont to spill over the border into Korea, subjecting the Koreans to increasing pressure over various concessions in the Yalu region. Such a resurgence of Russian influence was anathema to Japan, and thus the stage was set for either a compromise or a confrontation between the two imperial powers. As it turned out, they settled the issue through force and the Russo-Japanese War (1904 to 1905).[6]

The Objectives

It is difficult to determine what the mainspring of modern imperialism was: politics or economics, the systems or the individuals, needs or ideas. Perhaps all these factors were woven in an intricate pattern which is yet to be deciphered to the satisfaction of all. Here, however, we are not concerned with a general theory of imperialism. Instead, we shall inquire into the objectives of the Russians when they were extending their influence to the Far East. Attention will be focused on the three areas commonly accepted as most important in the study of imperialism: political, economic, and cultural.

The early political goal of the Russians in the Far East was outright absorption of contiguous territories, which were largely underpopulated and ill-defended. But once the Amur-Ussuri border was established in 1860, they made no attempt to extend their domain further into the populated areas of China or Korea. Here, neither the tsarist autocracy nor Russian nationalism provided much of a motive force for empire building. At least until 1890's, the Russians were not interested in carving out spheres of influence or exercising power through indirect control of governments in Peking or Seoul. For example, in the mid-1880's, when Korea, in an attempt to neutralize the conflicting pressures of China and Japan, broached the idea of a Russian protectorate over the country, the offer was declined.[7] Involvement in Korea was recognized as a political liability, and as for strategic considerations, the Russians simply did not care about the peninsula. Such a policy reflected perhaps more than anything else Russia's lack of interest at the time in its Far Eastern possessions; should there be a revival of Russian interest in these territories, Russia could be expected to take a very different attitude toward its Asian neighbors.

Whatever the tangled motives behind it, the decision to build a trans-Siberian railroad was a clear sign of Russia's renewed interest in Siberia, and a fresh outlook on the areas across the border was bound to result. In particular, the Russians discovered that their positions, both on land and on sea, were dangerously exposed. Increase of the Russian army and navy in the Far East was in order, but this would not suffice. They felt that the adjoining territory to the south was vital to their security and that some measures had to be taken there to improve the overall defense posture. Also, if the Russian fleet were to operate effectively, Russia had to have warm-water ports in the area.[8] Accordingly, the Russians set their sights on Manchuria and for the next fifteen years pressed on in this direction, gaining along the way the Chinese Eastern Railway (a short-cut to Vladivostok across Manchuria), the Liaotung peninsula (including Dairen and Port Arthur, ice-free outlets to the Yellow Sea), and the South Manchurian Railway. Then, in order to protect these acquisitions, the Russians introduced special railway guards and, later, regular troops into Manchuria, following up with attempts to assume police and administrative functions. In short, Russia was turning Manchuria into its sphere of influence.[9]

By extending itself in this manner, Russia could not help being caught up in the inexorable logic of imperialism. Russia was taking over Manchuria for the defense of Siberia, but this meant that Russia must go one step further if Manchuria, in turn, were to be kept secure. It was in this context that Russia's political objectives in Korea came to be defined. This is not to say, as popular views would have it, that Russia had specific designs to control the country politically or to obtain certain strategic advantages. Although such ends were perhaps regarded as desirable, the Russians did not pursue them with purpose even when they were in an excellent position to do so in the mid-1890's.

Instead, they allowed themselves to be involved in the affairs of the neighboring country from a largely preventive point of view: that is, Korea must not become a source of threat to Manchuria. What the Russians were concerned with, of course, was not Korea itself but Japan, whose power in the peninsula had been rapidly increasing since its Chinese rival had been overcome in 1895. The Russians were willing enough to acknowledge the considerable political and economic advantages that Japan had already gained in Korea during the preceding decades, but they could not accept the possibility that Japan's military strength might enable it to win preponderance in the strategic territory. Therefore, Russia's political aim in Korea between 1895 and 1904 was not attainment of an exclusive superior position for itself but denial of military advantage to Japan.[10]

In mid-nineteenth century, Russia's economic interests in Asia were intimately tied with two aspects of the economy at home. First, because of its belated economic development, Russia could not compete with its Western neighbors and therefore wanted to sell its products in the East. Second, the rapid industrialization of Russia required development of Siberia, and to this end the Amur was surely an important artery of communication and its river valley a potential food base. By 1860 the Russians met with preliminary successes on both counts. The commercial privileges they had gained in Sinkiang and Outer Mongolia—in addition to their share in the benefits of the treaty ports being opened up along the coast—promised great expansion of trade with China. Simultaneously, expectations were high for the exploitation of the Amur region, which was now in their hands. Soon, however, Russia had to face disappointments. Its economic weaknesses—lack of marketable products and the high cost of overland freight—were hindering the growth of its China trade; furthermore, the cold climate proved to be a serious impediment to their activities along the Amur. Inevitably, such economic setbacks produced a gradual loss of interest and Russia's attention was deflected from Asia for some time.

Ultimately, the Russians had to turn eastward again. The reason was clear: thwarted in the West, the Russians recognized that their economic progress hinged more than ever on extensive development of their Far Eastern possessions. In these territories, Russia was inadequate in the essential means—population, food supply, land transport, and naval power—and one way of overcoming these shortcomings was to build a railway linking European Russia with Siberia.[11] Such a project was bound to have much wider and more diverse repercussions than anticipated. From the economic point of view, the railroad, instead of being simply an internal line of communication, came to be envisaged as a connection between Europe and the Far East. Russia wanted to be the carrier of goods between the two points, replacing the maritime powers. Concomitantly, Asia was now seen afresh as a vast market for the manufactured goods of Russia.[12] Obviously, these possibilities had to wait for the railway to be completed (in 1904) and for the Russian industries to reach a fairly advanced stage. In the meantime, the predominant feature of Russian economic activities in China was participation in "the scramble for concessions"; out of it Russia emerged with a string of concession rights in Manchuria, ranging from railway construction to mining and lumbering. Some of these were relevant to Russian activities in Siberia, but most represented merely a future monopoly of investment opportunities.

In Korea, the Russians were for a long time lackadaisical in pursuing economic objectives. In the 1860's they tried to regularize border trade in order to get some supplies for the Maritime Province, and then, when their economic experiments in the Amur valley failed, Korea was suggested as the alternative source of grains and cattle for Siberia. But on both occasions Russia showed little inclination to act with persistence. As a market, moreover, the peninsula was totally neglected.[13] It was not until their political influence in Korea had risen sharply in the mid-1890's that the Russians began to pay more serious attention to economic matters in the country and belatedly entered the contest for concessions (in which other powers had been engaged for decades). In considerable favor with the Korean government at the time, the Russians soon received important concession rights to mines and timberlands near the Manchurian border. For years the Russians could not make much use of these concessions, however, because their economy at home was still too backward to support large-scale operations abroad and also because the limited resources they had at their disposal had to be devoted to priority enterprises in Manchuria. Therefore, only after they had launched an extensive lumbering project in south Manchuria in the early 1900's did the Russians become very active in Korea; they operated particularly on the south bank of the Yalu River, where, besides timber, they found a terrain convenient for building shipping depots. In 1903 they started settlements in the area and at the same time pressed the Korean government—without success—for the right to build a railroad and for a lease on an outlet to the sea.[14]

Since the early eighteenth century a Russian church and cultural mission had been continuously maintained in Peking, but these were for the benefit of Russian residents rather than for the sake of proselytizing. In the nineteenth century, however, the Russians began to put forward certain cultural goals, both to stimulate and to sustain their activities in Asia. Here, Pan-Slavism and the Orthodox religion, which in Europe were often the objective as well as the means of Russian imperialism, had little relevance. Instead, among the items invoked in support of expansion in the East were a wide range of newly developed assertions, reflecting various ideas then current in Russia.[15] Some believed that the tsarist empire was the first line of defense of Christian civilization against "the Yellow Peril" and that the best defense called for a positive policy. More German than Russian in origin, this concept did not become popular until Japanese power on the continent had grown measurably, and it was to gain wide acceptance only after the outbreak of the Russo-Japanese War. On the opposite end of the political spectrum could be found those who were progressive in outlook and felt that Russia should emancipate the "suppressed" peoples of the Orient. Apart from its incongruity in view of the Russian autocracy, such a cause could expect to receive little response from people outside the small circle of liberals.

The dominant and most appealing theme, after all, was that Russia had "a historical mission" to spread Western culture and to bring the blessings of an advanced civilization to the benighted populace of the East. The Asian ventures were therefore regarded as a noble undertaking, although to those who subscribed to this view such an aggressive altruism was perhaps more important in increasing their *amour propre* and in bolstering their doubting conscience than in its practical effect. No specific act of the Russians in China or Korea could be attributed to this cultural messianism, and yet, without the ideological milieu it created, Russian imperialism could not possibly have taken the road it did. Beneath the contradictory and ambivalent protestations lay a unique quality which set the Russian rationale apart from "the White Man's burden" or *mission civilisatrice*. Whether because Russia had "an Asian past," was located midway between Europe and Asia, or had physically become "an Asian power," the Russians felt that they were as much Asian as European, and hence they did not so much call for imposition of things Russian on the Asians as dwell on the kinship of Russia and Asia. "All these peoples of various races feel themselves drawn to us, and are ours, by blood, by tradition, and by ideas." [16] They envisioned not a one-sided advance but a mutual embrace, and in this emphasis on affinity one finds a striking similarity of outlook between Russian imperialism in the East and in the West.

THE MEN

In the preceding pages "Russia" and "the Russians" have been referred to as if the country or the people were acting as a unit. The objectives so far examined were, of course, neither preordained for Russia nor determined by a single will. Empire building was carried out by a small number of men, who represented diverse groups, ideas, and interests, sometimes cooperating but more often vying with one another for advantage. The nature of Russian expansionism, therefore, can be better appreciated if we gain some notion of what kinds of people were actively involved in formulating and carrying out the imperial policies.

The extension of Russian rule to Siberia had been accomplished by a succession of enterprising people who proceeded on their own and then turned the territories they occupied over to the tsar. The Russian advance into Asia in mid-nineteenth century likewise had its origin in personal initiative. The prime mover was Nicholas Muraviev, who became governor-general of Eastern Siberia in 1847.[17] Acting independently of the government, which at the beginning gave him scant backing, he sent his men out to the Amur region with a purpose of setting up a support area for Siberia. His operation resulted in the acquisition of a large territory, and by the time he retired in 1861 the Russian Far East was firmly established. Muraviev's successors, however, were of a different cast. Considerably lower in caliber and possessed of neither audacity nor imagination, they fitted the role of stodgy functionaries struggling with the difficult task of administering a frontier land. Even after a separate government for the cis-Amur region was established at Khabarovsk in 1884, the officials in the area were in the main concerned with affairs within the border, paying little heed to Manchuria, let alone Korea. A man of stature with wider authority was to come along much later, in 1903, when a viceroyalty was created at Port Arthur in order to unify all military, economic, and diplomatic affairs of Russian possessions east of Lake Baikal, but Admiral E. I. Alexeev, the viceroy, had hardly time to warm his seat before the war broke out between Russia and Japan.

Government bureaucrats on the scene were, of course, not the sole guardians or promoters of Russian interests in the Far East. In terms of the influence they had on government policy making and the effectiveness with which they executed the policies, the diplomats stationed in Asian countries were to render a far greater service to the cause of Russian expansionism. Especially in the early stage, when the government had little interest in and less knowledge about Asia, the professional expertise of these men was extremely valuable. For example, without the skill and perseverance of Nicholas Ignatiev, the envoy to Peking, in obtaining Chinese accession to a new border agreement, Muraviev's achievement would have been inconclusive, at best.[18] Being in the field and, therefore, immediately alive to the opportunities and dangers, the diplomats were on the whole more inclined toward a spirited approach in their dealings with foreign governments and in their recommendations to their superiors. For example, A. P. Cassini in China and Carl Weber and Alexis de Speyer in Korea were particularly earnest in calling for vigilance and pressed for active policies which would result in Russian involvement.[19] Russia's gains in Asia were thus very largely fruits of the diplomats' efforts, although their enthusiasm was by no means always reciprocated or their actions long sustained by their chiefs in St. Petersburg.

For decades after the Amur border had been established the foreign ministry was conspicuous for its detached posture where Far Eastern affairs were concerned. This was largely due to its preoccupation with the rapidly changing situation in Europe, but another important contributing factor was the strong guiding hand of Nicholas Giers. A dominant figure during his long tenure in the foreign ministry, first as assistant minister (1875 to 1882) and then as minister (1882 to 1895), he was an inveterate advocate of caution in diplomacy. Convinced that the Russian interest was best served by averting confrontation with other powers, he held fast to the dictum that Russia should make its position secure through quiet arrangement of defense alliances and should not allow itself to become an element disturbing to the peace. In Asia, this meant that preservation of the status quo was desirable and that Russia should refrain from precipitous involvement.[20] However, once Giers was gone, it was difficult to arrest a reverse trend. The ensuing quick turnover in the holders of the foreign affairs portfolio had the effect of gradually weakening the voice of the minister and also loosening the ministry's tight rein over the conduct of Russia's foreign policy. By far the most pronounced change to come about was espousal by the ministers themselves of more aggressive policies in Asia. In fact, they reflected the strong stand being taken by people outside the ministry, and this fact, together with the weakening of the restraining influence of the ministry, was a clear sign that the foreign ministry was increasingly obliged to share authority with others and defer to their views.

The group whose weight was most felt was the military. The army had indeed been long associated, if indirectly, with the administration of Siberia, for in the tsarist system generals were appointed as governors of the provinces. The role of the military, however, underwent a significant change after the development of the Russian Far East had started in earnest. Defense build-up could not but lead to a more direct involvement of the army in the affairs of the region. Moreover, Russian security was absorbed in the larger framework of a strategic concept in which both China and Korea were integrated, and this helped not only to extend the army's interest across the border but also to make the navy, which until then had counted for little in the East, to take on more and more importance. It was a measure of the influence of the military that the extension of Russian power into southern Manchuria and northern Korea became the very substance of Russian goals in Asia and was vigorously pursued over the objections of others.[21]

Among those who had doubts about such a deep thrust of Russian power into Asia was Sergei Witte, who, as finance minister (1892 to 1903) and a preeminent member of the government, was in a position to exert a decisive influence on Russian foreign policy, directly and indirectly. As one means of expediting the economic growth of Russia, which was his major concern, Witte had promoted the development of Siberia by encouraging settlement and railway construction. Expansionism in Asia as such was not his major objective, although he had some optimistic views about a future Russian monopoly of the East-West trade.[22] Nevertheless, economic activities in Siberia could not well be strictly confined within its borders. Their success, in one way or another, depended on making an effective use of the neighboring territories, and soon Witte pushed for and gained the right to build the Chinese Eastern Railway and organized the Russo-Chinese Bank to finance the project. He thus launched a limited economic penetration of northern Manchuria, but the interest he aroused and the trend he set were to carry the Russians far beyond. It was, therefore, ironic that he later found himself forced to resist what he regarded as reckless attempts to spread Russian influence into southern Manchuria and northern Korea. After his failure to prevent the takeover of the Liaotung peninsula, he proposed to resign from office but, dissuaded from doing so, proceeded to make the most of the situation by lending his authority to the rapid development of Russian interests in the area.[23]

To reconcile and adjust such conflicting policy recommendations and competing political pressures, Russia had the tsar, who, theoretically, held the ultimate authority in foreign policy decisions. Practice, however, belied the absolutist façade. Russia pursued a consistent policy under Alexander III (1881 to 1894), who depended almost entirely on Giers, his foreign minister. Nicholas II (1894 to 1917), too, followed the counsel of senior ministers in the early days of his reign, but soon he began to advance independent ideas and promote pet projects. His oblique intervention—he did not attempt to overrule his ministers or supersede the apparatus of the national government—had the deleterious effect of compounding the diversity of Russian aims abroad. Where Asia was concerned, Nicholas regarded himself as something of an expert, on the strength of his experiences as the tsarevich: he had traveled in the Far Eastern countries and served as chairman of the control committee of the Trans-Siberian Railway. The fact of the matter was that, having neither a clear-cut concept of Russian interest in the East nor a deep understanding of Asian countries, he lacked consistent determination and was likely to be swayed by those who were around him and gained his ear.

A man who had considerable influence on Nicholas in Eastern matters was Esper Ukhtomskii. A prominent member of high society and a close friend of both the tsar and Witte, he represented the Vostochniki (Easterners), a vocal group who advocated Russia's "mission" to expand in Asia.[24] Under Nicholas their ideas began to be translated into official policies, and also opportunities arose for them to participate directly in expansionist activities. Ukhtomskii, for example, became the first chairman of the Russo-Chinese Bank and a director of the Chinese Eastern Railway. Many others in the tsar's entourage were also to gain notoriety in connection with various schemes in Asia; the best-known group was the one usually associated with the name of Alexander Bezobrazov.[25] Promoters of business deals involving concession rights in Manchuria and Korea, they found in Nicholas a valuable sponsor and, after Witte's retirement in 1903, their ascendancy was assured where charting of Russian policy in Asia was concerned. Although much maligned as irresponsible, adventurous imperialists, in point of fact the Bezobrazov group were hardly prime movers of Russian expansion; they came in too late, with too little, and most of the projects they were backing were not carried out. Their role, therefore, was essentially a negative one, in that they, in league with the tsar, succeeded in disturbing the normal functioning of the government at a critical juncture and thereby helped to exacerbate the mounting international tensions that had resulted from a decade of Russian advances into the region.[26]

The Setting

Russian expansion in Asia can not be properly judged without also taking into consideration the circumstances in which it occurred, for in history design and chance play equally important roles. As a matter of fact, the expansionist objectives were both engendered and delimited by changing conditions that were not necessarily of Russia's making and were beyond its control. Two kinds of shifting situations provided the scene in which Russian imperialism was to be played out. The first was the consequence of a general decline in power of the Asian countries, leading to a breakdown in the international order and internal political systems. The second was produced by the domestic and external problems Russia had to face in Europe, for these inevitably had repercussions in Asia in the form of imperial competition or the absence thereof.

The Far Eastern international order of the nineteenth century was quite different from the modern nation-state system of the West. China's position was central, and it was the acknowledged suzerain over its smaller neighbors, such as Burma, Vietnam, and Korea.[27] The introduction of Western powers into the region meant that this relationship would come to an end; the countries on the periphery of the much-weakened China would be weaned, sooner or later, and made to fend for themselves. In the case of Korea, the government tried in vain to ward off foreign encroachments by persisting in the policy of national seclusion behind the protective cover of China. The country was forced open and exposed to the storm of international rivalry that raged around it. The initial contestants were China, which wanted to hold on to its residual influence; and Japan, which, for both military and economic reasons, was aiming to get exclusive control of the strategic peninsula. Japan's bid for the dominant position in Korea following its victory over China in 1895 was countered by Russia, which regarded this new move of a potent Japan as a threat to its Far Eastern interests in general. Attempts at a compromise solution were made, but the issue had to await the outcome of the Russo-Japanese War for the final settlement.[28]

The centrifugal force generated by the decline in China's power affected not only its hold on the tributary states but also its control over the frontier regions. Because difficulties in the center of the country made it impossible for the government in Peking to give adequate attention to such outlying territories as Tibet, Sinkiang, Mongolia, and Manchuria, situations arose which either invited or facilitated foreign interventions and intrusions. The absence of effective representation of the central government enabled outside powers to intimidate local officials into signing treaties advantageous to themselves; the prime example was the treaty of Aigun of 1858, concluded between the Russians and the local Chinese general, which China had to accept eventually.[29]

Also, Peking's inability to handle public disorders provided the occasion for the Russians to step in. When the Chinese authorities failed to suppress a Muslim rebellion in Sinkiang late in the 1860's, Russia sent in troops to occupy Ili, the strategic point near the Russo-Chinese border. Likewise, when the Boxer Rebellion erupted in 1900, Manchuria came under Russian military occupation. The Russians left Ili in 1881 after much pressure, but evacuation of troops from Manchuria, although promised, was delayed under one excuse or another and thereby created an issue that foreshadowed the war between Russia and Japan.[30]

The difficulties China was experiencing were basically due to its weakness in the home provinces. The old Confucian order was in the throes of collapse, and the government was incapable of meeting the challenges of the new age. The lessening of government power and the general breakdown in public order worked hand in hand to create conditions that foreign powers could exploit. Time and again, ensuring the safety of their nationals, particularly the missionaries, was used as the immediate reason for landing troops in China or taking over ports and other territories. The stationing of foreign military contingents and naval units on Chinese territory became a permanent feature of China's relations with the outside world. More serious in their consequences were the large-scale rebellions. These proved such a drain on the government that it could not energetically resist outside pressures for concessions. Like other powers, Russia gained most when China was plunged in grave domestic crises: the Taiping and other rebellions which lasted from the 1850's until the 1870's and the Boxer uprising at the turn of the century.

The trouble, however, was not limited to internal disorder. Faced with crisis, the debilitated *ancien régime* was deeply divided within itself over what remedial course to take. In the context of international rivalry over China at the time, such differences were bound to breed factionalism, each Chinese group opposing or favoring a particular foreign country over the rest. Depending on how they analyzed the situation, the Chinese were divided among those who were opposed to all foreigners, those who regarded Japan as the most immediate threat, those who feared Russian advances, and those who were afraid that China was most vulnerable to the maritime powers, particularly Great Britain. All of these factions had powerful protagonists, but it so happened that Li Hung-chang, a leader of the anti-Japanese group, emerged as the dominant figure in China's foreign relations in the latter part of the nineteenth century. This was a great boon to Russia, for in order to oppose Japan, China wanted to ally with Russia. Under Li's guiding hand, China pursued a consistently pro-Russian policy, from which Russia naturally profited a great deal, particularly in Manchuria.

In Korea, too, the domestic troubles and factionalism often invited foreign interventions. The Yi dynasty (1392 to 1910) was showing signs of superannuation; the country was politically moribund and economically stagnant. The monarchy was weak and inefficient; the old, hereditary ruling class of *yangban* was divided and self-serving; and the majority of the population, the peasantry, was suffering from heavy taxes, official corruption, famine, pestilence, and banditry. Under such circumstances, pressure was bound to build up for change. In 1862 and 1863 a large-scale peasant-based rebellion, led by a religious cult, broke out in the southeastern provinces. Known as the Tonghak (Eastern Learning) party, the rebels were subdued by the government for a while but proved to be sturdy enough to rise up again in 1894, at which time the disturbance they caused was used as a pretext by Japan to dispatch troops to Korea, thereby raising the curtain on a clash with China and eventually a war against Russia. Apart from the Tonghak rebellion, the inability of the weak government to maintain civil order, protect aliens, and control its military gave foreign powers excuses to introduce military guards. Given the unsettled condition prevailing at the time, the presence of foreign troops, instead of restoring order, further complicated the already tangled affairs of the conutry.[31]

With respect to internal division, Korea was in even worse shape than China. Since the sixteenth century the country's ruling class had been suffering from a chronic case of factionalism. The factions were hardened, and hereditary groups remained in permanent rivalry; bound by an intricate network of family and regional loyalty, obligations and expectations, they thoroughly undermined the orderly processes of the monarchical government. Their partisan strife, which cut across the entire life of the land, could not but affect foreign relations and vice versa, and the country was split among those who were for or against China, Japan, or Russia, the three countries which had the greatest stakes in the peninsula. In Korea, however, no single group or person gained enough ascendancy for a long enough time to steady the course, for better or worse. Instead, throughout the last quarter of the nineteenth century Korea was the scene of kaleidoscopic turnovers in political power, punctuated by intrigues and little coups involving swiftly changing combinations of various Korean factions and their foreign partners. The pro-Russian faction gained the upper hand briefly, twice. The earlier attempt to place Korea under Russian protection (1884 to 1886) did not succeed for lack of a positive response from Russia, but between 1896 and 1898 Russia was the predominant influence in the kingdom.

The opportunities for Russia arose not merely from the internal breakdown of China or Korea but also from the fact that these countries were periodically under attack by other powers. The Anglo-French military campaign against China from 1856 to 1860 allowed Russia to advance into the Amur region with impunity and also enabled the Russian ambassador to China to play a shrewd role of mediator, thereby earning China's gratitude; this he cashed in for still greater gains for Russia in Manchuria and Siberia.

Similarly, China's defeat by Japan in 1895 offered Russia a chance to emerge as China's protector; and having successfully persuaded Japan to retrocede the Liaotung peninsula, Russia could garner another reward from the grateful China in the form of the right to build the Chinese Eastern Railway across Manchuria.[32] Excesses of the Japanese in Korea in the same period—the Japanese were, for instance, responsible for the murder of the intractable Korean queen—literally drove the Koreans into the arms of Russia. The king himself sought protection of his person with the Russians, and for over a year he and his ministers ruled the country out of the Russian legation in Seoul.[33]

The fortunes of Russia in Asia were also greatly affected by the rivalry among the Western powers in Europe, for their shifting political alignments had immediate reflections in the East. In the last decades of the nineteenth century, Russia found itself strenuously opposed by Great Britain, whereas France and, to a certain degree, Germany, showed friendship and support. Be it for underwriting railroad projects in Siberia and Manchuria or for helping China pay her indemnities, the ready availability of the franc was crucial to the success of Russian Far Eastern policies. Also, the participation by both France and Germany was instrumental in making Japan bow to the Triple Intervention over the Liaotung peninsula.

Russia had to cope with the perennial obstacle of Great Britain, however. British encouragement of the Muslim rebels in Sinkiang in the 1860's and the dispatch of an armed expedition to Tibet in 1904 were both designed to forestall the Russians. Above all, the British were concerned over Russia's gaining access to the sea, and whenever such a possibility arose, they quickly resorted to counteraction. In 1885 the mere talk of Russia's getting a port on the east coast of Korea prompted British occupation of an island at the mouth of the Sea of Japan; the Russian takeover of Port Arthur and Dairen in 1897 was followed by British acquisition of Weihaiwei on the opposite shore of the Yellow Sea; and, on a much larger scale, Great Britain in 1902 entered into an alliance with Japan against Russia.[34]

The last but not the least important factors governing Russia's behavior in Asia were the changes both in domestic conditions and in overall relations with the outside world. Whether or not Russia was active in certain areas at a given time was to a large measure dictated by the priorities and exigencies of the country. In the mid-nineteenth century, when Russian prestige in Europe was at its lowest after the Crimean War, Russia was looking elsewhere for fresh opportunities, and it was in the easterly direction that it made the greatest gains. Russia's push into Asia, however, could not long be sustained, and for almost three decades Russia was cast in a relatively minor role in that area. The reasons were mostly to be found in the events taking place at the other end of the empire. In the 1860's repercussions of domestic reforms and the Polish rebellion tied the hands of the tsarist government, and then, through the 1870's and 1880's, Russia's energy had to be devoted to attending to problems beyond its borders. Difficulties with Turkey in the Balkans and the foundering and eventual collapse of the Dreikaiserbund kept Russia occupied in Europe. Russia's renewed prominence in the Far East in the 1890's followed restoration of surface calm at home by the victory of the reaction and a general impasse in relations with its neighbors in Europe.

The Means

Modern imperialism has taken many forms, depending on the parties involved, the area, and the period. The means employed by Russian imperialism in Asia were naturally determined to a large extent by the goals, the participants, and the circumstances; however, by comparing the Russian methods with those of other imperial powers, the nature of Russian expansionist undertakings can be brought into sharper relief. Some were direct means used to gain specific imperial advantages, while others were designed to help Russia maintain general superiority of power in order to facilitate attainment of long-range political and economic objectives.

Although in the popular notion Russian activities in Asia are associated almost exclusively with covert scheming, the methods employed by the Russians were in fact quite diverse. And it must be pointed out that diplomacy has been the most important of them, be it in gaining advantage from neighbors in difficulties or in dealing with troublesome competitors. The most significant example is the Triple Intervention of 1895, an international demarche instigated by Russia. To be sure, Russia considered it so vital to its defenses to keep Japan out of the Liaotung peninsula that the government was ready to take whatever action was necessary, including the bombardment of Japanese ports. Yet the major thrust was in the diplomatic field.

Diplomatic moves, however, were not always as open as the Triple Intervention. Many were secret. For instance, in the aftermath of the Sino-Japanese War, the Chinese were desirous of having Russia as an ally, while Russia, for its part, was anxious to take advantage of China's difficulties to win a concession to extend the Trans-Siberian Railway across Manchuria. The issues involved were such that wide international repercussions and some adverse reaction were likely if the terms of agreement were publicly divulged in advance; both sides therefore resorted to secret talks. The occasion for negotiations came at the time of the coronation of Nicholas II in 1896. At the request of Russia, Li Hung-chang was designated head of the Chinese mission. Li, who was also scheduled to visit Britain, France, Germany, and the United States, was "intercepted" by the Russians so that he would visit Russia ahead of the other countries; the Russians wanted to make sure that Li would not be swayed by what might be anti-Russian bias of the other powers. By the time Li reached London and Paris, the secret treaty of alliance between China and Russia was a *fait accompli*.[35]

Where compromise with potential rivals was involved, the Russians also made use of secret negotiations. In the aftermath of the Korean king's move into the Russian legation in 1896, the Japanese were anxious to come to terms with the Russian protectors, who for their part were also in favor of negotiated settlement of differences with the Japanese. A series of secret agreements of 1896 and 1898 represented a Russo-Japanese bargain over Korea, touching on stationing of the military, financial assistance, training of military and police force, maintenance of communications lines, and so forth.[36]

Diplomacy was supplemented by intrigue. The Korean king's move into the Russian legation was no doubt the product of secret maneuvers. Although specific details are not yet clear, there are many reasons to believe that the Russians and the Korean king, or his representatives, must have had prior consultation.[37] A more widely suspected Russian intrigue of 1884 and 1885, involving the establishment of a Russian protectorate in Korea, however, was not Russian in origin. The proposal was initiated by Paul G. von Möllendorf, a former member of the German consular service, who held a Korean foreign ministry position; he represented neither the Germans nor the Russians but what he believed to be the best interest of his host country.

Two minor but important aids in Russian diplomatic moves were money and arms. At the time the secret treaty between China and Russia was signed in 1896, the Chinese plenipotentiary, Li Hung-chang, was said to have accepted a Russian bribe of $1.5 million, although this was denied by Sergei Witte. In 1898, when the lease of the Liaotung peninsula and construction of the South Manchurian Railway were being negotiated, Witte bribed the two Chinese negotiators, Li Hung-chang and Chang Yin-huan, with 500,000 and 250,000 rubles apiece.[38] On other occasions a cheaper means was open display of military might. At the time of protracted negotiations over Ili in 1880, Russia sent warships to China as a naval demonstration.[39] The Chinese could not maintain a strong stand because they greatly feared the possibility of a Russian naval attack, along with an army thrust overland to Manchuria and Peking. Later, at the time of the Triple Intervention, the Russians tried to give visible backing to their demand by recalling warships from the Chinese and Japanese harbors, declaring Vladivostok a war zone, and gathering troops there. A show of arms was useful even when extracting economic concessions, as was the case in Korea in 1900 when the Russian naval squadron showed up off Inch'on, the port of the capital city of Seoul, to persuade the reluctant Koreans to accord Russia concessions along the Yalu River.[40]

If need be, Russia was willing to go beyond a demonstration of military power and put troops into action. The occupation of Ili is an example. Then, in 1897, when the Germans seized Kiaochow and compelled the Chinese to lease it, Russia, under the pretext of protecting China from the Germans, sent troops to occupy Port Arthur and Dairen, in spite of the fact that Russia was honor-bound to respect Chinese territorial integrity. Shortly thereafter, the Russians extended the occupied zone to the adjacent areas as well, and eventually exacted an agreement from China on Manchuria. Similar military occupation of Chinese territory took place in Manchuria in 1900, at the time of the Boxer Rebellion.

Finally, although less often than other powers, Russia resorted to an array of familiar indirect, "peaceful" means of imperialism. Unhappy over the large number of foreign, particularly Japanese, "advisers" in Korea, the Russians tried to introduce their own men.[41] In 1896 a Russian colonel, assisted by three commissioned officers and ten noncommissioned officers, undertook to organize a royal bodyguard in Seoul. In the meantime, attempts were made to substitute a Russian for an Englishman who was supervising Korea's financial affairs. For a short while, in 1897 and 1898, K. A. Alexeev, a Russian customs official, did enjoy virtually the status of minister of finance to the king. The tenure of Russian advisers, however, was usually short. Another method was economic penetration. Concession rights to railway construction, mines, and timberland were the more important means to extending Russia's economic power into Manchuria and northern Korea. In this regard the Russo-Chinese Bank was of particular significance. Although outwardly represented as a joint, private bank, it was in fact an adjunct of the Russian treasury, serving the cause of Russian imperialism in Manchuria.[42]

Russia in Retreat

The imperialist competition between Russia and Japan over Manchuria and Korea was finally resolved through the war of 1904 to 1905. The Portsmouth treaty, which ended the war, and subsequent agreements entered into by the two powers made one thing clear: Russia's advance into the Far East, which had been so notable in the preceding ten years, came to a halt and a movement in the reverse direction started. Russia not only acknowledged a paramount interest of Japan in Korea but also turned over to Japan its interests in southern Manchuria (the Liaotung peninsula and the South Manchurian Railway).[43] It was not a rout, however. Having yielded to Japan, Russia persuaded Tokyo to make good on its prewar offer to have Manchuria divided into two spheres of influence. The Russo-Japanese Convention of 1907 assured Russia a special interest in northern Manchuria (Outer Mongolia was added later); furthermore, both sides went on to recognize the right of each power, within its sphere, freely to take all measures necessary to safeguard and defend its interests.[44] This arrangement was to last until World War I and the Revolution, but for all practical purposes, troubles at home put Russian operations in Asia on ice after 1905.

When tsarist Russia's imperialism in Asia is reviewed in its entirety, from its inception to its end, its peculiarities emerge more clearly. First, it was active for only a short period of time (1854 to 1860 and 1895 to 1904), some fifteen years altogether; and for a stretch of thirty-five years the Russian presence was little felt in East Asia. Deep involvement in Manchuria and Korea was therefore not the norm in

Russia's overall relations with its Asian neighbors in the last half of the nineteenth century. Second, on balance, economic penetration, in spite of all the attention it attracted, was not as important as strategic considerations, which invariably took precedence in the mind and actions of the Russians.

This leads to the third point: Russian expansion in Asia was essentially tied to Siberia. What the Russians looked for in the 1850's and what they settled for in the 1900's equally reflected their basic concern, which was over their sprawling territory in the East. And, finally, the Russian experience is a classic case of how an imperial power, operating in a political vacuum, failed to draw the line on where to stop and therefore overextended itself, with all this meant in terms of a relative weakening of its position and the courting of strong counteractions from other powers. Ironically, responsibility for such a gross discrepancy between the nation's interest and commitment lay not so much with the autocratic centralization of power as with the lack of unitary authority in the tsarist government.[45]

Another interesting evaluation of Russian imperialism can be made by comparing the records of Russia with those of its major adversaries in Asia, Great Britain and Japan. Extensive though they were, particularly the acquisition of eastern Siberia, the Russian gains examined in this chapter were in many respects far exceeded by those of the British or the Japanese. The British, starting in 1800's, were most active in China: they waged at least two military campaigns against China (the Opium War of 1840 to 1842 and the Arrow War of 1856 to 1860), exacted millions of dollars in indemnities, acquired the island of Hong Kong, gained leaseholds on Kowloon and Weihaiwei, fixed Chinese tariff and then supervised the Chinese customs service; and above all, using extraterritoriality and superiority in commerce to advantage, they made deep and extensive economic inroads in the Yangtze valley, which was turned into a British sphere of influence.

As for Japan, its gains in China were for the time being limited to Taiwan, the Liaotung peninsula, and subsidiary rights in Manchuria; but in Korea it was first among foreign powers where political and economic encroachments were concerned. Having opened the country by using military threats, Japan made a quick dash for preeminence by pouring in thousands of its nationals, who eventually dominated commerce and trade in the country. Meanwhile the Japanese government obtained numerous concession rights in railways, telegraph lines, mines, and timberlands. Moreover, the Japanese—government officials as well as civilians—were constantly involved in political intrigues and machinations, to the great detriment of the country's political stability.

Perhaps the most distinctive characteristic of Russian imperialism in Asia, however, was that it did not benefit from either nationalism or capitalism, the two elements that are widely held to be responsible for modern imperialism. With its multinational composition and its dynastic regime, tsarist Russia was not a nation-state; indeed, nationalism would only have led to destruction of the empire. In Europe, to be sure, Russian activities had certain nationalistic connotations, but Russian expansionist projects in Asia were hardly manifestations of nationalism. Likewise, the Russian economy during the period under study was so backward that it would be a gross misstatement to describe it as capitalistic. Russia was enmeshed in capitalistic undertakings only to the extent that it served as the conduit for French capital for investment in Asia, but on the whole Russian activities in Manchuria or Korea were not related to the search for a monopoly of the market for surplus good, capital, and people, or for a controlled source of natural resources. Instead, Russian imperialism in Asia was primarily an outgrowth of expansionism of much earlier origin, and it did not quite fit the type of the Age of Imperialism.

An understanding and evaluation of Russian imperialism would not be complete without also taking note of its impact. In more than one sense, the Russo-Japanese War was a watershed in history. Thereafter, Russia was unmistakably in retreat in Asia, and the trend continued for the next forty years. The Soviets returned only after World War II to perform a role very similar to the one in which their tsarist predecessors had failed. Within Russia itself, the failure of imperialism in the East had the effect of hastening the downfall of autocracy; the 1905 revolution was but a dress rehearsal of the fatal one to come in 1917. The empty space the Russians had left in Asia was to be filled by the Japanese. Korea was first made into a Japanese protectorate and then annexed outright in 1910. Two years later, in China, the Manchu dynasty collapsed under the pressure that had been mounting throughout the preceding century, and in the course of the prolonged internal turmoil that ensued, the Japanese made enormous gains at China's expense in Manchuria and North China. Japan, however, was to travel the same route tsarist Russia had gone. Ultimately, imperialism destroyed the imperial power itself.

Notes

INTRODUCTION

1. *Encyclopaedia of the Social Sciences,* ed. Edwin B. A. Seligman and Alvin Johnson, 8 vols. (New York: Macmillan), V, 505.

2. Henri Brunschvig, *L'Impérialisme colonial français* (Paris: Armand Colin, 1960), pp. 186–187.

3. Claude G. Bowen, *Beveridge and the Progressive Era* (Boston: Houghton Mifflin, 1932), pp. 69 f., 74 f., 134. Mark Sullivan, *Our Times,* 6 vols. (New York: Scribner, 1929–1935), I, 50. See A. K. Weinberg, *Manifest Destiny* (Baltimore: Johns Hopkins Press, 1935); Julius W. Pratt, "The Ideology of American Expansionism," *Essays in Honor of William E. Dodd,* ed. Amory Graven (Chicago: University of Chicago Press, 1935); Ernest Leo Tuveson, *Redeemer Nation, the Idea of America's Millennial Role* (Chicago: University of Chicago Press, 1968).

4. Egon Caesar Conte Corti, *Mensch und Herrscher: Wege und Schicksale Kaiser Franz Josephs I. Zwischen Thronbesteigung und Berliner Kongress* (Graz: Styria, 1952), pp. 436 f.

5. Theodore Poesche and Charles Goepp, *The New Rome, or the United States of the World* (New York: Putnam, 1853), pp. 16, 59, 62, 87 f., 99 f., 177. "A people can not forego its mission, and the mission of the American people is not bounded by oceans" (*ibid.,* p. 20)

6. The Fourth Crusade, which was launched at the initiative of Pope Innocent III, was diverted by the Venetians, who sought economic advantages in Constantinople. The Crusaders took the city in 1204 and held it until 1261. Throughout this period the Venetians enjoyed a virtual economic monopoly.

7. Friedrich von Gentz is quoted in Golo Mann, *The Secretary of Europe* (New Haven: Yale University Press, 1946), pp. 276–277.

8. The articles by Marx were reprinted in *The Eastern Question,* ed. Eleanor Marx Aveling and Edward Aveling (London: Swan Sonnenschein, 1897). Russia's "plan" to conquer all of Europe was submitted to the French government in 1797 by a Polish general as a document in which he incorporated the so-called Testament of Peter the Great. Supposedly the testament had been among secret Russian documents in Warsaw in April, 1794. Proof that it was a forgery was published in Harry Breslau in the *Historische Zeitschrift* in 1879. How many "secret" documents have played a nefarious role in history!

9. On Jules Michelet, see Hans Kohn, *Prophets and Peoples* (New York: Macmillan, 1946), pp. 43–76, 172–182; on Giuseppe Mazzini and Russia, see pp. 94, 188.

10. František Palacky, *Radhost,* 3 vols. (Prague: B. Tempsky, 1873), III, 10–17. On the possibility of the survival of the Habsburg empire, see Hans Kohn, "Was the Collapse Inevitable?" in *Austrian History Yearbook* (Houston, Tex.: Rice University, 1967), III, pt. 3, pp. 250–266.

11. R. W. Seton-Watson, *Masaryk in England* (Cambridge: Cambridge University Press, 1942), pp. 127 f., 124, 132 f.

12. Pogodin's "Letter on Russian History" in Nikolai Platonovich Barsukov, *Zhizn i trudy M. P. Pogodina,* 22 vols. (St. Petersburg, 1888–1910), V, 165–175; English trans. in Hans Kohn, ed., *The Mind of Modern Russia* (New Brunswick, N.J.: Rutgers University Press, 1955), pp. 58–68.

13. Nikolai Iakovlevich Danilevskii, *Rossiia i Evropa: Vzgliad na kulturnie i politicheskie otnosheniia Slavianskago mira k Germano-Romanskomu,* ed. Nikolai Nikolaevich Strakhov, with notes by K. N. Bestuzhev-Riumin, 5th ed. (St. Petersburg, 1895). In the last issue of his *Journal of an Author,* published at the end of January, 1881, Dostoevsky favored Russia's turning to Asia, which would become Russia's America. Here the Russians would, with the help of science, produce immense wealth. This New Russia in Asia would regenerate old Russia and make its masses understand Russia's destiny. *Dnevnik Pisatelia,* vol. V of *Polnoe sobranie sochinenii* (published by Dostoevsky's widow, St. Petersburg, 1886), pp. 815 ff.

14. Nicholas Muraviev's "Rescript of the Russian Emperor, August 24, 1898," in James Brown Scott, *The Hague Peace Conferences of 1899 and 1907,* 2 vols. (Baltimore: Johns Hopkins Press, 1909), II, 1–2.

15. See Richard Pipes, *The Formation of the Soviet Union: Communism and Nationalism, 1917–1923,* rev. ed. (Cambridge, Mass.: Harvard University Press, 1964), p. 1, text and footnote.

16. Thornton Anderson, *Russian Political Thought* (Ithaca, N.Y.: Cornell University Press, 1967), pp. 184, 185.

17. K. B. Pobedonostsev, *Reflections of a Russian Statesman,* trans. Robert Crozier Long (London: Richards, 1898), p. 36.

18. Timothy Dwight, *Greenfield Hill: A Poem in Seven Parts* (New York: Childs and Swaine, 1794), p. 157.

19. On Nicholas Chernyshevskii's novel *What Is To Be Done?,* see Hans Kohn, ed., *The Mind of Modern Russia* (New Brunswick, N.J.: Rutgers University Press, 1955), pp. 138–154.

20. *Ibid.,* p. 150. The profound web of interest on the two shores of the North Atlantic was foreseen by the great Russian liberal Alexander Herzen, who then lived in London and wrote about the first transatlantic cable that connected England and North America in 1858: "What can a country which feels the beat of an uninterrupted pulse with America not do, for the ocean will become an internal system! In truth there are not two states but two different shores, belonging to the Anglo-Saxons." David Hecht, *Russian Radicals Look to America, 1825–1894* (Cambridge, Mass.: Harvard University Press, 1947), p. 29.

THE ORIGINS OF RUSSIAN IMPERIALISM

1. Philip E. Mosely, "Aspects of Russian Expansionism," *American Slavic and East European Review,* VII (October, 1948), 197–213.

2. Oscar Halecki, "Imperialism in Slavic and East European History," *American Slavic and East European Review,* XI (February, 1952), 1–26.

3. *Ibid.,* p. 1.

4. Nicholas V. Riasanovsky, "Old Russia, the Soviet Union and Eastern Europe," *American Slavic and East European Review,* XI (October, 1952), 171–188.

5. John A. Hobson, *Imperialism,* 3d ed. (London, 1938), pp. 8–11.

6. A point discussed in greater detail by Oswald P. Backus, III, "Was Muscovite Russia Imperialistic?" *American Slavic and East European Review,* XIII (December, 1954), 522–534.

7. Robert J. Kerner, *The Urge to the Sea* (Berkeley, Calif., 1942), p. 103.

8. *Ibid.,* pp. 103–104.

9. Nikolai Berdiaev, "O vlasti prostranstv nad russkoi dushoi," in *Sudba Rossii, opyty po psikhologii voiny i natsionalnosti* (Moscow, 1918), p. 62.

10. Boris Brutkus, "The Historical Peculiarities of the Social and Economic Development of Russia," in *Class, Status and Power,* ed. Reinhard Bendix and Seymour Martin Lipset (New York, 1953), pp. 517–518.

11. V. O. Kliuchevskii, *Sochineniia* (Moscow, 1956), I, 32.

12. A. Kizevetter, "Obshchie postroenniia russkoi istorii v sovremennoi literature," in *Istoricheskie siluety. Liudi i sobytiia* (Berlin, 1931), pp. 285–286.

13. Compare maps Nos. 3 and 4 in Allen F. Chew, *An Atlas of Russian History* (New Haven, 1967). Also see maps Nos. 9 and 10 in *Atlas istorii SSSR* (Moscow, 1954), pt. 1; and P. Kovalevsky, *Atlas historique et culturel de la Russe et du monde slave* (Paris, 1961), pp. 23, 43.

14. See maps in Kerner, *Urge to the Sea,* pp. 55, 57. For information on the defense line, see N. A. Popov, ed., *Akty moskovskogo gosudarstva* (St. Petersburg, 1890), I, 1–17.

15. George V. Lantzeff, *Siberia in the Seventeenth Century* (Berkeley, Calif., 1943), p. 155.

16. N. M. Iandritsev, *Sibir kak koloniia* (St. Petersburg, 1882), pp. 190–191.

17. For a full discussion of the history of this period of expansionism, see George Vernadsky, *Kievan Russia* (New Haven: Yale University Press, 1948), pp. 19–42.

18. There is much controversy still whether Sviatoslav had a definite plan of conquest in mind or merely improvised. For a bibliography of this problem, consult A. D. Stokes, "The Background and Chronology of the Balkan Campaign of Svyatoslav Igorevich," *Slavonic and East European Review,* XL (December, 1961), 95, nn. 3, 4. I subscribe to the positive interpretation of Sviatoslav's imperial designs as demonstrated by Stokes in "The Balkan Cam-

paigns of Svyatoslav Igorevich," *Slavonic and East European Review,* XL (June, 1962), 466–693.

19. On the Volga campaign, see Samuel H. Cross, ed. and trans., *The Russian Primary Chronicle* (Cambridge, 1953), p. 250, nn. 665, 666; also Gerhard Laehr, *Die Anfänge des russischen Reiches* (Berlin, 1930), p. 138, n. 8; and A. A. Vasiliev, *The Goths in the Crimea* (Cambridge, 1936), pp. 119–131.

20. Cross, ed., *Russian Primary Chronicle,* p. 86.

21. *Ibid.,* p. 243, n. 84. His 985 campaign against the Volga Bulgars, though a military success, failed to conquer and annex the region.

22. I. P. Shaskolskii, "Dogovory Novgoroda s Norvegiei," *Istoricheskie Zapiski,* XIV (1946), 24.

23. For a general survey of the period, see A. I. Nikitskii, *Istoriia ekonomicheskago byta velikago Novgoroda* (Moscow, 1893).

24. *Pamiatniki russkago prava,* II (Moscow, 1933), 117–118.

25. Kerner, *Urge to the Sea,* p. 29; and C. Raymond Beazley, "The Russian Expansion Towards Asia and the Arctic in the Middle Ages to 1500," *American Historical Review,* XIII (October, 1907–July, 1908), 731–741.

26. *Polnoe sobranie russkikh letopisei* (Moscow and Leningrad, 1962), XXIX, 174 ff. [Hereafter cited as *PSRL.*]

27. K. Waliszewski, *Ivan the Terrible* (London, 1904), p. 168. The consolidation of Muscovite trade interests is clearly discernible in the official chronicle reports; *PSRL,* XIII, 235–236, 265–266.

28. Thomas Esper, "Russia and the Baltic, 1494–1558," *Slavic Review,* XXV (September, 1966), 461.

29. Walther Kirchner, *Commercial Relations Between Russia and Europe, 1400 to 1800* (Bloomington, Ind., 1966), p. 12.

30. S. M. Solovev, *Istoriia Rossii s drevneishikh vremen,* 2d ed. (Moscow, 1959–1966), Bk. 3, vol. VI, 500 ff.

31. Kirchner, *Commercial Relations,* pp. 59–77.

32. Stuart Ramsay Tompkins, *Alaska: promyshlennik and Sourdough* (Norman, Okla., 1952), p. 17.

33. *PSRL,* XIII, 248; *Istoriia Sibirii,* I (Leningrad, 1968), 371.

34. Michael Cherniavsky, *Tsar and People* (New Haven, 1961), pp. 5–43.

35. Cross, ed., *Russian Primary Chronicle,* p. 129.

36. *Ibid.,* p. 200.

37. *Ibid.,* p. 205.

38. *The Song of Igor's Campaign,* trans. Vladimir Nabokov (New York, 1960), p. 72.

39. M. S. Hrushevskyi, *Istoriia Ukrainy-Rusy,* 2d ed., III (Lvov, 1905), 11–12.

40. Cherniavsky, *Tsar and People,* pp. 22–23.

41. *PSRL,* XXV, 200–203.

42. G. P. Fedotov, *The Russian Religious Mind* (Cambridge, 1966), p. 226.

43. J. L. I. Fennell, *Ivan the Great of Moscow* (New York, 1961), pp. 211–214.

44. Bjarne Norretranders, *The Shaping of Czardom under Ivan Groznyi* (Copenhagen, 1964), p. 41.

45. *Russkaia istoricheskaia biblioteka,* VI (St. Petersburg, 1878), cols. 795–796. [Hereafter cited as *RIB.*]

46. V. Malinin, *Starets Filofei i ego poslaniia* (Kiev, 1901), App. IX, pp. 49–55.

47. Savva, formerly Metropolitan Spiridon of Kiev, wrote his epistle in the Ferapon Monastery in Beloozero, in semiretirement and semiconfinement. The text of the tract is in P. R. Dmitrieva, *Skazanie o kniaziakh Vladimirskikh* (Moscow, 1955), pp. 159–170.

48. Nikolay Andreyev, "Filofey and His Epistle to Ivan Vasil'yevich," *Slavonic and East European Review,* XXXVIII (December, 1959), 1, 25. See also N. S. Chaev, *Moskva-tretii rim v politicheskoi praktike moskovskogo pravitelstva* (Paris, 1947), pp. 10–13.

49. *RIB,* VI, col. 633.

50. Malinin, *Starets Filofei,* pp. 166–170.

51. *Ibid.,* pp. 45–56.

52. Dimitri Stremeoukhoff, "Moscow the Third Rome: Sources of the Doctrine," *Speculum,* XXVIII (January, 1953), 91–93.

53. J. L. H. Keep, "The Regime of Filaret, 1619–1633," *Slavonic and East European Review,* XXXVIII (June, 1960), 357.

54. K. V. Kharlampovich, *Malorossiiskoe vliianie na velikorusskuiu tserkovnuiu zhizn* (Kazan, 1914), pp. 26–27.

55. Stremeoukhoff, "Moscow the Third Rome," p. 100.

56. A theme pursued by M. A. Diakonov, *Vlast moskovskikh gosudarei. Ocherk iz istorii politicheskikh idei drevnei Rusi do kontsa XVI veka* (St. Petersburg, 1889); Stremeoukhoff, "Moscow the Third Rome," p. 100.

57. George Vernadsky, *The Mongols and Russia* (New Haven: Yale University Press, 1953), p. 206.

58. *Dukhovnye i dogovornye gramoty vilikikh i udelnykh kniazei XIV–XVI vekov* (Moscow and Leningrad, 1950), p. 11. [Hereafter cited as *DDG.*]

59. *PSRL,* IV, 349.

60. *DDG,* p. 59.

61. *PSRL,* XII, 175, and *PSRL,* XV, col. 500.

62. *Sbornik Mukhanova* (Moscow, 1836), No. 27, p. 39.

63. *DDG,* pp. 295, 301.

64. *DDG,* p. 329.

65. *Akty otnosiashchiesia k istorii zapadnoi Rossii,* I (St. Petersburg, 1846), No. 69. [Hereafter cited as *AZR.*]

66. Dmitrieva, *Skazanie o kniaziakh Vladimirskikh,* pp. 159–170. This secular counterpart of the Third Rome theory became especially popular in a new version after the coronation of Ivan IV in 1547 (Dmitrieva, pp. 171–178).

67. Francis Dvornik, *The Slavs in European History and Civilization* (New Brunswick, N.J., 1962), p. 272.

68. Ivan III began the subtle process of establishing claims over Livonia by insisting that it refer to him as tsar, thereby inferring a form of vassalage;

H. Uebersberger, *Österreich und Russland seit dem Ende des 15. Jahrhunderts* (Vienna, 1906), I, 84, 277. Ivan IV made outright claims upon Livonia as his historical heritage, and so referred to it in his correspondence with the monarchs of Denmark, England, Poland, and Sweden, among others, from the mid-1550's. For example, in 1558 he spoke of it as "unser grosfürsten veterlich erbe" (A. Bergengrün, ed., *Aufzeichnungen des rigaschen Ratssekretär Johann Schmied zu den Jahren 1558–1562* [Leipzig, 1892], p. 31). A detailed discussion of this is to be found in Fritz T. Epstein, ed., *Heinrich von Staden* (Hamburg, 1964), App. 5, pp. 244–250, also pp. 32–33.

69. Michael Cherniavsky, "Khan or Basileus: An Aspect of Russian Medieval Political Theory," *Journal of the History of Ideas,* XX (October–December, 1959), 462–464.

70. *PSRL,* VI, App. B, p. 90.

71. *AZR,* I, No. 69.

72. In fact, following the conquest of the khanate of Kazan in 1552, Ivan IV was hailed throughout the steppe and western Siberia as "Belyi Tsar"—"White Tsar"; and in 1555 he assumed the title of Lord of Siberia after its khan had placed himself under Ivan's protection; *PSRL,* XIII, 248.

73. W. Philipp, *Ivan Peresvetov und seine Schriften zur Erneuerung des moskauer Reiches* (Berlin, 1935), p. 117; and A. A. Zimin, ed., *Sochineniia Ivana Peresvetova* (Moscow and Leningrad, 1956), pp. 131–161.

74. In this respect, Ivan III was the first of the Muscovite rulers to invite foreign technicians and through them introduced foreign technology into Muscovy. It was this process that ultimately swung the balance of power in favor of Muscovy, to the East as well as to the West.

75. For an analysis of Ivan III's foreign policy, the best study is still K. V. Vazilevich, *Vneshniaia politika russkogo tsentralizovannogo gosudarstva. Vtoraia polovina XV veka* (Moscow, 1952). See also George Vernadsky, *Russia at the Dawn of the Modern Age* (New Haven: Yale University Press, 1959), pp. 67–95; and Fennell, *Ivan the Great.*

76. Vernadsky, *Russia at the Dawn of the Modern Age,* pp. 150–157. The most thorough study of Vasilii's foreign policy remains Solovev's in his *Istoriia Rossii s drevneishikh vremen,* Bk. 3, vol. V, pt. 2, chaps. 1, 2.

77. In 1541 the Crimea mounted a major attack, and throughout the remainder of the decade Kazan sent out large expeditions almost every year. It was reported that up to 100,000 Muscovite prisoners were kept in Kazan.

78. *Ocherki istorii SSSR* (Moscow, 1955), pp. 355 ff.

79. George Vernadsky, *The Tsardom of Moscow, 1547–1682* (New Haven: Yale University Press, 1969), pt. 1, pp. 87–88. On the politics of the dispute, refer to I. I. Smirnov, *Ocherki politicheskoi istorii russkogo gosudarstva 30–50kh godov XVI veka* (Moscow and Leningrad, 1958).

80. This is discussed in the chapter on the Ukraine and Muscovite expansion, below.

81. The fullest discussions on the Livonian War are found in Vol. I of G. V. Forstén, *Baltiiskii vopros v XVI i XVII stoletiiakh* (St. Petersburg,

1893); and E. Donnert, *Der livländische Ordensritterstaat und Russland 1558–1583* (Berlin, 1963).

82. Keep, "The Regime of Filaret," p. 337.

83. On Golitsyn's foreign policy, see C. Bickford O'Brien, *Russia under Two Tsars, 1682–1689* (Berkeley, Calif., 1952), pp. 89, 91–97, 101–104, 127, 128–150.

84. The most thorough analyses of Peter's foreign policy are to be found in B. H. Summer, *Peter the Great and the Ottoman Empire* (Oxford, 1950); B. Kafengauz, *Vneshniaia politika pri Petre I* (Moscow, 1942); W. Mediger, *Moskaus Weg nach Europa* (Braunschweig, 1952). An excellent and concise survey of the consequences of Peter's war with Sweden seen in the context of all Europe is Penfield Robert's *The Quest for Security, 1715–1740* (New York, 1947).

PAN-SLAVISM OR PAN-RUSSIANISM

1. F. Tiutchev, *Polnoe sobranie sochinenii,* ed. P. Bykov (St. Petersburg, 1912), p. 294.

2. Johann Gottfried von Herder, *Sämtliche Werke,* ed. Bernard Suphan (Berlin: Weidmann, 1877–1913), XVII, 58 ff.

3. Svetozar Hurban-Vajansky is quoted by Hans Kohn, *Pan-Slavism: Its History and Ideology* (New York, 1960), p. 19.

4. N. Ustrialov, "Natsionalnaia problema u pervykh slavianofilov," *Russkaia Mysl* (Moscow), X (1916), 1. For native sources of Russian nationalism, see Hans Rogger, *National Consciousness in Eighteenth-Century Russia* (Cambridge, Mass.: Harvard University Press, 1960).

5. O. I. Herzen, *Mynule i dumy* (Kiev: Derzhavne Vydavnytsvo Kh. Literatury, 1957), pp. 303, 313.

6. Peter Chaadaev is quoted in Hans Kohn, ed., *The Mind of Modern Russia* (New Brunswick, N.J.: Rutgers University Press, 1955), pp. 39, 42.

7. Herzen, *Mynulc i dumy,* p. 305.

8. Friedrich Hertz, *Nationalgeist und Politik* (Zürich, 1937), p. 310.

9. Nikolai Barsukov, *Zhizn i trudy M. P. Pogodina* (St. Petersburg, 1880–1910), V, 467.

10. Rogger, *National Consciousness in Eighteenth-Century Russia,* p. 84.

11. For an instructive discussion of the problem by a leading Slavophile, Ivan V. Kireevski, see Marc Raeff, ed., *Russian Intellectual History: An Anthology* (New York, 1966), pp. 199–205.

12. In accordance with the messianic claims of the Slavophiles, only Orthodoxy represented true Christianity. Cf. *Biografiia Aleksandra Ivanovycha Kosheleva* (Moscow, 1892), II, 74.

13. Edward Chmielewski, *Tribune of the Slavophiles: Konstantin Aksakov* (Gainesville: University of Florida Press, 1961), p. 83; Ivan Aksakov, *Sochineniia* (Moscow, 1886), IV, 251.

14. Orest Miller, "Osnovy ucheniia pervonachalnykh slavianofilov,"

Russkaia Mysl, I (1880), 80–81; Emanuel Sarkisyanz, *Russland und der Messianismus des Orients* (Tübingen: J. C. Mohs, 1955), p. 110.

15. Nicholas Berdyaev, *The Russian Idea* (Boston: Beacon Press, 1962), p. 51. For the Slavophiles, the family, as the ultimate expression of communality and organic wholeness (*sobornost*), became not only "the prototype of the 'ideal society'," but also "a model of the good state." See Vladimir C. Nahirny, "The Russian Intelligentsia: From Men of Ideas to Men of Convictions," *Comparative Studies in Society and History: An International Quarterly* (The Hague), IV (July, 1962), 410–411.

16. Nicholas V. Riasanovsky, *Russia and the West in the Teaching of the Slavophiles* (Cambridge, Mass.: Harvard University Press, 1952), p. 135.

17. Peter K. Christoff, *An Introduction to Nineteenth-Century Russian Slavophilism: A Study of Ideas* (The Hague: Mouton, 1961), pp. 126, 138–141, 153.

18. D. I. Chizhevskii, *Gegel v Rossii* (Paris, 1939), pp. 165–166; P. N. Miliukov "Razlozhenie slavianofilstva," *Voprosy Filosofii i Psikhologii* (Moscow), May, 1893, pp. 48–49; K. P. Petrov, "Slavianofilskoe uchenie," *Istoricheskii Vestnik,* LXXXV (September, 1901), 902, 915.

19. Cf. S. A. Vengerov, *Peredovoi boets Slavianofilstva: Konstantin Aksakov* (St. Petersburg, 1912), pp. 142, 180, 181, 185, 187. Also S. Levitskii, *Pravoslavie i narodnost* (Moscow, 1888), pp. 210–211.

20. Professor Venturi has referred to the Slavophile projection of preconceived ideas as "an idealization of Russia's origins on an unhistorical myth." Franco Venturi, *Roots of Revolution: A History of the Populist and Socialist Movements in Nineteenth-Century Russia* (New York, 1966), p. 22.

21. P. G. Vinogradov, "I. V. Kireevskii i nachalo moskovskago slavianofilstva," *Voprosy Filosofii i Psikhologii,* January, 1892, p. 102.

22. Ivan Aksakov, *Sochineniia,* I, 680, 681, 746.

23. Barsukov, *M. P. Pogodina,* I, 56.

24. *Ibid.,* IX, 229–231.

25. Kohn, ed., *The Mind of Modern Russia,* p. 84.

26. *Ibid.,* p. 88.

27. Professor Miliukov refers to Slavophilism as the religious-philosophical nationalism which ended in 1850, giving way to an original national creativity. See P. N. Miliukov, *Natsionalnyi Vopros* (Prague, 1925), pp. 130, 135.

28. See A. N. Pypin, *Panslavism v proshlom i nastoiashchem* (St. Petersburg, 1913), p. 101.

29. For the changing nature of Slavophilism, see E. Mamonov, "Slavianofily," *Russkii Arkhiv* (Moscow), No. 11 (1873), 2489–2490.

30. For the Slavophile attitude toward state, autocracy, and politics, see N. I. Brodskii, ed., *Rannie Slavianofily: A. S. Khomiakov, I. V. Kireevskii, K. S. i I. S. Aksakovy* (Moscow, 1910), pp. 69–96.

31. A French royalist who went on a political pilgrimage to the Russia of Nicholas I found it terrifying "that for such a great multitude of arms and legs there is only one head." Cf. *Journey for Our Time: The Russian Journals of the Marquis de Custine* (Chicago, 1951), p. 80.

32. M. Pogodin, *Istorico-politicheskie pisma i zapiski vprodolzhenii Krymskoi Voiny, 1853–1856* (Moscow, 1874), pp. 10–11.

33. Kohn, *Pan-Slavism,* pp. 141–146.

34. F. K. Neslukhovskii, "Iz vospominanii," *Istoricheskii Vestnik,* XL (April, 1890), 143.

35. Barsukov, *M. P. Pogodina,* VI, 291.

36. "Vospominaniia F. V. Chizhova," *Istoricheskii Vestnik,* XI (February, 1883), 257. A. N. Pypin refers to this type of Russian Pan-Slavism as Pan-Russianism. Cf. Pypin, *Panslavism,* p. 153.

37. Nicholas V. Riasanovsky, *Nicholas I and Official Nationality in Russia, 1825–1855* (Berkeley and Los Angeles: University of California Press, 1961), pp. 163–164.

38. M. I. Sukhomlinov, "I. S. Aksakov v sorokovykh godakh," *Istoricheskii Vestnik,* XXXI (1881), p. 343.

39. *Vospominaniia Borisa Nikolaevicha Chicherina: Moskva sorokovykh godov* (Moscow, 1929), II, 148.

40. Kohn, ed., *The Mind of Modern Russia,* p. 108.

41. Pypin, *Panslavism,* p. 97.

42. Pogodin, *Istoriko-politicheskie pisma,* pp. 186–187.

43. Michael Boro Petrovich, *The Emergence of Russian Pan-Slavism* (New York: Columbia University Press, 1958), p. 242.

44. As a zealous nationalist, Ivan Aksakov always upheld the primacy of Russia. For him, "to say 'Russia'—means to say: The Orthodox-Slavic world. . . ." Cf. Ivan Aksakov, *Sochineniia,* I, 749. Equating Slavs with the Russians was an intransitive relationship, however; for one could not say that the Slavs equaled Russia, just as one could not say that the Russian Emperor was the ruler of the Slavs. Indeed, "The Russian Emperor is the Russian ruler, and not a collective one. . . ." *Ibid.,* II, 215.

45. Stephen Lukashevich, *Ivan Aksakov, 1823–1886: A Study in Russian Thought and Politics* (Cambridge, Mass.: Harvard University Press, 1965), p. 119; also "Perepiska dvukh slavianofilov," *Russkaia Mysl,* IX (1916), 3.

46. Boro Petrovich, *Russian Pan-Slavism,* p. 151.

47. *Ibid.,* pp. 145–146.

48. Nil Popov, *Iz istorii Slavianskago blagotvoritelnago komiteta v Moskve; pervoe piatiletie, 1858–1862* (Moscow, 1871), p. 45.

49. N. M. Druzhinin, ed., *Slavianskii sbornik: Slavianskii vopros i russkoe obshchestvo v 1867–1878 godakh* (Moscow, 1948), p. 6; also D. D. Rudin, "Epizody iz politicheskoi zhizni Bosnii i Gerzegoviny v posledniia tridtsat let," *Istoricheskii Vestnik,* XXVII (March, 1887), 652.

50. Pogodin is cited by Boro Petrovich, *Russian Pan-Slavism,* p. 162. See also M. P. Pogodin, "Otryvki iz pisem o polozhenii slavian v Europe," *Russkaia Beseda* (Moscow), I (1859), 63–64.

51. V. I. Lamanskii, *Natsionalnost italianskaia i slavianskaia v politicheskom i literaturnom otnosheniiakh* (St. Petersburg, 1865), p. 17; also his "Izuchenie Slavianstva: russkoe narodnoe samosoznanie," *Zhurnal Ministerstva Narodnago Prosveshcheniia,* January, 1867, p. 152.

52. Anton Budilovich, "Ob izuchenii Slavianskago mira," in *Slavianskii sbornik* (St. Petersburg, 1877), II, 2.

53. *Ibid.*, pp. 3–4.

54. Druzhinin, *Slavianskii sbornik*, p. 8.

55. Postlethwayt is cited by E. M. Winslow, *The Pattern of Imperialism* (New York: Columbia University Press, 1950), p. 14.

56. Lukashevich, *Ivan Aksakov*, p. 113.

57. *Ibid.*, p. 110; see also Barsukov, *M. P. Pogodina*, IX, 231.

58. *Sobranie sochinenii A. Hilferdinga* (St. Petersburg, 1868), II, 313–314.

59. *Ibid.*, p. 315.

60. Lukashevich, *Ivan Aksakov*, p. 90.

61. *Ibid.*, pp. 90–95.

62. B. E. Nolde, *Iurii Samarin i ego vremia* (Paris, 1926), p. 152. Michael Pogodin, historian though he was, sought to mitigate the Russo-Polish problem by modifying history. According to him, Russia had not violated the basic rights of Poland, nor had it participated in any partitions. What had really happened, according to him, was that "Russia and Poland had united . . . on the basis of the natural order of things. . . ." Cf. M. Pogodin, *Istoriko-kriticheskie otryvki* (Moscow, 1846), I, 423, 432.

63. General Rostislav Fadeev, *Opinion on the Eastern Question* (London, 1876), p. 78.

64. *Ibid.*, p. 76.

65. *Ibid.*, pp. 71, 74. See also Orest Miller, *Slavianstvo i Evropa* (St. Petersburg, 1877), pp. 92–93.

66. For data on the participants in the 1848, 1867, and 1868 Slav Congresses, see Stanley Bukholz Kimball, "The Prague 'Slav Congress' of 1868," *Journal of Central European Affairs*, XXII (April, 1962), 195–199.

67. For details, see *Vserossiiskaia etnograficheskaia vystavka i Slavianskii sezd v maie 1867 goda* (Moscow, 1867), pp. 87, 96–97, 197–199, 258–259, 280–281.

68. *Ibid.*, pp. 299–301. The views of Rieger coincided remarkably with the ideology of the Ukrainian Pan-Slavists who were organized in the Brotherhood of Saints Cyril and Methodius. See John P. Sydoruk, *Ideology of Cyrillo-Methodians and Its Origin* (Winnipeg, 1954), p. 11.

69. K. Pigarev, "F. I. Tiutchev i problemy vneshnii politiki tsarskoi Rossii," *Literaturnoe Nasledstvo* (Moscow), XIX–XXII (1935), 236.

70. S. A. Nikitin, "Slavianskie sezdy shestidesiatykh godov XIX veka," in *Slavianskii sbornik* (Moscow, 1948), p. 36.

71. Druzhinin, *Slavianskii sbornik*, p. 8.

72. Fedor Dostoevsky, *The Devils*, trans. David Magarshack (Bungay, Suffolk: The Penguin Classics, 1962), p. 253.

73. Dostoevsky's dialogue is quoted by Ernest J. Simmons, *Dostoevsky: The Making of a Novelist* (New York: Vintage Books, 1962), p. 280.

74. Dostoevsky, *The Devils*, p. 258. For a contrastic interpretation, see

Vladimir S. Solovev, *F. M. Dostoevsky kak propovednik vsclenskago pravoslaviia* (Moscow, 1908), pp. 47–48.

75. For an analysis of the contradictory messianic claims of the Slavophiles, see *Sobranie sochinenia Vladimira Sergeevicha Soloveva* (St. Petersburg, 1883–1897), V, 167, 174–175, 197, 199.

76. Dostoevsky, *The Devils,* p. 257. Shatov's negation of Stavrogin's observation was merely a question of semantics, for he himself stated that "God is the synthetic personality of the whole people, taken from its beginning to its end." *Ibid.,* p. 256.

77. *Ibid.,* p. 258.

78. *Ibid.,* p. 253.

79. Kohn, *Pan-Slavism,* p. 211.

80. *Ibid.,* p, 213.

81. Dostoevsky's letter is cited in Hans Kohn, "Dostoevsky and Danilevsky: Nationalist Messianism," in *Continuity and Change in Russian and Soviet Thought,* ed. Ernest J. Simmons (Cambridge, Mass.: Harvard University Press, 1955), p. 502.

82. *Ibid.,* p. 503.

83. Danilevskii is quoted in Robert E. MacMaster, *Danilevsky: A Russian Totalitarian Philosopher* (Cambridge, Mass.: Harvard University Press), p. 256.

84. N. Ia. Danilevskii, *Rossiia i Evropa: vzgliad na kulturnyia i politicheskiia otnosheniia slavianskago mira k germano-romanskomu* (St. Petersburg, 1895), II, 468.

85. For Leontiev's views, see Nikolai Berdyayev, *Konstantin Leontiev* (Paris, 1926), pp. 196–199.

86. Compare Danilevskii's aspirations with Tiutchev's vision:

> Seven internal seas and seven great rivers! . . .
> From the Nile to the Neva, from the Eloe to China —
> From the Volga to the Euphrates, from the Ganges to the Danube
> This is Russian tsardom . . . and it will not disappear with the ages
> As the Holy Spirit foresaw and Daniel foretold.

Quoted by Riasanovsky, *Nicholas I and Official Nationality in Russia,* pp. 152–153.

87. Danilevskii, *Rossiia i Evropa,* II, 395.

88. *Ibid.,* II, 420.

89. *Ibid.,* II, 445.

90. *Ibid.,* II, 420.

91. *Ibid.,* II, 410.

92. *Ibid.,* II, 416.

93. "Zapiski Grafa N. P. Ignatieva," *Istoricheskii Vestnik,* CXXXV (1914), 49.

94. "Zapiski Grafa N. P. Ignatieva," *Istoricheskii Vestnik,* CXLIV (May, 1916), 346. Also S. A. Nikitin, "Diplomaticheskie otnosheniia Rossii s Iuzhnymi

Slavianami v 60-kh godakh XIX v," in *Slavianskii sbornik* (Moscow, 1947), pp. 275, 284, 285.

95. "Zapiski Grafa N. P. Ignatieva," *Istoricheskii Vestnik,* CXXXV (1914), p. 54. See also K. Leontiev, *Vostok, Rossiia, i Slavianstvo: Sobranie sochinenii,* V (Moscow, 1912), 107.

96. *Istoricheskii Vestnik,* CXXXV (1914), p. 56.

97. B. H. Sumner, *Russia and the Balkans, 1870–1880* (Hamden, Conn.: Archon Books, 1962), p. 188.

98. *Ibid.,* pp. 189–190.

99. David MacKenzie, *The Serbs and Russian Pan-Slavism, 1876–1878* (Ithaca, N.Y.: Cornell University Press, 1967), pp. 95–96.

100. *Ibid.,* pp. 118–119.

101. David MacKenzie, "Panslavism in Practice: Cherniaev in Serbia (1876)," *Journal of Modern History,* XXXVI (September, 1964), 292–293.

102. *Ibid.,* p. 285. This was echoed in the writings and pronouncements of other Russian writers and statesmen. Thus in 1885 Alexander III is to have said: "We ought to have one principal aim: The occupation of Constantinople so that we may once for all maintain ourselves at the Straits and know that they will remain in our hands . . . everything else that takes place in the Balkan Peninsula is secondary to us. . . . The Slavs in the Balkans must now serve Russia and not we them." Cited in Arthur J. May, *The Hapsburg Monarchy, 1867–1914* (Cambridge, Mass.: Harvard University Press, 1951), p. 275.

103. MacKenzie, "Panslavism in Practice," p. 286.

104. See Michael Pavlovitch, "Romanisme et réalisme dans l'impérialisme russe," *Revue Politique Internationale* (Paris), II (1914), 219.

105. MacKenzie, *The Serbs and Russian Pan-Slavism,* p. 156.

106. Hans Kohn, "The Impact of Pan-Slavism on Central Europe," *Review of Politics,* XXIII (July, 1961), 326.

107. See Louis Levine, "Pan-Slavism and European Politics," *Political Science Quarterly,* December, 1914, p. 684.

108. "It has been estimated that the growth of the Russian Empire between the end of the fifteenth and the end of the nineteenth century proceeded at the rate of 130 square kilometers or fifty square miles a day." See Richard Pipes, *The Formation of the Soviet Union: Communism and Nationalism, 1917–1923* (Cambridge, Mass.: Harvard University Press, 1954), p. 1.

RUSSIA AND THE BALTIC

There exists, to the best of my knowledge, no scholarly study of Russia and the Baltic covering the whole of the modern period; nothing to compare with, e.g., F. A. Golder, *Russian Expansion on the Pacific* (Cleveland, O., 1914); B. H. Sumner, *Tsardom and Imperialism in the Far and Middle East* (London, 1940); D. F. Dallin, *The Rise of Russia in Asia* (New Haven, 1949); or G. A. Lensen, *The Russian Push Towards Japan* (Princeton, N.J., 1959).

For the eighteenth century there are, however, two recent articles of significance: W. Mediger, "Russland und die Ostsee im 18. Jahrhundert," *Jahrbücher für Geschichte Osteuropas* (Wiesbaden) (1968), pp. 85–104, and L. R. Lewitter, "Russia, Poland and the Baltic, 1697–1721," *Historical Journal* (London) (1968), pp. 3–34. Most of the articles in the periodical *Skandinavskii Sbornik* (published in Tallinn from 1956 onwards) are also relevant to Russia and the Baltic; for a convenient summary of many of them, see Erkki Kuujo's review article in *Jahrbücher für Geschichte Osteuropas* (1968), pp. 56 ff. The general studies on the struggle for the Baltic—e.g., E. Hornborg, *Kampen om Östersjöen* (Stockholm, 1945), and W. Sobieski, *Der Kampf um die Ostsee* (Leipzig, 1933)—are of necessity brief; though we have many important studies of specific periods of the struggle—e.g., G. V. Forstén, *Baltiiskii vopros v XVI i XVII stoletiiakh,* 2 vols. (St. Petersburg, 1893–1894); W. Kirchner, *The Rise of the Baltic Question* (Newark, Del., 1954); M. A. Polievktov, *Baltiiskii vopros v russkoi politike 1721–1725* (St. Petersburg, 1907)—as well as of relations between Russia and a specific Baltic power in a given period—e.g., K. Forstreuter, *Preussen und Russland von den Anfängen des Deutschen Ordens bis zu Peter dem Grossen* (Göttingen, 1955); T. M. Kopreeva, *Russko-polskie otnosheniia vo vtoroi polovine XVII v* (Warsaw, 1952); B. G. Porshnev, "Moskovskoe gosudarstvo i vstuplenie Shvedtsii v 30 letn. voinu," *Istoricheskii Zhurnal* (Moscow) (1945), and the same author's "Borba vokrug shvedsko-russkogo soiuza v 1631–1632 gg," *Skandinavskii Sbornik* (Tallinn) (1956); Caspar von Saldern, *Der Kampf um die Ostsee am Vorabend der Französischen Revolution* (Copenhagen, 1933); A. Szelągowski, *Der Kampf um die Ostsee, 1544–1621* (Munich, 1921); U. Voges, *Der Kampf um das Dominium Maris Baltici, 1629–1645* (Zeulenroda, 1938).

For the seventeenth century, G. V. Forstén's study, "Datskie diplomaty pri Moskovskom dvore vtoroi polovine 17 veka," in *Zhurnal Ministerstva Narodnago Prosveshcheniia* (St. Petersburg, 1904), is particularly illuminating, as is Klaus Zernack, *Studien zu den Schwedisch-Russischen Beziehungen in der 2. Hälfte des 17. Jahrhunderts* (Giessen, 1958). Wider in approach, but utilizing Swedish archive material from the same century to good purpose, are several articles by G. V. von Rauch, reprinted in *Studien über das Verhältnis Russlands zu Europa* (Darmstadt, 1964). An important investigation into the motives for the expansion of Russia into the Baltic region is that by S. Svensson, *Den merkantile bakgrunden till Rysslands anfall på den livlandska ordensstaten 1558. En studie til den ryska imperialismens uppkomsthistoria* (Lund, 1951). Erik Hornborg's *Sverige och Ryssland,* 2d ed. (Stockholm, 1942), is especially helpful for Russo-Finnish border disputes, though it lacks scholarly apparatus. The older Russian work by N. N. Bantysh-Kamenskyi, *Obzor vneshnikh snoshenii Rossii po 1800 god,* four volumes of which appeared between 1899 and 1902, is a mine of information, as are the volumes of S. M. Solovev, *Istoriia Rossii s drevneishikh vremen,* available in a 1959–1966 edition of the nineteenth-century one.

In modern Russian general histories the following have material or express points of view of interest for the subject: P. I. Liashchenko, *Istoriia narodnogo khoziaistva SSSR* (Moscow, 1952); L. G. Beskrovnyi, *Russkaia armiia i flot v XVIII veke* (1958); A. I. Pashkova, ed., *Istoriia russkoi ekonomicheskoi mysli. Epokha feodalizma,* vol. I: *IX–XVII vv.* (1955); V. O. Kliuchevskii, *Kurs russkoi istorii,* vols. III and IV of his collected works (Moscow, 1957–1958); there is a translation of vol. III of 1968 by N. Duddington.

Of recent research the following are especially valuable for given topics within the general field: K. F. Bazilevich, "Elementy merkantilizma v ekonomicheskoi politike Alekseia Mikhailovicha," in *Uchenie zapiski Moskovskogo gosudarstvennogo universiteta* (1914); S. A. Feigina, "Pervyi russkii kantsler A. L. Ordyn-Nashchokin," *Istoricheskii Zhurnal* (1941); E. Amburger, *Die Familie Marselis. Studien zur russischen Wirtschaftsgeschichte* (Giessen, 1957); S. P. Luppov, *Istoria stroitelstva Peterburga pervoi chetverti XVIII veka* (Moscow, 1957); M. Bogucka, "Zboz rosyjskie na rynku amsterdamskim w pierwszej polowie XVII wieku," *Przegląd Historyczny* (Warsaw) (1962); Erich Donnert, *Der livländische Ordensritterstaat und Russland, 1558–1583* (Berlin, 1963); C. Bickford O'Brien, "Russia and Eastern Europe. The View of A. L. Ordin-Naščókin," *Jahrbücher für Geschichte Osteuropas* (1969); R. Wittram, *Peter I. Czar und Kaiser,* 2 vols. (Göttingen, 1964); W. Mediger, *Mecklenburg, Russland und England-Hannover, 1706–1721* (Hildesheim, 1967); J. Kulischer, *Russische Wirtschaftsgeschichte* (Jena, 1925); and R. Wittram, *Baltische Geschichte* (1954).

Some Russian publications of documents (for Karelia in 1948, for Russo-Swedish economic relations in the seventeenth century in 1960) should also be noted. Good guides to Russian publications in general can be found in *The American Bibliography of Russian and East European Studies* and in the five bibliographical articles by Walter Leitsch in the 1961 to 1964 volumes of the *Jahrbücher für Geschichte Osteuropas.* Polish, German, Finnish, Swedish, and East Baltic historians have naturally contributed much to our knowledge of Russian policy in and attitude toward the Baltic, whether directly by area trade studies or through their work on national history, and it is well worth following up the publications of A. Attman, E. Dunsdorfs, B. Fahlborg, J. Gierowski, E. Hassinger, K.-G. Hildebrand, G. Jensch, F. Kalisch, H. Kellenbenz, W. Lechnickii, O. H. Mattiesen, G. Mickwitz, W. Müller, H. Piirimae, K. Piwarski, A. Soom, A. Öhberg, and S. E. Åström.

1. B. H. Sumner, *Survey of Russian History* (London, 1947), p. 260.

2. The best synthesis, with excellent maps of this network, is by Robert J. Kerner, *The Urge to the Sea. The Course of Russian History. The Role of Rivers, Portages, Ostrogs, Monasteries, and Furs* (Berkeley, Calif., 1942).

3. Lionel Kochan, *The Making of Modern Russia* (Pelican ed., London, 1963), p. 28; based on the fuller quotation in Kerner, *The Urge to the Sea,* p. 33.

4. For the Order, see Friedrich Benninghoven, *Der Order der Schwertbrüder. Fratres milicie Christi de Livonia* (Cologne and Graz, 1965). For a recent analysis of the role of both the Teutonic Order and the Order of the

Knights of the Sword, see George von Rauch, *Der Deutsche Orden und die Einheit des baltischen Landes* (Hamburg, 1961).

5. See Hornborg, *Sverige och Ryssland genom tiderna,* pp. 25 ff., for these raids. See also Kauko Perinen, "Die finnisch-russische Grenze vor den Frieden von Täyssinä, 1595," *Jahrbücher für Geschichte Osteuropas* (Wiesbaden) (1969).

6. Since 1386 it had become the custom for Poland and Lithuania to elect the same prince as ruler, although the formal union did not take place till 1569.

7. George Vernadsky, *Russia at the Dawn of the Modern Age,* vol. IV of his *A History of Russia* (New Haven, 1959), pp. 36 ff., is particularly successful in his treatment of the Novgorod-Muscovy struggle, contrasting the federative idea of the Rus union of the former with the union by absorption of the latter.

8. J. L. I. Fennell, *Ivan the Great of Moscow* (London, 1961).

9. Tver was annexed in 1845; Chernigov in 1503; and Pskov in 1510.

10. The title of Tsar was not, however, meant to signify "Emperor," but "King": H. Schaeder *Moskau das dritte Rom* (Darmstadt, 1929), chap. 3; Tsar Peter was the first to adopt officially the title of *Imperator* in 1721, but used the title of Emperor in the Baltic Provinces after 1710.

11. The Order of the Knights of the Sword dissolved itself in 1561.

12. See, e.g., the letter (contemporaneously translated from the Latin) that King Sigismund Augustus wrote to Queen Elizabeth in 1569; printed by Giles Fletcher, *Russia at the Close of the Sixteenth Century* (London: Hakluyt Society Publication, 1856), p. xvii: "We know and feele of a surety, the Muscovite, enemy to all liberty under the heavens, dayly to grow mightie by the increase of such things as be brought to the Narve [Narva], while not onely wares but also weapons heretofore unknowen to him, and artificers and arts be brought unto him; by meane whereof he maketh himself strong to vanquish all others. . . . If so be that this navigation of the Narve continue, what shall be unknowen to him? . . . we do foresee, except other princes take this admonition, the Muscovite, puffed up in pride with those things that be brought to the Narve, and made more perfect in warlike affaires, with engines of ware and shippes, will make assault this way on Christendome, to slay and make bound all that shall withstand him: which God defend."

13. Note that in its early stages this expansion to the East was the result of private enterprise which secured government support when successful: Svensson, *Den merkantile bakgrunden till Rysslands, passim.*

14. The so-called Seven Years Northern War (1563 to 1570).

15. Kexholm had fallen to the Swedes in 1580, and Narva was taken by storm in 1581, the Swedes being helped by Muscovite preoccupation with Báthory's siege of Pskov, which, however, failed.

16. A Swedish *riksdag* of 1599 declared Sigismund deposed, and in 1600 chose Charles king, with the succession in his own line (as Sigismund Vasa had ignored an offer of the crown for his son Władysław conditional on the boy's being brought up in the Lutheran faith). Charles took charge of the government but did not assume the title of king till 1604. The delay can, in part, be explained by the fact that John III had left a son (from a second

marriage) who was only eleven years old at this time: Charles felt it prudent to wait in case a strong claim should be put forward on his behalf.

17. For Narva's position, see W. Kirchner, "Narvas Bedeutung im 16. Jahrhundert," *Historische Zeitschrift* (Munich) (1951); E. Dunsdorfs, "Merchant Shipping in the Baltic during the Seventeenth Century," *Contributions of Baltic University* (Hamburg, 1947); and S. E. Aström, *From Cloth to Iron* (Helsinki, 1936), pp. 124 ff.

18. Gustavus Adolphus made this remark in a speech to the *riksdag* in August, 1617; a rather stiff translation of it is given in Kerner, *The Urge to the Sea,* pp. 49 ff.

19. Among modern specialists, Zernack, *Schwedisch-Russischen Beziehungen,* p. 32 and n. 78, is in favor of the term; Michael Roberts, *Gustavus Adolphus. A History of Sweden,* I (London, 1953), 89–90, is not.

20. *Axel Oxenstiernas skrifter och brefväxling,* 1st ser., II, 371, letter of November 15, 1616; given here in the translation by Michael Roberts, *Gustavus Adolphus,* p. 86, n. 1.

21. Riga fell to the Swedes in 1620, and at the peace of Altmark in 1629 Sigismund III recognized the whole of Livonia to be Swedish and permitted occupation of the West Prussian ports (with their rich tolls) for six years as compensation for Gustavus Adolphus' expenses in the war.

22. These successes were only made possible by Sweden's gains in the Empire: Pomerania and Wismar to the east of Denmark, and Bremen and Verden to the west, giving Sweden (in conjunction with its alliance with the dukes of Holstein-Gottorp) a backdoor entry into Jutland, from which the freak hard winter of 1658 permitted the army of Charles X to cross the frozen seas and threaten Copenhagen.

23. Note that recent Swedish research has tended to minimize the actual help given by Muscovy to Gustavus Adolphus in the form of cheap grain: the figures quoted by B. F. Porshnev, "Russkie subsidii Shvetsii vo vremia tridtsiatiletnei voiny," in *Izvestiia Akademii Nauk: Seria Istorii i Filosofii* (Moscow, 1945), have been found too high.

24. Bohdan Kentrschynskyj, "Karl X Gustaf inför krisen i öster, 1654–1655," *Karolinska Förbundets Årsbok* (1956), considers these fears more justified than do earlier Swedish historians.

25. Zernack, *Schwedisch-Russischen Beziehungen,* pp. 46–47.

26. *Ibid.,* pp. 67–68.

27. For Courland, see W. Eckert, *Kurland unter dem Einfluss des Merkantilismus* (Riga, 1927), and J. Kalisch, "Pläne zur Belebung des Orienthandel über Kurland und Polen am Ausgang des 17. Jahrhundert," in *Hansische Studien* (1961).

28. For the Dutch Republic, see W. J. Kolkert, *Nederland en het Zwedzche imperialisme* (Deventer, 1908).

29. Cited from the protocol by Zernack, *Schwedisch-Russischen Beziehungen,* p. 77, n. 249, and p. 80.

30. For these issues, see my *Europe in the Age of Louis XIV* (London, 1969), pp. 91 ff.

31. See K. Rasmussen, "Danske i den azovske flåde 1696–98," *Historisk Tidsskrift* (Copenhagen) (1965), pp. 462–481.

32. Wittram, *Peter I,* I, 129 ff., considers that these activities were the real purpose of the trip.

33. See my *Charles XII of Sweden* (London, 1968; New York, 1969), pp. 69 ff.

34. E. Olmer, "Om ryssfruktan i Sverige för 200 år sedan," *Historisk Tidskrift* (Stockholm) (1903), pp. 295 ff.

35. Denmark-Norway acceded to this treaty in January, 1700.

36. See Hatton, *Charles XII,* pp. 102 ff. and p. 538, n. 48, for the contention that the architects of the anti-Swedish coalition were, successively, the Danish kings Christian V and Frederick IV.

37. E. Hassinger, *Brandenburg-Preussen, Schweden und Russland, 1700–1713* (Munich, 1953), p. 51, n. 16, quoting Tsar Peter's comment to a Russian diplomat.

38. E.g., L. A. Nikiforov, *Russko-angliiskie otnosheniia pri Petre I* (Moscow, 1950); E. Tarle, *Severnaia voina i shvedskoe nashestvie na Rossiiu* (Moscow, 1958); S. Feygina, *Alandskii Kongress* (Moscow, 1959).

39. Wittram, *Peter I,* I, 244 ff.

40. *Ibid.,* p. 263.

41. See Hatton, *Charles XII,* pp. 241 ff.

42. See R. Wittram, "Die Unterwerfung Livlands und Estlands, 1710," *Geschichte und Gegenwartsbewusstsein. Festschrift für H. Rothfels zu 70. Geburtstag,* ed. W. Besson and F. H. von Gaertingen (Göttingen, 1963); cf. the same author's *Peter I,* I, 344 ff.

43. A siege of Stralsund, in 1712, in which Russian troops participated, had failed, but Tsar Peter's forces had forced the Swedes to leave Elbing (1710), and that town had been restored to King Augustus II of Poland (1712); Denmark had occupied Bremen and the territories of the duke of Holstein-Gottorp; while Hanover and Prussia (acting ostensibly as Sweden's friends) had managed, respectively, to occupy Verden and to sequester Stettin.

44. Erik XIV of Sweden had plans for a canal via the Göta River to the Bothnian Sea to avoid the Sound; and Holsteiners had, in vain, before 1714 tempted Tsar Peter to support their cause against Denmark by stressing the utility of a canal through Sleswig territory to bypass the Sound.

45. Mediger, *Mecklenburg, Russland und England-Hannover, 1706–1721,* pp. 176 ff., in contrast to the views of Wittram, *Peter I,* II, 276 ff.

46. For Charles' views, expressed in a conversation with Axel von Löwen, see the Löwen *Mémoires,* ed. F. Adler and S. Bonnesen, *Karolinska Förbundets* (Årsbok, 1929), p. 34.

47. Claude Nordmann, *La Crise du Nord au début du XVIIIe siècle* (Paris, 1962), pp. 147 ff.

48. For the general background of this peace plan, see my *War and Peace, 1680–1720* (London, 1969), pp. 21 ff.; for a recent analysis of its failure, see L. R. Lewitter, "Poland, Russia and the Treaty of Vienna, 1719," *Historical Journal* (London) (1970), pp. 3–30.

49. A Swedish party in the 1720's and 1730's aimed to nominate as heir to the throne Duke Charles Frederick of Holstein-Gottorp, living as a refugee in Russia and married (since 1725) to Anna, a daughter of Tsar Peter; the son of this marriage, Duke Charles Ulric Peter, was nominated in 1743, but the Tsarina Elizabeth had forestalled the Swedes by making him her own heir: he adopted the Orthodox faith and took the name of Peter, succeeding as Tsar Peter III in 1762.

50. This "equivalent" plan had first been mooted during Peter the Great's reign at the Åland Islands conferences; for Gustavus III's commitment to it, see Stewart Oakley, "Gustavus III's Plans for War with Denmark in 1783–84," *Studies in Diplomatic History, Essays in Memory of David Bayne Horn,* ed. Ragnhild Hatton and M. S. Anderson (London, 1970), pp. 268 ff. When Norway was obtained in 1814 (though on terms less favorable to Sweden than expected), it was with Russian diplomatic support, as an equivalent for Finland.

51. See Wittram, *Baltische Geschichte,* pp. 133 ff.

52. Note the correction (in a downward direction) to the hitherto accepted export figures for Russian iron in M. T. Florinsky, *Russia: A Short History* (New York, 1964), p. 182 and note.

53. I owe this information to J. E. O. Screen, who is engaged on a doctoral dissertation (London University) entitled "Finnish Officers in the Russian Army, 1815–1918."

54. See, e.g., Torvald Höjer, *Den Svenska Ultrikespolitikens Historia,* III, pt. 2 (Stockholm, 1954), pp. 258 ff., for the influence of Russia on Charles XIV's policy in respect of the South American independence struggle.

55. See my "Palmerston and Scandinavian Union," *Studies in International History,* ed. K. Bourne and D. C. Watt (London, 1967), pp. 123, 128–130, and works there cited.

56. For the Crimean War period, see, briefly, *ibid.,* pp. 130 ff. and, fully, C. F. Palmstierna, *Sverige, Ryssland och England 1833–1855* (Stockholm, 1932), and S. Ericsson, *Svensk diplomati och tidningspress under Krimkriget* (Uppsala, 1939); for the 1863–64 crisis, see my "Charles XV in 1863," *Historisk Tidskrift* (Stockholm) (1966), pp. 312–327.

57. See Folke Lindberg, *Kunglig Utrikespolitik* (Stockholm, 1953), pp. 63 ff., for Fårösund, the Gotland harbor utilized by Anglo-French naval forces during the Crimean War, being declared a Swedish naval base and thus made unavailable for foreign warships in the 1885 to 1887 crisis.

58. See Folke Lindberg, *Scandinavia in Great Power Politics, 1905–1908* (Stockholm, 1958), *passim;* cf. Walther Hubatsch, *Unruhe des Nordens* (Göttingen, 1956).

59. Though note, from Sumner, *Survey of Russian History,* p. 266, and p. 478 n., for further references, that when the Danish Sound tolls were abolished, Russia paid the second largest sum (the largest was paid by Great Britain) as its share of compensation agreed on in proportion to ships using the Sound.

60. Ordyn-Nashchokin is cited by Bickford O'Brien, "Russia and Eastern Europe. The view of A. L. Ordin-Naščókin," pp. 377–378.

61. Juhani Paasivirta, *Finland år 1918* (Helsinki, 1962), pp. 120 ff.

62. Sumner is of the opinion that these East Baltic states saved Russia in World War II, since on their territory the Russian army was able to hold up the German advance.

63. Cited by Lewitter, "Russia, Poland and the Baltic, 1697–1721," *Historical Journal* (London) (1968), p. 14.

64. G. Maude, "Finland and Britain, 1854–1914" (University of London Ph.D. thesis, 1970).

65. Lolo Krusius-Ahrenberg, "Finnischer Separatismus und Russischer Imperialismus im vorigen Jahrhundert," *Historische Zeitschrift* (Munich) (1959), pp. 249–288.

66. This was the thesis of P. Nyström, "Mereatura Ruthenica," *Scandia* (Stockholm) (1937), pp. 257–296.

67. See Mediger, "Russland und die Ostsee im 18 Jahrhundert," p. 89.

68. For this sense, see my "Louis XIV and his Fellow-Monarchs," in *Louis XIV and the Craft of Kingship,* ed. John C. Rule (Columbus, O., 1970), pp. 159 ff.

69. Cited by E. Hassinger, *Brandenburg-Preussen, Schweden und Russland 1700–1713* (Munich, 1953), p. 68, n. 35. Cf. Mediger, *Mecklenburg, Russland und England-Hannover,* p. 76, for Tsar Peter's liking to compare himself with Louis XIV.

RUSSO-POLISH CONFRONTATION

1. Adam Gurowski, *La Vérité sur la Russie et sur la révolte des provinces polonaises* (Paris, 1834), pp. 2–3. In literal translation Gurowski's statement reads: "From the time of their appearance in history, it was to be decided to which of the two states the empire of the reunited Slavic races would belong. Perhaps without being conscious of it from the beginning, they were pushed into the arena by destiny to debate this great question. Such is the fateful origin of the wars between Russia and Poland, which, above all from the sixteenth century, became for one of the two a question of political life or death."

2. Władysław Konopczyński, *Dzieje Polski nowożytnej,* 2 vols. (Warsaw, 1936), I, 356. For more recent estimates with somewhat different results, see Irena Gieysztorowa, "Research into the Demographic History of Poland," in *Acta Poloniae Historica,* XVIII (Warsaw, 1968), 5–17. Sources in these notes are limited to those which contain special material not found in the standard works for the history of both countries. Since the question of territorial changes is crucial to this study, the following two books may be recommended: Jan Natanson-Leski, *Rozwój terytorialny Polski od czasów najdawniejszych do okresu przebudowy państwa w latach 1569–1572* (Warsaw, 1964); R. Flaes, *Das Problem der Territorialkonflikte. Eine Untersuchung über ihre Grundlagen und Eigenschaften am Beispiele der Territorialgeschichte Polens* (Amsterdam, 1929). For the western border, see Gerard Labuda, *Polska granica zachodnia. Tysiąc lat dziejów politycznych* (Poznan, 1971). The most recent bibliographies

on the topic are Henryk Łowmiański, "Dzieje narodów ZSRR oraz stosunki polsko-ruskie i polsko-rosyjskie (do konca XVIII w.) w historiografii Polski Ludowej," *Z dziejów stosunków polsko-radzieckich. Studia i materiały,* V (1969), 3–17; Mirosław Wierzchowski, *Historia Rosji i ZSRR 1795–1939 w pracach historyków polskich* (zestawienie bibliograficzne 1944–1966) (Warsaw, 1968); Mieczysław Tanty, "Historia ZSRR i stosunków polsko-rosyjskich i radzieckich XIX–XX wieku w historiografii Polski Ludowej," *Z dziejów stosunków polsko-radzieckich,* V (1969), 19–34.

3. For the Russo-Polish relations up to 1401, see Gotthold Rhode, *Die Ostgrenze Polens. Politische Entwicklung, kulturelle Bedeutung und geistige Auswirkung,* vol. I: *Im Mittelalter bis zum Jahre 1401* (Cologne and Graz, 1955) (Ostmitteleuropa in Vergangenheit und Gegenwart, II); Henryk Paszkiewicz, *The Making of the Russian Nation* (London, 1963), pp. 336–397.

4. M. D. Priselkov, *Troitskaia letopis: Rekonstruktsiia teksta* (Moscow, 1950), p. 432.

5. Akademiia Nauk SSSR, *Polnoe sobranie russkikh letopisei,* XXVII (Moscow and Leningrad, 1962), 82, 256. [Hereafter cited as *PSRL.*]

6. *Ibid.,* XXV (1949), 213.

7. It is not clear whether Lithuanian Catholics or Poles are meant. *Ibid.,* XXV, 231; XXVII, 91 (here *inovernykh*).

8. Priselkov, *Troitskaia,* pp. 461, 468; *PSRL,* XXVII, 95; XXV, 234, 238.

9. *PSRL,* XXV, 247.

10. Akademiia Nauk SSSR, *Dukhovnye i dogovornye gramoty velikikh i udelnykh kniazei XIV–XVI vv.* (Leningrad, 1950), No. 15, p. 41; No. 37, p. 105; No. 59, pp. 187, 190; No. 63, pp. 202, 205; No. 79, p. 296. The passage is lacking in 1449, and only Casimir and the order of the Teutonic Knights are mentioned (*ibid.,* No. 54, p. 163).

11. *Ibid.,* No. 47, p. 142 (1447). In 1402 only Tatars are mentioned, but in line with the times the princes of Riazan are given the option of entering into relations with Witold (*ibid.,* No. 19, pp. 53, 55).

12. A. M. Sacharov, "Über den Kampf gegen das 'Lateinertum' in Russland am Ende des 15. und zu Beginn des 16. Jahrhunderts," in *Ost und West in der Geschichte des Denkens und der kulturellen Beziehungen* (Berlin, 1966), pp. 92–105 (Quellen und Studien zur Geschichte Osteuropas, XV).

13. For the policy of Ivan III, see K. V. Bazilevich, *Vneshniaia politika russkogo tsentralizovannogo gosudarstva. Vtoraia polovina XV veka* (Moscow, 1952). The English-speaking reader can brief himself in J. L. I. Fennell, *Ivan the Great of Moscow* (London, 1961); Oswald P. Backus, *Motives of West Russian Nobles in Deserting Lithuania for Moscow, 1377–1514* (Lawrence, Kans., 1957). For a discussion of the problem whether the political programme of Ivan III should be called imperialistic or not, see O. Halecki, "Imperialism in Slavic and East European History," *American Slavic and East European Review,* XI (1952), 1–26; Nicholas V. Riasanovsky, "Old Russia, the Soviet Union and Eastern Europe," *ibid.,* XI (1952), 171–188; Oswald P. Backus, "Was Muscovite Russia Imperialistic?", *ibid.,* XIII (1954), 522–534.

14. Hans Uebersberger, *Österreich und Russland seit dem Ende des 15. Jahrhunderts,* vol. I: *Von 1488–1605* (Vienna, 1906), 22.

15. *Sbornik Imperatorskogo Russkogo Istoricheskogo Obshchestva,* XXXV (St. Petersburg, 1882), 282. [Hereafter cited as *SIRIO.*]

16. *SIRIO,* XXXV, 380.

17. *SIRIO,* XXXV, 460.

18. *SIRIO,* XXXV, 509. Originally neither did Ivan IV extend his claims to the Polish parts of Rus. *SIRIO,* LIX, 274 (1549).

19. *SIRIO,* LXXI, 172 (September 10, 1563).

20. *SIRIO,* LXXI, 260 (December 11, 1563). Ivan IV repeated the demand in 1566 and 1570 (*ibid.,* pp. 361–362, 648).

21. The following presentation adheres substantially to Jan Natanson-Leski, *Dzieje granicy wschodniej Rzeczypospolitej,* Pt. I: *Granica Moskiewska w epoce Jagiellońskiej* (Lvov and Warsaw, 1922).

22. Erich Donnert, *Der livländische Ordensritterstaat und Russland. Der livländische Krieg und die baltische Frage in der europäischen Politik, 1558–1583* (Berlin, 1963), pp. 239–241.

23. *SIRIO,* XXXV, 481–482.

24. Uebersberger, *Österreich und Russland,* pp. 400–447: V. Novodvorskii, *Borba za Livoniiu mezhdu Moskvoiu i Rechiu Pospolitoiu (1570–1582): Izsledovanie istoriko-kriticheskoe* (St. Petersburg, 1904), pp. 12–32 (Zapiski istoriko-filologicheskago Fakulteta imperatorskago S.-Peterburgskago Universiteta, XXII).

25. Jan Natanson-Leski, *Epoka Stefana Batorego w dziejach granicy wschodniej Rzeczypospolitej* (Warsaw, 1930) (Rozprawy Historyczne Towarzystwa Naukowego Warszawskiego, 9/2); Académie Polonaise des Sciences et des Lettres, *Etienne Batory, roi de Pologne, prince de Transylvanie* (Cracow, 1935); B. Floria, "Rossiia, Rech Pospolitaia i konets Livonskoi voiny," *Sovetskoe Slavianovedenie,* XVIII, 2 (1972), 25–35.

26. S. M. Solovev, *Istoriia Rossii s drevneishikh vremen,* 15 vols. (Moscow, 1959–1966), IV, 213–227. Boris Floria, "Rosyjska kandydatura na tron polski u schyłku XVI wieku," *Odrodzenie i reformacja w Polsce,* XVI (1971), 85–95.

27. Kazimierz Tyszkowski, *Poselstwo Lwa Sapiehy w Moskwie 1600 r.* (Lvov, 1927) (Archivum Towarzystwa Naukowego we Lwowie, Pt. II, 4/1).

28. Walter Leitsch, *Moskau und die Politik des Kaiserhofes im XVII. Jahrhundert,* vol. I (1604–1654) (Graz and Cologne, 1960), pp. 26–29 (Wiener Archiv für Geschichte des Slawentums und Osteuropas, IV). See also in the foregoing the literature for the first half of the seventeenth century: Jarema Maciczewski, *Polska a Moskwa 1603–1618, Opinie i stanowiska szlachty polskiej* (Warsaw, 1968).

29. For the events of 1655 to 1660, see Polska Akademia Nauk, Instytut Historii, *Polska w okresie drugiej wojny północnej 1655–1660,* vols. I–III (Warsaw, 1957). The older literature is noted in an extensive bibliography.

30. Zbigniew Wójcik, *Traktat Andruszowski 1667 roku i jego geneza* (Warsaw, 1959).

31. *Ibid.,* pp. 159–161. See also I. V. Galaktionov, "Rossiia i Polsha naka-

nune peregovorov v Andrusove," *Uchenye Zapiski Instituta Slavianovedeniia,* XVIII (1959), 191–249, esp. 218–223; Tatiana Koprejewa, "Starania Rosji o sojusz ekonomiczny z Polską w walce z władztwem szwedzkim na Bałtyku (Projekt zwołania konferencji w Kurlandii w 1668 r.)," *Kwartalnik Historyczny,* LXVI (1959), 52–71, esp. 59–60.

32. Uebersberger, *Österreich und Russland,* p. 39.

33. *SIRIO,* LIX, 572. For the plan of an accord with the tsar against the Emperor in 1570 and 1571, see Stanisław Bodniak, "Najdawniejszy plan porozumienia Polski z Moskwą przeciw Niemcom," *Pamiętnik Biblioteki Kórnickiej,* IV (1947), 77–92.

34. Natanson-Leski, *Dzieje granicy,* p. 145.

35. Władysław Godziszewski, *Polska a Moskwa za Władysława IV, Rozprawy Wydziału Historyczno-Filozoficznego,* Polska Akademja Umiejetności, LXVII (1930), 457–526, esp. 520–523.

36. Wójcik, *Traktat Andruszowski,* pp. 22, 184, 187, 201–202, 231, 250–251, 256. In the subsequent two interregna Tsar Alexis again made efforts for the election of his son Fedor to the Polish throne; in the period 1667 to 1669 this even involved great expenditure of money. Zbigniew Wójcik, *Między traktatem andruszowskim a wojną turecką. Stosunki polsko-rosyjskie 1667–1672* (Warsaw, 1968), pp. 127–164. For the election in 1673 and 1674, see Solovev, *Istoriia Rossii,* VI, 505–511.

37. Wójcik, *Między traktatem, passim.*

38. Janusz Woliński, "Komisja Andruszowska 1674 roku," in *Księga pamiątkowa ku uczczeniu dwudzięstopiecioletniej działalności naukowej Prof. Marcelego Handelsmana* (Warsaw, 1929), pp. 501–511; A. Popov, *Russkoe posolstvo v Polshe v 1673–1677 godakh. Neskolko let iz istorii otnoshenii drevnei Rossii k evropeiskim derzhavam* (St. Petersburg, 1854).

39. E. Zamyslovskii, "Snosheniia Rossii s Polshei v tsarstvovanie Feodora Alekseevicha," *Zhurnal Ministerstva Narodnago Prosveshcheniia,* 254 (1888), 1–23; 255 (1888), 464–485; 256 (1888), 161–197, and esp. 22–23; L. R. Lewitter, "The Russo-Polish Treaty of 1686 and Its Antecedents," *Polish Review,* IX, 3–4 (1964), 1–40.

40. C. Bickford O'Brien, *Russia under Two Tsars, 1682–1689. The Regency of Sophia Alekseevna* (Berkeley and Los Angeles, 1952), pp. 85–104.

41. For the decline of Poland, see Zbigniew Wójcik, "Zmiana w układzie sił politycznych w Europie środkowowschodniej w drugiej połowie XVII wieku," *Kwartalnik Historyczny,* LXVII (1960), 25–57.

42. Reinhard Wittram, *Peter I. Czar und Kaiser. Zur Geschichte Peters des Grossen und seiner Zeit,* 2 vols. (Göttingen, 1964), I, 148–149. About the election 1697, see L. R. Lewitter, "Peter the Great and the Polish Election of 1697," *Cambridge Historical Journal,* II (1956), 126–143.

43. Wittram, *Peter I,* I, 216–217. For the further negotiations and the treaty of October 1/12 (or October 10 st.n.), 1703, see V. D. Koroliuk, "Russkaia diplomatiia i podgotovka vstupleniia Rechi Pospolitoi v Severnuiu voinu. (Vosstanovlenie russkosaksonskogo soiuza 1702–1703 gg.)," *Uchenye Zapiski Instituta Slavianovedeniia,* VII (1953), 210–276.

44. V. D. Koroliuk, "Vstuplenie Rechi Pospolitoi v Severnuiu voinu," *Uchenye Zapiski Instituta Slavianovedeniia,* X (1954), 239–347; parts of this article are in German translation: V. D. Koroljuk, "Der Eintritt der Rzeczpospolita in den Nordischen Krieg," in *Um die polnische Krone. Sachsen und Polen während des Nordischen Krieges 1700–1721,* ed. J. Kalisch and J. Gierowski (Berlin, 1962), pp. 129–160; also Andrzej Kamiński, "Początki antyszwedzkiego sojuszu. Ze stosunków polsko-rosyjskich 1704–1706," *Przegląd Historyczny,* LX (1969), 291–313.

45. Józef Feldman, *Polska w dobie wielkiej wojny północnej 1704–1709* (Cracow, 1925), pp. 200–254; *Lysty Petra Velykoho do A. M. Siniavskoho,* ed. Stefan Tomashivskyi, in *Zapysky naukovoho tovarystva imeny Shevchenka,* XVIII (1909), 194–238, esp. 196–198; Józef Gierowski, "From Radoszkowice to Opatów—The History of the Decomposition of the Stanisław Leszczyński Camp," in *Poland at the XIth International Congress of Historical Sciences in Stockholm* (Warsaw, 1960), pp. 217–237; Andrzej Kamiński, *Konfederacja sandomierska wobec Rosji w okresie poaltransztadzkim 1706–1709* (Wrocław, Warsaw and Cracow, 1969) (Polska Akademia Nauk—Oddział w Krakowie, Prace Komisji nauk historycznych, XXIII); V. A. Artamonov, "Russko-polski soiuz v kampanii 1708–1709 godov," *Sovetskoe Slavianovedenie* VIII, 4 (1972), 42–55.

46. Wittram, *Peter I,* I, 324–325.

47. L. R. Lewitter, "Russia, Poland and the Baltic, 1697–1721," *Historical Journal* (London), XI (1968), 3–34, esp. 13–14.

48. Wittram, *Peter I,* I, 387.

49. Solovev, *Istoriia Rossii,* VIII, 396–406.

50. Lewitter, "Russia, Poland and the Baltic," pp. 17–24; Solovev, *Istoriia Rossii,* VIII, 415–427.

51. Konopczyński, *Dzieje Polski,* II, 169–175.

52. See Wittram, *Peter I,* II, 440–441.

53. N. N. Bantysh-Kamenskii, *Obzor vneshnikh snoshenii Rossii,* IV (Moscow, 1902), 43.

54. Solovev, *Istoriia Rossii,* IX, 407–417. The efforts to establish a protectorate over the Orthodox in Poland-Lithuania never ceased from the mid-seventeenth century. For the beginnings in diplomatic relations, see Sergei Solovev, *Istoriia padeniia Polshi* (Moscow, 1863), p. 26.

55. V. Gere, *Borba za polskii prestol v 1733 godu* (Moscow, 1862); Szymon Askenazy, *Elekcya Augusta III,* in *Biblioteka Warszawska,* LX (1900), 197–215, 430–464.

56. Mieczysław Skibiński, *Europa a Polska w dobie wojny o sukcesyę austryacką w latach 1740–1745,* 2 vols. (Cracow, 1912), I, 747–748.

57. Władysław Konopczyński, *Polska w dobie wojny siedmioletniej,* 2 vols. (Cracow and Warsaw, 1909–1911), II, 96 *et passim* (Monografie w Zakresie Dziejów Nowożytnych, 7–8, 16).

58. *Ibid.,* I, 18–19, 143.

59. N. D. Chechulin, *Vneshniaia politika Rossii v nachale tsarstvovaniia*

Ekateriny II. 1762–1774 (St. Petersburg, 1896), pp. 208, 231–232 (Zapiski istoriko-filologicheskago fakulteta imp. S. Peterburgskago universiteta, XL).

60. *Ibid.*, pp. 126–146.

61. *Ibid.*, p. 139.

62. *Ibid.*, pp. 221, 227.

63. *Ibid.*, pp. 237–238.

64. *Ibid.*, p. 228.

65. Robert Howard Lord, *The Second Partition of Poland: A Study in Diplomatic History* (Cambridge, 1915), pp. 49–50; Alkar [Aleksander Kraushar], *Książę Repnin i Polska w pierwszem czteroleciu panowania Stanisława Augusta (1764–1768)*, 2 vols. (Cracow, 1897), I, 166–167.

66. Chechulin, *Vneshniaia politika Rossii*, p. 285.

67. Kraushar, *Repnin*, I, 360; II, 73–89.

68. *Ibid.*, II, 58–59, 127, 156–157, 228, 253–254, 299, 303–304; a recently published source is Stanisław Lubomirski, *Pod władzą księcia Repnina. Ułamki pamiętników i dzienników historycznych (1764–1768)*, ed. Jerzy Łojek (Warsaw, 1971).

69. Władysław Konopczyński, *Konfederacja Barska*, 2 vols. (Warsaw, 1936–1938); Wacław Szczygielski, *Konfederacja barska w Wielkopolsce 1768–1770* (Warsaw, 1970); Jerzy Michalski, *Schyłek konfederacji barskiej* (Wrocław, Warsaw and Cracow, 1970).

70. For the oldest plan, see Hildegard Schaeder, *Geschichte der Pläne zur Teilung des alten polnischen Staates seit 1386*, vol. I: *Der Teilungsplan von 1392* (Leipzig, 1937) (Deutschland und der Osten, V).

71. Lord, *Second Partition of Poland*, p. 44.

72. *Ibid.*, pp. 50–51.

73. Chechulin, *Vneshniaia politika Rossii*, pp. 222–224.

74. *Ibid.*, 377; Lord, *Second Partition of Poland*, p. 52.

75. Chechulin, *Vneshniaia politika Rossii*, pp. 449–451; Lord, *Second Partition of Poland*, pp. 54–55; for the attitude of Europe towards the three partitions, see Marian Henryk Serejski, *Europa a rozbiory Polski. Studium historiograficzne* (Warsaw, 1970).

76. K. M. Morawski, *Prokonsulat Stackelberga* (Przyczynek z archiwum spraw zagranicznych w Moskwie), in *Biblioteka Warszawska*, LXXI (1911), pp. 560–568.

77. Lord, *Second Partition of Poland*, pp. 92–127; *Źródła do dziejów drugiego i trzeciego rozbioru Polski*, ed. Bronisław Dembiński, vol. I: *Polityka Rosyi i Prus wobec Polski od początków Sejmu Czteroletniego do ogłoszenia Konstytucyi Trzeciego Maja. 1788–1791* (Lvov, 1902), pp. 503, 523.

78. *Źródła do dziejów drugiego i trzeciego rozbioru Polski*, p. 46.

79. Lord, *Second Partition of Poland*, pp. 243–275; Władysław Smoleński, *Konfederacya Targowicka* (Cracow, 1903).

80. Lord, *Second Partition of Poland*, pp. 480–482.

81. *Mémoires du prince Adam Czartoryski et correspondance avec l'Empereur Alexandre I*, preface by Charles de Mazade, 2 vols. (Paris, 1887), I, 96–97; for the following, see also Marceli Handelsman, *Adam Czartoryski*, ed.

Stefan Kieniewicz, 3 vols. (Warsaw, 1948–1950) ; Charles Morley, "Alexander I and Czartoryski: The Polish Question from 1801 to 1813," *Slavonic and East European Review,* XXV (1946), 405–425; M. Kukiel, *Czartoryski and European Unity, 1770–1861* (Princeton, N.J., 1955).

82. Hedwig Fleischhacker, *Russische Antworten auf die polnische Frage 1795–1917* (Munich and Berlin, 1941), pp. 8–9, 16–19.

83. *Ibid.,* p. 10; Morley, "Alexander I and Czartoryski," p. 412.

84. Szymon Askenazy, *Rosja-Polska 1815–1830* (Lvov, 1907), p. 65.

85. *Ibid.,* pp. 86, 88, 89, 107. For the Eastern territories, see also Adam Żółtowski, *Border of Europe: A Study of the Polish Eastern Provinces* (London, 1950).

86. Kukiel, *Czartoryski,* p. 103.

87. Fleischhacker, *Russische Antworten,* p. 40.

88. Askenazy, *Rosja-Polska,* pp. 115–117.

89. See Alexander's very interesting statement in *Doneseniia avstriiskago poslannika pri russkom dvore Lebcelterna za 1816–1826 gody,* ed. [Velikii kniaz] Nikolai Mikhailovich (St. Petersburg, 1913), p. 60.

90. Hugh Seton-Watson, *The Russian Empire, 1801–1917* (Oxford: Oxford University Press, 1967), p. 174; see also Helena Wieckowska, "Przemiany myśli politycznej w Królestwie Kongresowem," in *Pamiętnik V Powszechnego Zjazdu Historyków Polskich w Warszawie 28 listopada do 4 grudnia 1930 r,* vol. I: *Referaty* (Lvov, 1930), 595–612.

91. Fleischhacker, *Russische Antworten,* p. 40; N. K. Shilder, *Imperator Nikolai Pervyi. Ego zhizn i tsarstvovanie,* II (St. Petersburg, 1903), p. 383.

92. Shilder, *Nikolai Pervyi,* II, 348–349.

93. Irena Koberdowa, *Wielki książe Konstanty w Warszawie 1862–1863* (Warsaw, 1962) ; Julian Komar, *Warszawskie manifestacje patriotyczne 1860 1861* (Warsaw, 1970) ; Franciszka Ramotowska, *Rząd carski wobec manifestacji patriotycznych w Królestwie Polskim w latach 1860–1862* (Wrocław, Warsaw, Cracow and Gdansk, 1971) ; Stanisław Bóbr-Tylingo, "La Russie, l'Eglise et la Pologne, 1860–1866 (Rapports des consuls français)," *Antemurale,* XIII (1969), 49–299.

94. R. F. Leslie, *Reform and Insurrection in Russian Poland, 1856–1865* (London, 1963) (University of London Historical Studies, XIII) ; Stanislaw Kutrzeba, *Sprawa polska w Królestwie Polskiem 1815–1915* (Lvov, 1916) ; Erazm Piltz, "Rosyjskie rządy w Polsce w latach 1864–1904," *Świat Słowiański,* V (1909), I, 363–381; Mieczysław Tanty, *Panslawizm, carat, Polacy. Zjazd Słowiański w Moskwie 1867 r.* (Warsaw, 1970).

95. I. I. Kostiushko, *Krestianskaia reforma 1864 goda v Tsarstve Polskom* (Moscow, 1962).

96. Mirosław Wierzchowski, *Sprawy polskie w III i IV Dumie Państwowej* (Warsaw, 1966) (Rozprawy Uniwersytetu Warszawskiego, XII) ; also *Sprawa poska w programach i taktyce rosyjskich partii politycznych w latach 1905–1914, Studia z dziejów ZSRR i Europy środkowej,* II (Warsaw, 1967), 81–101; Leon Wasilewski, *Rosya wobec Polaków w dobie "konstytucyjnej"* (Cracow,

1916); Edward Chmielewski, *The Polish Question in the Russian State Duma* (Knoxville, Tenn., 1970).

97. Irena Spustek, *Sprawa polski w polityce Rosji w roku 1916, Najnowsze Dzieje Polski. Materiały i Studia z okresu 1914–1939,* II (1959), 5–34, esp. 26–31; Titus Komarnicki, *Rebirth of the Polish Republic: A Study in the Diplomatic History of Europe, 1914–1920* (London, 1957), pp. 30–63; Kazimierz Grzybowski, "The Jakhontov Papers: Russo-Polish Relations (1914–1916)," *Journal of Central European Affairs,* XVIII, 1 (1958), 3–24.

98. Fleischhacker, *Russische Antworten;* Wacław Lednicki, *Russia, Poland and the West: Essays in Literary and Cultural History* (New York [1953]); Michael Boro Petrovich, *The Emergence of Russian Pan-Slavism, 1856–1870* (New York, 1956), pp. 172–197; Peter Brock, "Polish Nationalism," *Nationalism in Eastern Europe,* ed. Peter F. Sugar and Ivo J. Lederer (Seattle and London, 1969), pp. 310–372; Stephen Lukashevich, *Ivan Aksakov, 1823–1886: A Study in Russian Thought and Politics* (Cambridge, Mass., 1965), pp. 76–95; for the years immediately after 1917, see the two most recent studies: Piotr S. Wandycz, *Soviet-Polish Relations, 1917–1921* (Cambridge, Mass., 1969); M. K. Dziewanowski, *Joseph Piłsudski: A European Federalist, 1918–1922* (Stanford, Calif., 1969).

THE UKRAINE AND MUSCOVITE EXPANSION

1. The most recent Soviet example is the two-volume *Istoriia Ukrainy* (Moscow: Akademiia Nauk, 1969).

2. The most comprehensive study of this period is V. T. Pashuto, *Ocherki po istorii Galitsko–Volynskoi Rusi* (Moscow: Akademiia Nauk, 1950), pp. 289–305.

3. Horst Jablonski, *Westrussland zwischen Wilna und Moskau* (Leiden, 1955), pp. 11–12.

4. By the treaty of 1503, Lithuania ceded the Chernigov-Severia region, most of which had already been annexed as a result of defection by local aristocrats to Muscovy. *Sbornik Imperatorskogo Russkogo Istoricheskogo Obshchestva,* XXXV (St. Petersburg, 1882), 398–402. [Hereafter cited as *SIRIO.*]

5. This transfer of allegiance has been studied in minute detail by Oswald P. Backus, *Motives of West Russian Nobles in Deserting Lithuania for Moscow, 1377–1514* (Lawrence, Kans., 1957), pp. 94–106.

6. *Polnoe sobranie russkikh letopisei* (Moscow and Leningrad, 1962), XII, 233. [Hereafter cited as *PSRL.*]

7. M. K. Liubavskii, *Ocherk istorii Litovsko-Russkago gosudarstva do liublinskoi unii vkliuchitelno* (Moscow, 1910), pp. 189–190.

8. Though the Third Lithuanian Statute of 1588 formally established serfdom, peasant bondage had existed since the beginning of the century. I. P. Novitskii, "Ocherk istorii krestianskogo soslovia iugozapadnoi Rossii," *Arkhiv Iugo-Zapadnoi Rossii* (Kiev), VI, pt. 1 (1876), 136.

9. Both in Lithuania and in Muscovy, this term originally meant merely any region beyond delineated frontiers, not just the steppeland to the south.

10. For a definitive study of the origins of the Cossacks, see G. Stöckl, *Die Enstehung des Kosakentums* (Munich, 1953). For the rise of the Cossacks in the Dnieper valley, see N. Kostomarov, "Bogdan Khmelnitskii," *Sobranie Sochinenii* (St. Petersburg), IV (1904), 1–9.

11. Stöckl, *Die Enstehung des Kosakentums,* p. 116.

12. *SIRIO,* XLI, 194–196.

13. *PSRL,* VI, 213; XIII, 38–43.

14. Dashkevich had fled Lithuania in 1503 to serve Ivan III of Muscovy. In 1508 Vasilii III sent him to help Glinsky's conspiracy, after which Dashkevich once again swore allegiance to Lithuania. W. Pochiecha, "Daszkiewicz," *Polski Slownik Biograficzny,* IV (1938), 444–447.

15. *PSRL,* XIII, 271.

16. *PSRL,* XIII, 286–288, 296.

17. After hearing that Vyshnevetskyi had sworn allegiance to King Sigismund Augustus (V. A. Golubinskii, *Zaporozhskoe kazachestvo* [Moscow, 1957], pp. 82–83), Ivan showed his contempt for him by instructing his ambassador to refer to Vyshnevetskyi as an unprincipled adventurer: "He came like a dog and fled like one" (*SIRIO,* LXXI, 156).

18. E. Lassota von Steblau, *Tagebuch* (Halle, 1866), pp. 210–212.

19. This system was first tried out in 1572 with the formation of a corps of 300 mercenary Cossacks, which was disbanded three years later. In 1578 a permanent unit of 500 men was established under a Polish officer. D. Doroshenko, *Narys istorii Ukrainy,* I (Warsaw, 1932), 157–158.

20. *Listy Stanislawa Żolkiewskiego, 1584–1620* (Cracow, 1868), No. 17, p. 27, and No. 18, p. 34. [Hereafter cited as *LSZ.*]

21. *Istoriia Ukraini v dokumntakh i materialakh,* III (Kiev, 1941), 27.

22. *LSZ,* No. 17, pp. 26–27.

23. M. Hrushevskyi, *Istoriia Ukrainy-Rusy* (Moscow, 1935), VII, 200–239.

24. George Vernadsky, *Russia at the Dawn of the Modern Age* (New Haven: Yale University Press, 1959), pp. 270–271.

25. A general survey of the *bratstvo* movement is A. Papkov, *Bratstva* (Moscow, 1900), and I. Isaievych's more recent *Bratstva ta ich rol v rozvytku Ukrainskoi Kultury XVI–XVIII st.* (Kiev, 1966).

26. On the *bratstva* in Lvov, see A. Krilovskii, "Lvovskoe stavropigalnoe bratstvo," *Arkhiv Iugo-Zapadnoi Rossii,* X (1904), pt. 1.

27. Contemporary reports on the Council of Brest in Polish and in Russian are in *Russkaia Istoricheskaia Biblioteka,* XIX, cols. 83–376 and 477–982. The best survey in English of this topic is Oscar Halecki, *From Florence to Brest, 1439–1596* (New York, 1959).

28. Much of the early polemics of this period reveals the ambiguity of identity other than the religious. Calls for the liberation of "Rus," and "Malaia Rus," and for the defense of "naroda russkogo volnosti" were politically vague and were openings for any movement choosing to represent these interests. Both Muscovy and Cossackdom were ready to assume this role. O. I. Biletskii,

Khrestomatiia davnoi Ukrainskoi literatury (*doba feodalizmu*) (Kiev, 1949), pp. 112–118 and 131–134.

29. A. I. Baranovich, ed., *Vossoedinenie Ukrainy s Rossiei* (Moscow, 1954), I, 3–7. [Hereafter cited as *VUR.*]

30. Patriarch Theophanes, before his departure, asked that the Cossacks make common cause with Muscovy in the defense of Orthodoxy, refusing to distinguish the Cossacks and Muscovy as separate political entities and clearly indicating that in his estimation Muscovy had earned the title of capital for the Orthodox. Hrushevskyi, *Istoriia Ukrainy-Rusy,* VII, 45.

31. *VUR,* I, 47–48.

32. In 1640, Mohyla offered to send several monk-scholars from the academy to Moscow in order to found a similar school. In 1649 Tsar Alexis requested that two monks be sent to carry out such an assignment. *VUR,* II, 197–198. The most extensive study on Mohyla is still S. Golubev, *Mitropolit Petr Mogila i ego spodvizhniki,* 2 vols. (Kiev, 1883).

33. The flow of churchmen who elected to live in Muscovy, however, included the noted Lavrentii Zizanii. Their refined scholarship exerted considerable influence upon the Muscovite Orthodox Church. K. B. Kharlampovets, *Malorossiiskoe vliianie na velikorusskuiu tserkovnuiu zhizn* (Kazan, 1914), I, 106–107; I. P. Kripiakevich, *Zviazky zakhidnoi Ukrainy z Rossieiu do seredyny XVII st.* (Kiev, 1953), p. 30.

34. *Dyaryusz . . . Symona Okolskiego* (Cracow, 1858), pp. 10–14.

35. *VUR,* I, Nos. 145, 153, 178, 195, and 196.

36. Since 1639, sporadic peasant uprisings had gathered force. V. Shutoi, "Kanum osvoboditelnoi voiny," *Istoricheskie Zapiski,* No. 46 (1954), 271–272.

37. *Pamiatniki, izdannye kievskoi komissiei dlia razbora drevnikh aktov* (Kiev, 1898), I, 175; O. Pritsak, "Der erste türkisch-ukrainische Bündnis (1648)," *Oriens,* VI (1953), 266–298.

38. *Akty Iugo-Zapadnoi Rossii,* III, 129–130; *VUR,* II, 32–33.

39. George Vernadsky, *The Tsardom of Moscow, 1547–1682* (New Haven: Yale University Press, 1969), Bk. I, p. 454. Additional pressure to align itself with Muscovy came from Patriarch Paisios of Jerusalem, who felt that Orthodoxy in Poland had been too much exposed to Catholicism. Within the context of Muscovy, Orthodoxy would be relatively free from these influences.

40. The report of the Muscovite embassy headed by the shrewd boiar V. V. Buturlin is in *VUR,* III, No. 205.

41. *VUR,* III, No. 205.

42. The power to increase the number of registered Cossacks lay with the tsar in Moscow, where leading registered Cossacks argued against opening their ranks to what they contemptuously called *guliai* (tramps). *Akty Iugo-Zapadnoi Rossii,* IV, 108.

43. Khmelnytskyi had to pass special legislation against the seizure of those lands, thereby seriously compromising his claim as a popular leader. V. A. Miakotin, *Ocherki sotsialnoi istorii Ukrainy v XVII–XVIII v.v.* (Prague, 1942), I, 53–66 and 70–73.

44. One of Khmelnytskyi's plans was to seize Belorussia and make it part

of his hetmanate, thereby challenging Muscovy's own intentions to annex the area. O. Ohloblyn, *Dumky pro Khmelnychchynu* (New York, 1957), pp. 83–84.

45. *Akty Iugo-Zapadnoi Rossii,* VII, 184, 193, and 210.

46. N. Kostomarov, "Getmanstvo Vygovskogo," *Sobranie Sochinenia,* I, 345–346.

47. V. Harasimchuk, "Vyhovskyi i hadiatskyi Traktat," *Zapysky naukovoho tovarystva imeni Shevchenka* (Lvov, 1909), pp. 87–89.

48. *Polnoe sobranie zakonov rossiiskoi imperii,* I (St. Petersburg, 1885–1916), 475–487; N. Kostomarov, "Getmanstvo Iurii Khmelnitskogo," *Sobranie sochinenii* (Kiev, 1903–1906), 102–104.

49. *Polnoe sobranie zakonov rossiiskoi imperii,* I, 656–669.

50. *Sobranie gosudarstvennykh gramot i dagovorov,* IV, 231–248; Doroshenko, *Narys istorii Ukrainy,* II, 86–7.

51. Vernadsky, *The Tsardom of Moscow,* Bk. II, pp. 630–634.

52. Relative peace came to the southern frontier in 1681 with the signing of the treaty of Bakhchisarai between Muscovy and Turkey. The twenty-year truce recognized that the entire left bank, including the Zaporozhian Cossacks, was within Muscovy's sphere of influence. N. Iorga, *Geschichte des osmanischen Reiches,* IV (Gotha, 1912), 181–182.

53. R. Stupperich, "Kiev—das zweite Jerusalem," *Zeitschrift für Slawische Philologie,* XII (1935), 332–354.

54. C. Bickford O'Brien, *Russia under Two Tsars, 1682–1689* (Berkeley, Calif., 1952), p. 46.

55. *Ibid.,* p. 48.

56. Considerable pressure to place only Russians in the hierarchy of the church came from the Patriarch in Jerusalem, who considered Ukrainians unreliable. S. F. Platonov, *Moskva i zapad* (Moscow, 1912), p. 139.

57. P. K. Shchebalskii, *Pravlenie Tsarevny Sofii* (Moscow, 1856), p. 82.

58. N. Storozhenko, "Reformy v Malorossii pri Grafe P. Rumiantseve," *Kievskaia Starina* (1891), No. 3.

59. N. Vasylenko-Polonska, "Z istorii ostannikh chasiv Zaporozha," *Zapysky Akademii Nauk* (Kiev), IX (1927).

60. A 1739 ukaz enserfing the entire Ukrainian peasantry was reappealed in 1742. However, by 1763 when Catherine made her first move to terminate free peasantry, there were fewer than 2,000 free peasant households in the Ukraine. Jerome Blum, *Lord and Peasant in Russia from the Ninth to the Nineteenth Century* (New York: Atheneum, 1965), p. 417. Her latest decree in 1783 coincided with the annexation of the Crimea, which opened the door to complete Russification of the steppelands. V. I. Semevskii, *Krestianskii vopros v Rossii v XVIII i pervoi polovine XIX veka* (St. Petersburg, 1888), I, 148–152.

61. In 1786 church and monastic estates were secularized, as they had been in the rest of the empire in 1764. The peasants from these lands were placed under state supervision. V. I. Semevskii, *Krestiane v tsarstvovanie Ekateriny II* (St. Petersburg, 1901), II, 193–195.

62. The preferential customs tariff of 1775 sparked a veritable boom attracting thousands of merchants and speculators from central Russia to the South, thereby assisting in the economic integration of the Ukraine.

RUSSIAN DOMINATION IN THE BALKANS

1. N. V. Gogol, *Sobranie sochinenii,* vol. v: *Mertvye dushi: Poema* (Moscow: Gosudarstvennoe izdatelstvo khudozhestvennoi literatury, 1953), pp. 229–230, 258.

2. Fernand Braudel, *Civilisation matérielle et capitalisme (XV*[e]*–XVIII*[e] *siècle)*, I (Paris: Armand Colin, 1967), 314.

3. N. A. Smirnov, *Rossiia i Turtsiia v XVI–XVII vv* (Moscow, 1946), II, 18.

4. J. C. Hobhouse, *A Journey Through Albania, and Other Provinces of Turkey in Europe and Asia, to Constantinople, During the Years 1809 and 1810,* 2d ed. (London: Printed for J. Cawthorne, 1813), pp. 977–978.

5. Paul Rycaut, *The History of the Turkish Empire from the Year 1623 to the Year 1677* (London: Printed by J.M. for John Starkey, 1680), pp. 6–7. For further comments on the villages of Yeni Köy (or Yeniköy), Büyük Dere (or Büyükdere), and İsteniye, see Robert Mantran, *İstanbul dans la seconde moitié du XVII*[e] *siècle,* Bibliothèque Archéologique et Historique de l'Institut Français d'Archéologie d'Istanbul, XII (Paris: Adrien Maisonneuve, 1962), pp. 83–85. Wealthy or otherwise privileged Stambouliotes had established summer residences in such villages, but these settlements also performed other functions. Yeni Köy, for example, was the place of residence of many captains and owners of merchant ships. Büyük Dere provided shelter to vessels when a storm threatened from the north. İsteniye was a shipbuilding village whose craftsmen were especially skilled in the construction and repair of caiques.

6. B. H. Sumner, "Peter the Great," *History,* XXXII (March, 1947), 42–49.

7. Joseph A. Schumpeter, "The Sociology of Imperialism," *Imperialism, Social Classes: Two Essays by Joseph Schumpeter,* introd. Bert Hoselitz, trans. Heinz Norden (New York: Meridian Books, 1955), pp. 6, 62–65.

8. François Perroux, "Esquisse d'une théorie de l'économie dominante," *Economie Appliquée,* I, 2–3 (April–September, 1948), 243–300. See also Raymond Aron, "Nations et empires," *Dimensions de la conscience historique* (Paris: Plon, 1961), p. 209. Aron's article first appeared in *Encyclopédie Française,* XI (1957), 11-04-1 to 11-06-8.

9. A. A. Novoselskii, *Borba moskovskogo gosudarstva s tatarami v pervoi polovine XVII veka* (Moscow: Akademiia Nauk SSSR—Institut Istorii, 1948), pp. 293–307; B. H. Sumner, *Peter the Great and the Ottoman Empire* (Oxford: Basil Blackwell, 1949), p. 16.

10. Fred Cottrell, *Energy and Society: The Relation Between Energy, Social Change, and Economic Development* (New York: McGraw-Hill, 1955), pp. 19–20; Braudel, *Civilisation matérielle,* I, 116.

11. Braudel, *Civilisation matérielle,* pp. 18–42; Voltaire, "Histoire de l'Empire de Russie sous Pierre le Grand," *Œuvres historiques,* ed. René Pomeau (Paris: Gallimard, 1957), pp. 354–355, 377–378; Jerome Blum, *Lord and Peasant in Russia from the Ninth to the Nineteenth Century* (New York:

Atheneum, 1965), pp. 121–122; Traian Stoianovich, *A Study in Balkan Civilization* (New York: Alfred A. Knopf, 1967), pp. 162–164.

12. W. E. D. Allen, *The Ukraine* (Cambridge: Cambridge University Press, 1941), pp. 66–67; Peter I. Lyashchenko, *History of the National Economy of Russia to the 1917 Revolution,* trans. L. M. Herman (New York: Macmillan, 1949), pp. 344–345; Irena Gieysztorowa, "Guerre et régression en Masovie aux XVIe et XVIIe siècles," *Annales (Economies, Sociétés, Civilisations)*, XIII, 4 (October–December, 1958), 651–668.

13. Boris Nolde, *La Formation de l'Empire Russe: Etudes, notes et documents,* 2 vols. (Paris: Institut d'Etudes Slaves, 1952–1953), II, 140–144, 147–152, 193–195, 229–258; N. D. Polonska-Vasylenko, "The Settlement of the Southern Ukraine (1715–1775)," *The Annals of the Ukrainian Academy of Arts and Sciences in the United States,* IV–V (Summer–Fall, 1955), 272–275; V. M. Kabuzan, *Narodonaselenie Rossii v XVIII-pervoi polovine XX v.* (Moscow: Akademiia Nauk SSSR, 1963), p. 164; William H. McNeill, *Europe's Steppe Frontier, 1500–1800* (Chicago: University of Chicago Press, 1964), pp. 191–202.

14. Edward Louis Keenan, Jr., "Muscovy and Kazan: Some Introductory Remarks on the Patterns of Steppe Diplomacy," *Slavic Review,* XXVI, 4 (December, 1967), 557.

15. McNeill, *Europe's Steppe Frontier,* p. 186.

16. Richard Hellie, ed. and trans., *Readings for Introduction to Russian Civilization: Muscovite Society* (Chicago: Syllabus Division of the College of the University of Chicago, 1967), p. 26.

17. James H. Billington, *The Icon and the Axe: An Interpretive History of Russian Culture* (New York: Alfred A. Knopf, 1966), p. 40; Bertrand Gille, *Histoire économique et sociale de la Russie du Moyen Âge au XXe siècle* (Paris: Payot, 1949), pp. 67–69; Carlo M. Cipolla, *Guns, Sails, and Empires: Technological Innovation and the Early Phases of European Expansion, 1400–1700* (New York: Pantheon Books, 1965), pp. 59–60, 144–145.

18. Gille, *Histoire économique,* pp. 88–90, 96–101; Roger Portal, *L'Oural au XVIIIe siècle: Etude d'histoire économique et sociale* (Paris: Institut d'Etudes Slaves, 1950); Roger Portal, *Les Slaves: Peuples et nations* (Paris: Armand Colin, 1965), pp. 156–159; Arcadius Kahan, "Continuity in Economic Activity and Policy During the Post-Petrine Period in Russia," *Journal of Economic History,* XXV, 1 (March, 1965), 72–77.

19. Traian Stoianovich, "The Conquering Balkan Orthodox Merchant," *Journal of Economic History,* XX (June, 1960), 254–59; Stoianovich, *Balkan Civilization,* p. 87; Cipolla, *Guns, Sails, and Empires,* pp. 92–99.

20. [Pierre Chevalier,] *A Discourse of the Original, Countrey, Manners, Government and Religion of the Cossacks, with Another of the Precopian Tartars* [trans. Edward Brown] (London, 1672), preface by Edward Brown, cited by Lubomyr Vynar, "The Question of Anglo-Ukrainian Relations in the Middle of the Seventeenth Century," *The Annals of the Ukrainian Academy of Arts and Sciences in the United States,* VI, 3, 4 (21, 22) (1958), 1411–1418. Comparisons between the sea and the steppe have been made repeatedly. One of the most interesting, drawn in 1918, identified "the main conditioning feature"

of the nomadic societies of the Eurasian steppe as their "openness to traffic—the general absence of obstacles and the existence of easy routes in every direction—that tends to keep peoples who commit themselves to it in a permanent state of vagrancy; and this vagrancy, once set up, helps in turn to keep the country open by discouraging settlement and cultivation, which are greater obstacles to nomadism than any physical barriers.

"The command of this open steppe country is in some respects more like sea power than power on land. Like sea power, it is ultimately indivisible. The whole breadth of the steppe, from north to south, is needed for the nomad's summer and winter pasturage, and as his flocks and families increase, he is bound to come into conflict with his neighbours east and west, for in steppe herdsmanship there is practically no possibility of intensive exploitation. Such conflicts arise periodically, and the weaker tribe is either pushed off the steppe altogether or decimated and incorporated by the conqueror. And the conqueror of the steppe, like the master of the sea, can operate at will on any of its coasts, for movement across the steppe involves merely the expenditure of time and not the surmounting of obstacles."

The above article also makes a careful distinction between the Cossacks—"borderers between steppe and forest"—and the nomads: "The unit of the nomadic tribe is the *kibitka* or movable felt hut, the Cossack unit is the *stanitsa* or palisaded village; and a series of these fortified posts constitutes a Cossack 'host.' The *stanitsas* are generally echeloned along the banks of a river, for the Cossacks have been rivermen since the days when they issued from the Russian forests; and the rivers running out across the steppe from the forests to the Black Sea, at right angles to the path of nomad invasion, are natural lines of defence." See the unsigned article, "Russia, Germany, and Asia," *Round Table. A Quarterly Review of the Politics of the British Empire,* VIII (June, 1918), 528, 539, 540.

21. Cipolla, *Guns, Sails, and Empires,* pp. 100–103, 145, 160–162; Fernand Braudel, *La Méditerranée et le monde méditerranéen à l'époque de Philippe II,* 2d rev. and enlarged ed., 2 vols. (Paris: Armand Colin, 1966), II, 282–284, 392–398; Traian Stoianovich, "L'Economie balkanique aux XVIIe et XVIIIe siècles" (unpublished doctoral dissertation, University of Paris, 1952), pp. 139–51.

22. Karl Marx, "The Background of the Dispute (1853–1854)," in *The Russian Menace to Europe by Karl Marx and Friedrich Engels: A Collection of Articles, Speeches, Letters, and News Dispatches,* selected and ed. Paul W. Blackstock and Bert F. Hoselitz (Glencoe, Ill.: The Free Press, 1952), p. 141. Article first published in the New York *Tribune,* June 14, 1853.

23. Montesquieu, *L'Esprit des lois,* 2 vols. (Paris: Garnier Frères, 1922), I, Bk. 9, chap. 6, and Bk. 10, chap. 9.

24. Jacob Friedrich von Bielfeld, *Institutions politiques,* 2 vols. (The Hague: P. Gosse, 1760), II, chap. 4, sec. 20, p. 89.

25. C. E. Vaughan, *The Political Writings of Jean Jacques Rousseau (Edited from the Original Manuscripts and Authentic Editions),* 2 vols. (Cambridge, 1915), I, 100, 297, 321.

26. Albert Sorel, *L'Europe et la Révolution Française,* vol. I, *Les Mœurs politiques et les traditions* (Paris: Plon [1885]), pp. 30–33; L.[eften] S. Stavrianos, *The Balkans since 1453* (New York: Holt, Rinehart and Winston, 1958), p. 193. For a systematic study of the theory and practice of balance of power, 1600–1800, see Edward Vose Gulick, *Europe's Classical Balance of Power: A Case History of the Theory and Practice of One of the Great Concepts of European Statecraft* (Ithaca, N.Y.: Cornell University Press, 1955, by the American Historical Association; published as a paperback in 1967 by W. W. Norton, New York).

27. On liberty and collective liberties in European history, see S. Baille, F. Braudel, and R. Philippe, *Le Monde actuel: Histoire et civilisations* (Paris: Librairie Classique Eugène Belin, 1963), pp. 333–341.

28. Charles Verlinden, "Les Origines coloniales de la civilisation atlantique: Antécédents et types de structure," *Cahiers d'Histoire Mondiale, Journal of World History, Cuadernos de Historia Mundial,* I, 2 (October, 1953), 381–384.

29. Arnold van Gennep, *The Rites of Passage,* trans. Monika B. Vizedom and Gabrielle L. Caffee (London: Routledge and Kegan Paul, 1960), pp. 15–16.

30. Jacques Le Goff, *La Civilisation de l'Occident médiéval* (Paris: Arthaud, 1964), pp. 195–196.

31. Albert Howe Lybyer, *The Government of the Ottoman Empire in the Time of Suleiman the Magnificent,* Harvard Historical Studies, XVIII (Cambridge, Mass.: Harvard University Press, 1913), p. 29.

32. Veselin Čajkanović, "Gostoprimstvo i teofanija," *Studije iz religije i folklora* (Belgrade: Srpska Akademija Nauka, 1924), pp. 1–24, 169–171; Norman Cohn, *The Pursuit of the Millennium* (London: Secker and Warburg, 1957), p. 164.

33. P. B. Struve, *Sotsialnaia i èkonomicheskaia istoriia Rossii s drevneishikh vremen do nashego, v sviazi s razvitiem russkoi kultury i rostom rossiiskoi gosudarstvennosti* (Paris: n.p., 1952), pp. 89–90.

34. Clarence Dana Rouillard, *The Turk in French History, Thought, and Literature (1520–1660),* Etudes de Littérature Etrangère et Comparée, 13 (Paris: Boivin, foreword dated 1938 [pub. 1940?]), pp. 112–113.

35. *Ibid.,* p. 140.

36. Nicéphore Moschopoulos, *La Terre Sainte: Essai sur l'histoire politique et diplomatique des lieux saints de la Chretienté* (Athens: n.p., 1956), p. 203; Stoianovich, "The Conquering Balkan Orthodox Merchant," p. 240.

37. Stoianovich, "The Conquering Balkan Merchant," p. 288; Gabriel Noradounghian, ed., *Recueil d'actes internationaux de l'Empire Ottoman,* vol. I, *1300–1789* (Paris, 1897), pp. 324–352; George Young, *Corps de droit ottoman* (Oxford: Clarendon Press, 1905–1906), III, 68; [Antoine-Ignace] Anthoine, baron de Saint-Joseph, *Essai historique sur le commerce et la navigation de la Mer Noire,* 2d rev. ed. (Paris: Vve Agasse, 1820), pp. 156–157.

38. Stoianovich, "The Conquering Balkan Orthodox Merchant," pp. 254–260. For an ampler discussion of the unfavorable effects of the "capitulatory" regime on Ottoman manufactures and the Ottoman economy in general, see Osman Nebioglu, *Die Auswirkungen der Kapitulationen auf die türkische*

Wirtschaft, Probleme der Wirtschaft—Schriften des Instituts für Weltwirtschaft an der Universität Kiel, 68 (Jena: Gustav Fischer, 1941).

39. Robert J. Kerner, "Russia's New Policy in the Near East after the Peace of Adrianople; including the Text of the Protocol of 16 September 1829," *Cambridge Historical Journal,* V, 3 (1937), 280–290.

40. B. H. Sumner, *A Short History of Russia,* rev. ed. (New York: Harcourt, Brace and World, 1949), pp. 24–25.

41. G. A. Olivier, *Voyage dans l'Empire Othoman, l'Egypte et la Perse, fait par ordre du Gouvernement, pendant les six premières années de la République* (Paris: chez H. Agasse, year IX), pp. 233–234.

42. Archives Nationales (Paris), Affaires Etrangères [hereafter cited as A.N., Aff. Etr.], B^{III} 239, memoir on Ottoman trade with Russia, *c.* 1751–1753.

43. A.N., Aff. Etr., B^{1} 905, letter from Amoreux, July 23, 1776.

44. N. G. Svoronos, *Le Commerce de Salonique au XVIIIe siècle* (Paris: Presses Universitaires de France, 1956), pp. 209, 239.

45. Sumner, *Peter the Great and the Ottoman Empire,* pp. 17–25.

46. Stoianovich, "The Conquering Balkan Orthodox Merchant," pp. 273–276.

47. N. S. Derzhavin, "Russkii absoliutizm i iuzhnoe slavianstvo," *Izvestiia Leningradskogo Gosudarstvennogo Universiteta,* I (1928), 66.

48. S. K. Bogoiavlenskii, "Sviazi mezhdu russkimi i serbami v XVII–XVIII vv.," in *Slavianskii Sbornik* ([Moscow:] OGIZ, 1947), pp. 260–261. For the life of Šćepan Mali, see in particular Michael Boro Petrovich, "Catherine II and a False Peter III in Montenegro," *American Slavic and East European Review,* XIV (1955), 169–194.

49. Derzhavin, "Russkii absoliutizm," pp. 79–81.

50. Archives Nationales (Paris), Archives de la Marine [hereafter cited as A.N., A.M.], B^{7} 453, memoir by de la Colinière on the trade of Kherson in 1785.

51. A.N., Aff. Etr., B^{III} 242, memoir by Fourcade on the commerce of Smyrna, *c.* 1810.

52. A. N., A.M., B^{7} 453, memoir by de la Colinière on the trade of Kherson.

53. Jan Reychman, "Le Commerce polonais en Mer Noire au XVIIIe siècle par le port de Kherson," *Cahiers du Monde Russe et Soviétique,* VII (1966), 243.

54. A.N., Aff. Etr., B^{III} 242, "Etat des consuls et des agents français à Smyrne et dans les diverses îles de l'Archipel grec," joined to the memoir by Fourcade on the commerce of Smyrna, *c.* 1810.

55. Stoianovich, "L'Economie balkanique," pp. 45–50; Stoianovich, "The Conquering Balkan Orthodox Merchant," pp. 273–274.

56. Young, *Corps de droit ottoman,* III, 65–68; G. I. Brătianu, "Les Observations de M. de Peyssonnel en 1777 sur l'exécution du traité de Koutchouk-Kaïnardji," *Revue Historique du Sud-Est Européen,* VI (1929), 347–348.

57. Stoianovich, "The Conquering Balkan Orthodox Merchant," pp. 288–89.

58. A.N., Aff. Etr., B^{1} 446, letter from St. Priest, January 10, 1783.

59. E. Rodocanachi, *Bonaparte et les îles ioniennes: Un Episode des conquêtes de la République et du Premier Empire (1797–1816)* (Paris: Félix Alcan, 1899), pp. 116–169; S. T. Lascaris, *Capodistrias avant la révolution grecque* (Lausanne: Imprimerie Centrale, 1918), pp. 9–12; Edouard Driault, *Napoléon et l'Europe: Tilsit, France et Russie sous le Premier Empire; la question de Pologne (1806–1809)* (Paris: Félix Alcan, 1917), pp. 267–268.

60. Cited by Stavrianos, *The Balkans since 1453,* p. 208.

61. Count John Capodistrias (to His Majesty the Emperor), "Aperçu de ma carrière, depuis 1798 jusqu'à 1822," *Sbornik Imperatorskogo Russkogo Istoricheskogo Obshchestva,* III (1868), 209–212.

62. Vernon J. Puryear, "Odessa: Its Rise and International Importance, 1815–50," *Pacific Historical Review,* III (1934), 193–194.

63. On the introduction of fashion in the Balkans and the Ottoman Empire, see Traian Stoianovich, "Theoretical Implications of Braudel's *Civilisation matérielle,*" *Journal of Modern History,* XLI, 1 (March, 1969), 68–70; Traian Stoianovich, "Material Foundations of Preindustrial Civilization in the Balkans," *Journal of Social History,* IV, 3 (Spring, 1971), 246–248.

64. On the Ottoman system of social statuses, see Stoianovich, *Balkan Civilization,* pp. 131–133; Stanford J. Shaw, "The Ottoman View of the Balkans," in Charles and Barbara Jelavich, eds., *The Balkans in Transition: Essays on the Development of Balkan Life and Politics since the Eighteenth Century* (Berkeley and Los Angeles: University of California Press, 1963), pp. 58–61.

65. Reychman, "Le Commerce polonais en Mer Noire," p. 248; Stoianovich, "The Conquering Balkan Orthodox Merchant," p. 289.

66. Puryear, "Odessa," p. 197.

67. *Ibid.,* pp. 195–97; Grigorii Nebolsin, *Statisticheskoe obozrenie vneshnei torgovli Rossii,* 2 vols. (St. Petersburg: Department of Foreign Trade, 1850), I, 2–4, 11–12, 53, 121; II, 457–458; Lyashchenko, *History of the National Economy of Russia,* pp. 367, 520; Margaret Miller, *The Economic Development of Russia, 1905–1914,* 2d ed. (London: Frank Cass, 1967), p. 73; Gille, *Histoire économique,* p. 209. For an overall view of Russia's Mediterranean grain trade, see Patricia Herlihy, "Russian Grain and Mediterranean Markets, 1744–1861," unpublished doctoral dissertation, University of Pennsylvania, 1963.

68. Nebolsin, *Statisticheskoe obozrenie,* I, 151.

69. Vernon John Puryear, *International Economics and Diplomacy in the Near East: A Study of British Commercial Policy in the Levant, 1834–1853* (Stanford, Calif.: Stanford University Press, 1935), p. 136.

70. Thibault-Lefebvre, "Le Commerce de la Valachie," *Journal des Economistes: Revue de la Science Economique et de la Statistique,* 2d ser., 3d year, vol. IX (1856), 398–418.

71. S. Grosul, "Istoricheskoe znachenie prisoedineniia Bessarabii k Rossii dlia sudeb moldavskogo naroda," *Voprosy Istorii,* No. 7 (July, 1962), 53.

72. Blackstock and Hoselitz, eds., *The Russian Menace,* p. 187.

73. Dietrich Gerhard, *England und der Aufstieg Russlands: Zur Frage des Zusammenhanges der europäischen Staaten und ihres Ausgreifens in die aus-*

sereuropäische Welt in Politik und Wirtschaft des 18. Jahrhunderts (Munich and Berlin: R. Oldenbourg, 1933), p. 98.

74. Frank Edgar Bailey, *British Policy and the Turkish Reform Movement: A Study in Anglo-Turkish Relations, 1826–1853* (Cambridge, Mass.: Harvard University Press, 1942), pp. 83–86.

75. Thibault-Lefebvre, "Le Commerce de la Valachie," pp. 398–418.

76. Arno Mehlan, "Mittel- und Westeuropa und die Balkanjahresmärkte zur Türkenzeit," *Südostdeutsche Forschungen,* III (1938), 105.

77. Marx, "The Background of the Dispute," in Blackstock and Hoselitz, eds., *The Russian Menace,* pp. 130–131. Article first published in the New York *Tribune,* April 12, 1853.

78. Puryear, "Odessa," pp. 206–207.

79. *Ibid.,* p. 214.

80. Charles Morazé, *Histoire des faits économiques et sociaux* (Paris: Université de Paris—Institut d'Etudes Politiques, 1950–1951, "Les Cours de Droit"), fasc. III, pp. 294–303; L. Tikhomirov, *La Russie politique et sociale* (Paris: E. Giraud, 1886), pp. 231–232; Lyashchenko, *History of the National Economy of Russia,* p. 520; William Woodruff, *Impact of Western Man: A Study of Europe's Role in the World Economy, 1750–1960* (New York: St. Martin's Press, 1967), pp. 268–269.

81. P. A. Khromov, *Ekonomicheskoe razvitie Rossii* (Moscow: Izdatelstvo Nauka, 1967), pp. 332, 355.

82. Morazé, *Histoire des faits économiques,* pp. 294–303; Richard E. Pipes, "Domestic Politics and Foreign Affairs," in Ivo J. Lederer, ed., *Russian Foreign Policy: Essays in Historical Perspective* (New Haven: Yale University Press, 1962), p. 152.

83. Charles Morazé, *Les Bourgeois conquérants: XIXe siècle* (Paris: Armand Colin, 1957), p. 361.

84. Lyashchenko, *History of the National Economy of Russia,* pp. 518–519; Hugh Seton-Watson, *The Russian Empire, 1801–1917* (Oxford: Clarendon Press, 1967), pp. 530, 660.

85. Nebolsin, *Statisticheskoe obozrenie,* II, 452–453.

86. Ia. Zakher, "Konstantinopol i Prolivy," *Krasnyi Arkhiv,* VI (1924), 58.

87. *Ibid.,* p. 49.

88. Nebolsin, *Statisticheskoe obozrenie,* II, 454, 466.

89. Eugène Zaleski, *Les Courants commerciaux de l'Europe danubienne au cours de la première moitié du XXe siècle* (Paris: R. Pichon et R. Durand-Auzias, 1952), pp. 44–45, for the Bulgarian figure.

90. Charles and Barbara Jelavich, "Jomini and the Revival of the *Dreikaiserbund,* 1879–1880," *Slavonic and East European Review,* XXXV, 85 (June, 1957), 529.

91. Zaleski, *Les Courants commerciaux,* p. 48.

92. Danica Miljković, "Prilozi za rasvetljanje privrednih odnosa Srbije i Rusije u XIX veku," in Srpska Akademija Nauka, *Gradja* (*Documents*), XII, Istoriski Institut, 9, *Mešovita gradja* (*Miscellanea*) (Belgrade, 1956), p. 87.

93. *Ibid.*, p. 9.

94. For a bibliography, see Ivo J. Lederer, "Russia and the Balkans," in Lederer, ed., *Russian Foreign Policy,* pp. 425–426. See also Barbara Jelavich, *Russia and the Greek Revolution of 1843* (Munich: R. Oldenbourg, 1966), pp. 19, 21–22; Mirko Lamer, "Die Wandlungen der ausländischen Kapitalanlagen auf dem Balkan," *Weltwirtschaftliches Archiv,* XLVIII, 3 (November, 1938), 470–522.

95. Barbara Jelavich, *Russia and the Greek Revolution,* pp. 95–97.

96. Charles and Barbara Jelavich, eds., *The Education of a Russian Statesman: The Memoirs of Nicholas Karlovich Giers* (Berkeley and Los Angeles: University of California Press, 1962), pp. 220–221. The Memoirs conclude with the above reflections.

97. Puryear, *International Economics,* pp. 132–136, 207–209.

98. Edward Krehbiel, "The European Commission of the Danube: An Experiment in International Administration," *Political Science Quarterly,* XXXIII, 1 (March, 1918), 43–47; Noradounghian, ed., *Recueil d'actes internationaux,* III (1902), 76, 319–320, 335.

99. Archives du Ministère des Affaires Etrangeres (Paris), Correspondance Commerciale, Belgrade, vol. II, letters from Théodore Goepp, October 18, 1850, and October 26, 1850; letters from Limpérani, December 1, 1850, and March 9, 1851.

100. Count Chedomille Mijatovich (Čedomilj Mijatović), *The Memoirs of a Balkan Diplomatist* (London: Cassell, 1917), pp. 18–22.

101. Arthur J. May, "Trans-Balkan Railway Schemes," *Journal of Modern History,* XXIV, 4 (December, 1952), 352–367; Wayne S. Vucinich, *Serbia Between East and West: The Events of 1903–1908* (Stanford, Calif.: Stanford University Press, 1954), p. 106.

102. Charles Jelavich, *Tsarist Russia and Balkan Nationalism: Russian Influence in the Internal Affairs of Bulgaria and Serbia, 1879–1886* (Berkeley and Los Angeles: University of California Press, 1958), p. 69.

103. J. H. Jensen and Gerhard Rosegger, "British Railway Building along the Lower Danube, 1856–1869," *Slavonic and East European Review,* XLVI, 106 (January, 1968), 118–122.

104. Melvin C. Wren, "Pobedonostsev and Russian Influence in the Balkans, 1881–1888," *Journal of Modern History,* XIX, 2 (June, 1947), 130–141.

105. David S. Landes, "The Nature of Economic Imperialism," *Journal of Economic History,* XXI, 4 (December, 1961), 499.

106. Gille, *Histoire économique,* p. 209. German exports to Russia rose from 194.8 million marks in 1894 to 315.5 million in 1904 and 880.0 million in 1913, while German imports from Russia rose during the same years from 543.9 to 818.7 and 1,426.6 million marks. See W. F. Bruck, *Social and Economic History of Germany from William II to Hitler, 1888–1938: A Comparative Study* (Cardiff: University Press Board; Oxford University Press, 1938), p. 118.

107. Lyashchenko, *History of the National Economy of Russia,* p. 724.

108. Edward Mead Earle, *Turkey, the Great Powers, and the Bagdad Rail-*

way: A Study in Imperialism (New York: Macmillan, 1924), pp. 36, 101–107; A. D. Novichev, *Ocherki ekonomiki Turtsii do Mirovoi Voiny* (Moscow, Leningrad: Akademiia Nauk SSSR, 1937), pp. 180–181; B. M. Tupolev, *Ekspansiia germanskogo imperializma v iugo-vostochnoi Evrope v kontse XIX—nachale XX v.* (Moscow: Izdatelstvo "Nauka," 1970), pp. 219–256 on German capital investments and trade in Turkey and p. 250 in particular on foreign trade statistics. Official statistics underestimate Germany's trade with Turkey, however, in view of the fact that much of it passed through Austria-Hungary.

The United States State Department quotes a slightly edited account of the London *Times* of October 28, 1898 ("German Enterprise in the East," by the *Times'* Berlin correspondent), on the growth of German exports to the Levant after the entry into the Ottoman economy, in 1888, of the Deutsche Bank. The report provides an excellent account of the German economic penetration of the Ottoman Empire. For details, see United States State Department, *Consular Reports* (January, 1899), LIX, 220, 149–151.

109. Zakher, "Konstantinopol i Prolivy," pp. 48–76.

110. Earle, *Turkey, passim;* Sydney Nettleton Fisher, *The Middle East: A History* (New York: Alfred A. Knopf, 1959), pp. 333–336.

111. Fisher, *Middle East,* pp. 327–329; William Yale, *The Near East: A Modern History,* new ed. rev. and enlarged (Ann Arbor: University of Michigan Press, 1968), pp. 92–96.

112. Lederer, "Russia and the Balkans," pp. 439–443.

113. G. H. Bolsover, "Aspects of Russian Foreign Policy," in Richard Pares and A. J. P. Taylor, eds., *Essays Presented to Sir Lewis Namier* (London: Macmillan; New York: St. Martin's Press, 1956), p. 341; Barbara Jelavich, *A Century of Russian Foreign Policy, 1814–1914* (Philadelphia and New York: J. B. Lippincott, 1964), pp. 272–273.

114. Derzhavin, "Russkii absoliutizm," p. 51.

115. I. Dujčev, "La Conquête turque et la prise de Constantinople dans la littérature slave contemporaine," *Byzantinoslavica,* XIV (1953), 46.

116. Eudoxiŭ de Hurmuzaki, *Documente privitóre la istoria Românilor,* II, pt. 3 (Bucharest, 1892), pp. 614, 617–618, 623–624.

117. Derzhavin, "Russkii absoliutizm," pp. 52–61.

118. Bogoiavlenskii, "Sviazi mezhdu russkimi i serbami," pp. 252–261.

119. Mita Kostić, "Serbische Studenten an den Universitäten Halle, Leipzig und Göttingen im 18. Jahrhundert," *Südostdeutsche Forschungen,* III (1938), 352.

120. Joseph Rothschild, *The Communist Party of Bulgaria: Origins and Development, 1883–1936* (New York: Columbia University Press, 1959), p. 10.

121. L. S. Stavrianos, *Balkan Federation: A History of the Movement Toward Balkan Unity in Modern Times,* Smith College Studies in History (Northampton, Mass.), XXVII (October, 1941–July, 1942) (Menasha, Wisc.: Printed by George Banta, 1944), p. 119. For a history of Russia's Slavic societies, see S. A. Nikitin, *Slavianskie komitety v Rossii v 1858–1876 godakh* (Moscow: Moskovskii Universitet, 1960).

122. Jevrem Grujić, *Zapisi,* I (Belgrade: Buducnost, 1922), 54.

123. Archives du Ministère des Affaires Etrangères (Paris), Correspondance Commerciale, Belgrade, vol. I, fol. 415, letter from Limpérani, *élève consul* in charge of the management of France's consulate in Belgrade, November 18, 1847.

124. *Ibid.*, vol. II, letter from Théodore Goepp, *gérant* of the French consulate in Belgrade, January 16, 1850.

125. *Ibid.*, letter from Goepp, February 20, 1850.

126. Olga Mučalica, "Osnivanje katedre narodne istorije i književnosti i njen prvi profesor u Liceju," *Arhivski Almanah*, No. 1 (Belgrade, 1958), 177–190.

127. Grujić, *Zapisi*, I, 54.

128. Woodford D. McClellan, *Svetozar Marković and the Origins of Balkan Socialism* (Princeton, N.J.: Princeton University Press, 1964), pp. 42–43, 47–48; B. H. Sumner, "Russia and Panslavism in the Eighteen-Seventies," *Transactions of the Royal Historical Society*, 4th ser., XVIII (London, 1935), 44–46.

129. Traian Stoianovich, "The Pattern of Serbian Intellectual Evolution, 1830–1880," *Comparative Studies in Society and History*, I, 3 (March, 1959), 259–260.

130. Peter F. Sugar, "The Southern Slav Image of Russia in the Nineteenth Century," *Journal of Central European Affairs*, XXI, 1 (April, 1961), 45–52.

131. David McKenzie, *The Serbs and Russian Pan-Slavism, 1875–1878* (Ithaca, N.Y.: Cornell University Press, 1967), pp. 145–146.

132. Stevan K. Pavlowitch, *Anglo-Russian Rivalry in Serbia, 1837–1839: The Mission of Colonel Hodges* (Paris, The Hague: Mouton, 1961), p. 63, n. 1.

133. Nicholas V. Riasanovsky, *Nicholas I and Official Nationality in Russia, 1825–1855* (Berkeley and Los Angeles: University of California Press, 1967; paperback edition), pp. 262–265.

134. Barbara Jelavich, *Russia and the Greek Revolution*, pp. 17–18; Stavrianos, *The Balkans since 1453*, pp. 467–468; George G. Arnakis, "The Role of Religion in the Development of Balkan Nationalism," in C. and B. Jelavich, eds., *The Balkans in Transition*, p. 134.

135. Stoianovich, "The Pattern of Serbian Intellectual Evolution," p. 247.

136. Jovan Cvijić, "Izlazak Srbije na Jadransko More," *Govori i članci*, 2 vols. (Belgrade: Napredak, 1921), II, 9–25. Cvijić first published this article in a 1912 issue of the *Glasnik Srpskog Geografskog Društva* as an expanded version of an article for *Petermanns Mitteilungen* (December, 1912).

137. George Peabody Gooch and Harold Temperley, eds., with the assistance of Lillian M. Penson, *British Documents on the Origins of the War, 1898–1914*, IX, 2 (London: His Majesty's Stationery Office, 1934), p. 234, No. 313.

138. Stjepan Radić, *Moderna kolonizacija i Slaveni*, Poučna Knjižnica "Matice Hrvatske," XXX (Zagreb: Matica Hrvatska, 1904), pp. 220–221, 255–258.

139. D. Tucović, *Srbija i Arbanija: Jedan prilog kritici zavojevačke politike srpske buržoazije* (Belgrade: Save Radenkovića i braća, 1914);

Dimitrije Djordjević, *Révolutions nationales des peuples balkaniques, 1804–1914* (Belgrade: Institut d'Histoire, 1965), p. 226.

RUSSIAN PENETRATION OF THE CAUCASUS

1. N. A. Smirnov, *Politika Rossii na Kavkaze v XVI–XIX vekakh* (Moscow, 1958), p. 10.

2. Boris Nolde, in *La Formation de l'Empire Russe* (Paris, 1953), vol. II, discusses at some length Russia's relations with the peoples of the Northern Caucasus in the sixteenth century.

3. *Ibid.*, pp. 303–304.

4. Smirnov, *Politika Rossii,* p. 27.

5. *Ibid.*, p. 41.

6. Cited in Nolde, *Empire Russe,* II, 310–311.

7. *Ibid.*, II, 317–318. The number of Kabardians who took part in the operation seems exaggerated.

8. S. A. Belokurov, *Snosheniia Rossii s Kavkazom* (Moscow, 1889), various documents in vyp. 1, 1578–1613; Nolde, *Empire Russe,* II, 320–323; Smirnov, *Politika Rossii,* pp. 45–47.

9. Smirnov, *Politika Rossii,* pp. 46–47.

10. B. H. Sumner, *Peter the Great and the Emergence of Russia* (London, 1956), p. 171.

11. S. M. Solovev, *Istoriia Rossii s drevneishikh vremen* (St. Petersburg, 1894), IV, 665 ff.

12. For these and related events, see *Akty sobrannye Kavkazskoiu Arkheograficheskoiu Kommissieiu,* 12 vols. (Tiflis, 1868–1904); V. P. Lystsov, *Persidskii pokhod Petra I, 1722–1723* (Moscow, 1951); D. M. Lang, *The Last Years of the Georgian Monarchy, 1658–1832* (New York, 1957); and Nolde, *Empire Russe.*

13. T. Iuzefovich, *Dogovory Rossii s Vostokom* (St. Petersburg, 1869), pp. 202 ff., as cited in Nolde, *Empire Russe,* II, 339. For an account of the Persian revival, the sad fate of the Russians in the Caspian provinces, and the treaty of Ganjeh, see L. Lockhart, *Nadir Shah* (London, 1938).

14. Münnich to Bühren (Minikh to Biron), August 14, 1736, as cited in Nolde, *Empire Russe,* II, 341.

15. *Ibid.*

16. See Smirnov, *Politika Rossii,* pp. 87–90.

17. *Sbornik Russkogo Istoricheskogo Obshchestva,* XXVII, 177–178, in Smirnov, *Politika Rossii,* pp. 116–117.

18. Smirnov, *Politika Rossii,* p. 147. The above account of Shaykh Mansur's "rebellion" follows Smirnov's, which is based on his research in the Central State Archive of Old Records (TsGADA) in Moscow (*ibid.*, pp. 138–162).

19. The best account in English of the complicated events leading to the annexation of Georgia is in Lang's *Georgian Monarchy.* See also W. E. D.

Allen, *A History of the Georgian People* (London, 1932), and Z. D. Avalov, *Prisoedinenie Gruzii k Rossii* (St. Petersburg, 1906).

20. "Notions abrégées sur la Perse," October 15, 1795, French Foreign Ministry. Mémoires et Documents, Perse, I, 147, as cited in Lang, *Georgian Monarchy,* p. 219.

21. The classic English account of this and subsequent wars in the Caucasus is J. F. Baddeley's *The Russian Conquest of the Caucasus* (London, 1908). See also P. M. Sykes, *A History of Persia* (London, 1915), vol. II; and M. S. Ivanov, *Ocherk istorii Irana* (Moscow, 1952).

22. A. A. Tsagareli, *Gramoty,* II, pt. 2, p. 287, as cited in Lang, *Georgian Monarchy,* p. 231.

23. See n. 21 above. For a Persian view of the wars, see Jamil Qozanlu, *Jange dah-sale ya jange avvale Iran ba Rus* (Tehran, 1937), and *Jange Iran-Rus, 1825–1828* (Tehran, 1938).

24. *Akty sobrannye Kavkazskoiu Arkheograficheskoiu Kommissieiu,* II, No. 1414.

25. A. V. Fadeev, *Rossiia i Kavkaz v pervoi treti XIX* v. (Moscow, 1960).

26. *Ibid.,* pp. 316–317.

27. *Akty sobrannye Kavkazskoiu Arkheograficheskoiu Kommissieiu,* VII, No. 873.

28. *Arkhiv Raevskikh* (St. Petersburg, 1910), IX, No. 505, as cited in A. V. Fadeev, *Rossiia i Kavkaz,* p. 309.

29. A. A. Veliaminov to Rozen (Rosen), May 20, 1833, in D. I. Romanovsky, *Kavkaz i kavkazskaia voina* (St. Petersburg, 1860), p. XXV of the Appendix, quoted in Smirnov, *Politika Rossii,* p. 194.

30. A. V. Fadeev, *Rossiia i Kavkaz,* p. 340.

31. *Ibid.,* pp. 52–53.

32. *Ibid.,* p. 56.

33. Cited in M. K. Rozhkova, *Ekonomicheskaia politika tsarskogo pravitelstva na Srednem Vostoke vo vtoroi chetverti XIX veka i russkaia burzhuaziia* (Moscow, 1949), p. 60. The circular argument—"We must expand our borders to make our trade secure, and we must expand our trade to make our borders secure"—does not seem to have bothered anyone. The significant thing is the conscious noneconomic use of trade.

34. *Obozrenie Rossiiskikh vladenii za Kavkazom,* pt. 1, pp. 12–13, cited in A. V. Fadeev, *Rossiia i Kavkaz,* p. 72.

35. *Akty sobrannye Kavkazskoiu Arkheograficheskoiu Kommissieiu,* VII, No. 108. See also A. V. Fadeev, *Rossiia i Kavkaz,* p. 73.

36. A. V. Fadeev, *Rossiia i Kavkaz,* p. 36.

37. *Ibid.,* p. 47.

38. S. K. Bushuev, *Borba gortsev za nezavisimost pod rukovodstvom Shamilia* (Moscow, 1939), p. 75.

39. Mirza Hasan Effendi, *Asar-i-Daghestan,* as cited in Bushuev, p. 75.

40. Baddeley's *Russian Conquest of the Caucasus* remains, after sixty-five years, the best work on the Causasian wars in English. The most comprehensive

work in Russian is N. Dubrovin's *Istoriia voiny i vladychestva russkikh na Kavkaze,* 6 vols. (St. Petersburg, 1871–1888).

41. All subsequent quotations from Mochulskii are taken from Bushuev, *Borba gortsev za nezavisimost,* pp. 98–104.

42 Not all, or even a majority of Russian participants in the war, shared such views. R. Fadeev, an officer in the Caucasus, wrote: "Russia can be proud of the subjugation of the Caucasus, not only as of a great political achievement but also as of a great moral deed that gives the full measure of the power of the spirit that she can expect from her sons. . . . The Caucasian soldier [Russian soldier in the Caucasus] manifested to the world the union of all the qualities of an incomparable fighter. . . ." R. Fadeev, *Pisma s Kavkaza k redaktoru Moskovskikh Vedomostei* (St. Petersburg, 1865), pp. 45–46.

43. *Ibid.,* p. 29.

44. *Ibid.,* p. 76.

45. *Ibid.,* p. 134.

46. Smirnov, *Politika Rossii,* p. 220.

47. R. Fadeev, *Pisma s Kavkaza,* p. 154.

RUSSIAN CONQUEST AND COLONIZATION OF CENTRAL ASIA

1. Geoffrey Wheeler, *Modern History of Soviet Central Asia* (London: Weidenfeld and Nicolson, 1964), p. 227.

2. *Aziatskaia Rossiia* (St. Petersburg, 1914), p. 29.

3. Wheeler, *Soviet Central Asia,* p. 37.

4. M. Viatkin, *Ocherki po istorii Kazakhskoi SSR* (Leningrad: Ogiz Gospolitizdat, 1941), chaps. VI and VII.

5. Wheeler, *Soviet Central Asia,* p. 242.

6. *Ibid.*

7. N. A. Khalfin, *Politika Rossii v Srednei Azii 1857–1868* (Moscow, 1960), p. 198.

8. V. V. Barthold, *Four Studies on the History of Central Asia,* vol. I (Leiden: Brill, 1956).

9. This was an investigating commission under Senator Count K. I. Pahlen dispatched by the Russian government to Turkestan in 1908 following on reports of maladministration and corruption and of weakness shown by the authorities in dealing with unrest and disturbances in 1905 to 1907. A report in nineteen volumes was published in St. Petersburg in 1909 and 1910.

10. To Kaufman more than to anyone else was due the pacification of Turkestan which made the eventual Soviet take-over possible. It is significant that his name was omitted from the second edition of the *BSE* (Great Soviet Encyclopaedia) and from the *MSE* (Smaller Soviet Encyclopaedia). In the first edition of the *BSE* (1936) there is a brief reference to him as having "carried out a cruel colonialist policy." His name reappeared in the *Sovetskaia*

Istoricheskaia Entsiklopediia of 1964 as "a prominent representative of the colonialist and offensive policy of tsarism."

11. Exceptions were the Turgai and Uralsk oblasts, where direct rule was not established until 1869.

12. *Aziatskaia Rossiia*. For an English translation of the relevant extract, see Wheeler, *Soviet Central Asia*, pp. 235–244.

13. C. P. von Kaufman, *Proekt vsepoddaneishago otcheta general-adiutanta C. P. von Kaufman I-go po grazhdanskomu upravleniiu i ustroistvu v oblastiakh Turkestanskogo general-gubernatorstva, 7 noiabria 1867–25 marta 1881 gg.* (St. Petersburg, 1885), p. 76.

14. D. S. M. Williams, "Native courts in Tsarist Central Asia," *Central Asian Review*, XIV, 1 (1966), 6–19.

15. K. I. Pahlen, *Mission to Turkestan* (London: Oxford University Press in association with the Central Asian Research Centre, 1964), p. 228.

16. Richard A. Pierce, *Russian Central Asia, 1867–1917* (Berkeley and Los Angeles: University of California Press, 1960), p. 78.

17. Quoted by Pierce; *ibid.*, p. 181.

18. Khalfin, condensed version of his *Russia's Policy in Central Asia, 1857–1868* (London: Central Asian Research Centre, 1964), p. 76.

19. Violet Conolly, *Beyond the Urals* (London: Oxford University Press, 1967), p. 27.

20. Eugene Schuyler, *Turkistan*. Condensed version edited by Geoffrey Wheeler (London: Routledge and Kegan Paul, 1966), p. 283.

21. *Aziatskaia Rossiia*, pp. 425–426; quoted by Pierce, *Russian Central Asia*, p. 199.

22. Pierce, *Russian Central Asia*, p. 107.

23. Pahlen, *Mission to Turkestan*, p. 174.

24. According to the Soviet census of 1959, the total of Russian and Ukrainian settlers in the whole region was approximately 7.5 million, of whom 1.5 million were in the territory formerly occupied by the Turkestan province and the khanate of Bukhara.

25. See particularly P. I. Liashchenko, *Istoriia Narodnogo Khoziaistva SSSR* (Moscow, 1956), II, 515; quoted by Conolly, *Beyond the Urals*, p. 29.

26. Wheeler, *Soviet Central Asia*, p. 237.

27. "Tsarist Policy Towards Islam: the Soviet Version," *Central Asian Review*, VI, 3 (1958), 242–252.

28. Pierce, *Russian Central Asia*, p. 204.

29. Alexandre Benningsen and Chantal Lemercier-Quelquejay, *Islam in the Soviet Union* (London: Pall Mall Press in association with the Central Asian Research Centre, 1967), p. 14.

30. *Ibid.*, p. 15.

31. V. V. Barthold, *Istoriia kulturnoi zhizni Turkestana* (Leningrad: Academy of Sciences, 1927), pp. 143–144.

32. *Central Asian Review*, XIV, 2 (1966), 151. Translation of relevant passages from Alexandre Benningsen and Chantal Lemercier-Quelquejay, *La*

pp. 277–289; also see report of Walter C. Hillier, the British consul general in Seoul, in Great Britain, Foreign Office, *Confidential Papers,* reproduced in George Alexander Lensen, ed., *Russia's Eastward Expansion* (Englewood Cliffs, N.J., 1964), pp. 104–111.

34. Written statement of Foreign Minister Jutarō Komura on the proposed Anglo-Japanese Alliance, dated December 7, 1901, in *SB,* I, 201–203.

35. Yarmolinsky, *Memoirs of Witte,* pp. 85–89.

36. Understandings reached between Komura and Weber on May 14, 1896, and between Yamagata and Lobanov on June 6, 1896, and the Nishi-Rosen protocol of April 25, 1898, in *SB,* I, 174–176 and 186–187.

37. Harrington, *God, Mammon, and the Japanese,* pp. 288–289.

38. Yarmolinsky, *Memoirs of Witte,* pp. 95 and 103.

39. Li Chien-nung, *Chung-kuo chin pai-nien chêng-chih shih,* I (Shanghai, 1947), 141.

40. *Kuhan'guk Oekyo Munsŏ,* XVII, 651.

41. *Ibid.,* pp. 302–303.

42. Von Laue, *Sergei Witte,* p. 150.

43. The Russo-Japanese treaty of September 5, 1905, in *SB,* I, 245–249.

44. The Russo-Japanese conventions of July 30, 1907, and July 4, 1910, *ibid.,* pp. 280–282 and 336–337.

45. Hugh Seton-Watson, *The Russian Empire, 1801–1917* (Oxford, 1967), p. 589.

About the Authors

SUNG-HWAN CHANG was born in Seoul and educated at Yonsei and Columbia Universities, receiving his Ph.D. in 1972. After serving as government information officer and staff member of a daily newspaper in Korea, he came to the United States. A specialist in Far Eastern international relations, he has taught Asian politics and history at Columbia and Rutgers Universities (1961 to 1970) and is currently engaged in research for a book.

RAGNHILD MARIE HATTON is professor of international history at the University of London. She has taught at the London School of Economics and Political Science since 1949 and also offers Senate House lectures and a research seminar at the Institute of Historical Research. She was a visiting professor in the United States in 1964 and 1968, and frequently lectures in Scandinavian universities under the auspices of the Northern Studies Scheme and by invitation. She is a Fellow of the Royal Historical Society and a foreign corresponding member of the Swedish Academy.

Mrs. Hatton's main research field is the period 1660 to 1720, but she also has a strong interest in nineteenth-century international relations, particularly the great power rivalry in the Baltic. She is the author of numerous essays, books, and articles dealing with Anglo-Dutch diplomatic relations, with Louis XIV and his fellow monarchs, and with Sweden's rise and fall as a great power. Among her books are *Charles XII of Sweden* and *Europe in the Age of Louis XIV*. She is also coeditor of *William III and Louis XIV: Essays by and for Mark Thomson*, and of *Studies in Diplomatic History: Essays in Memory of David Bayne Horn*. She is presently at work on biographies of George I of Hanover-Britain and Louis XIV of France.

TARAS HUNCZAK has taught Russian and East European history at Rutgers University since 1960 and currently serves also as chairman of the Newark history department and director of the East European and Soviet Areas Studies Program at Rutgers. He holds B.S. and M.A. degrees from Fordham University and his Ph.D. degree from the University of Vienna. He is the editor of the two-volume *Ukraine and Poland in The Light of Documents* (in press), and will shortly finish a book to be entitled *From Riga to Potsdam: A Study of Soviet-Polish Relations*. His articles and reviews have appeared in *Slavic Re-*

view, Jewish Social Studies, East European Quarterly, Journal of Modern History, Ukrainskyi Istoryk, Zeszyty Historyczne, The Russian Review and *Canadian-American Slavic Studies.*

HENRY R. HUTTENBACH teaches Russian history at the City College of the City University of New York, where he has been chairman of the graduate program in history since 1968. He is a graduate of Gonzaga University and completed his graduate studies at Fordham University and the University of Washington, receiving his Ph.D. in 1961. He has published articles on East European culture and intellectual history, particularly for the Muscovite period, in the *Slavonic and East European Review,* the *American Historical Review,* and other scholarly journals, and is preparing a definitive edition of the correspondence of Elizabeth I and Ivan IV. Professor Huttenbach spent the year 1964–65 in the Soviet Union as a United States State Department Exchange Scholar at Moscow State University. He has also taught at the University of Seattle, East Texas State University, and Louisiana State University.

FIRUZ KAZEMZADEH was born in 1924 in Moscow. He has taught Russian history at Yale University since 1956, serving also as director of graduate studies in the Russian and East European Program and as chairman of the Council of Russian and East European Studies. He holds A.B. and A.M. degrees from Stanford and a Ph.D. from Harvard (1951), and he has been at various times research fellow at the Hoover Institution, Stanford, and the Center for Middle Eastern Studies and the Russian Research Center at Harvard. Before going to Yale he was with Radio Free Europe and an instructor in history and literature at Harvard. Professor Kazemzadeh has also been visiting lecturer or professor at Harvard, Columbia, Stanford, the University of Southern California Law School, and Lewis and Clark College. His publications include *The Struggle for Transcaucasia, 1917–1921* and *Russia and Britain in Persia, 1864–1914: A Study in Imperialism,* as well as many articles and contributions to collective volumes.

HANS KOHN was born in Prague in 1891, and died in Philadelphia in 1971. He received his doctorate in jurisprudence from the German University at Prague in 1923. In a long and distinguished career as professor of modern European history in the United States, he held posts at the New School for Social Research, Smith College (1934–1949), and The City College of New York (1949–62). He was also a visiting professor or lecturer at many other institutions all over the country, including Harvard University, the University of California, the University of Denver, and Mount Holyoke College. He was a Guggenheim Fellow in 1940–41 and a member of the Institute for Advanced Studies in 1948 and 1955.

Hans Kohn's numerous books include *Pan-Slavism, Its History and Ideology, The Idea of Nationalism: A Study in Its Origins and Background, The Mind of Modern Russia: Historical and Political Thought of Russia's Great Age,* and *Basic History of Modern Russia: Political, Cultural, and Social Trends.*

WALTER LEITSCH received his Ph.D. in East European history and Slavic philology in 1954. During his postgraduate studies at Vienna's Research Institute for Austrian History he was appointed assistant in the Institute for East European History and Southeastern Research of the University of Vienna, and in 1965 became professor and director of the Institute. Professor Leitsch is the author of *Moskau und die Politik des Kaiserhofes in XVII Jahrhundert* (1960) and of numerous articles in *East European Quarterly, Jahrbücher für Geschichte Osteuropas,* and *Österreichische Osthefte.*

EMANUEL SARKISYANZ has been director of the political department of the South Asian Institute of the University of Heidelberg since 1967. He was born an Iranian citizen in Kharkov in 1923 and received his Ph.D. in 1952, following studies in archeology and history at the University of Teheran, the Asia Institute of New York, and the University of Chicago. In the years 1956 to 1958 he was associated with the German Foreign Policy Association and in 1959 held a Guggenheim Fellowship for field research in Burma. Before going to Heidelberg he taught at Bishop College, Dallas, the University of Kansas, and the Universities of Kiel and Freiburg. Professor Sarkisyanz is the author of *Russland und der Messianismus des Orients, Geschichte der orientalischen Völker Russlands bis 1917, Südostasien seit 1945,* and *Buddhist Backgrounds of the Burmese Revolution.*

TRAIAN STOIANOVICH is a graduate of the University of Rochester and received his advanced degrees from New York University and the University of Paris (Doctorat de l'Université, 1952). He has been a member of the history department at Rutgers University since 1955 and has also taught at New York University, the University of California at Berkeley, Stanford University, and Sir George Williams University, Montreal. He was a Fulbright Research Fellow in Salonika in 1958–59 and a Rutgers Faculty Research Fellow in 1965–66, and has been an active participant at the sessions of the international conference of historians held since 1960. He is the author of *A Study in Balkan Civilization,* as well as of numerous articles on cultural, social, and economic history. A new book—an interpretative study of European civilization—is in preparation.

LIEUTENANT COLONEL GEOFFREY WHEELER founded the Central Asian Research Centre in London in 1953, following thirty-eight years in British government service, spent mainly in Asian countries. He directed the center until 1968 in association with St. Antony's College, Oxford, and was joint editor of the *Central Asian Review.* He is the author of *Racial Problems in Soviet Muslim Asia, The Modern History of Soviet Central Asia,* and *The Peoples of Soviet Central Asia.*

Index